ECONOMIC ANALYSIS FOR FISHERIES MANAGEMENT PLANS

Edited by
LEE G. ANDERSON

ANN ARBOR SCIENCE
PUBLISHERS INC / THE BUTTERWORTH GROUP

Library of Congress Catalog Card Number 80-68820
ISBN 0-250-40389-7

Butterworths, Ltd., Borough Green, Sevenoaks,
Kent TN15 8PH, England

PREFACE

It would be fair to say that there exists among the economics staff of the National Marine Fisheries Service, the staffs of the various councils, and other organizations and individuals interested in the economic aspects of fisheries management, the belief that the amount of economic analysis currently being done to implement the Fisheries Conservation and Management Act is less than sufficient and, more than likely, it is less than called for in the act. This is not to say that the implementation of the act has been a failure or that good economic analysis has not been done. It simply means that there is room for improvement. In November 1980 a workshop was held at the University of Delaware which addressed these issues in a straightforward manner. The meeting was sponsored by the University of Delaware Sea Grant College Program and the National Marine Fisheries Service. I am grateful to Richard Gutting and Morton Miller for their help and encouragement in organizing this effort. This volume is the product of that workshop. It contains all of the papers presented and, where appropriate, comments on them by preassigned discussants. Although I selected the discussion topics and provided a suggested analytical framework, credit for the substance of this volume belongs entirely to the individual authors. I am grateful for their efforts.

I am also indebted to many people at the College of Marine Studies at the University of Delaware for their help in planning and holding the workshop and in publishing these proceedings. William Lovejoy, Pat Lavin, David Rockland and Mark Holliday helped with the conference logistics; Pam Donnelly did the typesetting for the book; and Lois Butler did much of the drafting. My able and unflappable secretary, Ruth Leo, provided services above and beyond the call of duty with respect to correspondence, hotel reservations and just simply reminding me what things had to be done. I am especially grateful for her help. Bruce Lee of the CMS communications group did much of the technical work of putting this volume together. The conference was held in November and I went on sabbatical leave to Norway on January 3, 1981. Before I left I was able to edit and review all of the papers and set up the book's general format. I then set the pile of papers on Bruce's desk and he did an admirable and completely professional job of turning those papers into this completed volume. I am very grateful for his help.

Lee G. Anderson

EDITORIAL INTRODUCTION

The Fisheries Conservation and Management Act has been in effect for about four years at this writing. Just after the law was passed, but before it went into effect, a symposium was held at the University of Delaware entitled "Economic Impacts of Extended Fisheries Jurisdiction." The purpose of that symposium was to provide a general economic analysis of the law. The purpose of this workshop was to analyze, from an economist's point of view, the implementation of the Fisheries Conservation and Management Act by studying some actual plans that have resulted, as well as the process of developing and reviewing them. In addition, several special topics related to the economic analysis for fisheries management plans were selected for study. The authors were selected for their knowledge of the particular plan or issue under consideration. Each of them was given the following general format to follow in the preparation of their papers:

1. Outline the issues that have economic content or are amenable to economic analysis.
2. Review the appropriate economic theory that applies and show the specific application to the issues at hand.
3. Describe how you would ideally go about applying this theory. Your description should include data sources, types of data manipulations, display procedures, etc. An actual example with real numbers would be most useful.
4. Since it is often the case that council staffs will not be able to use the ideal methodology due to data shortages, time shortages, or lack of professional expertise, make specific suggestions as to how to come as close to the ideal methodology given the relevant constraints. In other words, how can the best possible economic work be done in a less than perfect world?
5. If the descriptions in number 3 and 4 above vary considerably, suggest a plan that will eliminate these differences over time. This plan should include data collection needs and procedures, training programs, etc.
6. With respect to items 3 and 4, pay special attention to ways in which the proper economic analysis can be presented to noneconomists in the clearest manner possible. Also, try to point out where the concepts discussed are generally applicable to other problem areas or management plans.

It is left to the reader to be the final judge of exactly how well the authors achieved these goals. In general, however, it must be conceded that no one succeeded on all accounts. This, I think, is an indication of the complexity of the issues. All of the problems cannot be resolved simply by holding a single workshop. There is certainly a lot more theoretical and empirical work that needs to be done before proper economic analysis for fisheries management plans is possible. Indeed, because economic analysis is costly, more work needs to be done before we can really know what the optimal kinds and amounts of economic analyses are. However, the analyses provided in this volume are a step forward in our understanding of the overall problem.

The book is divided into four main sections; the first gives a general introduction to the topic. Mueller and Wang first provide a review of economic analysis in the fishery management plan process. They discuss such issues as the role of economic information, the nature of the economic analysis to provide it, and the types of methodologies and data needs required for the analysis. In the second paper, Siegel describes the federal regulatory policy on marine fisheries management and examines how well it is being carried out, as well as some of the impacts of this policy.

The second section contains four papers devoted to the economic analysis contained in specific management plans. There were many plans to choose from, and the basis for selection was geographical location and usefulness of the analysis to a wide range of management plans. In the first paper, Huppert discusses the Northern Anchovy Management Plan. He provides a description of the fishery and shows how economic theory can be tailored to specific management problems. Finally he shows the types of possible analytical results. In the next paper, Griffin and Stoll describe the Gulf of Mexico Shrimp Management Plan. They show how economic analysis can be used as an educational tool for explaining peculiarities of the fishery. They also present a model of the multipurpose nature of the fishery and a simulation tool that can be used in policy analysis. Next, the Atlantic Surf Clams Plan is discussed by Strand, Kirkley and McConnell. After providing a general description of the fishery, they discuss such issues as the usefulness of the moratorium, the substitutability of inputs, and the problems caused by potential monopsony power. In the final paper Rettig discusses Salmon Management Plans. He shows several reasons why salmon species are subject to distinct types of management problems. He also covers methodological issues in impact assessment and details some economic research specific to impacts of regulation on particular resource uses.

The third section of the book contains two papers which provide perspectives on economic analysis for fishery management plans from other countries. Hannesson discusses management issues and fishery economics research in Norway and Iceland. In a similar manner Mitchell analyzes fishery management and economics research in Canada.

The fourth section of the book covers selected economic issues related to most management plans. In the first paper in this section, Bishop, Bromley and Langdon discuss the problem of specifying management goals. They point out that managers are interested in a range of issues, including economic efficiency, distribution of benefits and costs, and biological effectiveness. They stress that proper management will not be possible until we know the relative importance of these for the various fisheries. A methodology for obtaining this information is provided. The second paper in this section, by Wang and Mueller, stresses that management must be a dynamic phenomenon taking into account how optimal yields are to be set over a period of years. They demonstrate several types of methodologies that can be used to investigate these intertemporal issues.

The economic aspects of managing marine recreational fishing are discussed in the next paper by McConnell and Strand. They stress that successful long-run management of recreational fish stocks requires that managers know several critical relationships including those between the value of recreational fishing days and catch rates and between catch rates and stock size. They describe the relevance of these relations to management and present cost effective ways of managing recreational fisheries taking them into account. In the next paper, Stokes discusses fishery development issues in the context of management. He uses the Alaska groundfishery as an example and explains how development and management merge with respect to optimal yield adjustments, joint ventures and protection of incidental species.

The final paper was not prepared in advance for the workshop. It is an outgrowth of a particular topic that was raised many times during the workshop. The issue related to the role of economics and the economist in fisheries management. Many of the participants felt that it was sometimes an uphill battle to get councils and the central office of National Marine Fisheries Service even to consider economics at all, to say nothing of worrying about the proper way to use economics. Stokes took it on himself to address the feelings and issues related to this topic.

Lee G. Anderson is Associate Professor of Economics and Marine Studies in the College of Marine Studies at the University of Delaware, where he received the 1975 Excellence in Teaching Award. He has also taught at the University of Washington and the University of Miami.

Dr. Anderson received his BS in Economics from Brigham Young University and his PhD from the University of Washington—also in Economics.

Currently, he is an advisor to the National Commission on Water Quality, and a referee for *Land Economics*. He has served on Advisory Committees for the National Science Foundation and the National Academy of Sciences.

A member of the American Economic Association and the Canadian Economic Association, he is the author of 20 articles and two books on marine economics and fisheries management including the Ann Arbor Science publication, *Economic Impacts of Extended Fisheries Jurisdiction*. His areas of current research include extended jurisdiction fisheries management and economic studies of environmental pollution.

CONTENTS

CHAPTER 1

ECONOMIC ANALYSIS IN FISHERY MANAGEMENT PLANS: AN OVERVIEW

J. J. Mueller
> National Marine Fisheries Service

D. H. Wang
> New England Fishery Management Council

On April 13, 1976, President Ford signed into law PL 94-265, which extended the U.S. jurisdiction over the living marine resources from the previously established 12-mile seaward limit to 200 miles. The law was designated the Fisheries Conservation and Management Act, and had as its principal goal the conservation and management of the fishery resources off the coasts of the United States. To achieve this goal, the act called for the establishment of Regional Fishery Management Councils whose responsibilities included (in cooperation with the Secretary of Commerce) the preparation and implementation of fishery management plans (FMP).

The purpose of this chapter is to discuss and review the role of economic analysis in the FMP process. To achieve this, the paper will:

1. provide a brief description of the FMP process itself;
2. identify the role of economic information in this process;
3. identify the economic analysis required to provide the information;
4. identify the methodological and data needs to provide the requisite information; and
5. identify the further research and data collection efforts that need to be undertaken immediately to rectify the identified problems.

2 FISHERIES MANAGEMENT PLANS

THE FMP PROCESS

The road from initiation of a FMP to its implementation can be long and confusing. The major procedural phases are detailed in Table I. Plan preparation and implementation include Phases I to V. A summary explanation of each of these phases follows.

1. Preplanning: the actions required before preparation of the FMP, including the identification of the management unit and the preparation of a work plan.
2. Draft FMP Development: development of the draft FMP, including the environmental impact statement (EIS) and the regulatory analysis (RA).
3. Public Review and Comment: review of the draft plan by the public and NOAA/NMFS, the transformation of the draft plan to a final plan, and the adoption of the final plan by the council.
4. Secretarial Review: review of the FMP by the Secretary of Commerce.
5. Regulation Promulgation: public review of the approved FMP and proposed regulations, and the issuance of the final EIS and the final regulations.

In terms of the necessary time, NMFS estimates that approximately 250-300 days are required from the time a draft FMP is submitted by a council to promulgation of the regulations implementing the FMP.

ROLE OF ECONOMIC INFORMATION IN THE FMP PROCESS

Ideally, the use of economics should be ubiquitous throughout all phases of the FMP process, since economic information should help guide the decision process. By regulating the available volume and timing of raw material (fish) flow to industry, the councils (and the Secretary of Commerce) are operating in the mode of industrial control. For example, when quarterly quotas are set, seasonal prices and revenues are affected. Thus, it is imperative that the decision-makers have a clear understanding of the extant economic condition of the industry to be regulated, and an understanding of the consequences of imposing alternative "conservation" strategies on the industry in question. Depending on the availability of data, this may require substantial economic analysis. As will be discussed below, it is the authors' position that the economic information required for FMP preparation and implementation was insufficient prior to 1977, and, under current levels of effort, economic information is slowly gaining significance.

The role that economics is required to play can be viewed procedurally and topically. Procedurally, economic information must enter the FMP process in all of the five phases.

Table I. Overview of the Fishery Management Plan Process (under FCMA, EO 12044, NEPA and Other Requirements)

PHASE I	PHASE II	PHASE III	PHASE IV	PHASE V	PHASE VI	PHASE VII
PRE-PLANNING	DRAFT FMP DEVELOPMENT	PUBLIC REVIEW AND COUNCIL ADOPTION	SECRETARIAL REVIEW	REGULATION PROMULGATION	CONTINUING FISHERY MANAGEMENT	FMP AMENDMENTS
• Identification of FMU (Council)	• Preparation of DFMP — incorporating EO 12044 (RA) and NEPA (DEIS) requirements (Council)	• Publication of DEIS/DFMP and DPR availability in Federal Register (NMFS)	• Official secretarial review of FMP (NMFS)	• Publication of approved FMP in the Federal Register (NMFS)	• Implementation of management measures (other than regulations) identified in approved FMP, i.e., research, data collection, socio-economic studies (Council, Secretary, NOAA, NMFS and others)	• Decision to amend the FMP (Council)
• Decision to initiate pre-planning activities (Council)	• Preparation of DPR (Council, with assistance from RD and NOAA general counsel)	• Publication of public hearings in Federal Register (NMFS)	• FMP approval, partial disapproval or disapproval (NMFS)	• Publication of PR (NMFS)		• Application of "Significance" under EO 12044 and NEPA (Council)
• Decision to prepare an EIS, and processing NOI (Council)	• Activities assoc. w/releasing DEIS (Review — NMFS) (Approval — NOAA)	• Public review period (NMFS)	• Consultation — If partial or full disapproval, and possible resubmission (Council, NMFS)	• Public review of FMP and PR		• Concurrence with council determination (NOAA/NMFS)
• Decision to prepare an EA and NONSI (Council)		• Public hearings (Council)	(NOTE: Secretarial FMP preparation authorized under FCMA when plans are disapproved)	• Compilation and assessment of public comments — preparation of FR (NMFS)	• Implementation of FMP monitoring procedures as delineated in FMP (Council, NMFS)	• Preparation of FMP amendment (Council)
• Processing and approval of EA and NONSI (Processing — NMFS) (Approval — NOAA)		• Agency advance review* of DFMP — Comments to council (DOC's chief economist, NOAA, NMFS, CG & DOS)	• Preparation of PR (NOAA/NMFS)	• Final consistency review of PR with FCMA (NOAA/NMFS)	• Refinements to regulations, i.e. notice actions, regulatory changes (Council, NMFS)	— Restarts all or portions of the FMP process, depending on whether the NEPA/EO 12044 procedures will be instituted.
• Conduct scoping meetings (Council)		• Compilation and assessment of public and agency comments (Council)		• Approval of FR and RA (NOAA- A)		
• Work plan activities (Preparation — Council) (Processing — NMFS) (Approval — NOAA, A)		• Preparation of FMP (Council)		• Publication of FR in Federal Register (NMFS)		
		• Approval & submission of FMP (Council)		• FEIS notice availability in Federal Register (NMFS)		
				• APA and NEPA (simultaneous) 30-day "cooling off" period		
				• Regulations effective		
(No set time frame)	(Preparation of DFMP — 6 mos to 2 years; Activities associated with DEIS release takes approx. 20 days)	(Approximately 75 days) *This NMFS coordinated advance review may precede the public review period — at the Council's discretion	(Approximately 27 days)	(Approximately 128 days)	(No set time frame - varies from plan to plan)	(No set time frame — varies from plan to plan)

4   FISHERIES MANAGEMENT PLANS

Phase I

Two major activities in Phase I (preplanning) include (1) identification of those fishery management units (FMU) in need of management, and (2) specification of work plans to direct the development of the FMP. In regard to item 1, it may be the case that some fisheries are not in need of management. That is, the benefits to be gained (viewed either in a single time period or a multiple time period context) may simply not be worth the costs that must be incurred by both taxpayers and industry to achieve certain objectives. Thus, the initial problem faced by a council is to determine which species or species constellations that fall under their jurisdictional purview are worth the cost of managing. This determination should, in part, be based on the findings of a brief economic assessment of the need to manage.

At this phase then, the responsibility of council staff economists is to provide the council with at least a reasonably substantive description of the industry, its problems, and identification of alternative strategies available to address the problems, and preliminary calculations of the benefits and costs for various candidate management strategies. These calculations should be completed before the end of this *"scoping" process*.

Assuming that a positive decision has been made to go forward with FMP development, economic information and analysis should be used in developing the *work plan*. Although the major focus of the work plan may be to redraw the council's attention to the major issues or problems in the fishery, the economists involved should use it as a vehicle for planning in terms of model development, methodology specification and data management. That is, after having completed their initial analysis of the fishery during the scoping process, and after there is a *general determination* of the objectives to be achieved by the council and the strategies to be examined, the economists involved should develop detailed work plans as to the further analytic tasks that must be carried out to provide the necessary support for council decision-making.

Phase II

During Phase II (draft FMP development), the economists involved in plan development should execute all of those activities detailed in the work plan to provide requisite inputs into the FMP, EIS and the RA. The essence of the economic analysis should satisfy the requirements for each of these documents. This is because the economic criteria (to be detailed later) utilized in the analysis are fundamental in nature, robust with respect to alternative objectives and relevant irrespective of the institutional position of the decision-maker.

Specifically, the economist involved should ensure that they contain (1) a concise statement on the *economic problem* that necessitates action; (2) a statement of the adopted council objectives and how they relate, if at all, to the economic problem identified; (3) a rationale for the alternative strategies to be considered for addressing the problem and its relation to the objectives; (4) a detailed, rigorous, and comprehensive analysis of the consequences of each alternative relative to the criteria selected; and (5) an *economic rationale* for strategy selection or rejection.

Phase III

During Phase III (public review and council adoption), the burden of economic inputs is shifted somewhat to Commerce/NOAA/NMFS economists. The FMP is reviewed in the NMFS region and the Washington office. The Department of Commerce Chief Economist is one of the major reviewers, who reviews those sections of the submitted documents that constitutes the RA. To expedite the process, the RA must be quite clear in articulating the issues and alternatives at hand, in providing a rationale for the analytic approaches taken in the document, and exhibit an understanding of the implications of the analysis. It should not be a document for justification of a council's decision after the fact.

Phase IV

Phase IV constitutes the secretarial review. A critical step in this phase is the "decision meeting" conducted in NMFS Plan Review Section. Reviewers within NOAA/NMFS and other agencies provide their views on the subject document. At this time the principal economic inputs into the decision process should be provided by the NMFS staff economist. The staff economist should summarize the issues at hand, address whether the economic analysis is adequate and supportive of the recommended decision, and provide a recommendation for specific further steps, if any, that need to be taken in regard to the document, either for rejection or approval.

Phase V

Phase V is the FMP implementation phase, if the FMP is approved. At this point, the economic information required in relation to the recommendations must be detailed in the FMP. For example, based on the alternatives examined, the FMP may contain a data collection program and/or the establishment of an economic monitoring system to provide guidance to the steps that may be needed in the future.

REQUIRED ANALYSIS

Up to this point, we have not discussed what kind of economic analysis should exactly be conducted. PL 94-265 is rather vague on this matter. Sections 301 (a)(5) and (7) state that "Conservation and management measures shall, where practical, promote efficiency in the utilization of fishery resources; except that no such measure shall have economic allocation as its sole purpose," and "conservation and management measures shall, where practicable, minimize costs and avoid unnecessary duplication." Section 303 (a)(2) states that an FMP must contain a description of the fishery. Section 303 (a)(3) calls for the specification of optimum yield or MSY modified by relevant economic and social factors, and for an estimate of U.S. capacity to exploit the OY.

In discussing the option of limited access provisions (a requirement of the act), the act calls for the recognition of "historical fishing practices in, and dependence on, the fishery." Based on the above, the act suggests that the issues of efficiency and distribution be addressed in the FMP. The other issues relate to the secondary impacts on other user groups of the resource under management. Therefore, the issues of efficiency, distribution and secondary economic impacts require economic analyses and will be discussed.

Efficiency

A rather succinct summary of the notion of "efficiency" in applied fishery economics works (except for Anderson [1977], which was theoretical), was compiled by Bromley and Bishop [1977]. A representative sample of these would be:

1.   Crutchfield and Zellner [1962], Pacific Halibut:

    If we may assume that market prices for goods reflect with reasonable accuracy the preferences of consumers, the basic economic objective from the standpoint of society is to see that fisheries maximize net economic yield—the difference between the aggregate money value of output and the aggregate money cost of input needed to produce it (excluding, of course, money returns based on monopolistic restriction of output).

2.   Bell [1972], Northern Lobster:

    The optimum management strategy for any fishery is to permit effort to expand to the point where the marginal cost of the resources (capital and labor) needed to produce a pound of fish is equal to the price consumers are willing to pay for that last pound of fish.

3.   Gates and Norton [1974], Yellowtail Flounder:

Gates and Norton have studied the New England yellowtail flounder fishery by estimating various economic parameters under free entry, limitation of entry to the maximum sustainable yield, and limitation of entry into the level of effort which produces maximum economic efficiency. The latter is defined as that position where price equals marginal cost.

4.   Anderson [1977]:

In a static sense, a fishery should be operated at that level where the price that consumers are willing to pay for the last unit produced just equals the marginal cost of producing it. This point represents the maximum sum of profit to the fishery and consumer surplus.

The reason that the equation, price = marginal cost, is viewed to be that point of maximum efficiency is that the value to society of the last unit of fish (the price) is equal to the marginal cost of producing it, which is equivalent to the maximization of consumer and producer surplus.

This issue is illustrated in Figure 1 for a commercial fishery and in Figure 2 for a recreational fishery. Figure 1 depicts the demand and supply curves for a commercial fishery. The line labeled D is the demand curve for fish, the one labeled MCF indicates the marginal cost of output (fish), and the one labeled ACF is the average cost of output. See Anderson [1977, Chapter 2]. The economic efficiency optimum position is at the point where price = marginal cost. The area under the marginal cost curve, i.e., the cross-hatched area labeled TC, represents the total costs of producing output Q*, and includes a normal profit. The area labeled A represents the consumer surplus and the area labeled B the producer surplus. In essence, the amounts contained in areas A and B represent the amount that consumers and producers would pay (over and above production costs) to retain the ability to produce and consume Q* units of fish products. The net value to society for this fishery would then be areas A + B less any management costs not borne by the industry, such as regulation and enforcement costs paid by the government. In instances where management actions affect the productivity of the vessels, the cost curves would shift, thus resulting in reductions in consumer and producer surplus. These would be management costs paid by the industry.

Figure 2 depicts the demand curve for *user days* by recreational fishermen. This example characterizes a particular fishery for which no fee is charged for the right of access to the fishery. The price Pa (vertical scale) relates to the cost of gear, equipment, etc., necessary to participate in the recreational fishery when total user days equals Qa. This does not include the price for the right to fish. The position and slope of the demand curve is a function of a variety of factors that could include income, the success rate, and the availability of alternative fisheries. One way of viewing the net economic value of this fishery at this particular output level would be to determine the area

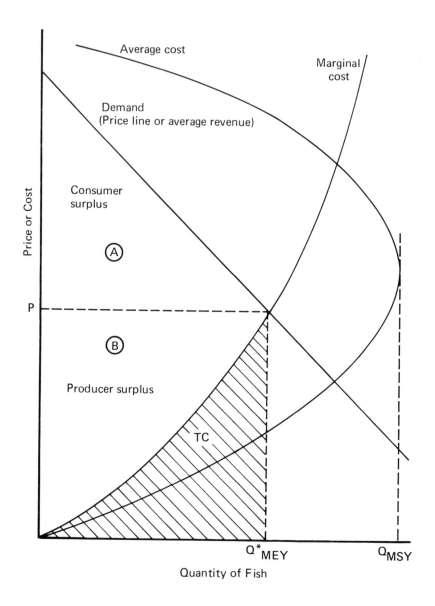

Figure 1.   Demand curve and supply curve in a commercial fishery.

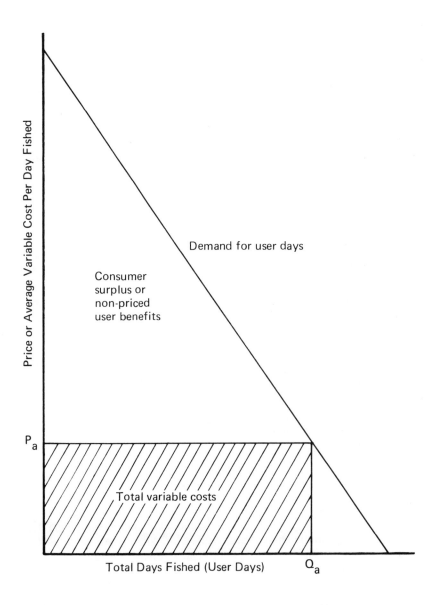

Figure 2.   Relation of average variable costs and total days fished for a recreational fishery.

under the demand curve that is above the present variable costs. From society's perspective any other management costs (not shown in Figure 2) not borne by the anglers would be deducted from this total to determine the true net economic value. Thus, if management actions are taken that affect a factor such as the catch rate, the demand curve could shift, and the user benefits could be affected. For a more detailed analysis of recreational fisheries, see McConnell and Sutinen [1979], Bishop and Samples [1980] and Anderson [1980a,b].

The economic efficiency analysis then should concentrate on the impacts of alternative strategies relative to the achievement of the maximum economic efficiency in the fishery. However, the steady-state model referred to above may lose its applicability in complex fisheries when the time dimension must be considered. A deviation from the steady-state model can lead to models of varying degrees of complication and sophistication, and which may suggest conclusions completely different from the conclusions derived from the steady-state model. The revised model could be a dynamic adjustment model, a stochastic model, or an intertemporal model. For more on this see Chapter 10 of this book.

Distribution

As noted by Bromley and Bishop [1977], the issue of income distribution has been somewhat ignored in the recent fisheries economics literature. They suggest that

> the solution lies, we believe, in making the distributional implications of alternative courses of action as explicit as possible even if economics yields no clear advice about which course of action is distributionally preferable. Only in this way will it be possible to approach, as nearly as we can at this stage in the development of economics, the conclusion of welfare economics that social welfare is based on both *efficiency* and *equity*.

It is clearly suggested that fishery management should encompass an objective which is not always measurable in a single dimension. In a formal terminology we may denote the welfare results of a fishery program as $W = W(Z_1, Z_2, \ldots . Z_n)$ where the Zs are different desirable outcomes including economic efficiency, contribution to net economic output, income distribution, balance of payment equilibrium, reduction in structural employment, freedom from arbitrary government action, etc. Therefore, economic efficiency does not necessarily dictate the socially desirable course of action in the face of the income distribution issue.

Secondary Economic Impacts

This section draws on discussion from Rothschild, Gates, and Carlson [1977]. An important issue in the analysis of recreational or commercial fishing is the valuation of what might be called "downstream" economic impacts. For example, if a fisherman (either recreational or commercial) sells his catch he generates a primary impact. A portion of this primary impact may be used to buy fuel and thus a secondary impact is generated. The food and lodging consumed by recreational fishermen may also be considered as "downstream" impacts. Similarly there are "downstream" impacts associated with the commercial fisheries sector.

The analysis of primary, secondary, tertiary, and successive impacts involves input-output (I-O) analysis. In this analysis primary and secondary impacts are usually identified, but higher order impacts are aggregated and referred to as induced impacts. All second and higher order impacts will be termed induced impacts in order to economize on words. For an excellent introduction to I-O analysis see Miernyk [1965].

The purchase of fish at dockside is termed a transaction and involves an expenditure or flow of money. The fisherman in turn uses this revenue in subsequent transactions to buy fuel, bait, ice, nets, twine and food, in transactions with grocery stores, merchants and banks.

The stores and banks generate further transactions. This sequence of transactions continues indefinitely, but the process has a limit. This limit is expressed as a matrix of multipliers. The matrix can be used to calculate the indirect and induced impacts of expenditures in any sector on other sectors or on the total economy of a region or nation. I-O analysis must therefore begin by recording all transactions as outputs from a particular sector and inputs into another sector, or into final consumption. These transactions can be written as a transaction matrix. The transaction matrix can be used to derive a sequence of induced transactions or impacts.

It is important, however, to point out various nuances in this approach. We have used as an implied criterion for evaluating "value," the concept that a policy decision is "good" if it makes society "better off." If fish stocks are reduced, all other things being equal, commercial fishermen would, in the short run, incur higher expenditures to catch the same number of fish. In this short-run case, the expenditures would rise but the price would not, and the profitability of the fishing fleet would be reduced. However, if the quantity of fish that are being caught also fell (and the ex-vessel price rises), then the consumer would also be hurt, for he would experience a loss of consumer surplus. This is obviously not a desirable outsome. However, in an I-O analysis, the higher expenditures could generate more required regional inputs in terms of employment, gear, etc., to produce the fish. Thus, a reduced catch rate could have a greater short-term induced impact than a catch rate at a higher level, if we ignore the alternative uses to which additional employment and commitment of resources could have been put and the impacts which these alternative uses would have generated. Another example would be an increase in expenditures incurred by recreational fishermen, i.e., fuel and travel costs, or costs of charter vessels and fishing gear. If these expenditures increase, so would the induced impacts from an increase in recreational fishing in the region in question. It does not seem sensible, however, to suggest that a rise in these costs makes recreational fishermen "better off" (note that the recreational consumer surplus would decline). In summary, the results of an impact analysis have to be placed in the proper perspective. However, it is easy to see why, from the point of view of local economies, they are so important.

METHODOLOGIES AND DATA NEEDS

Given the set of issues that must be addressed in the FMP, it is necessary to (1) specify the specific performance or economic measurements that can be used to determine the economic consequences of alternative management action; (2) develop the appropriate methodologies for conducting the analyses; and (3) to indentify and collect the requisite data.

The determination of the performance indicators guide the selection of the methodologies and data collection efforts. The performance indicators that could be used for a commercial fishery for short-run analysis include:

1. price changes;
2. net income to the harvesting sector;
3. employment in the harvesting sector;
4. labor income in the harvesting sector;
5. net income in the processing sector;
6. employment in the processing sector;
7. labor income in the processing sector;
8. regional income;
9. consumer surplus;
10. management and enforcement costs; and
11. trade flows.

All of these should be presented to the decision-makers in both an aggregate and disaggregate mode (distribution aspects).

It should be noted that we have not assigned any weights to the above criteria. Essentially, what we are suggesting is that these indicators can be included as some of the arguments in the social welfare function. Theoretically, through the FMP process, the weights are implicitly assigned and the function is maximized.

The above performance indicators have considerable implications in terms of the requisite methodology and data. For example, referring to Figure 1 on the efficiency question, the analyst should develop the appropriate price and supply functions. In regard to the supply estimation, this can be complex, especially for a multiple-species fishery where the underlying production functions are not generally well understood. Indeed, even developing a clear definition of fishing effort and estimating the factor cost of effort is extremely complex. The same complexities can arise in estimating the price equations, since our knowledge of the structure of most markets is often parochial.

However, the problem of analysis is made more complex by the fact that in any FMP, there is (or should be) a set of alternative strategies to be examined. These may include area closures, quotas, vessel allocations, etc. The next questions are, of course, how do these strategies theoretically affect supply and demand, and is there any way of estimating the impacts of such regulatory measures on the parameters of the model. These questions can be empirically impossible to answer with existing methodologies and data.

In regard to the distribution issue, what do we currently know about the income distribution in the fleet? How has it been changing over time? What are the factors causing the change? How will the alternative strategies impact the future distribution of income?

So how do we get started? A logical first step would be an inventory and descriptive analysis of the data base for all the different sectors involved. Recently, the NMFS undertook a nationwide study on the economic data needed for fisheries managmenet, its priority, its availability, and a plan for securing the deficient data. The areas of data needs are listed in Table II. Clearly, these data categories are quite relevant for the quantitation of the performance indicators stated previously, for they constitute the "guts" of the models to be built which will be used to generate the indicators. Unfortunately, glaring deficiencies exist in many major topic areas.

The next step is to try to specify the assumed behavioral relationships that exist among various categories of data and, empirically estimate these relationships. In doing this, the analyst should be mindful of the underlying constraints similar to those in Figure 1. In the work that we now are undertaking in the Northeast Region for our short-run analysis, we are trying a multi-step approach to the problem. (This may not be the most desirable way to do it.) However, the notions involved seem reasonably sound, and we follow the rule "if it works, use it."

Table II. Data Priorities for New England Region

Data Topic Area	Atlantic Fisheries	Pollock	Redfish	Silver Hake	Other Hake	Sea Scallops	Herring
Number of Vessels and Gear	1	1	1	1	1	1	1
Detailed Vessel Inventory	1	1	1	1	1	1	1
Costs and Earnings	1	1	1	1	1	1	1
Employment	1	1	1	1	1	1	1
Income Level and Distribution	1	1	1	1	1	1	1
Age, Education and Experience	2	2	2	2	2	2	2
Cultural Characteristics	2	2	2	2	2	2	2
Capacity Considerations	1	1	1	1	1	1	1
Landings and Effort	1	1	1	1	1	1	1
Production and Prices	1	1	1	1	1	1	1
Number of Processors, Etc.	1	1	1	1	1	1	1
Processing and Marketing Costs	1	1	1	1	1	1	1
Product Flows	1	1	1	1	1	1	1
Processing Employment	1	1	1	1	1	1	1
Processing Employee Char.	2	2	2	2	2	2	1[a]
Processing Capacity	1	1	1	1	1	1	1
Fleet Size and Composition	1[a]	1[a]	1[a]	–	–	NA	NA
Costs and Earnings	1[a]	1[a]	1[a]	–	–	NA	NA
Expenditures in Support Ind.	1[a]	1[a]	1[a]	–	–	NA	NA
Detailed Economics of Support Ind.	1[a]	1[a]	1[a]	–	–	NA	NA
Employment	2	2	2	–	–	NA	NA
Employee Characteristics	2	2	2	–	–	NA	NA
Sales of Rec. Caught Fish	2	2	2	–	–	NA	NA

Home Consumption	1[a]	1[a]	1[a]	1[a]	1[a]	1[a]	1[a]
Rest./Inst. Consumption	1[a]	1[a]	1[a]	1[a]	1[a]	1[a]	1[a]
Industrial Use	2	2	2	2	2	2	1[a]
Imports	1	1	1	1	1	1	1
Exports	2	2	2	2	2	2	1[a]
Transfers to Foreign Ships	3	3	3	–	–	3	3
Foreign Production	1[a]	1[a]	1[a]	1[a]	1[a]	1[a]	1[a]
Foreign Market Data	2	2	2	2	2	2	1[a]
Local Economic Data	2	2	2	2	2	2	2
Cultural Values	2	2	2	2	2	2	2
Expenditures in Comm. Support Industries	1[a]	1[a]	1[a]	1[a]	1[a]	1[a]	1[a]

[a]Within category 1, these data topics are less important.
– = Currently unimportant, but may soon become important.
NA = Not applicable.
Not included in this table are data for the red crab, which was the subject of a single-industry study.

A number of different sector models are being specified. These include:

1. price equations at the various market levels;
2. short-run fishery production functions;
3. applied effort functions;
4. change in the capital stock function (vessels);
5. cost models or financial simulators for the harvesting and processing sectors;
6. employment response functions;
7. share models for the processing sector and harvesting sectors; and
8. capacity models.

While these are not being combined in exactly the way that Figure 1 suggests, the framework should prove useful for providing quantitative estimates of some of the performance indicators.

PROBLEM AREAS AND NEEDED RESEARCH

In the opening scene of the movie "Love Story," Oliver asserts, "Where do I begin, to tell the story of . . . ." We feel the same way in discussing the problems that we have identified in attempting to conduct economic analyses for fisheries management purposes. The story starts essentially with Phase I of the FMP process, namely, defining the problem. Specifically, the information base that was in place in 1977 was so deficient that there was no way to ascertain the extant financial condition of the harvesting or processing sectors of the industry at the level necessary for problem definition and scenario evaluation purposes. There had been little price analyses work completed since the 1960s. There were no cost/earning models for the harvesting or processing sectors. There were not enough industry structure studies available for the harvesting or processing sectors. Our knowledge of products was (and continues to be) inadequate. In many fisheries, there were no time series available on catch and effort. Our knowledge of foreign markets was nonexistent.

Because of this, many of the economists were simply unable to provide the requisite information when it was required and the quality of the FMP and RA suffered accordingly. No doubt many management decisions have been made with a lack of adequate economic information.

These continuing deficiencies in our information base were further highlighted this summer. The NMFS established a task force to determine the economic problems being faced by the industry, nationwide, during the recession. The members of the task force queried the NMFS regional and center economists to receive a status report on the current performance of various industry sectors. In short, the response was disappointing and disconcerting. While our collective ignorance of the industries that we are regulating may not be growing, our collective wisdom is still in its infancy.

The factors that limited our information base in 1977 and which continue to limit it today is a topic of great concern. An understanding of these limitations is essential to their resolution. To begin to rectify this situation, we feel an enhanced and well-directed effort must be initiated immediately to develop an industry financial monitoring system that is capable of providing key information for decision making purposes in our major fisheries. The information system would provide disaggregated performance data similar to that found in annual corporate reports. In addition, monthly or at least quarterly updates of the information base should be available. This information would be used for problem definition, model estimation and system monitoring. Such an endeavor would again highlight the specific data deficiencies that we all face, and we hope, be a vehicle for channeling necessary resources to correcting these problems.

On the marketing side, it is hoped that the current efforts of the NMFS consumption survey will rectify the deficienceis in our knowledge of market information.

CONCLUSION

The purpose of the workshop is to discuss the economic analysis in the FMP and RA. With these opening remarks, we have attempted to outline the FMP process itself, the preceived role of economic information in the process, the specific types of information that should be supplied, some of the approaches that we are using to supply the information in the Northeast, the problems that we perceive in supplying this information, and some suggestions for addressing these problems. Generally, we feel that there is a major problem with the scope and quality of work that is being produced nationwide. However, we also feel that the problems are tractable.

REFERENCES

1. Anderson, L. G. 1977. *The Economics of Fisheries Management* (Baltimore, MD: The Johns Hopkins Press).
2. Anderson, L. G. 1980a. "Estimating the Benefits of Recreation under Conditions of Uncertainty: Comments and Extension," *J. Environ. Econ. Management* 7(4):400-405.
3. Anderson, L. G. 1980b. "An Economic Model of Recreational Fishing," University of Delaware (unpublished).
4. Bell, F. 1972. "Technological Externalities and Common Property Resources: An Empirical Study of the U.S. Northern Lobster Fishery," *J. Polit. Econ.* 80:148-158.

5. Bishop, R. C., and K. C. Samples. 1980. "Sport and Commercial Fishing Conflicts: A Theoretical Analysis," *J. Environ. Econ. Management* 7(3): 220-233.
6. Bromley, D. W., and R. C. Bishop. 1977. "From Economic Theory to Fisheries Policy: Conceptual Problem and Management Prescription," in *Economic Impacts of Extended Jurisdiction*, L. G. Anderson, Ed. (Ann Arbor, MI: Ann Arbor Science Publishers, Inc.).
7. Clawson, M. 1959. *Methods of Measuring the Demand for and Value of Outdoor Recreation*, (Washington, DC: Reprint #10—Resources for the Future).
8. Crutchfield, J. A., and A. Zellner. 1962. "Economic Aspects of the Pacific Halibut Fishery," *Fishery Ind. Res.* 1(1):1-173.
9. Gates, J. M., and V. Norton. 1974. "The Benefits of Fishery Regulation: A Case Study of the New England Yellowtail Flounder Fishery," University of Rhode Island Marine Technical Report No. 21.
10. McConnell, K. E., and J. G. Sutinen. 1979. "Bioeconomic Models of Marine Recreational Fishing," *J. Environ. Econ. Management* 6(1):127-139.
11. Miernyk, W. H. 1965. *The Elements of Input-Output Analysis* (New York: Random House).
12. Rothschild, B. J., J. M. Gates and A. M. Carlson. 1977. "Management of Marine Recreational Fisheries," in *Marine Recreational Fisheries*, H. Clepper, Ed. (Washington, DC: Sport Fishing Institute).

COMMENT–CHAPTER 1

Giulio Pontecorvo

Graduate School of Business
Columbia University

May I begin by congratulating the authors on both an excellent paper and on how carefully they followed the instructions laid down by Dr. Anderson. I have six comments, some of which apply directly to the paper; others, however, extend beyond the guidelines the authors were asked to follow.

DE FACTO AND DE JURE CONDITIONS

We need a better exposition than has been provided of how things actually work in the reviewing of fishery plans by the National Marine Fisheries Service, the National Oceanic and Atmospheric Administration and the Department of Commerce. We need to understand the de facto operating conditions, not a review of de jure procedures. Mueller and Wang tell us that the Department of Commerce Chief Economist is the Chief Reviewer. Our instincts suggest that this is not the case. But if it is, does the Chief Economist or the staff understand the complexities of fisheries management? Are fishery plans reviewed *sui generis* or are they compared to each other? What are the criteria for protection of the general welfare? Who does the review? How much time do they have to do the work? What pressure may be applied to the reviewers? Is the review process a rationalization for protection of the status quo? What are the implications of the process for income distribution, etc., etc.? What is called for is an articulation and evaluation of what is accomplished in the "black box" described as the review process.

STATICS AND DYNAMICS

Mueller and Wang note that the equilibrium model utilized "may lose its acceptability in complex fisheries where the time dimension is considered." In my opinion, the paper would be strengthened by just referring to the equilibrium model, which is well established in the literature, and starting with a discussion of the implications of a dynamic multispecies fishery.

SECONDARY IMPACTS

What Mueller and Wang call secondary impacts raises an important point concerning the examination of both the immediate and secondary economic benefits that flow to the economy from operation of the fishery. This point is *critical* in any evaluation of the economic costs and benefits of the councils themselves and in regulation of the fishery in general. Specifically, it opens up the question of the relationship of the cost of the regulation to the value of output from the fishery.

The authors suggest recourse to input-output tables to make those calculations. For several reasons, both theoretical and empirical, I feel this is an inappropriate route to the calculation of the value of fisheries in the economy.

The same results may be obtained via national income accounting. See Pontecorvo et al. [1980]. In the cited analysis of the 1972 GNP data, the results indicate that the value of the output of fish was much less than indicated by the National Marine Fisheries Service using an input-output approach. The use of input-output raises questions about substitution, uniqueness of product, product transformation and very difficult definitional questions. It is these problems that account for the discrepancy between the two approaches to valuation.

DATA NEEDS

The authors present a table or list of the economic information needed for fisheries management. I count 33 items needed. A similar list of data requirements could be deduced as needed to understand the biological productivity and the underlying chemical/physical determinants of biological productivity in the area. What is missing here is a recognition of the primary importance of the cost of information—its initial cost and the cost of updating it in real time, maintaining it, storing it, etc.

Recognition of the need to consider the cost of information leads to a correlary proposition. Assume that the needed data in a multispecies fishery is made available free, i.e., the complete set of biological, economic and social parameters needed to manage the fishery under PL 94-265, and that these data were continuously available in real time and that the complex problem in control theory posed by attempting to manage a multispecies fishery could be fully articulated and solved. In these circumstances, I submit as a tentative hypothesis that the fishery still could not be managed efficiently.

> Were such information available, it would be possible theoretically to tailor the response of fishing effort to changes in composition and size of the biomass. The tracing of energy flows through the biomass should make possible the ultimate documentation of all the stock/stock and stock/biomass interactions so necessary to optimum biomass control. However, in our opinion the cost of information required to do this is today too high. Furthermore, the responses required of the fishing fleet, and the managers of the system, to these changes are today beyond both the economic and emotional capability of all concerned. [Donaldson and Pontecorvo 1980]

THE MACROECONOMICS OF FISHERY PLANS

I am concerned about the direction of drift of the entire management system. It is appropriate to be concerned with the needed economic input to one fishery plan. However, legitimate concern with individual plans is not enough. There is a macro problem as well; we must be able to see the forest as well as the trees. With the councils basically in the hands of the producers we run the risk that their interests dominate. Here the recent history of the fisheries in the Canadian Maritimes is interesting.

> In response, emergency federal financial subsidies of varying forms were enacted for which the total cost has been $130 million over the period July 1974-March 1977 alone. These subsidies are in addition to the customary aid of $140 million/year which would normally have been budgeted. To put the relative enormity of these sums in perspective, as noted above, the

total value of landings in the Atlantic provinces totaled only $171 million in 1973, with average prices surely lower in 1974. [Donaldson and Ponte-corvo 1980]

Developments in New England and Gulf Coast fisheries hint that we are moving in the direction of greater subsidization; in part, because our concern with micro problems (individual fishery plans) does not lead directly to analysis of the larger issues in fisheries management.

THE DEPARTMENT OF COMMERCE

The responsibility for fisheries management rests in Washington. The FCMA of 1976 introduces local concerns and interests, via the councils, into the fisheries management process. But the ultimate responsibility for seeing that the entire process of fisheries management acts in the public interest rests with the Secretary of Commerce; how and how well this responsibility is met is crucial to understanding the meaning of any fishery plan. Recognition of this responsibility is central in the insertion of economics into fishery plans.

REFERENCES

1. Donaldson and Pontecorvo. 1980. "Economic Rationalization of Fish-eries: The Problem of Conflicting National Interests on Georges Bank," *Ocean Devel. Int. Law J.* 8(2):149-170.
2. Pontecorvo, G. et al. 1980. "Contribution of the Ocean Sector to the United States Economy," *Science* 208:1000-1006.

CHAPTER 2

FEDERAL REGULATORY POLICY FOR MARINE FISHERIES

Robert A. Siegel
   Office of Resource Conservation and Management
   National Marine Fisheries Service

Under the authority of the Fishery Conservation and Management Act of 1976 (FCMA), the federal government has established a national program governing the uses of marine fishery resources in the United States fishery conservation zone (FCZ). (The FCZ is the area between the seaward boundary of each coastal state and a point 200 miles from the baseline used to measure the territorial area.) The objectives of this program are to prevent overfishing, rebuild overfished stocks, ensure conservation, promote the development of underutilized stocks and realize the full potential of the nation's fishery resources for present and future generations.

To meet the program objectives, the FCMA calls for the preparation of fishery management plans (FMP) by eight Regional Fishery Management Councils. The councils are responsible for preparing an FMP for each fishery in need of management within their respective geographical areas of authority. The Secretary of Commerce is empowered to approve, implement and enforce (with the Coast Guard) the provisions of each FMP.

Management of fishery resources for which FMP have been approved is accomplished through regulations issued by the Secretary of Commerce. Fishery regulations translate management measures selected by the councils into detailed rules governing allocations, catch levels, fishing strategies, fishing seasons and the conduct of joint ventures. The FCMA, therefore, provides the framework for controlling the activities of user groups in a fishery through council and federal intervention.

Regulations can be designed by the councils to enhance or restrict competition, improve or detract from the efficient use of resources, alter the market supplies of fish, and indirectly affect the level of exports and imports of fishery products. Council decisions thereby affect the allocation of fishery resources and the distribution of benefits. User groups participate in the regulatory decisions to the extent that their power and political leverage are expressed at public hearings and meetings on FMP, and through comments on proposed regulations.

The FCMA came into being partly because of the perception that the prevailing laissez-faire policy for marine fisheries did not adequately achieve societal objectives for the conservation and efficient use of fishery resources. The "invisible hand," in this instance, had failed to guide the market in fishery products and creation to a socially optimal solution. After more than three years under the FCMA, however, it is fair to ask whether the regulators (councils and the federal government) are making management decisions that adequately recognize the legitimate interests of participants in the fishery and the public at large. Do the regulators propose management strategies which correct perceived market imperfections and result in the equitable distribution of benefits among user groups, including consumers? Do the identifiable benefits of regulations outweigh the costs of developing the regulations and the costs of enforcement? Do regulations governing the use of fishery resources improve upon the existing allocation of resources and distribution of wealth in U.S. fisheries? The answers to these questions gives us a clue as to whether the FCMA as presently administered represents social progress.

The purpose of this chapter is to examine how well the federal regulatory policy on marine fisheries management is being carried out under the FCMA and to discuss some impacts of this policy. The first section addresses the rationale for federal intervention in fisheries from a general economic and social perspective. The second section outlines federal rulemaking requirements that must be followed when intervention is justified after an FMP is developed. The third section reviews the economic issues that affected the design of management strategies in some of the implemented FMP and also assesses whether the management regimes have complex regulatory controls or are nonrestrictive. The fourth section summarizes issues that should be considered in the development of an FMP to ensure that management of fishery resources yields net benefits to society.

THE RATIONALE FOR FEDERAL
INTERVENTION IN FISHERIES

Precedents For Regulation

Traditionally, the federal government assumed a major regulatory responsibility in four areas: antitrust, financial institutions, transportation and communication. Independent regulatory commissions were concerned primarily with issues such as abuses of market power and appropriate rates of return (fair and equitable) for specific industries. In recent years, the federal regulatory role has expanded to include wide areas of economic, environmental and social problems. Beginning in the 1960s, particular attention has been given to product safety, air and water pollution, waste of irreplaceable natural resources and energy.

Government intervention in the marketplace may be appropriate when the private market system does not provide the socially desirable output of goods, services and amenities for a variety of reasons. Certain conditions are prerequisite to efficient or properly functiong markets. A price system is necessary to provide correct signals on the values of resources or outputs; the consumer or producer must have adequate information to conduct a market transaction; and sufficient levels of competition must exist. In addition, where there is no market for certain goods and services (e.g., national defense or public recreation) there may be grounds for a government provision of these outputs. Market failure is the term often applied to situations where these free market conditions are absent.

A familiar example of market failure is the discharge of unacceptable levels of pollutants into the atmosphere that occurs in the absence of property rights because the price system signals that air is a free or undervalued resource. Similarly, the absence of property rights in marine fisheries has led to inefficient and wasteful use of resources. Other forms of market failure occur when: (1) consumers do not have sufficient technical information to make informed choices among products on the basis of prices, quality, hazards and side effects, and the absence of this information shifts the balance of market power in favor of the firm; (2) market power is concentrated with a small number of firms or in a natural monopoly; or (3) markets cannot be established to internalize externalities or even with the existence of a market, the transaction costs outweigh the benefits of having a market.

The government also may intervene to achieve broad social goals. Some groups may argue that it is in the public interest to alter the allocation decisions of the private market because of problems such as income distribution, standards of living, housing, discrimination and provision of services to small communities.

Attainment of national policy objectives through federal intervention in the market often requires the allocation of public and private sector resources through federal regulatory processes. As the scope of federal intervention has expanded, the number of regulatory agencies and the volume of regulations have proliferated. Between 1965 and 1975, the U.S. Regulatory Council estimated that 26 agencies were created to regulate pollution, energy, work place and product safety, discrimination, and other problems [U.S. Regulatory Council 1979]. During the fiscal years 1974-1979, the outlays of 41 agencies regulating business rose from $2.2 billion to $4.8 billion and the compliance costs of the private sector in fiscal year 1979 were estimated at $97.2 billion [Weidenbaum 1978].

An initial attempt to monitor the extent of this regulatory activity occurred in 1979. The U.S. Regulatory Council estimated that there were 58 regulatory agencies, including 18 independent commissions, which issued 7,000 rules and policy statements [U.S. Regulatory Council 1979].

The *Federal Register,* where all new regulations are printed, provides further evidence of the growth in federal regulations. In 1955 the *Federal Register* contained approximately 10,000 pages. Between 1955 and 1970, the number of pages had doubled to 20,000. By 1979, however, the number of pages was 77,000, almost four times the 1970 level.

Regulatory Reform

In response to the growth in government regulation and a greater awareness of the direct and indirect costs on different sectors of the economy, the Executive Branch and Congress proposed and initiated programs to overhaul the regulatory process. The program began when President Carter issued Executive Order 12044 [1978], "On Improving Government Regulations." The Executive Order requires, among other things, that regulations be designed to achieve legislative goals as efficiently as possible, to minimize reporting burdens and that a comparative analysis be performed on the benefits and costs of alternative regulatory schemes early in the decisionmaking process.

Policy objectives of the Executive Order emphasize that the need to regulate must be justifiable, i.e., existing market arrangements do not yield socially desirable outcomes. The Executive Order also requires that a regulatory analysis be prepared for certain categories of regulations. This analysis places increased emphasis on the benefits and costs of regulations and the need to examine a wide range of alternative means of achieving regulatory objectives. The Regulatory Flexibility Act (1980) established a similar policy with an emphasis on the impact of regulations on small businesses. This act specifically requires that federal agencies fit regulatory and informational requirements to the scale of the business, organizations, and governmental jurisdictions subject to the regulation. Federal agencies also are required to solicit and consider flexible regulatory proposals and to explain the rationale for their actions.

Subsequent to the Executive Order, laws have been implemented which aim to deregulate airlines (1978), crude oil and natural gas pricing (1978), and financial institutions (1979) [U.S. Regulatory Council 1980]. Regulatory reform programs also are being developed for trucking, railroads and the telecommunications industry.

The traditional approach to government involvement in market activities is through command and control techniques. This approach entails detailed specification of actions the regulated entity must follow and formal enforcement proceedings for noncompliance. The incentive structure affecting the regulated entity's activities is to comply with the regulations or face government sanctions such as civil penalties. Examples of command and control techniques include: control of entry and exit, licensing, setting prices or rates of return, and specifying quality or design standards.

The thrust of the regulatory reform programs is to deregulate those markets where government intervention has restricted competition needlessly, and to promote the use of innovative regulatory techniques which rely on market incentives. Regulatory alternatives to command and control techniques supplant or replace the government as a centralized decision-maker in certain types of market activities and use incentives similar to those of the private marketplace to achieve broad regulatory goals. Flexible regulatory techniques under consideration by Executive Branch agencies in rulemaking activities include [U.S. Regulatory Council 1980].

1. deregulation: dismantling of federal regulations that inhibit competition;
2. marketable rights: establishment of private property rights for certain classes of resources and allowing private parties to buy and sell government conferred rights;
3. economic incentives: correction of price signals through the use of fees, subsidies or allowing government sanctioned payments between private parties;
4. performance standards: instead of prescribing technologies for satisfying certain standards, allow firms greater flexibility in designing approaches to minimize costs of compliance; and
5. tiering: instead of having uniform regulations industrywide, it may be desirable to set standards according to the size of the firm or business.

These regulatory approaches do not apply to every industry where government intervention may be required. However, in rulemaking proceedings of federal agencies, these alternatives are being explored, even if the agency proposes a command and control mode of regulation.

In the design of management measures for FMP, the standard approach has been command and control regulations. Seldom has there been an attempt to explore regulatory techniques that maintain the incentive pattern of the marketplace.

The Perceived Need to Regulate
Marine Fishery Resources in the FCZ

The FCMA established a program for the conservation and management of fishery resources through the use of FMP developed by the councils. The FMP are implemented by federal regulations issued by the Secretary of Commerce. The regulations, which reflect the management strategy adopted by the councils in the FMP, can range from a nonrestrictive fishing environment to a detailed specification of the rules controlling all aspects of domestic and foreign fishing activity. The FCMA provides the council with the discretion to intervene in a preveiously unregulated fishery and supplement the existing market forces with other institutional mechanisms in order to "derive the greatest national benefit from the use of fishery resources." Management or intervention in a fishery may be justified when the benefit from correcting perceived problems or market imperfections exceed the administrative, compliance, and enforcement costs of the proposed regulatory regime, as compared to the costs of no intervention. This also assumes that the resulting distribution of benefits is politically acceptable.

The need to regulate U.S. fisheries traditionally has been justified on the basis of market failure problems stemming from the common property nature of fishery resources. The basic problem is the failure of the market to establish satisfactorily the property rights to fishery resources among different user groups. Intervention may be necessary because the "free" or unregulated market fails to provide incentives for efficient harvesting patterns of fishery resources (Gordon [1954], Scott [1955], Crutchfield and Zellner [1962], Christy and Scott [1965], Copes [1972] and Anderson [1977] provide detailed analyses of this problem). As a result, the individual fishermen have little incentive to consider the impact of their fishing effort on present or future yields. Without property rights, a participant in the fishery—either commercial or recreational—will not restrict effort in expectation of future returns because they perceive that what is left in the fishery for later in the season or the next fishing year, will probably be taken in the present by current fishermen. This type of market failure has resulted in depressed stocks of valuable fishery resources, overcapitalization, gear conflicts and excess effort in many developed U.S. fisheries.

In fully developed fisheries where the depletion of stocks or overcapitalization are serious problems, the regulatory scheme proposed by a council often will depend on the number of distinct user groups and their relative political power. The regulatory scheme may call for management measures to continue the status quo situation without treating the root problem. The council also may control the conduct of the fishery through the establishment of annual quotas, seasonal quotas, allocations among user groups or vessel classes, fishing seasons, and gear restrictions. Alternatively, the council could devise a regulatory scheme controlling entry coupled with quotas and allocations, or establish a system of property rights with the option of additional controls.

Some form of regulation also may be appropriate in fisheries that are underutilized or undeveloped from the standpoint of domestic user groups. However, the intent of the FMP and the regulatory scheme is to enable the domestic industry to enhance its economic and social well-being. For example, the optimum yield specified by councils in some FMP can be used to influence trade flows of fishery products between the United States and abroad. Two FMP have attempted to spur the development of export markets for U.S. fishery products through the allocation of fishery resources from foreign nations to domestic users. The total allowable level of foreign fishing in the Atlantic butterfish and Tanner crab fisheries was reduced significantly below levels that prevailed prior to the FCMA. Regulations also may be needed to avoid gear conflicts with foreign fleets and to ensure that foreign fleets do not overfish the stocks in the management unit. An innovative regulatory scheme for the Bering Sea clam FMP, which may be proposed by the North Pacific Council at a future date, is the possible leasing of clam beds in the FCZ. This probably could be accomplished with minimal regulations of fishing activity.

Government intervention in marine fisheries through FMP developed by the councils may be justified on either economic efficiency or economic de-development grounds. However, it must be recognized that the benefits of regulation cannot be obtained without incurring administrative, compliance, data collection and enforcement costs. Failure to consider these costs may result in greater losses to society than would a situation of no council and government intervention.

FEDERAL RULEMAKING REQUIREMENTS
FOR FISHERY MANAGEMENT PLANS

Rulemaking Requirements

Probably some of the least discussed aspects of the FMP process are the procedure for implementing fishery management regulations. These procedures, however, are a critical element in the final decisions by the Secretary of Commerce to approve an FMP and to implement management measures. During rulemaking proceedings, the problems and issues which necessitated the FMP become the focal point of public discussion, council decisions and approval by the Secretary of Commerce in terms of the choice of the proposed regulatory regime. The procedures which guide the rulemaking proceedings are found in the FCMA, the Administrative Procedures Act of 1946 (APA) and Executive Order 12044. In addition, the FMP must be consistent with other applicable laws such as the National Environmental Policy Act, the Endangered Species Act, the Marine Mammal Protection Act and the Regulatory Flexibility Act.

Under the FCMA, the councils may prepare FMP for fisheries they consider to be in need of management. When the FMP is being developed, the councils are required to conduct public hearings and to seek public comment on the proposed management strategy. When the council reaches its final decision on the course of action (i.e., the proposed management regime), there should be a straightforward explanation of the reasons for the decision and the rationale for rejecting alternative regulatory strategies.

In similar fashion, the Secretary of Commerce considers the available information contained in an FMP and supporting documents and evaluates the management regime on the basis of national standards in the FCMA, other applicable laws and administration policies. If the Secreatary approves the FMP, the next step is to translate the management measures adopted by the council into proposed regulations.

Procedural requirements for issuing proposed and final regulations implementing an FMP are covered by the APA and Executive Order 12044. The requirements of the APA are fairly simple. An agency must publish a notice of proposed rulemaking in the *Federal Register* and invite the interested public to offer written comments and information about the proposal. After a 60-day comment period, as required by Executive Order 12044, the Secretary may issue the final set of regulations. The decision to adopt the proposed regulations or revise them, is based on the public comment, the FMP, and a regulatory analysis, all of which are part of the public record. This is to ensure that the final decision is not arbitrary and capricious, and that the impacts of the regulation and alternatives have been considered in the rulemaking process.

Executive Order 12044 adds procedural requirements to informal rulemaking covered by the APA. To improve the federal regulatory process, the Executive Order requires that regulations should be as simple and clear as possible, achieve legislative goals effectively and efficiently, and should not impose unnecessary burdens on groups being regulated. Provisions of the Executive Order bearing directly on FMP concern oversight of the rulemaking process by the agency head, preparation of a regulatory analysis (RA) for each major rule, and the involvement of the public in regulatory decisions.

Rulemaking is a process by which the councils and the Secretary of Commerce obtain and test the information to support fishery management decisions. One of the reasons for the RA requirement in the FMP process has been the need for realistic assessments of the impacts of rules which are often based on complicated scientific and technical data and projections. Another function of the RA is to encourage the councils to indicate reasons for preparing an FMP, to discuss management alternatives, and to demonstrate that it has given special consideration to a particular problem area.

The Regulatory Analysis

The regulatory analysis requirement for an FMP is to ensure that new regulations or significant amendments to FMP that alter the management regime, are developed thoughtfully, openly and with maximum attention to the potential consequences of regulation before decisions are reached. In the U.S. Department of Commerce, the current framework for a regulatory analysis includes the guidelines discussed in the following paragraphs.

A Succinct Statement of the Problem That Necessitates Federal Action, or in the Case of an FMP, Council Action

What are the problems in the fishery that require a council to prepare an FMP? Some councils quote the FCMA [Section 301(h) (1)] which states that "each council shall prepare and submit to the Secretary a fishery management plan with respect to each fishery within its geographical area of authority. . ." Although a function of the councils is to prepare FMP, there should be a test to determine whether the expenditure of federal funds will produce gains to society in excess of the costs of regulation.

A Description of the Major Alternative Ways of Dealing with the Problems Being Considered by the Council

The RA should provide a description of each alternative management strategy which may be preferred by every group significantly affected by an FMP. The alternatives considered should be viable approaches to solving the problems in the fishery, rather than strawmen which are dismissed in a few summary paragraphs. One of the alternatives that should be discussed is the "no action" option. All the alternatives (benefits and costs) should be measured against the base case.

An Analysis of the Economic Consequences
(Direct and Indirect) of Each Regulatory Alternative

This analysis should compare the fishery without council action against alternative management strategies that require some form of regulation. The results of the analysis should point out the marginal effects of the alternatives and demonstrate that one of the alternatives is superior. Questions that should be addressed in the analysis include:

1. What types of burdens are placed on each user group as a result of the proposed and alternative management regimes (capital outlays, operating and maintenance costs and reporting burdens)?
2. What are the benefits of the regulations to each user group (income redistribution, employment)?
3. What are the specific economic impacts on the local, regional and national economies (prices, supplies, productivity, imports, exports, markets for complementary or substitute products)?
4. What are the alternatives ways of ensuring compliance (self regulation, incentives, market rights, reporting, inspection, observers)?
5. What are the administrative costs of implementing the FMP (enforcement, data collection, preparation of the FMP)?

A Detailed Explanation of the Reasons for Choosing the
Preferred Regulatory Alternative Over the Others

The final step in the RA is to demonstrate that one of the alternatives is superior to the others. Depending on the method used to evaluate each alternative, the selection criteria may include cost effectiveness, net present value, balance of payment gains, increases in productivity or other measures of gains in economic efficiency. On the other hand, FMP may contain management measures which do not necessarily foster economic efficiency, but only redistribute benefits by regulating user groups. In any case, the councils will make decisions involving tradeoffs among user groups and it is necessary to indicate the basis for this decision.

The RA attempts to introduce disciplined analysis into the rulemaking process. It requires the councils and the Secretary of Commerce to evaluate thoroughly the available information, and perhaps to take steps to obtain more. This type of analysis should, if done properly, result in a better definition of the issues involved, a better appreciation of the difficulties to be overcome in reaching the FMP objectives and a better understanding of the fishing industry.

The RA can be an effective means to guard against overregulation which occurs where the costs outweigh the beneficial effects. Even in fisheries where the benefits of regulation exceed the costs, it does not necessarily follow that the proposed set of regulations should be implemented. It may turn out that a less costly management alternative is available but was rejected or not even considered.

In several FMP, the practice of the councils has been to select a specific set of management measures—gear, seasons, quotas—without exploring alternative combinations of measures. As long as these measures result in gains to the fishery (however calculated), then this alternative is usually adopted. Under these circumstances, the RA and FMP are used to rationalize a specific approach rather than to objectively evaluate alternative approaches as required by Executive Order 12044 in the rulemaking process.

A PERSPECTIVE ON FISHERY
MANAGEMENT PLAN STRATEGIES

The decision of a council to prepare an FMP acknowledges that government intervention is necessary to provide a socially desirable allocation of resources in a particular fishery. To overcome market failure problems and move toward economic efficiency and fishery development goals, a choice must be made on the type of regulatory environment: command and control regulations for modifying institutional structure, or incentive programs. Virtually all implemented FMP have adopted a command and control regulatory approach to influence the behavior of the harvesting sector using management tools such as catch allocations, quotas, gear restrictions, regulation of incidental catches and discards, and area and landing restrictions.

Rarely have the councils considered the establishment of property rights or incentive oriented approaches. Although command and control techniques may be the best regulatory approach in some fisheries, they could lead to situations where the council actions "become a race between the ingenuity of the regulatee and the loophole closing of the regulator, with a continuing expansion in the volume of regulations as the outcome" [Schultze 1977]. This is often the result of a regulatory lag between the time the council diagnoses a problem through a biological assessment or by monitoring the economic performance of the fishery and the time when the regulations are implemented.

Atlantic Groundfish: A Case of Direct Control [Mueller and Vadaeus 1978]

The Atlantic Groundfish FMP (AGFMP) is a good example of a plan where the management strategy chosen by the council involves direct regulation of U.S. fishermen. The primary objective of the FMP is to "generate over the period of the plan the greatest possible joint economic and social benefits from the harvesting and utilization of the groundfish resources, ensuring that by the end of the period the relevant groundfish stocks shall be in conditions which will produce enhanced and relatively stable yields from the ground-fish fishery in future years" [New England Fishery Management Council 1979, 1980]. In pursuit of this goal, the AGFMP establishes an intricate quota system complete with allocations to specific vessel classes by management area and species. During 1977-1980, the council, through the Secretary of Commerce, undertook an estimated 43 regulatory actions affecting allocations, gear restrictions, fishing seasons, closures and optimum yield (OY), and also including corrections to previously published regulations.

The regulatory actions in this fishery are an example of an attempt to detail the particular actions that could achieve social efficiency (the greatest benefit to the nation as defined by the council), and then command their performance. However, these actions were undertaken with limited information on the regulatory impacts on the user groups. It is possible that some regulatory actions may not have been proposed if better information had been available. The New England Council is considering alternative management strategies in Amendment No. 5 which could reduce the degree of regulation in the AGF fishery and still achieve management goals.

The AGFMP is characterized by the classic problem of too many vessels fishery for a limited quantity of fish. In a period of rising prices for Atlantic groundfish, there has been a significant increase in the number of vessels entering the fishery, despite the uncertainty that satisfactory catch levels can be maintained indefinitely.

The regulatory policy adopted by the New England Council has been to permit an open access fishery while intervening to allocate the cod, haddock and yellowtail flounder to vessel class groups, and to impose trip limits as previously described. The council, acting through the federal government, has been making many of the basic decisions normally made independently by fishermen: catch rates, gear, seasons, number of trips and fishing areas. Council allocation decisions also affect the distribution of income in the fishery and it is not entirely clear whether the redistribution that has occurred under the current regulatory environment is any better than a system without regulations.

The major amendments to the AGFMP and the technical amendments were in response to either biological or economic emergencies in the fishery and problems caused by the regulatory lag. Justification for these actions gives the appearance of conflict. The biological emergency argument centered on the need to prevent catches from exceeding the OY or else risk the possibility of depleting the resource. The economic emergency actions were justified on the basis that if OY were not increased, fishermen would suffer reductions in income because of fishery closures. This raises the question of whether the OY were specified properly in the first place. In justifying the economic emergency actions, however, the regulatory amendments did not indicate whether net profits would be negative or whether they would be reduced from levels achieved because OY were not increased to prevent closures of the fishery. By the time the council had taken emergency action dealing with one set of problems, fishing effort always seemed to intensify forcing the council to again reconsider an adjustment to OY. The council, therefore, had to make frequent decisions on the optimal harvest rate in the fishery, i.e., balance the short-run welfare of the user against long-run gains from larger stock sizes.

One consequence of the council decision to prevent unjustifiable economic hardships on the industry (although never fully documented in the FMP or amendments) is to downplay the effect of the allocation and OY decisions on the prices and supply of groundfish to the consumer market. The regulatory changes proposed in Amendment No. 4 to the FMP, for example, alter the quarterly catch rates. Relative to the previous fishing pattern, the changes in the total allowable catches increase the quotas in quarters 1 and 2, and decrease them in quarters 3 and 4. The proposed amendment also would change the seasonal harvesting patterns for cod and haddock. Under the proposed quotas, it was estimated that average prices would increase between 12 and 29% depending on the species and the quarter. Further, it was expected that these price increases would be passed on to consumers.

The AGFMP raises the policy issue of how to weigh the impacts of management measures which may benefit fishermen but alter the historical supply pattern in the market and introduce new factors which cause retail prices to fluctuate. The management system adopted in the AGFMP appears to impose what can be described as a "regulatory externality" in which a set of regulations are designed to benefit one group but the costs are borne by a third party. Neither the FMP nor supporting analyses consider the inflationary impact of the management strategy as an important issue, which leaves open the questions of how the FMP achieves the OY to the nation.

Salmon: Regulations with Special Constraints

The salmon FMP addresses the need to control the ocean salmon fishery off the coasts of Washington, Oregon and California to achieve and maintain optimum spawning escapements [Pacific Fishery Management Council 1977, 1979]. The user groups include commercial troll, ocean sport, inside commercial and sport, and treaty Indians. A critical issue faced by the Pacific Council, in addition to the escapement problem, is the allocation of salmon among the user groups. Allocation is constrained by several federal court orders which reserve for certain treaty Indian tribes in Washington and Oregon the opportunity to make 50% of the harvest of salmon that is destined for the Indians "usual and accustomed" fishing areas. However, the court order did not specify the regulatory approach for making the allocation.

In the salmon FMP, the Pacific Council made implicit allocation decisions through detailed rules controlling fishing seasons, gear, size of fish, closures and permitted fishing areas. This raises the question of what is the best possible regulatory regime called for by economic efficiency considerations? Does this management regime allocate fishery resources such that user groups are better off than without the council allocation? What is the appropriate type of economic analysis that could aid the council in evaluating the tradeoffs among user groups that will achieve OY and provide the optimum benefits to the nation? How do consumers enter into the allocation problem, especially when fish transferred among groups could reduce the salmon availabe to the consumer and export markets? Does the council consider the effect of its management decisions on groups external to the fishery? It is possible that the council attempted to minimize the political problems that might occur if there was a movement away from the status quo situation in the fishery. Although the FMP has been in place since 1978 and amended each year through 1980, it is not clear whether any economic efficiency gains have been achieved. The FMP has been so controversial that the Secretary of Commerce has been sued by one or more groups every year since the FMP was first implemented.

The lawsuits raise the question of whether there are alternative management strategies which alter the institutional structure or change the incentive patterns that could achieve the FMP goals. Indeed, command and control techniques are the favored approach since they follow state management strategies. However, the FMP has not as yet demonstrated through an appropriate analysis that detailed regulations to achieve management objectives are superior to market-like instruments, nor whether there has been a marked improvement in the economic performance of the fishery compared to a "no regulation" alternative.

Surf Clam/Ocean Quahog: Complex Regulatory Control

The surf clam and ocean quahog FMP is another example where complex regulations control fishing behavior and allocations [Mid-Atlantic Fishery Management Council 1977]. This FMP has been amended twice since it was implemented in 1977. The primary objectives are to rebuild the declining surf clam populations and minimize short-term economic dislocations during the rebuilding process.

The FMP regulates all phases of fishing activity at the harvesting level. Management measures establish quarterly quotas, restrict the number of days fished, prohibit entry of new vessels into the fishery (but allows replacement of vessels that left involuntarily during the moratorium), impose minimum surf clam size limits, and establish conditions for closure of surf clam beds. A direct vessel allocation system and a limitation on dredged size were considered, but were rejected in the public review process. The moratorium is expected to be in place through 1981. In the interim, the council continues to review alternative approaches to managing the fishery. As in other fisheries, council decisions in the surf clam/ocean quahog fishery affect the distribution of income, the size of the product to be processed and market prices. These are important issues for management decisions because of the strong consumer demand for surf clam products and the substitutability between surf clams and ocean quahogs, and the minimum size of surf clams for efficient operation of the processing plants.

Management with Minimum Intervention

The FMP for Atlantic butterfish [Mid-Atlantic Fishery Management Council 1977] and Alaskan Tanner crab [North Pacific Fishery Management Council 1977] provide an interesting contrast to the management objectives and regulatory approaches in the AGF, salmon and surf clam FMP. The butterfish FMP was prepared in response to the objective of the Mid-Atlantic Council to provide an environment conducive to the development of a butterfish export market to Japan [Mid-Atlantic Fishery Management Council 1977]. Prior to the FCMA, the market in Japan was supplied by Japanese catches of butterfish in the FCZ (formerly statistical areas 5 and 6 of the International Commission for the Northwest Atlantic Fisheries). In the butterfish FMP, the council presumed a relationship between the growth of the U.S. export industry and the size of the total allowable level of foreign fishing, i.e., the higher the total allowable level of foreign fishing, the lower the foreign demand for U.S.-caught butterfish. Furthermore, the council assumed that the foreign demand for U.S.-caught butterfish was partially dependent on a potential reallocation of the total allowable level of foreign fishing from U.S. harvesting capacity during the fishing season.

The major issue in the FMP, therefore, was the specification of OY, U.S. harvesting and processing capacity, and the total allowable level of foreign fishing. The domestic harvesting capacity was estimated to be higher than the historical landing levels before the FMP. There are no regulations on effort, seasons or gear, and so U.S. fishermen can make the basic decisions on fishing strategy, catch rates and product quality. Consequently, the success of this FMP depends upon how effectively U.S. fishermen respond to the price signals of the Japanese market.

This management strategy has been in effect for the 1978-1979 and 1979-1980 fishing seasons. Amendment 1 also adopted the export development objective for the 1980-81 fishing season. Preliminary data show that U.S. catches were below projected estimates of harvesting capacity and that an insignificant quantity of butterfish was exported. Current data for the 1980-1981 fishing season suggest that U.S. catches and exports may be below projections in Amendment 1.

During the public comment period on proposed regulations, commenters on Amendment 1 indicated that a market for Atlantic butterfish products exists in Japan, but because of the poor quality of previous U.S. exports, the product cannot be marketed successfully in Japan. As a result, the commenters argued that there should be higher foreign allocations of butterfish. At least for the 1980-1981 fishing season, however, the fishery development objective will be pursued so that U.S. industry has every opportunity to refine its harvesting and processing techniques to produce a butterfish product of acceptable quality.

The Tanner crab fishery consists of *C. bairdi* and *C. opilio* (see North Pacific Fishery Management Council [1977]). Before the FCMA, the Japanese fishing fleet operating in the Gulf of Alaska and Eastern Bering Sea harvested *C. bairdi*, which generally was the preferred species in the Japanese market. In the Tanner crab FMP, the North Pacific Council eliminated the *C. bairdi* total allowable level of foreign fishing because U.S. fishermen had sufficient capacity to harvest all available *C. bairdi* and significant quantities of *C. opilio*. As U.S. fishing vessels entered the fishery, exports of Tanner crab to Japan between 1976 and 1979 increased from almost nothing to more than 47,000 metric tons.

The FMP, with minimal regulations, provided an opportunity for U.S. fishermen to penetrate an existing foreign market for Tanner crab. Although effort has been increasing, the council has not been confronted with the need to intervene directly in the fishery by making vessel allocations. However, this and potential open access over utilization are potential problems that must be considered if the Tanner crab market continues to growth both in Japan and the United States. The allocation problem raises questions on the type of management regime that may be implemented in future amendments. Does the council intend to become more involved in the allocation decisions or minimize its interference by establishing other types of market arrangements which rely on limited entry or property rights?

SUMMARY

In the FMP that have been implemented, the regulation of fisheries either involved the detailed specification of compliance actions or minimum interference with the market mechanism. The implications of the command and control FMP is that all phases of fishing activity will eventually be regulated. In the initial stages of an FMP, the fishery will usually be open-access with controls on seasons, gear and quotas. This has led, in some cases, to vessel class allocations, followed by restrictions on different components of effort (vessels, number of days fished, amount of gear, etc.). This may not be consonant with the intent of Congress as expressed in the FCMA and the recent efforts for regulatory reform.

None of the implemented FMP have carefully evaluated alternative regulatory approaches which may include licensing (with some other regulations as well), establishment of property rights or perhaps even specific vessel allocations. The councils have not clearly articulated tradeoffs between economic efficiency and other goals, nor have they provided any indication of a weighting scheme for making the choices among user groups.

The FMP process should place more emphasis on the analysis of alternative regulatory regimes focusing on issues such as: (1) the need for regulation as opposed to the status quo situation; (2) the state-federal relationship in the management of fishery resources that occurs in both state waters and the FCZ; (3) the need for more explicit recognition of commercial and recreational uses of fishery resources; (4) the need to integrate fishery development objectives into FMP; (5) the optimal catch levels taking into account the users and the consumers of the resource; (6) the open-access control problem; (7) the minimum cost enforcement program for a given management strategy; and (8) the feasible ways of allocating the total allowable catch among users. There is a need for careful analysis of these issues for each FMP so as to provide indications of where regulations can increase the benefits of fishery management to the nation. There may be fisheries where the net benefits of regulation are virtually nonexistent since all possible regulations impose very high administrative and enforcement costs. Efforts aimed at measuring the benefits and costs of regulation will have a high payoff in terms of avoiding unproductive regulations.

DISCLAIMER

This chapter expresses the views of the author, and does not necessarily reflect the policies of the National Marine Fisheries Service.

REFERENCES

1. Anderson, L. G. 1977. *The Economics of Fisheries Management* (Baltimore, MD: The Johns Hopkins University Press).
2. Christy, F. T., Jr., and A. Scott. 1965. *The Common Wealth in Ocean Fisheries: Some Problems of Growth and Economic Allocation* (Baltimore, MD: The Johns Hopkins University Press).

3. Copes, P. 1972. "Sole Ownership and the Optimum Level of Fisheries Exploitation," The Manchester School of Social and Economic Studies 40:145-163.
4. Crutchfield, J. A., and A. Zellner. 1962. "Economic Aspects of the Pacific Halibut Fishery," Fishery Ind. Res. 1(1).
5. Executive Order 12044. 1978. "On Improving Government Relations," Federal Register 43(58):12661-12669.
6. Gordon, H. S. 1954. "Economic Theory of a Common-Property Resource: The Fishery," J. Polit. Econ. 62:124-142.
7. Mid-Atlantic Fishery Management Council. 1977. "Atlantic Clam Fishery Management Plan."
8. Mid-Atlantic Fishery Management Council. 1978. "Final Environmental Impact Statement/Fishery Management Plan for the Butterfish Fishery of the Northwest Atlantic Ocean."
9. Mueller, J., and L. Vadaeus. 1978. "Management of the Commercial Groundfish Fishery off the U.S. Northeast Coast" (unpublished manuscript).
10. New England Fishery Management Council. 1979. "Final Supplement No. 3 to the Environmental Impact Statement and Amendment to the Atlantic Groundfish Fishery Management Plan."
11. New England Fishery Management Council. 1980. "Final Supplement No. 4 to the Environmental Impact Statement and Amendment to the Fishery Management Plan for Atlantic Groundfish."
12. North Pacific Fishery Management Council. 1977. "Fishery Management Plan and Environmental Impact Statement for the Tanner Crab off Alaska."
13. Pacific Fishery Management Council. 1977. "Draft Fishery Management Plan and Environmental Impact Statement for Commercial and Recreational Salmon Fisheries off the Coasts of Washington, Oregon, and California Commencing in 1978."
14. Pacific Fishery Management Council. 1979. "Supplement to the Final Environmental Impact Statement/Fishery Management for Commercial and Recreational Salmon Fisheries."
15. Schultze, C. L. 1977. "The Public Use of Private Interest," J. Gov. Society (September/October).
16. Scott, A. D. 1955. "The Fishery: The Objectives of Sole Ownership," J. Polit. Econ. 63:116-124.
17. Stigler, G. J. 1971. "The Theory of Economic Regulation," Bell. J. Econ. Management Sci. 2(1):3-21.
18. U.S. Regulatory Council. 1979. "Regulatory Reform: The President's Program," Washington, DC (unpublished report).
19. U.S. Regulatory Council. 1980. "Regulatory Reform Highlights: An Inventory of Initiatives 1978-1980," Washington, DC.
20. Weidenbaum, M. L. 1978. "The Impacts of Government Regulations," Working Paper No. 32, Center for the Study of American Business, St. Louis, MO.
21. Weitzman, M. L. 1978. "Optimal Rewards for Economic Regulation," Am. Econ. Rev. 68(14):683-691.

CHAPTER 3

ECONOMIC ANALYSIS FOR
NORTHERN ANCHOVY MANAGEMENT

Daniel D. Huppert
   Southwest Fisheries Center
   National Marine Fisheries Service

Published in July of 1978, the Pacific Fishery Management Council's management plan for the northern anchovy fishery off of California was the second plan (after salmon) to be implemented on the West Coast. The high priority given to the development of the anchovy plan was due largely to the apparent ecological importance of the fish stock and to the great political sensitivity of anchovy management issues in California. For the most part, traditional economic issues were drowned out by the noneconomic concerns of recreationists and public agencies. Nevertheless, a moderate amount of economic information was assembled and analyzed for inclusion in the plan that was eventually adopted. After the introduction of the planned regulations in September 1978, the economists and biologists responsible for most of the analysis at the National Marine Fisheries Service Southwest Fisheries Center continued to examine management strategies and issues pertinent to the northern anchovy. Most of the ideas, data, and analytical results presented in this paper resulted from the joint efforts of the management planning team at the Southwest Fisheries Center.[1]

This chapter is organized into four major sections. In the first section, five important economic issues are listed and described. Following that, a section is devoted to the presentation of biological, institutional and economic information providing a necessary real-world context for the management problems. In the third section economic theories are tailored to the specific needs of

41

anchovy management, and analytical results are presented. In applying economics to the fishery, areas of theoretical weakness and data deficiency are revealed. In the concluding section the strengths and weaknesses of the existing economic analyses are reviewed, and recommendations for further research are advanced.

ECONOMIC ISSUES FOR ANCHOVY FISHERY MANAGEMENT

While no short list of topics can fully represent the complex management issues at stake in the formulation of public regulations for northern anchovies, the following five points cover the most substantial areas for economic analysis:

1. evaluation of the aggregate harvest rate by the U.S. fishery;
2. allocation of the fish harvest among various end uses;
3. analysis of the optimum investment in harvesting and processing capacity;
4. formulation of regulatory mechanisms to achieve the desired objectives for catch, investment and so forth; and
5. design of management information and monitoring programs.

To analyze any of these issues one must adopt some criterion or objective for management. A single economic objective that will provide the framework for the following discussions is the traditional one of maximizing the economic value of goods produced, net of production costs. Within this objective is contained the requirement that the fishery achieve productive efficiency, the minimization of costs incurred in producing the desired level of output. Within this context the careful identification of costs and values is clearly a principal task. Since neither the fish stock nor the recreationally caught fish are traded in markets, the economic analysis must account for nonmarketed and unpriced goods as well as commercial product values. As any student of welfare economics knows, the adoption of this "net economic yield" criterion for management cannot be rigorously defended since the distribution of income will be influenced by the fishery policy and we have not determined what changes in income distribution are desirable. Bromley and Bishop [1977] examine this aspect in great detail, concluding that the traditional approach to fisheries economics by focusing on economic efficiency issues ignores income distributional impacts and much of economic welfare theory. Assuming that any income distributional consequences of anchovy management decisions are on a small scale and that these can be remedied by other means, however, the traditional efficiency objective will serve as a useful guide in the following discussion.

Much of the economic theory of fisheries is devoted to the first topic listed above—evaluation of aggregate harvest rates. Since many extensive reviews of this theory are available [Anderson 1977; Clark 1976; and Peterson and Fisher 1977], no lengthy theoretical treatise is called for here. In application, however, the theory leaves much to be desired. As noted by Peterson and

Fisher, the "functional forms are too simple and their empirical content too low." Institutional, geographical and organizational content is often sacrificed to preserve mathematical tractability or to allow two-dimensional, pedagogical diagrams. Since we are addressing an actual management problem, simplicity-destroying complications must be introduced in some fashion. Three apparently important complications arising in the anchovy fishery are (1) the multipurpose nature of the fishing fleet; (2) the stochastic variability of the stock; and (3) the importance of anchovies as forage. Economic implications of these are discussed below.

Allocation among end uses, the second topic, is an important consideration for anchovy management because the widespread use of anchovies for live bait by both recreational and commercial fishermen is politically and economically more significant than their use as meal and oil. Market values per unit weight for live bait are estimated to be 8-10 times the value of fish used by reduction plants. One might be tempted to assume, therefore, that the free market forces could be counted on to assure the proper allocation to live bait, reduction fish and other end uses. This is not the case, however, because the two products are produced by two separate groups of fishermen having different equipment, locations and alternative opportunities. Most importantly, there is no institutional framework within which the live-bait interests can bargain with the reduction fishery interests to assure that the reduction fishery does not take all the available fish. In part this is a problem caused by the existing management procedures. An annual quota is set in the fall, while the major live-bait market occurs in the summer months. If the quota is taken before the summer begins, live bait would not be available at the appropriate time. Thus a set of separate quotas, or some other allocative device, is needed.

The third issue has occupied fishery economists concerned with the problem of "overcapitalization." Under some regulatory schemes, the fishery may be induced to harvest the proper quantity of fish (by some definition) but private, profit-oriented fishermen will have strong incentives to construct and operate far more fishing vessels than necessary to take the allowable catch. Arbitrary limits on some inputs to the production function encourages greater (and uneconomic) use of other inputs. This breach of the productive efficiency criterion is especially likely when regulations rely on "standards" (like quotas, size limits and gear restrictions) rather than incentive-compatible mechanisms (like taxes and property rights) to achieve narrowly defined harvest goals. A public policy toward fishery inputs, however, must rely on a normative theory of optimum input use, especially the optimum level of capital investment. An important secondary issue is whether the expected extra cost associated with unregulated input use exceeds the benefits of regulation.

The fourth issue listed above is concerned primarily with the economic efficiency of the management operations once the specific objectives of management have been defined. Experience with regulatory programs elsewhere, especially in pollution control and environment regulation, has led most economists to recommend pricing mechanisms rather than absolute standards as regulatory tools. Others prefer property right arrangements. But as Scott [1979] points out, either system can achieve a given set of goals regarding efficiency, equity and conservation. One of the principal considerations in choice of regulatory tools must be the prospective cost (economic and political) of gathering and monitoring the data needed to assure that the regulations are being obeyed with sufficient regularity to support the management program. This issue has not received the extensive formal analysis that it deserves in the fisheries literature. The cost of running a successful management program with a given set of regulations probably depends crucially on the extent to which the rules incite individual fishermen to evade enforcement and monitoring efforts. And these incentives will depend on the physical ease with which rules can be broken without detection, as well as upon the financial consequences of rule-breaking behavior.

The final issue I have suggested for economic examination requires that the tools of economics be turned inward on the analysts themselves. One frequently hears that more economic data, better stock assessments and more extensive enforcement of regulations are "needed." These claims are sometimes motivated by requirements laid down in the Fishery Conservation and Management Act (FCMA), such as National Standard (2) (Sec. 301) calling for the use of the "best scientific information available," or the "optimum yield" definition [Sec. 3(18)] which requires the consideration of economic and social factors. But information is costly to obtain. Thus optimum yield cannot logically call for vast reservoirs of data which contribute little to the decision-making process. Similarly, "best" scientific information is not necessarily the most comprehensive or conclusive information, but rather the most appropriate level of knowledge, given cost and time constraints. The economic theory of information suggests that new data be valued by the expected increase in discounted future returns associated with the decisions dependent on that information. (See, for example, Hirshleifer and Riley [1979].) This opens up a relatively unexplored area for analysis in fisheries management, but one which could potentially contribute significantly to the efficiency of management operations.

There are undoubtedly fruitful areas for economic analysis in addition to the five discussed here. But these five seem sufficiently important to the management of northern anchovies to demand immediate attention. As implied in much of the earlier discussion, the author considers it to be crucial that economic analysis be guided by the biological, economic and institutional context in which the managed industry exists. To adequately understand the relative importance of various policy issues and to intelligently judge the adequacy of economic analyses, therefore, the reader must have a firm grasp of the situation faced by fishery managers in California. Consequently, the next section of the paper is devoted to a presentation of pertinent background information.

THE BIOLOGICAL, INSTITUTIONAL AND ECONOMIC CONTEXT

Biological Basis

Important characteristics of the fish stock include location, size, potential yield and function in the ecosystem. The following summary information on these characteristics for the anchovy stock is drawn from Huppert et al. [1980a] which is a slightly modified version of the Anchovy Fishery Management Plan [1978], and Huppert et al. [1980b], an updated investigation of the population dynamics model and other technical issues. These two reports rely upon the many scientific studies carried out by the California State Department of Fish and Game (CF&G), the National Marine Fisheries Service, Scripps Institution of Oceanography and California Academy of Sciences. The brief review contained below serves to place the discussion of fishery management in context, but is not a substitute for the more extended treatments available elsewhere.

The northern anchovy, *Engraulis mordax,* is a small, pelagic schooling fish occurring along the west coast of North America from Queen Charlotte Sound in the north to the southern tip of Baja California. Significant physical differences in the fish found within this range suggest the existence of three separate subpopulations [Vrooman and Paloma 1975]. As shown in Figure 1, the northern subpopulation occurs essentially north of San Francisco; the central subpopulation extends from San Francisco to Punta Baja; and the southern subpopulation stretches south from Punta Baja to the tip of the Baja California peninsula. The central subpopulation is the most abundant of the three, and it is the stock unit adopted for management by the Pacific Fishery Management Council (PFMC). The bulk of the population biomass is consistently located in the Southern California Bight, an area of approximately 20,000 square nautical miles bounded by Point Conception, California in the north and by Ensenada, Mexico in the south.

Estimates of the central subpopulation's spawning biomass (Table I) are based on anchovy larva abundance estimates derived from the ichthyoplankton collections of the California Cooperative Oceanic Fisheries Investigations (CalCOFI), a consortium of scientific research agencies involved in oceanographic research. The biomass estimates for the 1951-1966 period suggest a logistic-shaped growth path. After reaching a peak biomass of 4.7 million

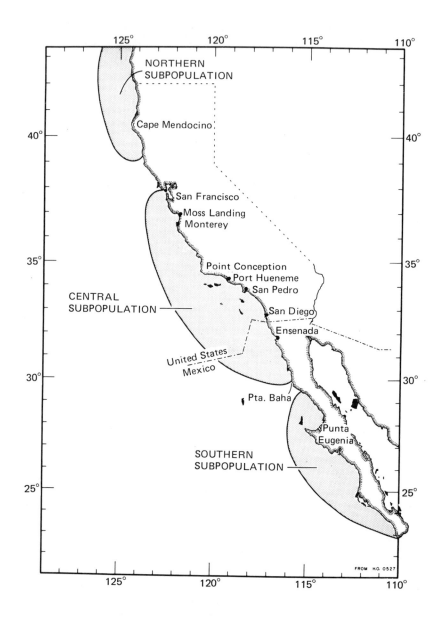

Figure 1.   Approximate location of three subpopulations of northern anchovy.

Table I.   Population Size and Harvests from the Central Subpopulation of
Northern Anchovies (in thousands of short tons)[a]

| Year | Estimated[b] Biomass | California Landings | | Ensenada Landings[c] |
		Commercial	Live-bait	
1951	180	3	5	–
1952	156	28	7	–
1953	510	43	6	–
1954	768	21	5	–
1955	845	22	6	–
1956	485	28	6	–
1957	1167	20	4	–
1958	1479	6	4	–
1959	1514	4	5	–
1960	1540	3	5	–
1961	1159	4	6	–
1962	2989	1	6	–
1963	4254	2	4	–
1964	2901	3	5	–
1965	4659	3	6	10
1966	3572	31	7	15
1967	--	35	5	25
1968	–	16	7	17
1969	2999	68	5	4
1970	–	96	6	6
1971	--	45	6	4
1972	2784	69	6	7
1973	--	133	6	2
1974	–	83	6	48
1975	3603	159	5	61
1976	–	122	5	79
1977	–	110	5	157
1978	1304	11	5	143
1979	1723	52[d]	5[d]	208[d]
1980	1775	--	–	–

[a]Sources: California Department of Fish and Game and Instituto Nacional de Pesca.

[b]After 1966 the ichthyoplankton cruises upon which the biomass estimates depend were
reduced from annual to tri-annual; in 1979 annual survey were resumed.

[c]Data not available for Ensenada before 1965.

[d]Preliminary estimates.

short tons in 1965, however, the stock has fluctuated and declined sharply. The 1978 biomass of 1.3 million tons was the smallest anchovy stock encountered since 1961. In addition to the spawning biomass measured by the larva census estimate, there is a substantial biomass of juvenile fish. In view of the rapid growth in juvenile anchovies, the cohort of immature fish probably reaches a maximum biomass slightly before the end of its first year of life. The fish mature between their first and second years, and the recruiting yearclass of fish begins to appear in the commercial catch a few months before it reaches one year of age. Thus the fishery could exploit a stock larger than the estimated spawning stock in the absence of any minimum size regulations to protect juveniles.

Although there was a small anchovy fishery for canning in the early 1950s, the fluctuations in biomass prior to the inception of the California reduction fishery in 1966 were due primarily to natural causes.[2] Additional evidence of natural fluctuations in stock size is provided by the anaerobic sediment data from Soutar and Isaacs [1974]. Smith [1978] converted the scale depositions in the sediment samples into biomass estimates for 38 five-year intervals from 1775 to 1970. The average anchovy biomass over this period is estimated to be 4.5 million metric tons with a coefficient of variation equal to 0.47.[3] This degree of variability is consistent with that observed in clupeoid fish stocks around the world [Murphy 1977].

The central subpopulation also undergoes north-south shifts. Stauffer [1978], again using CalCOFI larva census data, found that the percent of the standing stock of anchovy larvae north of the United States/Mexico boundary varied between 45 and 86% during the 1951-1975 period. Over the whole period combined 70% of the larvae were found in U.S. waters. Assuming that larva distribution is a good indicator of fish distribution, the data suggest that 70% of the fishable stock is within the United States jurisdiction.[4]

Published studies of the potential yield from the central subpopulation are based on a variety of population models and result in a disturbingly wide range of biological yield estimates. The most optimistic estimate was that of MacCall et al. [1976]. Using a crude, rule-of-thumb method suggested by Gulland [1970], MacCall et al. concluded that the potential yield of northern anchovy is over 2 million tons.[5] A cautionary note following the estimate suggested that this level of yield would not be sustainable due to the year-to-year fluctuations in the stock.

Radovich and MacCall [1979][6] presented a model based on the assumption that the stock observed during 1951-1975 followed a logistic growth equation. The estimated model is:

$$B(t) = B_{max}/[1 + e^{-r(t - t_o)}]$$
(1)

where B_{max} = 4.0 million tons

· r   = 0.36

t_o = the time at which the inflection in the growth curve occurs

The stock growth rate is given by the time derivative of the logistic equation. A maximum to the growth rate occurs at $B_{max}/2$ where dB/dt = 360,000 tons/yr. To calculate the potential yield from a fishery Radovich and MacCall assumed that the biomass measurement represents the spring spawning stock just after the new cohort of fish recruits to the spawning stock, and that the fishery takes fish from the stock at a steady rate during the year. Since the maximum annual growth represents the change in stock size at year-end, and the fishing mortality competes with natural mortality during the year, a fishery should be able to take more than the annual growth in equilibrium. Estimating that the excess of potential yield over potential growth at about 25%, Radovich and MacCall estimate MSY to be 450,000 short ton/yr.

In developing the yield estimates for the Anchovy FMP, MacCall modified his population model somewhat. The main innovation was the explicit treatment given to the size of and yield from the recruiting yearclass. Also, the logistic equation was reestimated after adjusting for the levels of harvest taken in California. The most recent estimates for the parameter of the logistic equation are B_{max} = 4.207 × 10^6 short tons and r = 0.3638 (see Huppert et al. [1980b]). A reparameterization allows the population transition equation to be written as:

$$B_{t+1} = B_t K/(H + B_t) \qquad (2)$$

where $K = B_{max}/(1 - e^{-r}) = 13.8 \times 10^6$ tons

$H = Ke^{-r} = 9.6 \times 10^6$ tons

The population transition equation applies to an unfished population.

Noting that the rate of natural mortality is due primarily to predation, starvation and other factors not related to the fishery, we assume that the percentage rate of mortality to the spawning biomass is constant. Since both somatic growth and mortality in numbers of fish occur simultaneously, we use a net mortality rate, (M-G), equal to 0.8 (see MacCall [1980]). If the measured spawning biomass disappears at this rate during a calendar year between biomass measurements, then any excess of biomass over adult fish survival appearing in accordance with Equation 2 must be recruitment. Thus recruitment can be expressed as a function of the previous year's biomass as follows:

$$R_{t+1} = B_t K/(H + B_t) - B_t e^{-(M - G)} \tag{3}$$

In the presence of a fishery which causes a constant percentage rate of mortality, denoted F, the population transition equation becomes:

$$B_{t+1} = B_t K/(H + B_t) - B_t e^{-(M - G)}(1 - e^{-F}) \tag{4}$$

where it is assumed that the juveniles are unaffected by the fishing. The catch taken during a year can be expressed as the following function of B_t and F:

$$Y_t = (F/F + M - G)(1 - e^{-(F + M - G)})B_t \tag{5}$$

Figure 2 depicts the equilibrium annual stock growth and the equilibrium yield curve given the parameter estimates noted above.

To examine the effects of harvesting juveniles Equations 3 to 5 must be modified to account for fishing mortality on juveniles. This involves specifying the relative availability of juveniles to the fishing effort. In MacCall [1978] and Huppert et al. [1980a,b] the juveniles are estimated to be available for 20% of the year with about 76% of the catchability of adults. Since the insertion of the juvenile harvest complicates the algebra while introducing no useful insight into the model, the interested reader is referred to the above-mentioned reports. The only important aspect of the harvest of juveniles is its impact on the equilibrium yield curve. As juveniles become more vulnerable the equilibrium yield from the fish stock falls as shown in Figure 2.

Another way of viewing the population dynamics shows the mortality of adults and recruitment to the stock as two separate components. In Figure 3, for example, the biomass at time T generates the recruitment at time T + 1 through the function labeled A. This recruitment function is just the graph of Equation 3, and the straight line out of the origin labeled "replacement" represents the total loss of adult biomass due to natural causes in a year. If the size of recruitment equals the total mortality, the population just maintains itself; hence the term "replacement." For spawning biomasses below the equilibrium level of 4.2 million tons, the recruitment exceeds the replacement level and net growth occurs. Two important issues regarding the validity of the estimated population model can be discussed with the aid of this figure. First, the estimated stock-recruitment relationship is not a very close "fit" to the 15 observations shown on the diagram, but the null hypothesis that recruitment is unrelated to spawning stock size can be rejected with better than 95% confidence.[7] Thus the statistically fitted equation can be used to make conditional predictions, but with a high degree of uncertainty. The standard deviation of the error about the recruitment function for the 15 observations

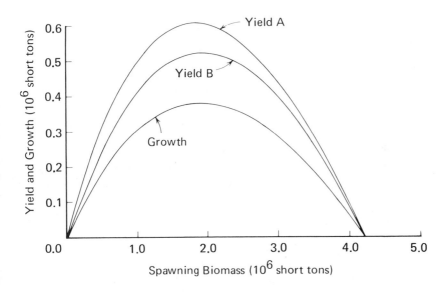

Figure 2.   Population growth and yield curves for the northern anchovy, central sub-population, with (Yield A) and without (Yield B) harvest of immature fish.

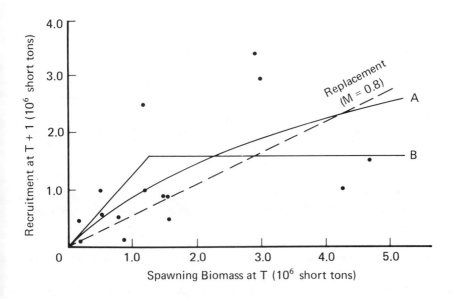

Figure 3.   Alternative stock-recruitment models. Model A is the logistic model, and Model B is the modified constant Recruitment Model.

is about 860,000 tons. Second, an alternative model of recruitment, which is labeled B in Figure 3 assumes that recruitment equals 1.247 times spawning biomass up to a biomass of 1.225 million tons and equals 1.527 million tons for larger stock sizes. This alternative model cannot be distinguished statistically from the original logistic-based model with a reasonable degree of confidence.[8] Given these two facts, the approach to management of the anchovy fishery must somehow recognize the level of uncertainty in the population model. One method described below is to adopt a stochastic decision-making framework.

One immediate consequence of the stochastic recruitment and yield curves is that the concept of sustainable yield is inapplicable. Although the peak of the yield curve may occur at 520,000 tons, this level of yield is in no sense sustainable. An attempt to take this "MSY" year after year can be expected to severely deplete the population within a short period of time. Although the theory of managing stochastic, fluctuating fish populations is not very well developed, the few published papers seem to support some general conclusions. Beddington and May [1977], for example, conclude that populations fluctuating due to environmental conditions will become unstable under either constant fishing effort or constant catch policies. They conclude that a feedback control policy should be adopted.

All the above comments address anchovy management solely in terms of the fish catch and the dynamics of the stock. But anchovies, like most clupeoid fishes, are a forage stock for many predators. In the California Current some of the known predators are commercially and recreationally important fish. These include tunas, barracuda, sea basses, jack mackerel, Pacific mackerel, Pacific bonito, yellowtail, striped bass, salmon, swordfish, striped marlin and others. Other known or suspected predators of northern anchovy include marine mammals (common dolphins, northern fur seals, California sea lions and others), and many varieties of marine birds including the brown pelican, a designated endangered species.

Anchovies are, of course, just one of a group of small schooling fish species that are preyed on by larger fish, birds and mammals. Other species are sardine, saury, mackerel, herring and lanternfish. In her "biomass budget" for the California Current Region, Green [1978] estimated that the total predation on small schooling fish amounts to at least 24 million ton/yr. Of this total estimated consumption of small fish only a small portion could be contributed by the anchovy stock.[9]

Management policies for anchovies should take into consideration the effect of reduced anchovy stocks on the food supply for, and resultant average stock size of predator species. But the available information is rather sparse and inconclusive regarding these interspecies impacts. Some predators may be much more dependent on the availability of anchovies than would be suggested by an examination of average food intake. For instance, there may be a short, but critical mating or spawning season during which the need for anchovy schools is essential. Comprehensive research may someday provide reliable, predictive models to reveal these ecosystem linkages. But current knowledge simply lacks the detail necessary to contribute quantitative models to the fishery management process.

Political/Institutional Setting

Management of the anchovy reduction fishery in California must, as Kaneen [1977] remarked, "walk in the shadow of the sardine fishery." Two legacies of the now-defunct sardine fishery play a significant role. First, the obvious failure of state authorities to prevent catastrophe in the sardine fishery, despite intense and lengthy scientific study, bolstered the mistrust of fisheries managers by recreational fishing and environmental groups. California sardines supported the United States' largest (by tonnage) fishery during the mid-1930s and early 1940s. The peak catch of 791,000 tons occurred in 1936-1937, and the average annual catch during 1934-1946 was 600,000 tons. A severe drop in stock size occurred in the late 1940s, followed by a moderate rebound in 1950-1951, and another collapse in 1952. After many years of small landings, sardine harvests were prohibited entirely in 1970. Years of scientific research resulted in some detailed post mortems [Murphy 1966; Ahlstrom and Radovich 1970], but the causes for the stock collapse are still not fully understood. Perhaps the most common view, as expressed by Murphy [1966; 1967; 1977], is that the fishery was extracting sardines faster than could be sustained during the 1940s until the recruitment of two successive poor year classes (1949 and 1950) reduced the stock to a size too small to generate large year classes. There is still controversy over the annual yield that the sardine population could have sustained (see Murphy, [1966] and MacCall, [1979]).

A second legacy from the sardine days is the institutionalized bias against the reduction of fish into meal and oil. Early in the sardine fishery the state legislature was persuaded to regulate the reduction fishery (without, of course, putting effective restraints on the fishing for canneries). Interested readers are directed to Schaefer et al. [1951] for a detailed account of these regulatory actions. The important fact is that producers, who had begun to pass a larger fraction of the fish through reduction plants, were prevented from utilizing the fish in the way they found most profitable. Mandel [1975] notes that this constituted a specific rejection of economic profit as a criterion for determining the best use of California resources. Clearly, this was not the only or most prominent rejection of simple economic criteria for resource allocation.

When the state legislature transferred control of the anchovy reduction fishery to the California Fish and Game Commission in 1965, it was largely motivated by the sharp and politically unrewarding controversy between commercial interests and recreational groups. Strengthening the commercial fishermen's argument for a reduction fishery was the scientific recommendation that a 200,000-ton experimental quota be established for anchovies. The CalCOFI committee had reasoned that the vastly expanded anchovy stock might be retarding the reestablishment of the more valuable sardine (see CalCOFI [1966]). A 200,000-ton catch was reckoned to be about 10% of the standing stock, a minimum withdrawal necessary to produce a measurable change in the anchovy/sardine system. The commission established an annual quota of 75,000 tons for the 1965-1966 season and maintained the quota until 1970 when the fishery expanded enough to justify larger quotas. The U.S. fishery has yet to reach a catch total of 200,000 tons.

Because of its ancestry, therefore, California's anchovy management program has had an undeniably conservative slant. Whether this is justifiable or not depends largely on subjective judgment. A sympathetic evaluation would emphasize the risk inherent in an aggressive fishery. Undetected failures of recruitment, combined with heavy fishing could easily lead to the demise of another fish stock. One suspects that rugged commercial fishermen, and perhaps society-at-large, would be willing to accept these risks in a simple commercial venture. The remaining unquantified factor, however, is the potential impact on other fish stocks and the subsequent deleterious effect on marine recreational and commercial fishing activities. As noted in the previous section of the paper, multispecies and ecosystem models are as yet unable to provide practical advice on these issues, and the possibility exists that some delicate balances in the system might be tipped inadvertently by a more extensive anchovy fishery.

Mexico's attitude toward the development of a reduction fishery for anchovies is spawned in a different environment. Establishment of income-generating fisheries is a key component in Mexico's national plan for marine resources. The Food and Agriculture Organization of the United Nations (FAO) assisted Mexico in developing plans for fishery development specific to the northern anchovy off of Baja California. Wadsworth [1974] outlined a plan for an eventual 500,000 ton/yr. fishery with 200,000 tons being produced at Ensenada and 100,000 tons at each of three more southerly ports. A later report [FAO-Mexico 1978] repeats the earlier plan and specifically mentions the fact that California does not intend to exploit its portion of the anchovy stock.

Mexico's plan for fishery development is reaching fruition through the efforts of Pesquera Zapata S.A. de C.V., a company jointly held by Mexican investors and Zapata Corporation of the United States. This new venture established a reduction plant in Ensenada and brought in six new U.S.-built purse seine vessels. Initial operations in 1976 were followed by rapid growth of the fishery to about 150,000 ton/yr. in 1977 and 1978 (see Table I). The Mexican fishery evidently takes some unknown fraction of its fish from the southern subpopulation, but most undoubtedly comes from the central sub-population. Because of the rapid diffusion of fish throughout their range, it can be expected that withdrawals to the south of the international border will affect the average abundance of anchovies to the north. Thus the need for some reconciliation of goal and procedures is clear. To date the United States government has been unable to induce Mexican officials to seriously consider a joint fishery management regime.

Economic Characteristics

The three main segments of the anchovy fishing fleet are (1) the so-called "wetfish" fleet in southern California[10]; (2) a smaller group of vessels in Monterey Bay; and (3) the live-bait fishing vessels scattered along the southern California coast in ports with substantial amounts of marine recreational fishing. All of these vessels use roundhaul nets, with the purse seine type predominating in the commercial reduction fishery and the lampara type being commonly used for live-bait fishing. Many of the wetfish vessels are survivors of the sardine fishery, but some are small tuna purse seiners and one is newly constructed specifically for the anchovy/mackerel fishery. As indicated in Table I, nearly all the anchovy catch is for the reduction processors. The U.S. reduction harvests are distributed geographically with 80% of the catch landed in Los Angeles, 16% in Port Hueneme and 4% in Monterey.

The number of vessels landing anchovies varies considerably from year to year. In 1975, the peak year for U.S. reduction fishery landings, 80 vessels participated, while only 29 reported landing anchovies for reduction during the 1979-1980 fishing season. Many of the vessels capable of fishing extensively for anchovies shift to the mackerel fishery (jack and Pacific mackerel) for substantial portions of the year and fish opportunistically for Pacific bonito, bluefin tuna and squid. Table II shows that anchovy landings generally account for the bulk of the wetfish landings by weight. But due to the lower prices received for anchovy (about $42 vs $160/ton for mackerel in 1980), the revenue derived from anchovy fishing is less than half of the total revenue for the fleet.

Live-bait operations generally consist of at least one roundhaul vessel and some bait receivers for holding the fish in good condition. Currently, there are 11 or 12 such live-bait operations. A major portion of the typical live-bait dealer's business is covered by contract obligations to local partyboat and charter boat businesses. Gruen, Gruen and Associates [1979] estimated the 1977 live-bait sales to be worth $2.6 million. Aggregate estimated live-bait landings have remained consistently between 500,000 and 700,000 tons over the past 10 years.

Although a wide range of vessel sizes and catch rates is exhibited in the anchovy reduction fishery, existing data are sufficient only to support a

Table II. Landings and Values of Wetfish Fleet in San Pedro and Port Hueneme, 1960-1979[a]

Landings (short tons)

Year	Anchovy[b] (Reduction)	Jack Mackerel[c]	Pacific Mackerel[c]	Pacific Bonito[d]	Bluefin Tuna[e]	Pacific Sardine[f]	Squid[g]	Total	Deflated Value[i]
1960	–	36,338	18,279	603	1,488	27,185	163	84,056	–
1961	–	46,968	22,011	4,199	2,553	21,006	3,299	100,036	--
1962	–	43,963	24,265	975	4,702	6,386	1,855	82,146	–
1963	–	46,895	20,109	1,964	4,441	2,895	2,337	78,641	–
1964	--	43,554	13,411	1,236	2,602	10,043	3,530	74,376	–
1965	171	31,957	3,517	2,729	1,881	792	4,695	45,742	–
1966	19,009	19,806	2,290	8,748	3,140	425	3,736	57,154	–
1967	23,952	18,623	571	7,714	1,528	70	3,799	56,257	–
1968	9,518	27,354	1,564	7,423	1,921	51	4,781	52,612	–
1969	62,390	25,736	1,173	6,340	2,008	41	4,256	101,944	–
1970	91,892	23,615	309	4,292	691	134	7,305	128,238	–
1971	42,288	29,854	77	4,684	1,211	82	2,598	80,794	–
1972	65,843	25,495	53	7,708	2,525	163	2,288	104,075	--
1973	126,082	10,016	27	9,203	1,911	66	1,278	148,583	--
1974	75,420	12,709	66	6,801	2,157	7	2,910	100,070	–
1975	148,516	18,370	142	1,680	3,796	3	4,350	176,857	–
1976	118,463	22,380	173	1,922	2,013	8	3,015	147,974	–
1977	101,402	52,288	3,650	1,334	868	2	4,709	164,253	–
1978	10,898	34,000	12,282	800	1,424	1	3,307	62,712	–
1979	48,545	17,575	29,503	250	1,597	17	2,260	99,747	–

Ex Vessel Value ($1000)

Year	Anchovy[b] (Reduction)	Jack Mackerel[c]	Pacific Mackerel[c]	Pacific Bonito[d]	Bluefin Tuna[e]	Pacific Sardine[f]	Squid[g]	Total	Deflated Value[i]
1960	–	1,534.1	751.1	34.9	362.7	1,117.7	7.6	3,808.1	9,177.5
1961	--	1,952.7	1,182.6	214.2	661.7	1,108.7	102.2	5,222.1	12,475.6
1962	–	1,826.3	1,024.9	55.6	1,320.7	408.7	46.5	4,682.7	10,985.6
1963	–	1,954.5	860.0	108.6	1,000.7	235.1	61.6	4,220.5	9,757.8
1964	–	2,048.2	666.2	60.3	633.1	456.2	86.0	3,950.0	8,990.2
1965	5.9	1,753.5	222.7	141.3	491.5	89.7	101.0	2,805.6	6,248.1
1966	388.2	1,377.9	185.8	694.5	920.9	147.0	104.1	3,818.4	8,232.4
1967	484.4	1,411.5	71.3	646.4	373.7	28.4	124.9	3,140.6	6,576.4
1968	167.0	2,085.4	167.3	616.2	584.3	14.5	142.8	3,777.5	7,570.1
1969	1,224.2	1,949.9	121.2	588.4	641.1	9.2	153.4	4,687.4	8,943.7
1970	2,030.1	1,860.6	49.1	609.3	258.4	57.7	291.6	5,156.8	9,344.0
1971	999.8	2,408.9	7.2	845.9	504.0	35.2	85.5	4,886.5	8,424.1
1972	1,566.0	2,147.6	6.0	1,403.5	1,086.7	48.9	81.9	6,340.6	10,493.7
1973	6,250.3	959.3	3.6	1,887.2	902.7	21.8	88.8	10,113.7	15,818.1
1974	3,076.6	1,493.6	10.6	1,811.6	1,238.5	0.9	215.8	7,847.6	11,198.1
1975	4,455.5	1,691.2	14.3	414.7	1,874.6	0.3	255.4	8,706.0	11,334.8
1976	4,326.3	2,237.3	18.1	524.3	1,215.1	0.7	149.4	8,471.2	10,487.2
1977	4,563.1	5,228.8	365.0	428.6	880.3	0.2	353.2	11,819.2	13,804.7
1978[h]	490.4	3,740.0	1,351.0	312.0	1,167.3	0.1	330.7	7,391.4	8,041.8
1979[h]	2,184.5	2,525.0	4,208.0	97.5	1,309.5	1.5	226.0	10,552.0	10,552.0

[a]Sources: California Department of Fish and Game, Fish Bulletins, California Marine Fish Landings, 1960-1976; Statistical Report of Fishery Products, 1977; unpublished preliminary estimates, 1978-1979; U.S. Dept. of Commerce, Fishery Statistics of the U.S., 1960-1975; Fisheries of the U.S., 1975-1979.
[b]Anchovy reduction landings, southern permit area.
[c]Total landings, all vessels.
[d]Total landings, all vessels, in California waters, 1960-1977; estimates for 1978-79.
[e]Landings by a group of vessels described by CF&G as wetfish, So. Calif. pelagic, or small (class 1 or 2) purse seiners, 1960-1976, estimates for 1977-1979.
[f]Total landings, all vessels.
[g]Landings by purse seine and lampara vessels, 1960-1975; estimates for 1977-1979 (excludes landings by dip and brail gear).
[h]Preliminary estimates, CF&G.
[i]Values adjusted for inflation by GNP implicit price deflator, 1979 = 100.

simple model of fishing costs representing a typical 58-ft purse seiner. Combs [1977] provides an estimate of minimum operating cost per ton landed of $24.58. Given that the better vessels averaged 78.1 ton/day fished in 1975, the daily operating cost is estimated to be about $1920. A vessel with this daily cost had a new price of about $425,000 in 1978.

The relationship between daily catch rate (i.e., catch per effort) and anchovy stock size has not been established, but MacCall [1976] has examined the relationship for sardines.[11] Since the sardine fleet operated in a fashion similar to that of the anchovy fleet, we may borrow the shape of the catch curve from the sardine fishery and then rescale it to the 1975 anchovy catch per effort. MacCall's equation introduces a nonlinear catch curve by specifying that the "catchability coefficient" be a function of fish stock biomass, B, so the catch equation becomes:

$$y = qfB \qquad (6)$$

with $\qquad q = aB^b$

Inserting the estimated value of b (= −0.6) into Equation 6 gives us

$$y = afB^{0.4} \qquad (7)$$

Catch per effort, y/f, of 78.1 tons in 1975 corresponds to a biomass of 3.6 million tons. Placing these values in Equation 6 allows us to solve for a = 0.186. Furthermore, noting that operating cost per day for a standard vessel is fixed at $1920, we can specify the operating cost per ton as the following function of stock biomass

$$C_1 = 10315 \, B^{-0.4} \qquad (8)$$

This operating cost function and the capital cost of $425,000 per vessel represents the known cost structure of the reduction fishing fleet.

Fish reduction plants in Los Angeles, Port Hueneme and Monterey produce fish meal, fish solubles and fish oil from anchovies. The product yields per ton of fresh fish processed varies among fish species, and, for a given species, among seasons of the year. The average product yields per ton of anchovy landed are:

Meal: 0.182 ton (348 lb)
Solubles: 0.112 ton (224 lb)
Oil: 0.0384 ton (76.8 lb)

Oil yield is especially variable, ranging from 140 lb/ton in September to 38 lb/ton of anchovy in the spawning season, February-April.

The meal and liquid solubles are sold as protein supplements for use in feeds for chickens, turkeys and freshwater fish. Local southern California poultry farmers buy most of the local fish meal and solubles. Imported anchovy, tuna/mackerel mix and menhaden meal from the Gulf and South Atlantic coasts are nearly perfect substitutes. Also, meat and bone meal from beef is a close substitute, and various vegetable protein meals (especially soybean and cottonseed meal) are readily available alternative sources of high-protein meal for poultry rations. Due to the cost-minimizing behavior of poultry growers and the ease of substitution, anchovy meal demand is naturally highly elastic. The only sources of market advantage for southern California anchovy meal seem to be (1) its higher protein content as compared with local tuna/mackerel and soybean meals, and (2) the cost of transporting fish meal to California from more distant production sites. A single-equation, linear least squares estimate of the inverse demand curve contained in Department of Commerce [1978] and Huppert et al. [1980a] is

$$p_m = 359.13 - 1.147 \, q_m \qquad (9)$$

where p_m is price per ton of meal and q_m is annual quantity of meal produced (in thousands of tons).

Neither the fish solubles nor oil markets for anchovy have been investigated sufficiently to yield similar, quantitative estimates of demand curves. Instead, we adopt a fixed-price for oil and solubles based on the average prices observed during 1970-1977. The average price of 12.87 ¢/lb for anchovy meal, implies a contribution of $9.88/ton of anchovies processed. Similarly, the average price for solubles was $105/ton, which converts to $11.76/ton of anchovies. Assuming these fixed prices, and converting the anchovy meal price equation to a function of fish landings (landings equal 5.5 times meal produced) we get a "value per ton landed" equation

$$v = 86.9 - 3.795 \times 10^{-5} \, y \qquad (10)$$

where y is annual landings. Although a more comprehensive study of the market demand would undoubtedly yield a more precise valuation procedure, Equation 10 provides a useful, rough estimate of the market value of reduction fishery harvests.

The industry structure in southern California is characterized by buyer and seller concentration in the raw fish sector, and by rigorous competition in the product markets. That is, the fishing fleet is organized by two unions—Fishermen's and Allied Workers Union (ILWU) and Fishermen's Union of America

(AFL-CIO)–and a vessel owners cooperative–the Fishermen's Cooperative Association of San Pedro. Fishermen in Monterey (or Moss Landing) are also represented by a chapter of the Fishermen's Union of America, but the few vessels landing at Port Hueneme apparently operate without benefit of a special organization. Buyers of anchovies for reduction are distributed as follows: one in Moss Landing, one in Port Hueneme and two in Los Angeles harbor. Competition in the fish meal and oil markets is assumed due to the large numbers of buyers and the plethora of alternative sources of both fish meal and other protein meals.

Because of the close-knit structure of the fishery/processor sector in all the reduction fishing ports, prices and wages are not a competitive market solution. Instead, the net value of the intermediate products sold is distributed to the various participants (reduction plant operators, fishing vessel owners, and crew members) through negotiated pricing and crewshare agreements. As is typical in marine fisheries, the crew members are paid a share of the landed value of the catch less direct operating expenses. Current arrangements call for a 58% share of the net landed value to be split among the 12-man crew.[12] The crewshare is negotiated between the Fishermen's Cooperative and the unions. Similarly, the Fishermen's Cooperative (with active guidance by the unions) negotiates a pricing formula for anchovy landings. The 1978 formula was

$$
p_f = \begin{cases} 25 + (p_m/65 - 3) \times 7.5 & \text{if } p_m/65 \geqslant 3 \\ 25. & \text{if } p_m/65 < 3 \end{cases} \tag{12}
$$

where p_f is price per ton of fish and p_m is price of fish meal quoted in the Department of Agriculture's *Feed Market News* (Los Angeles, California). Thus a meal price of \$390/ton results in a fish price of \$47.50/ton. This pricing agreement is analogous to the contingent contracts commonly signed by labor unions (see, e.g., Hall and Lilien [1979]). In this regard it is noteworthy that the minimum price of \$25 is just above the estimated minimum average cost of \$24.58/ton harvested. This strongly suggests that the ex-vessel fish price is related to the opportunity costs of fishing.

Processing of anchovies is estimated to cost \$23.30/ton of fresh fish landed (D. Cukierman, personal communication). This cost is, of course, dependent on the rate of flow through the reduction plant to some minor extent, but this fact will be ignored in subsequent discussions. Combining this constant processing cost, the fishing cost (Equation 8), and the gross market value (Equation 10), the net economic profit for the consolidated fishing/processing sector is expressed as

$$
NV = (63.6 - 3.795 \times 10^{-5}y)y - (10315B^{-0.4})y \tag{13}
$$

where capital costs of plant and vessels are not yet introduced.

The economic parameters and functional relationships described here are used in the following section on applications of economic theory to anchovy management. Table III presents a summary of these. Clearly, however, the broader economic concerns of nonreduction fishing and the ecological function of anchovies are as important as the quantified reduction fishery. The economic description of the fishery focused on the reduction fishery because the harvest for reduction is the major use of anchovies commercially, and because the data and analyses needed to quantitatively consider the other uses for anchovy are not available. As management analysts, however, economists must avoid the tendency to emphasize the importance of those things that are quantified to the neglect of those that are not.

THEORY AND ANALYSIS OF ECONOMIC ISSUES

Each of the five issues discussed in the second section above can be examined from the viewpoint of economic theory. The two issues which are most extensively and satisfactorily treated are those regarding optimum (i.e., economically efficient) reductions harvest rates and optimum investment in fishing capacity. Because these two issues are closely linked in the theoretical model they are combined in the first part of this section. Following this, the discussion turns

Table III.   Economic Parameters and Functions for the Anchovy Reduction Fishery

---

1. Inverse demand equation for processed products:

$$v = 86.9 - 3.795 \times 10^{-5} q_f$$

where v is value per ton of fish landed and q_f is tons of fish landed.

2. Average variable cost per ton landed:

$$c_1 = 10315 \, B^{-0.4}$$

where B is stock biomass

3. Capital cost of fishing fleet:

$$c_2 = 425,000 \, N$$

where N is number of fishing vessels in the fleet.

4. Cost of processing per ton landed:

$$c_3 = 23.30 \, q_f$$

to the allocation issue. Both the allocation of anchovies to the live-bait fleet and to the enrichment of the ecosystem are important aspects. A brief discussion of regulatory mechanisms for managing the fishery precedes the final section which presents an economic approach to determining the "best" level of precision to attempt in measuring the stock size. Where data and/or appropriate theory are lacking the deficiencies are noted.

Optimum Harvest Strategies and Fleet Size

The term optimum harvest *strategy* emphasizes the need for a contingency plan, that is, for a harvest plan which adapts to the unpredictable variations in fish stock size brought about by oceanographic and ecological events. A substantial portion of existing theory assumes a deterministic world in which biological and economic relationships are known and predictable. Even the more recent dynamic optimization theorists [Brown 1974; Clark 1976; Quirk and Smith 1970] examine the characteristics of the long-run steady-state in great detail, while treating very briefly the problem of approaching a steady-state, and ignoring entirely the need for adaptive control in a fluctuating environment. This is not to criticize the development of dynamic, capital-theoretic analysis of fisheries, because substantial gains in understanding have resulted from these developments. But recent papers by operations researchers and mathematicians have explored the theory and solution methods for stochastic optimizing models (cf. Walters [1975]; Walters and Hilborn [1976]; Reed [1979]; Mendelssohn [1980]). These focus on the derivation of optimum harvest strategies with uncertain biological production parameters. The consequences of market uncertainty, measurement error and social aversion to variability have yet to be adequately examined in the fisheries context.

The first step in applying an optimization method is, of course, the adoption of a management objective. Ignoring for the moment the nonreduction uses and ecological linkages important to anchovy management, we define an economically optimal harvest strategy as one which sets the harvest annually to maximize the expected discounted value of the fishery. In any year the net value of the fishery equals the net profit to the fishing industry plus any consumer's surplus obtained by those purchasing the fish meal, oil and solubles. Profit to the fishing industry was examined above, but the existence of surplus is less transparent because the usual notion of consumer's surplus applies only to markets for final consumption goods. Fortunately, Just and Hueth [1979] have shown that under certain conditions the overall welfare effect of a change in quantity of an intermediate good is represented by the usual "area under the demand curve" associated with consumer's surplus. The intermediate good must be in a vertical chain of markets none of which has a perfectly elastic demand curve.[13] An acceptable procedure, therefore, is to combine the area under the demand curve but above the current market price with the industry profits to obtain an overall economic value. Based on Equation 13 the resulting algebraic expression is:

$$NEV(y,B) = (63.6 - 1.8975 \times 10^{-5}y)y - (10315B^{-0.4}y) \qquad (14)$$

where we ignore capital costs for now.

The long-run objective, the net present value (NPV) of the anchovy fishery over a period of T years, is computed by the usual formula:

$$NPV(y,B) = \sum_{t=o}^{T} NEV(y_t,B_t) (1/1 + d)^t \qquad (15)$$

where d is a discount rate and $(1/1+d)^t$ is the discount factor applied to a monetary return occurring t years in the future. To introduce the random variability exhibited by the anchovy stock, the stock transition equation is multiplied by a lognormal error term ϵ.

$$B_{t+1} = g(y_t,B_t)\epsilon \qquad (16)$$

where ϵ has a mean value equal to one.[14] The function g( ) is the mean or expected stock transition function. Assuming that the public decision-maker is not averse to risk per se, the objective can be reexpressed as the expected net present value,

$$EPV = E(\sum_{t=o}^{T} NEV(y_t, B_t) (1/1 + d)^t) = \sum_{t=o}^{T} E (NEV(y_t, B_t) (1/1 + d)^t) \qquad (17)$$

The problem of maximizing the EPV subject to a stochastic stock transition equation can be decomposed into a sequence of annual decisions, each of which requires that the EPV be maximized for all future years, given the current stock biomass, B_t. Thus in year 1 the problem is to maximize

$$EPV_1 = NEV(y_1, B_1) + E(\sum_{i=2}^{T} NEV(y_i, B_i) (1/1 + d)^i) \qquad (18)$$

It is most practical to solve this sort of problem with stochastic dynamic programming methods. The reader is referred to Hillier and Lieberman [1967] for a thorough introduction to the mathematics, but a common sense interpretation of the process is attempted here.

Equation 18 indicates that there are two ways to utilize the available biomass in any year. One is to harvest the fish, thus enjoying an immediate economic return. The other is to leave the fish in the ocean to contribute to the stock available in future years, thus increasing the potential future economic value. The current value of harvesting fish is subject to diminishing returns, and is dependent also on the current fish stock biomass, since unit harvesting costs are lower with greater biomass. The diminishing marginal value of catch discourages any tendency to harvest all the fish at once, and the decrease in harvesting costs resulting from larger biomasses provides one incentive for maintaining a larger fish stock. In addition, the expected percentage rate of growth in the fish stock grows as the stock declines, thus increasing the incentive to "invest" in the stock rather than to "liquidate" it when the stock is small. These various incentives are countervailing to some extent. Larger biomass means lower harvesting costs, but also lower percentage returns to investment in the stock. Thus the optimum policy must choose a trade-off between current and future returns which properly accounts for the impact of current harvests on the future. At the optimum current year harvest, the marginal value of additional catch just equals the marginal decrement to expected discounted value from future years.

Since the current value of a given level of harvest is enhanced by increased biomass, and since the percentage rate of growth in the stock is negatively related to biomass, we should expect larger current year biomass levels to be associated with greater current year harvests in the optimal program. That is, the optimum harvest strategy (optimum harvest as a function of, or contingent upon biomass) has a positive slope. A second common sense result is that there may be a biomass level below which the marginal value of current harvest is less than the expected contribution of increased biomass to future return for *any* positive level of harvest. That is, below some minimum biomass the optimum decision is to harvest none at all.[15]

The optimal harvest strategy for the anchovy reduction fishery, assuming no fishing capacity constraint and no other users of the resource, is displayed as Strategy I in Figure 4. This optimal strategy was computed assuming a discount rate of 0.04,[16] and a standard deviation of 0.3 for the proportional random error term in the stock transition equation.[17] To facilitate an interpretation of this harvest strategy, the expected yield curve from Figure 2 is reproduced on Figure 4. According to this optimum strategy, when biomass is below 1.1 million tons, the potential future return from investment in the stock exceeds the current net economic value of even a small harvest. At biomass levels between 1.1 million and 2.6 million tons, the optimum harvest is less than the expected growth in the stock, thus reflecting investment in a larger stock. Above a biomass of 2.6 million tons the optimum strategy calls for a drawing down of the stock, or dis-investment in biomass.

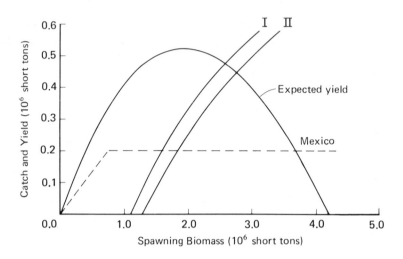

Figure 4.   Optimal harvest strategies for the U.S. reduction fishery. Curve I is for fishery without Mexican competition. Curve II assumes Mexico takes an amount represented by the broken line.

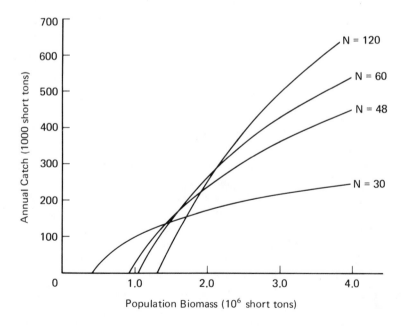

Figure 5.   Optimum harvest strategies for the U.S. reduction fishery with fleet size constraints ranging from 30 vessels to 120 vessels. (Still assume Mexican harvest is as depicted in Figure 4.)

As explained earlier, the Mexican fishery for anchovy reduction at Ensenada expanded to an annual harvest of around 200,000 tons, most of which is from the central subpopulation of anchovies. If we assume that Mexico will continue to take 200,000 tons per year, the optimum U.S. harvest strategy is altered. Since reduced stock size would affect the Mexican fishery, we assume that no more than 90% would be taken of the 30% of the stock below the U.S./Mexican border. Given this admittedly arbitrary assumption, the U.S. strategy calls for a lower U.S. catch at every stock size (approximately 50,000 ton/yr lower than without the Mexican fishery), and an increase in the fishery cut off level of biomass from 1.1 to 1.3 million tons. Additional consideration of international strategies for harvesting the jointly fished stock along lines outlined by Anderson [1975] may be useful, but this requires economic data regarding the Mexican fishery that are unavailable to the author.

In deriving harvest strategies I and II in Figure 4, only the operating costs for fishing vessels and reduction plants were subtracted from the gross value in computing NEV. This is equivalent to assuming that fishing effort is unlimited. But the capacity for catching anchovies is limited by both the number of vessels and the stock abundance. Assuming each vessel fishes 144 days per year, the amount of nominal fishing effort available per year is $N \times 144 = f_{max}$, where N represents number of homogeneous anchovy fishing vessels. Inserting this and the estimate value for the parameter "a" into Equation 7 yields the following capacity constraint:

$$y_{max} = 26.78 \, N \, B^{0.4} \tag{19}$$

The existence of such a constraint will alter the optimum strategy if some of the potential harvest rates along the unconstrained strategy curve (Strategy curve I in Figure 4) require more than the available fishing effort. With a fishing fleet of 48 vessels, for example, harvest strategy I exceeds the capacity output when biomass exceeds 2.57 million tons.

Optimum U.S. harvest strategies for a range of fleet sizes (and, again, assuming that Mexico harvests 200,000 tons) are displayed in Figure 5. As shown, diminishing fleet size dictates a falling harvest cutoff level and a lower peak catch level. For any one of these strategy curves the variations in biomass due to natural, unpredictable events will cause the fishery to harvest different amounts in different years. A frequency distribution of annual catches will be generated for any strategy and underlying error distribution in the biomass transition equation. Since the capacity constraint limits annual catch, it truncates the frequency distribution of catches on the righthand tail. A larger capacity, therefore, permits the fishery to take the larger catch consistent with large biomasses. But since the optimum strategy, with no capacity constraint, has an equilibrium harvest of around 470,000 tons (at an equilibrium biomass of 2.6 million tons), a capacity to take, say, one million tons might not be economical. A huge capacity would be used very infrequently; hence, the marginal expected value of an additional vessel must become very small for fishing fleets very much larger than that needed to take 470,000 tons.

One could define the optimum fleet size as that number of vessels which maximizes the net discounted value of the fishery minus the capital cost of building the fishing fleet. The curve labeled NPV in Figure 6 is the maximum net present value of the U.S. anchovy reduction fishery as related to fleet size. Each point represents NPV over a 25-year period. Only operating costs are considered in NPV, so the investment needed to build a fleet of N vessels is represented separately by the line labeled "capital cost." This line assumes each new vessel costs $425,000. It is easy to see that the maximum net difference between NPV and fleet capital cost occurs at a fleet size of about 48 vessels.

Assuming the absence of any recreational, ecological or income distributional concerns in the anchovy fishery, the economically efficient U.S. harvest strategy is the one labelled "N = 48" in Figure 5, and the optimum fleet size is 48. While this result is by no means conclusive (note the many qualifications in the previous statement), it provides a useful quantitative assessment of how economic considerations cause optimum yield to deviate from maximum sustained yield. Despite further modifications to incorporate noncommercial and noneconomic considerations into the optimum harvest strategy, two points will continue to be essential. First, the optimum harvest strategy is a contingency plan (or feedback control) which adapts current harvests to current stock levels for longer-term objectives. And, second, the optimum fleet size must be determined in a stochastic context which recognizes that all vessels will be fully utilized only infrequently.

Some of the key deficiences in the foregoing economic analysis are (1) the lack of multifishery interactions considered in the single-species optimizing framework; (2) the lack of market uncertainty in the model; and (3) the crudeness of estimated economic parameters such as those in the unit harvesting cost function, the demand function and the capacity relationship. Fishery interactions are particularly important for the southern California purse seine fleet as illustrated by the catch data in Table II. Since the capacity to fish is not specific to anchovy fishing, neither is the capital cost of the fleet. Furthermore, the opportunity costs of not fishing for, say, bonito or mackerel may frequently be greater than the current net return from anchovy fishing for many vessels. Thus the optimum rate of anchovy harvest ultimately depends on many other biological and market conditions. Before better multifishery models can be implemented, however, I think that additional serious theoretical development must ensue, possibly along lines suggested by Huppert [1979] or Anderson [1980]. More precise data on the fishing fleet economic parameters are needed, since the optimality of the given policies depends so critically on these values and the existing information is partly dependent upon extrapolations and secondary sources.

Allocation Among End-Uses

In a sense the allocation of fish among uses should be a part of the optimum harvest strategy. Any harvest by the reduction fishery clearly preempts some other use of the fish, and this is properly done only after comparison of the reduction fishery value to the opportunity costs associated with other uses. A

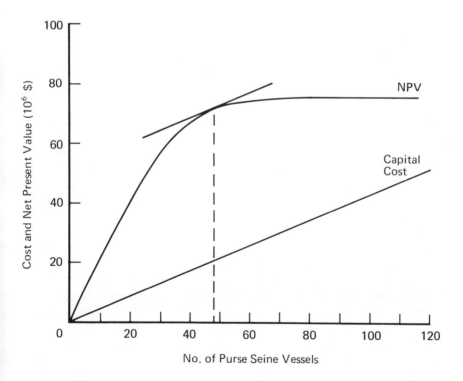

Figure 6.   Net present value of the U.S. reduction fishery versus capital cost of the fleet.

more complete derivation of optimum harvests, therefore, would involve a more complicated economic value equation containing separate components for each end-use, and an additional constraint requiring the sum of the harvests to equal the total withdrawal from the population. An optimum harvest strategy with two end uses, for instance, would maximize the sum of two value expressions, NEV_1 and NEV_2. In most circumstances one would expect the optimum strategy to occur with an allocation of catch between the two uses such that the marginal values of fish in the two uses are equal.[18] In considering the allocation of anchovy harvest between reduction and live bait, however, no such analysis was performed.

To implement the theoretical model several additional pieces of information would be needed: (1) a demand curve for live-bait; (2) the costs of fishing for live-bait and holding the fish live; and (3) the physical relationship between reduction and live-bait fishing in the ocean. Available information suggests that such a formal analysis may be unnecessary. First, with respect to the third point, much of the live-bait fishing takes place nearshore during the late spring, summer and early fall. The "availability" of anchovy schools in the narrowly circumscribed baiting areas seems to determine the success of the live-bait operators in meeting contractual commitments to partyboats and in supplying the general public. The little evidence available does not suggest that the success of live-bait fishing is related to the anchovy stock size. If bait supply does not depend directly on the biomass and indirectly on the reduction fishery harvests, the need for treating the two fisheries as two competing users in an analysis of optimum harvesting strategy is negated. Furthermore, the small size of the live-bait harvests means that there is no detectable impact directly on the fish stock and indirectly on the reduction fishery. Given this perception of the situation, the arbitrary assignment of a portion of the overall harvest quota to the live-bait fishery (which is essentially the procedure followed in the Anchovy Fishery Management Plan) may be a perfectly acceptable resolution to the problem.

The other form of allocation, between harvest of anchovies and forage for higher-level predators, is not so easily dispensed with, but is even less amenable to analysis with existing empirical knowledge. Again, the theoretical format for determining an optimal harvesting program would have to be extended to include other sources of economic value. Since anchovies are preyed on by many commercial and recreational fish, the number of values would be great. The problem is further compounded by the fact that the recreational values are difficult to measure and the ecological models available are only suggestive of the structure of the interspecies relationships, not useful, predictive tools of analysis. In a general, qualitative sense, however, an optimum harvest strategy recognizing the ecological-cum-commercial and recreational value of anchovies as forage would harvest the stock more conservatively than the strategies without such recognition.

Choice of Regulatory Tools

There are several good surveys of fishery regulations. Crutchfield [1961; 1979], Anderson [1977], and Clark [1980] are particularly complete. The usual array of management methods includes annual fishery quotas, individual fisherman quotas, limitations on the kinds of gear used, limitation of the numbers of fishermen or vessels licensed, restriction of the fishery to certain areas or seasons, taxes or royalties on fish landings, and license fees. A few generalizations can be gleaned from the literature. First, in the face of severe fish stock depletion under open competition, any aggregate limitation on total annual withdrawals from the fish stock is beneficial if it enables the fishery to sustain a much higher harvest level. More consumer's surplus is generated even if no further efforts are directed toward productive efficiency (cost minimization). Second, a complex set of physical restrictions on fishing activities (such as gear, season, area and size limit regulations) may maximize the physical yield of the fishery, but so long as other dimensions of fishing effort are open to manipulation (at a cost) a competitive fishing industry will be unlikely to achieve a high degree of economic efficiency. To approach the socially optimal configuration of productive factors in the fishery as well as the ideal harvest rate requires either (1) an infinite degree of control over the individual fishing operations, or (2) a set of rules and conditions which elicits fishermen behavior consistent with economic efficiency. A variety of taxing schemes and altered property rights regimes have been proposed in order to meet this second condition.

In the Anchovy Plan a great variety of regulations were proposed. These included (1) the establishment of a harvest strategy curve for the California fishery, (2) a size limit of five inches on the reduction fishery, (3) closure of nearshore areas to reduction fishing, (4) closure of the reduction fishery during the peak summer recreational fishing season and during the peak anchovy spawning season (February/March), (5) allocation of the quota to nonreduction fishermen and among reduction fisheries north and south of Pt. Buchon, (6) adjustment of the annual quota in response to imbalances in the ratio of male and female fish in the harvest, and (7) license limitation in the reduction fishery. Of these, only the last two were rejected by the Pacific Fishery Management Council. Economic analysis gave some support to the harvest strategy curve, but the fact that the curve finally adopted was nearly identical to the existing California state plan leaves open the possibility that inertia was the dominant factor. And the license limitation proposal which was motivated explicitly by the economic efficiency rationale found little support, ostensibly due to the absence of a hugely overcapitalized fleet. The slight support given the license limitation scheme came, ironically, from both the commercial and recreational groups. The commercial interests were presumably intrigued by the possibility of forming a closed shop, and the recreationists were willing to opt for any regulation limiting the size of the commercial fishery. Economic efficiency considerations, in other words, held little sway in the decision-making process.

The analysis of alternative kinds of economic regulations in the anchovy fishery suffers from fundamental defects stemming from inadequacies in the existing theory. Even the primary motivation for regulating the fishery could be given further attention. The usual argument is that a freely competitive fishery will overfish the stock, if not biologically then at least economically. But, as Scott [1955] pointed out, a sole owner would operate the fishery efficiently. And more recently Clark and Munro [1979] have suggested that a monopsonist fish processor may also run an economically efficient fishery. In the anchovy fishery we have neither a sole owner nor a true monopsonist fish buyer, but the number of participants in harvesting and processing is small enough to make one wonder whether the negotiating game among the few might not achieve a reasonable degree of commercial efficiency even without public regulations. Thus a satisfactory model of the industrial structure and behavior of the reduction fishery might have serious implications for management.

The biggest remaining difficulty, of course, is that a commercial fishery will be efficient only producing what it can sell. Recreation and enhancement of other fish stocks might require protection by a government agency even if overcapitalization and depletion in the usual sense is not threatened. Under the postulated condition of efficient execution of commercial fishing, but with too great an annual take, a quota system may very well be found to be an efficient management device. This line of reasoning bolsters my long-held belief that almost any kind of regulation can be efficient in some situation, and that the real need is for much more comprehensive empirical work which specifies the true situation and feasible set of alternatives.

Another of the basic weaknesses in the existing literature on fisheries regulation is that it is mostly based on a static model of the fishery (except for Clark [1980]), and always assumes a deterministic world. The unrealistic conditions assumed in the theory can lead to distortions in the conclusions regarding optimal regulatory policy. Weitzman [1978] shows that if the cost of deviating from a regulatory target (like not achieving the ideal harvest or fleet size) is a quadratic loss function, then the optimal selection of quantitative standards (like a quota) and pricing-type regulations (like royalities and license fees) generally includes a mix of both types. Presumably the regulatory analyst has some model of firm behavior which allows him to forecast the response of firms to new rules. To the extent that the behavioral model errs in predicting behavior, pricing-type regulations will result in missing the target. Quantitative rules may more reliably achieve targets in some circumstances. Whether reliance on quantity regulations is preferable to pricing depends on the cost of missing the target as well as the accuracy with which behavior can be predicted. If, for instance, a slight deviation is very costly (the weight attached to the squared term in the quadratic loss function is large), and firm behavior is predicted with large errors, quantitative restrictions on firms are preferable to price incentives. On the other hand, if the value of the regulated industry is fairly linear about the target and the regulator's model of the industry behavior is accurate, optimum regulations may rely heavily on price incentives.

Although this quick sketch does not reveal the full implications of Weitzman's work, and the results are not directly applicable to fisheries anyway, it does suggest some new directions for investigation. In particular, the seemingly vast gulf between adherents of the traditional quota/season-type regulations and the proponents of taxes and royalties may be partly bridged by a theory embedded in a world of uncertainty and stochastic decision-making. Both kinds of regulation may be optimal under some conditions, and a mix of regulations is probably called for in most situations. The ideal mix of regulations for the anchovy fishery have almost certainly not been found. To make much progress we need further conceptual thinking and data gathering. Until more is known about the system being managed and better management alternatives are devised, a rigorous case for different regulations in the anchovy fishery will not be developed.

Analysis of Management Information

Collection and analysis of management information is a continuing need under any kind of management program. It is needed to support law enforcement activities and regular changes in regulations and to enable the managing agencies to periodically assess the performance of the regulations and initiate significant reforms. Because the FCMA provides broad definitions and regulatory options, there is now increased pressure on fisheries managers to husband great masses of economic, social and ecological data along with the more traditional stock assessments. All this is, of course, essential if enlightened fishery policy is to address the wide range of issues required by law. But enlightenment is costly, and at some point the marginal cost of more information must exceed its marginal value. To determine the optimum amount of information-gathering in all the various fields of inquiry is a prodigious task. But some routine data-gathering activities having a clear purpose and a calculable impact can be evaluated with the help of decision theory and the economic theory of information.

Generally speaking, any decision-maker must continually choose among a variety of options based on more or less imperfect information. An important component of the uncertainty inherent in decision-making is uncertainty about objective facts, i.e., uncertainty about the "state of the world." Assuming that different decisions are optimal under different states, better decisions will be made when more precise information about pertinent aspects of the world is available. Decision theory provides a rational framework for using imperfect information, and, consequently, suggests a way to place an economic value on specific kinds of information.

To give an example from anchovy management, consider the annual quota decision which, according to the anchovy plan [Department of Commerce 1978], follows the rule

$$Q = \begin{cases} 0.333(B - 1,000,000) \text{ if } (B - 1,000,000) > 0 \\ 0. \qquad\qquad\qquad\quad \text{ if } (B - 1,000,000) \leqslant 0. \end{cases}$$

where Q is the annual quota and B is the estimated biomass. Since B is a statistical estimate based on ichthyoplankton surveys, it is at best correct on average. When biomass is over- or underestimated the assigned quota deviates from the level intended, and the expected economic value of the fishery presumably suffers. To evaluate the amount of information collection which is warranted on economic grounds, we need to demonstrate two relationships: (1) the relationship between the expected monetary value (EMV) of the fishery and the quantity of data collected; and (2) the correspondence between cost of data and quantity of data.

A rough, but illustrative, application of this approach can be developed by assuming that some elementary sampling theory applies to anchovy biomass estimation. First, we assume that the standard deviation of the biomass estimate about the true value is inversely related to the square root of the sample size. As the sample size gets larger the standard error of the estimate shrinks. This corresponds to collecting more data to get more precision. Table IV, columns 1 and 2 show the postulated relationship. Second, the cost of making the biomass estimate is assumed to be proportional to the sample size needed. (See Table IV, column 3.) Finally, the expected monetary value of the fishery is calculated as the annual average NEV defined as in Equation 14 above. The procedure for calculating these expected values involves a simulation program which is explained in detail by Huppert et al. [1980b]. As we should expect, the EMV (Table IV, column 5) for the fishery fall with decreasing accuracy of the estimate.

The payoff associated with increased data collection (i.e., larger sample size) for this example can be evaluated by comparing increased EMV with increased cost at successive levels of precision. The pertinent computations are given in Table IV, column 5. When the sample size is increased from 125 to 163, for instance, the cost of sampling grows from $139,000 to $181,000, while the EMV increases from $3.787 to $3.838 million for a net increase of $39,000. As is indicated in the table, collecting more than 222 samples may not be justified by the economic gain.

A more careful and thorough analysis is needed before reaching a final conclusion here, because nonreduction fishery values were not incorporated, and because an increased year-to-year variability in the quotas accompanies the decreased precision in estimation. An aversion to instability in the fishery would shift more emphasis onto the precision factor. Evaluation of other types of management information may be approached with the techniques outlined above.

SUMMARY AND RECOMMENDATIONS

A rich variety of economic issues and analytical techniques has been discussed or mentioned in the foregoing sections of the chapter. Existing applications to the anchovy fishery were summarized, deficiencies were identified and directions for improvement were suggested. Insufficient data are

Table IV.   Evaluation of Biomass Estimates for the Anchovy Reduction Fishery Management Program

Standard Error of the Estimate[a]	Sample Size[b]	Total Cost	Expected Monetary Value (EMV) ($1000)	Increase in EMV minus Increase in Cost
0.05	8000	8896	4155	−6647
0.10	2000	1113	4130	−1200
0.15	889	989	4095	−384
0.20	500	556[c]	4046	−141
0.25	320	356	3987	−71
0.30	222	247	3916	+12
0.35	163	181	3838	+39
0.40	125	139	3757	--

[a]Represents a proportional, not additive, error.
[b]Based on the assumption that 500 plankton samples yield a standard error of 0.2. Other values are computed by the use of the formula: $\sigma = \sqrt{s^2} / \sqrt{N}$.
[c]This is the estimated cost for annual survey in Department of Commerce [1978].

perhaps the commonest kind of problem, but this mainly affects the precision of certain estimated parameters and not the structure of the economic analysis or the kinds of management options evaluated. The methodological weaknesses, however, stem from more fundamental defects in applied fisheries economics. Three areas in particular need of further development are (1) the valuation of indirect impacts of commercial fishing and unpriced outputs; (2) a theory of multiple-use fishing vessels which addresses the problem of optimizing a mix of harvests under conditions of biological and market uncertainty; and (3) an investigation of the industry structure with implications for management strategy.

Obvious components of the first area of investigation are the extension of ecosystem models to predict interspecies effects of anchovy harvests, and development of recreational fishery evaluations to determine the importance of changes in angler success rates. The specification of predictive ecosystem models may be a distant goal, but current efforts in the area of recreational economics give some reason for optimism. Unless the impact of the anchovy fishery on recreationists can be assessed, however, the recreational economics work may not contribute significantly to management practice.

It is clear enough that a single species fishery with a single-purpose fishing fleet is an unrealistic abstraction. I think it is equally clear that the unpredictability of catch rates and the variability of fish prices provide sufficient motivation for the observed level of flexibility designed into the multipurpose southern California purse seine fleet. To manage adequately the harvest of any one target species in this situation has unavoidable implications for the others. A useful line of research, therefore, is one which seeks to capture the essential features of the fleet's economic strategies and to approach the fishery management question within a multidimensional model.

Behavior of the fishing industry is all too often assumed to be perfectly competitive. Cooperative behavior (or competition among a few participants) yields different conclusions regarding the need for public intervention, especially if a reasonable degree of control can be exercised by the industry over total fishery withdrawals. Externalities and indirect effects not valued by the commercial fishery may still justify public participation in fishery management, but industry behavior may be anticipated to solve some of the requirements for economic efficiency. Thus, the kinds of regulatory mechanisms proposed might reasonably avoid addressing many internal industry efficiency problems. A thorough examination of industry structure and market behavior along traditional lines could, depending on the finding, lead to a significant simplification in the kinds of regulations economists need examine.

NOTES

[1]Participating in the analysis of the anchovy fishery were, in addition to the author, Dr. G. D. Stauffer, A. MacCall and J. McMillan.

[2]The causes were natural in the sense that direct fishery-induced mortality was not responsible. The rapid growth of the stock in the early 1960s may have been partly due to the sardine stock collapse which may be attributable to the sardine fishery.

[3]A coefficient of variation equals the standard deviation divided by the mean.

[4]Although the presence of larvae is clear evidence of adults, there is some indication that anchovy schools tend to move farther north in the summer and south in the winter. Since the major spawning activity occurs during February-April, the larva distribution may be farther south than the average adult fish distribution.

[5]Gulland's method for estimating potential yield requires an estimate of unfished biomass. Since the anchovy stock biomass ranged from 2.6 to 4.0 million tons during the 1968-1972 period, the potential yield was given as a range of 1.5 to 2.4 million tons (MacCall et al. [1976], p. 7). Clearly, the unfished stock of anchovies was far smaller in the early 1950s than it was in later years.

[6]Radovich and MacCall [1979] was first presented at the 1976 CalCOFI Conference. Thus it predates MacCall [1980] and Department of Commerce [1978].

[7]The statistical test is of the hypothesis $H_0:E(R/B) = \bar{R}$. The following table from Huppert et al. [1980b] summarizes the results for both recruitment models in Figure 3.

Analysis of Variance for Recruitment Models
(Total sum of squares equals 14.078)

	Model A (logistic)		Model B	
Variance				
Explained (df)	4.506	(1)	3.875	(1)
Unexplained (df)	9.572	(13)	10.203	(13)
Mean Square				
Explained	4.506		3.875	
Unexplained	0.736		0.785	
F-statistic	6.12		4.94	
Approximate probability	0.028		0.045	

[8]The alternative recruitment model, B, was generated during a discussion of density-dependence at the Pacific Fishery Management Council's Scientific and Statistical Committee meeting in La Jolla, California on July 8, 1980. Below a biomass of 1.225 million tons the per capita recruitment is "density-independent" (i.e., not affected by the biomass of spawning fish), and above 1.225 million tons the absolute value of recruitment is density-independent. This model is a compromise between two extreme positions; one holding total recruitment to be completely independent, and the other holding recruitment to be strictly dependent via the logistic growth model.

[9]Green's estimated total predation was 3.5 times the estimated small school fish available to predators. The gap between these two figures illustrates the crude state of existing quantitative ecosystem models.

[10]The origin of the term "wetfish" is disputed among experts, but throughout this paper it stands for a group of fish species landed "wet" (i.e., in fresh seawater, without freezing) by purse seine vessels. These species include anchovy, jack mackerel, Pacific mackerel, Pacific bonito, bluefin tuna, Pacific sardine and squid. The "wetfish fleet" is that group of purse seiners which land these species *and* are smaller and less mobile than the tropical tuna vessels.

[11]An earlier unpublished paper by Fox [1974] precedes MacCall's work and the summary discussion by Gulland [1977] of the variable catchability model.

[12]The $24.58/ton average cost of fishing anchovies which was quoted earlier would correspond to an approximate $18,900/year wage per crew member. This assumes 48 weeks of fishing five days per week at 78.1 tons catch per day, direct operating costs of 15% of cost and 58% crew share for a 12-man crew.

[13]Strictly speaking, the Just and Hueth result applies only to a vertically structured competitive sector of an economy where each industry in the sector produces a single product using one major variable input produced within the sector and other variable inputs originating in other sectors of the economy. Since both the fishing fleet and the processing firms produce nonanchovy products, this use of their welfare measurement is not completely legitimate.

[14]Equation 15 can be derived from the stock transition Equation 4 and the catch Equation 5. Although we cannot algebraically solve Equation 5 for fishing mortality, F, as a function of y_t and B_t, there is a one-to-one correspondence between F and y_t and B_t which can be computed numerically and can be expressed as

$$F = f(y_t, B_t), y, B > 0$$

with $\quad \dfrac{\partial f}{\partial y} > 0, \dfrac{\partial^2 f}{\partial y^2} > 0, \dfrac{\partial f}{\partial B} < 0, \dfrac{\partial^2 f}{\partial B^2} = 0$

Substituting this function into Equation 4 yields

$$B_{t+1} = B_t K/(H + B_t) - B_t e^{-(M-G)} (1 - e^{-f(y_t, B_t)})$$

or $\quad B_{t+1} = g(y_t, B_t).$

[15]More formal derivation of these qualitative results proceeds as follows. The deterministic optimization problem is to maximize the following Lagrangian

$$L = \sum_{t=0}^{T} NEV(y_t, B_t) (\frac{1}{1+d})^t - Z_t [B_{t+1} - g(y_t, B_t)]$$

Necessary conditions for an interior maximum are

$$\frac{\partial L}{\partial y_t} = (\frac{1}{1+d})^t \frac{\partial NEV}{\partial y_t} + Z_t \frac{\partial g}{\partial y_t} \leqslant 0 \qquad (1)$$

$$\frac{\partial L}{\partial B_t} = (\frac{1}{1+d})^t \frac{\partial NEV}{\partial B_t} - Z_{t-1} + Z_t \frac{\partial g}{\partial B_t} \leqslant 0 \qquad (2)$$

$$\frac{\partial L}{\partial Z_t} = B_{t-1} - g(y_t, B_t) = 0 \qquad (3)$$

$$y, B > 0$$

If $\dfrac{\partial L}{\partial y_t} < 0$ for all $y > 0$, the nonnegativity constraint is effective, i.e., the optimum y is y = 0. Note that Z_t is the discounted value of having one more unit of biomass in year t + 1. If B_t is not so low as to require a zero harvest, Condition 1 must be an equality. An interpretation of this is that the marginal contribution of catch in year t to the discounted return must just equal the marginal contribution of leaving an additional unit (i.e., catching one unit less). The second term on the right side of Equation 1 equals marginal contribution of an additional unit of stock next year times the marginal effect of this year's catch on next year's stock.

[16]Choice of an appropriate discount rate involves several theoretical nuances that are not of great concern here, but which have occupied the journal literature [Baumol 1968]. The 4% rate of discount reflects the typical yield on Moody's corporate AAA Bonds during the relatively non-inflationary 1950-1965 period.

[17]A sample standard error of about 0.6 was computed for the residuals of the growth model [Huppert et al. 1980b]. A smaller standard deviation is assumed here because much of the variability in the fitted residuals appears to be due to the less accurate biomass estimates of the early 1960s which were based on far fewer plankton samples than are current estimates. It seems reasonable that at least half of the original standard error could be attributed to variability in the stock's real growth response.

[18]Using the terminology of note 15 and substituting the relationships,

$$NEV(y_t, B_t) = V_1(y_{1t}, B_t) + V_2(y_{2t}, B_t)$$

$$y_{1t} = S_1 y_t$$

$$y_{2t} = (1 - S_1)y_t$$

into the Lagrangian expression, the necessary conditions for an optimum include the following:

$$\frac{\partial L}{\partial y_t} = \frac{\partial V_1}{\partial (S_{1t} y_t)} y_t - \frac{\partial V_1}{\partial (1 - S_{1t})y_t} y_t \leqslant 0$$

In case this condition is satisfied as an equality, the marginal value of harvest in use 1 must equal the marginal value in use 2.

REFERENCES

1. Ahlstrom, E. H., and J. Radovich. 1970. "Management of the Pacific Sardine," in *A Century of Fisheries in North America,* American Fisheries Society Special Publication No. 7, pp. 181-193.
2. Anderson, L. G. 1975. "Optimum Economic Yield of an Internationally Utilized Common Property Resource," *Fish. Bull.* 70(1):51-66.
3. Anderson, L. G. 1977. *The Economics of Fisheries Management* (Baltimore, MD: The Johns Hopkins University Press).
4. Anderson, L. G. 1980. "The Economics of Multipurpose Fleet Behavior," College of Marine Studies, University of Delaware (unpublished).
5. Baumol, W. J. 1968. "On the Social Rate of Discount," *Am. Econ. Rev.* 58:788-802.
6. Beddington, J. R., and R. M. May. 1977. "Harvesting Natural Populations in a Randomly Fluctuating Environment," *Science* (July 29), pp. 463-465.
7. Bromley, D. W., and R. C. Bishop. 1977. "From Economic Theory to Fisheries Policy: Conceptual Problems and Management Prescriptions," in *Economic Impacts of Extended Fisheries Jurisdiction,* L. G. Anderson, Ed. (Ann Arbor, MI: Ann Arbor Science Publishers, Inc.).
8. Brown, G. M., Jr. 1974. "An Optimal Program for Managing Common Property Resources with Congestion Externalities," *J. Polit. Econ.* 82: 163-174.
9. California Cooperative Oceanic Fisheries Investigations (CalCOFI). 1966. *Reports.* 10:6-7.
10. Clark, C. W. 1976. *Mathematical Bioeconomics* (New York: John Wiley and Sons).
11. Clark, C. W. 1980. "Towards a Predictive Model for the Economic Regulation of Commercial Fisheries," *Can. J. Fish. Aquatic Sci.* 37:1111-1129.
12. Clark, C. W. and G. R. Munro. 1979. "Fisheries and the Processing Sector: Some Implications for Management Policy," University of British Columbia, Dept. of Economics Resources Paper No. 34.
13. Combs, E. R., Inc. 1977. "A Study to Evaluate the Economics of an Offshore Fishery for Anchovy and Jack Mackerel," Report to NMFS, Southwest Fisheries Center, La Jolla, CA.

14. Crutchfield, J. A. 1961. "An Economic Evaluation of Alternative Methods of Fishery Regulation," *J. Law Econ.* 4:131-143.
15. Crutchfield, J. A. 1979. "Economic and Social Implications of the Main Policy Alternatives for Controlling Fishing Effort," *J. Fish. Res. Board Can.* 36(7):742-752.
16. Department of Commerce, NOAA. 1978. "Implementation of Northern Anchovy Fishery Management Plan," *Federal Register* 43(141) Book 2: 31651-31879.
17. Food and Agricultural Organization-Mexico. 1978. "Investigacion y Desarallo de las Pesquerias Mexico, Resultados y Recommendaciones del Projecto," Programas de las Naciones Unidos para la Agricultura y la Alimentacion, Rome.
18. Fox, W. W. 1974. "An Overview of Production Modelling," Proceedings of the ICCAT Workshop on Tuna Population Dynamics, Nantes, France.
19. Green, K. A. 1978. "Ecosystem Description of the California Current," Final Report to Marine Mammal Commission, Contract No. MM7AC-026.
20. Gruen, Gruen and Associates. 1979. "The California Commercial Passenger Fishing Vessel and Southern California Live Bait Industry," NMFS, Southwest Fisheries Center, Administration Report LJ-79-31C.
21. Gulland, J. A. 1970. "Fish Resources of the Ocean," FAO Technical Report No. 97.
22. Hall, R. E., and D. M. Lilien. 1979. "Efficient Wage Bargains Under Uncertain Supply and Demand," *Am. Econ. Rev.* 69(5):868-879.
23. Hillier, F. S., and G. J. Lieberman. 1967. *Introduction to Operations Research* (San Francisco: Holden-Day, Inc.).
24. Hirshleifer, J., and J. G. Riley. 1979. "The Analytics of Uncertainty and Information: an Exploratory Survey," *J. Econ. Lit.* 57:1375-1421.
25. Huppert, D. D. 1979. "Implications of Multipurpose Fleets and Mixed Stocks for Control Policies," *J. Fish. Res. Board Can.* 36:845-854.
26. Huppert, D. D., A. D. MacCall, G. D. Stauffer, K. R. Parker, J. A. McMillan and H. W. Frey. 1980a. "California's Northern Anchovy Fishery: Biological and Economic Basis for Fishery Management," NOAA Technical Memorandum, NOAA-TM-NMFS-SWFC-1.
27. Huppert, D. D., A. D. MacCall and G. D. Stauffer. 1980b. "A Review of Technical Issues in the Anchovy Management Plan," NMFS Southwest Fisheries Center, Administrative Report No. LJ-80-12.
28. Just, R. E., and D. L. Hueth. 1979. "Welfare Measures in a Multimarket Framework," *Am. Econ. Rev.* 69(5):947-954.
29. Kaneen, R. G. 1977. "California's View of Anchovy Management," *CalCOFI Reports* 19:25-27.
30. MacCall, A. D. 1976. "Density-Dependence of Catchability Coefficient in the California Pacific Sardine *(Sardinops sagax caerulea)* Purse Seine Fishery," *CalCOFI Reports* 18:136-148.
31. MacCall, A. D. 1979. "Population Estimates for the Waning Years of the Pacific Sardine Fishery," *CalCOFI Reports* 20:72-82.
32. MacCall, A. D. 1980. "Population Models for the Northern Anchovy *(Engraulis mordax)*," Reports of the Meeting of the International Council for Exploration of the Sea 177 (in press).
33. MacCall, A. D., G. D. Stauffer and J. P. Troadec. 1976. "Southern California Recreational and Commercial Marine Fisheries," *Mar. Fish. Rev.* 38(1):1-32.

34. Mandel, P. I. 1975. "International Aspects of the Management of the California Current Anchovy Fishery," NMFS Southwest Fisheries Center, Anchovy Workshop Contribution No. 18.
35. Mendelssohn, R. 1980. "Using Markov Decision Models and Related Techniques for Purposes Other than Simple Optimization," *Fish. Bull.* 78(1):13-34.
36. Murphy, G. I. 1966. "Population Biology of the Pacific Sardine *(Sardinops caerulea)*," Proceedings, California Academy of Sciences 34(1):1-84.
37. Murphy, G. I. 1967. "Vital Statistics of the Pacific Sardine *(Sardinops caerulea)* and the Population Consequences," *Ecology* 48(5):731-736.
38. Murphy, G. I. 1977. "Clupeids," in *Fish Population Dynamics,* G. A. Gulland, Ed. (New York: John Wiley and Sons).
39. Peterson, F. M., and A. C. Fisher. 1977. "The Exploitation of Extractive Resources: a Survey," *Econ. J.* 87:681-721.
40. Quirk, J. P., and V. L. Smith. 1970. "Dynamic Economic Models of Fishing," in *Economics of Fisheries Management: A Symposium,* A. D. Scott, Ed. (Vancouver: University of British Columbia).
41. Radovich, J., and A. D. MacCall. 1979. "A Management Model for the Central Stock of the Northern Anchovy," *CalCOFI Reports* 20:83-88.
42. Reed, W. J. 1979. "Optimal Escapement Levels in Stochastic and Deterministic Harvesting Models," *J. Environ. Econ. Management* 6:350-363.
43. Schaefer, M. B., O. E. Sette, and J. C. Marr. 1951. Growth of Pacific Coast Pilchard Fisheries to 1942. U.S. Fish and Wildlife Service, *Research Report 29.* U.S. Gov't Printing Office.
44. Scott, A. D. 1955. "The Fishery: the Objectives of Sole Ownership," *J. Polit. Econ.* 63(2):116-124.
45. Scott, A. D. 1979. "Development of Economic Theory on Fisheries Regulation," *J. Fish. Res. Board Can.* 36:725-741.
46. Smith, P. E. 1978. "Biological Effects of Ocean Variability: Time and Space Scales of Biological Response," Report of the Meeting on the International Council for Exploration of the Sea 173:117-127.
47. Soutar, A., and J. D. Isaacs. 1974. "Abundance of Pelagic Fish During the 19th and 20th Centuries as Recorded in Anaerobic Sediment off the Californias," *Fish. Bull.* 72(2):257-273.
48. Stauffer, G. D. 1978. "The Proportion of the Spawning Biomass of the Anchovy Central Subpopulation in Mexico and U.S. 200-mile Fishery Zones," NMFS Southwest Fisheries Center Administrative Report LJ-78-1.
49. Vrooman, A. M. and P. A. Paloma. 1975. "Subpopulations of Northern Anchovy *(Engraulis mordax)*," NMFS Southwest Fisheries Center Administrative Report LJ-75-62.
50. Wadsworth, P. A. 1974. "Anchovy Fishery Development in Mexico: Potential and Strategies," Mexico PNUD FAO Programa de Investigacion y Fomento Pesquerias.
51. Walters, C. J. 1975. "Optimal Harvest Strategies for Salmon in Relation to Environmental Variability and Uncertain Production Parameters," *J. Fish. Res. Board Can.* 32:1777-1784.
52. Walters, C. J., and R. Hilborn. 1976. "Adaptive Control of Fishing Systems," *J. Fish. Res. Board Can.* 33:145-159.
53. Weitzman, M. L. 1978. "Optimal Rewards for Economic Regulation," *Am. Econ. Rev.* 68(4):683-691.

CHAPTER 4

ECONOMIC ISSUES PERTAINING TO THE GULF OF MEXICO SHRIMP MANAGEMENT PLAN

Wade L. Griffin
Department of Agricultural Economics
Texas A&M University

John R. Stoll
Department of Agricultural Economics
Texas A&M University

When fisheries are compared on the basis of total value of landings, the Gulf of Mexico constitutes the most important fishery in the United States. Within the Gulf of Mexico fishery, shrimp comprise the most significant portion of total harvest value. In 1978 U.S. fishermen landed over 6.0 billion pounds of seafood valued at $1.85 billion, including 423 million pounds of shrimp valued at $385.6 million. During this same year Gulf fishermen landed 248 million pounds of shrimp (58.6% of the U.S. total) which were valued at $319.6 million or 82.9% of the total value of U.S. shrimp landings [U.S. Department of Commerce 1979].

According to the Fishery Conservation and Management Act of 1976, the Gulf of Mexico Fishery Management Council was charged with the responsibility to develop and implement a plan for the management of the Gulf Coast shrimp fishery. Subsequently, the "Environmental Impact Statement and Fishery Management Plan for the Shrimp Fishery of the Gulf of Mexico, United States Waters" was developed under contract by the Center for Wetland Resources [1979] at Louisiana State University. After approval by the Gulf Council, the final plan was submitted to the Secretary of Commerce in January of 1980. The plan was approved by the Secretary of Commerce, and proposed federal regulations have been published in the *Federal Register* for public comment.

Two of the proposed regulations involve (1) closure of a nursery area in the Tortugas fishing grounds off the coast of Florida and (2) closure of the offshore Fishery Convervation Zone (FCZ) of Texas for periods of 45-60 days to protect small brown shrimp. Since development of the plan, two amendments have been proposed which would allow in-season adjustments of the closure periods. The Gulf Council has also been impressed by the lack of substantive economic content in the plan and has taken measures to increase the economic input to a current revision.

ECONOMIC ISSUES

A review of the shrimp management plan [Center for Wetland Resources 1979] reveals four basic areas where economics can play a major role in the drafting and implementation of the plan. The first area is the description and interpretation of existing data. A very large section of the shrimp management plan consists of tables, charts and figures of varying economic content.[1] Economists should be responsible for the construction and interpretation of these. Economists can play a role in determining the usefulness of the current data base, and can suggest data to be collected in the future. Sections of the shrimp management plan which present these data are handled fairly well, with some minor exceptions. The Gulf Council has recognized the need for these improvements, and is in the process of trying to incorporate many of them into the forthcoming revision of the management plan.

Economics is also important for determining which previous economic studies are relevant to the objectives of the plan and, thus, should be included. Although the bibliography of the plan contains much relevant economic literature, in some cases the important results of studies and their implications for the plan are overlooked. For example, there are several previous studies pertaining to vessel cost and return, demand analysis and utilization of finfish discards, the results of which could have been incorporated into the text of the management plan. Since its initial writing, additional studies have been completed and are currently being considered for inclusion in the revised plan.

Economic education is a third area that is important in the shrimp management plan. There are certain areas within the shrimp plan where a brief explanation of economic theory would help the council and other laymen understand changes that have taken place in the shrimp fishing industry. Two situations amenable to the useful application of economic principles are: (1) the continued expansion of effort in the fishery;[2] and (2) the determination of ex-vessel price of shrimp.[3] The plan does contain a helpful discussion of market structure, overcapitalization, optimum yield, maximum economic yield and economic efficiency.

The fourth area for economic input is the evaluation of problems in the fishery that could be solved or at least improved through different management policies.[4] Some of these are: (1) interaction with other sectors that affect shrimp fishing, e.g., loss of trawling grounds or gear due to manmade underwater obstructions or altered quantity or quality of estuaries; (2) the existence of regulatory practices that prohibit the landing of undersized shrimp (this later policy exists in Texas and Florida where it is estimated that several million pounds of shrimp are discarded annually); and (3) conflicts among competing user groups.

In the Gulf shrimp fishery, significant user conflicts exist and are of three basic types. The first is a gear conflict. Florida stone crab fishermen and shrimp fishermen are interrelated because shrimp trawls inadvertently destroy crab pots. The second type of user conflict results because the by-catch of the users of one fishery affects another fishery stock. Shrimp fishermen catch both shrimp and finfish, but discard the finfish. Groundfish fishermen claim that this has reduced their yield. The final type of user conflict is between user groups within the shrimp fishery itself. In the shrimp fishery there are bay, gulf, bait, and recreational fishermen, all competing for the harvest of a single biological resource: the shrimp biomass.

In the following three sections of this paper, two of these issues will be discussed. The first section illustrates how economic theory can be used within the shrimp management plan as an educational tool. In this section economic theory will be used to explain the continued expansion of effort in the fishery and the equilibrium which results under conditions of open access. The second section develops a general theory for the evaluation of conflict among user groups within a fishery and seasonal regulation analysis. The third section applies this theory to the evaluation of two proposed policy measures designed to: (1) mitigate conflict between bay and offshore shrimpers and (2) protect small shrimp and reduce discards.

ECONOMICS AS AN EDUCATIONAL TOOL:
EXPANSION AND CONTRACTION
IN THE SHRIMP INDUSTRY

Equilibrium in an open-access common property resource as well as the effects of increasing or decreasing unit prices (input and output) are discussed in this section. It is often stated that in times of economic hardship, "marginal producers and processors may go—but the remainder of the industry will stay"

[Prochaska and Cato 1975]. This discussion is intended as an educational tool to help the reader understand the rapid expansion of effort under favorable economic conditions and the very slow decline in effort during unfavorable economic conditions.

Figure 1 gives hypothetical curves for the Gulf of Mexico shrimp fishery. The horizontal axis measures effort expended in the fishery and the vertical axis represents costs and revenues. The total value of product curve (TVP^1) is calculated as price times the quantity of shrimp landed. The total cost curve (TC) represents total cost incurred by fishermen at different levels of effort. The TC curve includes the opportunity cost of fishermen's labor and capital. The intersection of the TC and TVP^1 curves at point A means that equilibrium in the open access fishery will occur when E^1 units of effort are used. Now suppose that the price of shrimp increases, causing the total value product curve to shift from TVP^1 to TVP^2. If effort remains at E^1, excess rents will be earned. These excess rents will cause additional effort to be added to the fishery, i.e., vessels, labor, time, etc., until equilibrium is once again reached at E^2 units of effort.

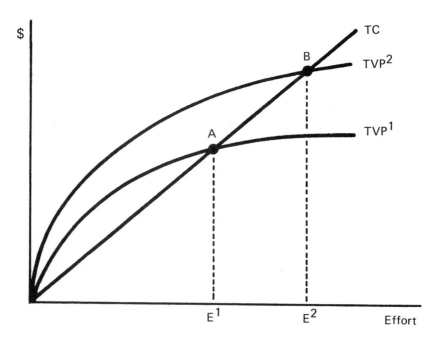

Figure 1.   Industry equilibrium in an open access fishery.

Using the same logic in reverse, if the fishery is at equilibrium at point B and the price of shrimp declines so that the total value of product curve shifts from TVP^2 to TVP^1, negative rents are incurred and fishermen reduce effort until equilibrium is once again restored at E^1. However, contraction of effort is somewhat more complex than this. The reason is the existence of fixed assets, a problem similar to that confronted by agricultural enterprises, as originally explained by Johnson [1958]. Asset fixity, the inability of vessels to move out of the shrimp industry, hinges on the concept of acquisition cost and salvage value. Acquisition cost is what a vessel owner has paid for his shrimp vessel or would have to pay to acquire more of that particular asset. Salvage value is what the vessel owner could get for the asset if it were sold rather than used in the production of shrimp landings.

The above logic holds only if markets are such that the purchase and selling prices of an input by an entrepreneur are identical. In actuality this is often not the case. When economic conditions are favorable, revenue often increases at a faster rate than it costs the industry to expand effort (add more vessels to the fleet). This is illustrated by a movement from point D to A on TC_a in Figure 2, where TC_a includes the acquisition cost of a vessel. Older vessels may actually appreciate in value under favorable economic conditions. When economic conditions become unfavorable, the value of vessels declines and they are more difficult to sell. Assuming the shrimp industry is in equilibrium at point A in Figure 2, let the price of shrimp decline. This causes the total value of product curve to shift from TVP^1 to TVP^2. TC_a represents total costs including the acquisition price of the shrimp vessels, and TC_s represents total costs incorporating the salvage value of the shrimp vessels. In this situation, vessel owners would continue to exert E^3 units of effort in the fishery since the value of the vessel in fishing (point B) is equal to or greater than its salvage value. If the price of shrimp had declined such that TVP^3 was the appropriate curve, then vessel owners would reduce effort to E^2 by selling some vessels or retiring them, which still exceeds effort level E^1. Because of asset fixity, vessels enter quite rapidly under favorable economic conditions but are reluctantly removed under unfavorable economic conditions.

Figure 3 illustrates a combination of short- and long-run effects. Assume the industry is at equilibrium at point A. The price of shrimp falls so that the total vlaue of product curve shifts downward from TVP^1 to TVP^2. In the short run shrimpers are at point B. However, at point B they are not recovering their variable costs (TVC) so they reduce effort by tying up their boats during part or all of the year. In this way they reduce effort from E^2 to E^3 (point C). If conditions remained unfavorable into the long run (perhaps, two to four years) some vessels would exit from the fishery because revenues would not be covering costs including salvage costs (TC_s) and a new equilibrium would be established at point D (representing E^4 units of effort). As capital

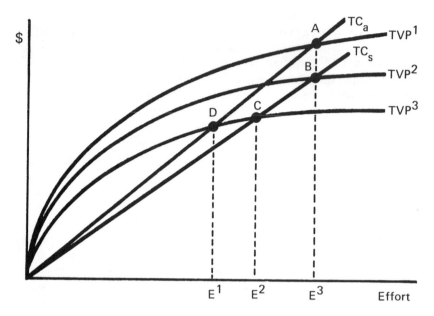

Figure 2.   Quantity of effort used when acquisition and salvage prices are unequal for the industry.

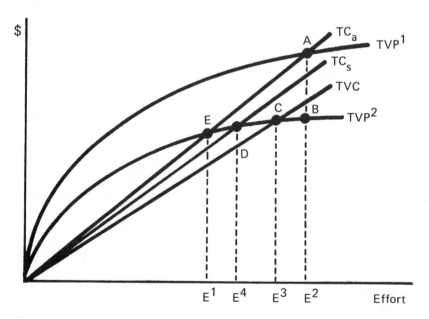

Figure 3.   Quantity of effort used when acquisition and salvage prices are unequal for the industry, short run considered.

is used up (vessels wear out) in the very long run there would be a gradual decrease in effort from E^4 to E^1 as some vessels are not replaced (point D to point E).

A REALISTIC MODEL OF THE GULF SHRIMP FISHERY

In the Gulf Coast fishery two distinct users, Bay and Gulf shrimpers, are associated with the single fishery resource. These users attempt to exploit the fishery at different points in the life cycle of the species, under different fishing conditions, using somewhat different technology. The fishing effort expended by one user group and the associated harvest have a significant impact on the other. To the extent that each group has a vested interest in the continuance of current practices, significant conflict arises when public policies to manage the fishery are considered.

In the empirical application to be presented in the following section, two policy alternatives will be examined. Given conditions of open access to the fishery, it is recognized that many of the impacts of these policies will be distributional and, in the long run, a new equilibrium will be established without any rent accruing to the biological resource being exploited. Thus, these particular policies do not represent movements from situations of inefficiency to situations of efficiency (although they could conceivably be closer to economic efficiency, if that can be said to have desirable consequences). Rather, they represent movement from one inefficient situation to another. Normative judgments regarding the desirability of these alternative results will not be presented here. However, judgments do need to be made in policy decisions, and inefficient outcomes may still have socially desirable distributional consequences. For an interesting perspective on this problem in fisheries economics the reader is referred to Bromley and Bishop [1977].

Another interesting facet of the shrimp fishery is the nature of the population dynamics. Shrimp populations constitute an annually renewable resource, which is uniquely different from many other biological resources. This difference arises in that the linkage between present rates of harvest and future recruitment is believed to be insubstantial [Center for Wetland Resources 1979; Anderson 1977]. Thus, current harvest rates are only of importance with respect to their impact upon the shrimp biomass for the remainder of the annual life cycle.

The multiple use nature of the fishery taking this type of population dynamics into account can be modeled as follows. The yield for each of the two segments of the fleet can be represented as:

$$y_1 = E_1 * g_1 * w_1 (E_1, E_2) \qquad (1)$$

$$y_2 = E_2 * g_2 * w_2 (E_1, E_2) \tag{2}$$

where

y_1, y_2 = yields of bay and gulf shrimpers, respectively

E_1, E_2 = effort of bay and gulf shrimpers, respectively

g_1, g_2 = catchability coefficient for bay and gulf shrimpers, respectively

$w_1 (E_1, E_2), w_2 (E_1, E_2)$ = average size of the fishable stock available to bay and gulf shrimpers, respectively

$*$ = a multiplication operation

Effort will be defined identically for each group, although the input mix used to produce effort may vary. The catchability coefficient can be assumed constant within user groups but will vary among user groups due to variations in the gear employed and areas fished. To capture the effect that harvest by one group will have on the yield of the other, the average stock size available to each is described as a function of effort produced by both.[5] The partial derivatives of both w_1 and w_2 with respect to E_1 and E_2 are assumed to be negative.

The price per pound of shrimp increases with the average size of the individual shrimp. For simplicity here it will be assumed that the demand for shrimp in each size class is perfectly elastic. Therefore, the prices received by the bay and gulf shrimpers can be represented by $p(z_1)$ and $p(z_2)$ where z_1 and z_2 represent the average size caught by the two groups respectively. To complete the model assume that the unit cost of effort is r_1 and r_2 for the bay and gulf shrimpers, respectively.

When a shrimp fisherman makes decisions regarding the level of effort to produce, he does not consider the external effects of his behavior on other users. The individual shrimper and, therefore, the industry, will only give credence to the private revenues and costs generated by additional effort. Note that not only factor costs differ between user groups but also the total value products differ due to (1) differences in gear and fishing methods employed and (2) harvesting of different size mixes of the shrimp. Thus, the open-access equilibrium with multiple users will usually have an equilibrium solution characterized by varying revenue, cost, harvest, and effort levels among user groups.

The long run open-access equilibrium will occur where total value product is equal to total factor cost for each user group (see Anderson [1975] for an analogous treatment with multiple species). This equilibrium condition is stated as:

$$p(z_1) * [E_1 * g_1 * w_1(E_1, E_2)] = r_1 * E_1 \tag{3}$$

and

$$p(z_2) * [E_2 * g_2 * w_2(E_1, E_2)] = r_2 * E_2 \tag{4}$$

If this set of simultaneous equations possesses a unique solution with both E_1 and E_2 greater than zero, both groups will operate in the open access fishery. This is indeed the situation that occurs in the Gulf shrimp fishery. This open access equilibrium is depicted as points A and B in Figure 4. Note that the yield curve for each group will vary depending on the level of effort produced by the other.

The usefulness of this model for policy analysis can be demonstrated using the following example. Assume that bay shrimping effort is reduced to E_1^2 by management edict. The effect of this on the two sectors can be represented by points C and D in the diagram. As can be seen, both groups will be earning an economic rent at these points. The existence of this rent provides an incentive for additional effort to be expended by gulf shrimpers until they once again attain an open-access equilibrium (point E). If the restriction of bay shrimping effort is strictly binding, then some bay shrimpers will continue to capture an economic rent if their factor cost curve lies below the total value product curve (point F). However, if the restriction of effort is caused by regulations affecting the inputs used to produce effort (e.g., length of season), the bay shrimpers will substitute other inputs in the production of effort to make up for the effect of the decreased season length. In this latter case, the total factor cost curve for bay shrimpers will shift up leading to a new and unique open-access equilibrium. This equilibrium will be arrived at through a process of iterative reactions between bay and gulf shrimpers, resembling a Cournot type process (see Koutsoyiannis [1975] for a description of the Cournot duopoly model).

This model can also be used to describe the efficient utilization of this multiple user fishery. If economic efficiency is the stated management goal, the fishery should be operated such that the potential rent is maximized. Technically society wishes to maximize[6] :

$$R = p(z_1)*[E_1{}^*g_1{}^*w_1(E_1,E_2)] + p(z_2)*[E_2{}^*g_2{}^*w_2(E_1,E_2)]$$

$$- (r_1{}^*E_1 + r_2{}^*E_2) \tag{5}$$

The first-order conditions for a maximum to the above are:

$$p(z_1)*[g_1{}^*w_1(E_1,E_2) + \frac{\partial w_1}{\partial E_1}*E_1g_1] + p(z_2)*E_2{}^*g_2{}^*\frac{\partial w_2}{\partial E_1} = r_1 \tag{6}$$

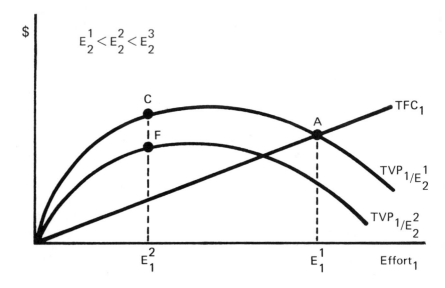

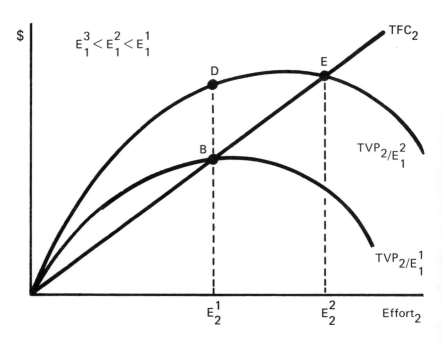

Figure 4.   Open-access equilibrium with multiple users and interactive biomass efforts.

$$p(z_2)^* [g_2^* w_2(E_1,E_2) + \frac{\partial w_2}{\partial E_2}^* E_2 g_2] + p(z_1)^* E_1^* g_1^* \frac{\partial w_1}{\partial E_2} = r_2 \qquad (7)$$

The simple interpretation of these equations is that effort should be expand-ed in both segments of the fleet until the value of the extra harvest is equal to the cost of producing it. Note that specific concern must be given to technical effects each group has on the other. The first term on the left side of both equations represents the value of extra harvest to the specific user group. The second term represents the negative effect an extra unit of effort in each will have on the value of catch in the other.

If the set of simultaneous equations formed by the two first-order conditions possesses a unique nonnegative solution, both groups will have a role in the optimal utilization of the fishery. Such a solution is represented by point A in Figure 5. It is possible, of course, that the solution will occur where the value of only one of the effort levels is positive, in which case, only that group should operate at the optimal point.

ECONOMIC APPLICATION TO MANAGEMENT PROBLEMS

Two management policies involving the competitive groups who use Texas waters for shrimp fishing will be addressed in this section. Before doing so, however, a more detailed description of the Texas fishery is needed.

Description of the Texas Shrimp Fishery

The Texas shrimp fishery can be divided into two major fleets: gulf and bay. In general, gulf trawlers (vessels) are larger and more powerful. They stay out of port several days to several weeks at a time and have greater facilities for storage of fuel, supplies, ice, and catch. These vessels fish almost exclusively in the offshore waters of Texas and harvest mostly brown shrimp (Table I). When they finish a fishing trip, these vessels unload at dockside. The shrimp are generally unloaded heads-off and packed in ice. The nonshrimp catch is discarded at sea. The primary season for shrimping by gulf vessels is from late spring through early or midwinter, although some gulf shrimp are taken throughout the year if weather and economic conditions are suitable.

Bay boats are smaller and less powerful than gulf vessels, and return daily to the docks to unload their catch. Their catch, unlike gulf vessel catch, is usually smaller and is unloaded heads-on. These boats trawl in the inshore waters of several major bay systems along the Texas coast and occasionally work the offshore gulf waters adjacent to the bays. In Texas there is a spring

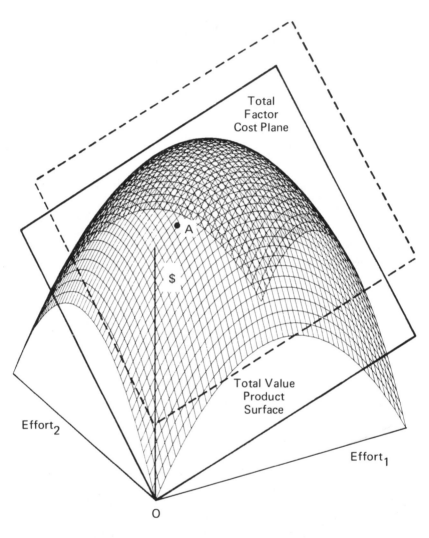

Figure 5.   Rent maximizing equilibrium (A) with multiple users and interactive biomass effects.

bay season for shrimping from about May 15 to July 15 when mainly brown shrimp are harvested. During a four-month fall season beginning around August 15 the catch is mostly white shrimp [Christmas and Etzold 1979].

One of the most important aspects of the bay shrimp fishery is the function of the "bay" itself in the life cycle of shrimp. The relatively shallow and protected waters of the major bay systems serve as nursery areas during the early stages of shrimp growth. As shrimp mature, they move from the bays to the offshore waters of the Gulf. Brown shrimp tend to leave the bay waters at a smaller size than white shrimp and head very quickly for 40-fathom-deep water. White shrimp migrate when they are larger and do so more slowly, generally staying within the 20-fathom line.

The two management policies mentioned earlier revolve around brown shrimp. Recognizing the fact that large shrimp have higher market value than small shrimp, both management policies have as their goal to protect young brown shrimp in the bays until they grow to larger sizes. Thus, potentially, a greater offshore harvest of brown shrimp is yielded which sells for a higher price per unit. Specifically the two policies are different types of closures of the fishery. The first is to close the bays during the spring season (May 15 to July 15), and the second is to close the offshore area during June and July. This virtually eliminates bay shrimpers from harvesting brown shrimp, and enables gulf fishermen to harvest them exclusively. The outcome of these policies are uncertain—thus causing heated arguments between bay and gulf shrimpers.

The Model

This model is designed to represent, in simplified form, the major biological and economic aspects of the Texas shrimp fishery. An essentially management-oriented model, it provides a framework for analyzing and predicting the effects of changes in key biological and economic parameters. In addition, the model may be used to generate statistics on landings and revenues for given time periods and levels of fishing effort. These statistics can aid resource planners in forecasting the effects of proposed policy changes in the fishery.

Table I.   Landings and Days Fished from Texas Waters by Species, Area and Vessel Class (1963-1974 Average)

	Boats		Vessels	
	Landings (million)	Days Fished (1000)	Landings (million)	Days Fished (1000)
Inshore				
Brown	1.24	1.81	0.01	0.06
White	4.18	10.18	0.13	0.05
Offshore				
Brown	0.34	0.64	28.31	40.73
White	0.43	0.85	4.58	8.59

A simplified representation of the key biological and economic aspects of the Texas shrimp fishery is presented in Figure 6. The biological submodel represents recruitment, offshore movement, growth, natural mortality and fishing mortality (harvest) of both brown and white shrimp.

The rate of recruitment for each species into the bays is a function of environmental factors, and is an external factor incorporated into the model. In the Gulf, some recruitment occurs through the immigration of shrimp to the Texas offshore waters from other regions of the Gulf Coast. However, shrimp also emigrate from Texas waters to other regions, and for the purposes of this model, it is assumed that these movements offset each other. Tagging studies to help determine shrimp movement are being conducted, but results are not yet available.

Treating initial recruitment for the two species as the driving variables, individual shrimp enter the simulation model after they are recruited into the bays. Having entered the model, shrimp grow, migrate to Gulf waters, and are subjected to natural and fishing mortality, both in the bays and the Gulf. Fishing mortality in an area is a function of the level of fishing effort applied to the shrimp biomass, and is determined by both economic and regulatory factors.

The model used to simulate the Texas brown/white shrimp industry is an adaptation of a previous model developed at Texas A&M University [Isakson et al. 1980]. It has been called the General Bioeconomic Fisheries Simulation Model (GBFSM), and examples of its applications have been previously reported [Grant and Griffin 1979; Blomo et al. 1978; Griffin et al. 1979]. With one exception, each of the applications involved single-species shrimp fisheries. In Griffin et al. [1979] a three-species fishery was examined; but in this study the model did not differentiate between depths or fishing areas. The GBFSM is a highly flexible model which can be adapted for use in simulating recruitment, growth, mortality harvest and fishing economics in practically any annual crop fishery.

In the present analysis, the GBFSM is applied to a two-species shrimp fishery harvested by two separate groups. Both of the user groups operate in overlapping but generally separable areas. An attempt was made to adapt the model to a semiweekly time step involving 26 time periods per year; in previous applications, the 12-month time step was used when data limitations were encountered. A 12-month time step was finally specified so that seasonal regulations in the bay and gulf fisheries could be simulated with reasonable accuracy. (For a complete mathematical description of the biological model see Warren [1980].)

Economic components of the model are linked to the biological submodel through fishing effort and harvest (landings). The level of fishing effort is treated as a driving variable, determined externally, before being incorporated into the model (see appendix). Prices for shrimp are also considered external to the model and are developed from National Marine Fisheries Service (NMFS)

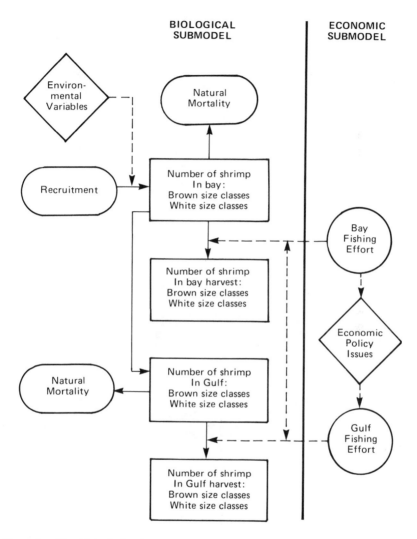

Figure 6.   Key biological and economic aspects of the Texas shrimp fishery simulation model (adapted from Warren [1980]).

data which is categorized by shrimp size class, time period and species [U.S. Department of Commerce 1977]. Unit costs of fishing are developed from budgets previously reported [Warren 1979]. The unit cost is defined as the sum of variable and fixed costs per vessel per time period. Variable cost for a given vessel class is the product of variable cost per day fished, number of nominal days fished per vessel and number of vessels in that class.

$$VC_k = VDF_k * NDF_k * NVES_k \qquad (8)$$

where
VC_k = variable cost of all vessels of class k

VDF_k = variable cost per nominal day fished per vessel of class k

NDF_k = number of nominal days fished in bays of gulf by the "average" type k vessel during the time interval

$NVES_k$ = number of type k vessels in the bay or gulf fishery during the time interval.

Fixed cost for a class of vessels is the product of the fixed cost per vessel and the number of vessels.

$$FC_k = FV_k * NVES_k \qquad (9)$$

where
FC_k = fixed cost of the class k vessels

FV_k = fixed cost per vessel of class k

Total cost for a given vessel class (TC_k) equals the sum of variable and fixed costs.

$$TC_k = VC_k + FC_k \qquad (10)$$

Revenues are a function of price and landings. For a given vessel class k, total revenue equals the product of shrimp price and quantity harvested (by size class and species).

$$TR_k = \sum_{ij} (P_{ij} * WT_{ijk}) \qquad (11)$$

where
TR_k = total revenue for vessel class k

P_{ij} = price of shrimp of species i, class j

WT_{ijk} = pounds of shrimp of species i, class j, landed by vessels in class k

Rent captured by a given vessel class in the fishery is represented as the difference between total revenue and total cost.

$$RENT_k = TR_k - TC_k \qquad (12)$$

where
$RENT_k$ = economic rents (profits) captured by vessel class k

Results

Basic Simulation

The model was adjusted so as to achieve a satisfactory simulation of average 1963-1974 (excluding 1967) performance in the Texas shrimp fishery. A brief summary of the results of this tuning exercise is presented in Table II. As predicted by the model, landings values categorized by species, vessel class and shrimp size class, are compared to average values from actual NMFS data. Size class 1 represents the large shrimp, and size class 5 the smaller. In this basic simulation mode, the model does very well in approximating actual values.

Because of the importance of seasonality in the fishery, the model was also tuned to monthly variations in landings within each species, vessel class and size class category. In the monthly adjustments, no effort was made to duplicate the actual landings by month and category, but relative magnitudes and variations between months in the data were approximated by the simulation. Figure 7 shows that predicted and actual monthly landings for brown and white shrimp do not diverge substantially.

Table II.   Results of Basic Model Simulation of Average Shrimp Fishery Conditions, Texas, 1963-1976.

Category	Landings by Shrimp Size Class (1000 lb)				
	1	2	3	4	5
Brown Shrimp					
Inshore					
Predictions	0.0	1.5	58.3	92.2	1,096.8
Actual data		0.7	29.6	145.6	1,066.6
Offshore					
Predictions	3,031.4	9,318.7	12,386.4	1,859.8	410.5
Actual data	4,035.1	9,121.0	11,593.5	1,939.7	190.7
White Shrimp					
Inshore					
Predictions	190.4	753.9	1,615.3	1,208.7	717.8
Actual data	117.7	962.6	1,654.9	973.8	782.5
Offshore					
Predictions	1,509.6	1,636.2	1,459.8	520.9	27.1
Actual data	1,423.7	1,898.4	1,443.1	279.8	124.0

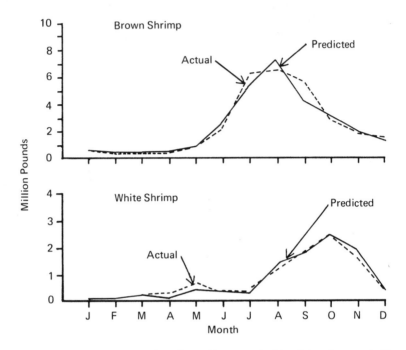

Figure 7.   Actual and predicted landings of brown and white shrimp by month, Texas, 1963-1974 average.

Baseline Simulation

To put the model to more practical use in evaluating a series of policy alternatives, it is necessary to develop a baseline version of the model upon which to test the impact of selected changes in fishery management. To reflect adequately previous fishing patterns, averages of data for five years (1970-1974) are used to generate the model baseline simulation. Since policy analysis is concerned with changes that occur when a policy is implemented, the base model is forced into open access equilibrium by adjusting the opportunity cost of the vessel owner/operator's labor. The model uses 1979 monetary data. After adjustments were made in the model to reflect the most recent effort data, the simulation was run as a baseline.

Policy Analysis

Two management alternatives for the Texas shrimp fishery have been suggested and discussed. Issues relating to shrimp seasonality and growth are important considerations in policy analysis for the industry, and are basic to the rationale for closing existing open seasons. The policies to be tested are:

1. close the spring bay season entirely (May 15 - July 15); and
2. close the offshore season from June 1 to July 31.

The shrimp management plan clearly shows that there is excess capacity in the shrimp fleet. Thus, for analysis of policy 2, it is assumed that vessels will increase their days fished by 10% during the remaining ten months the offshore fishery is open. This assumption seems reasonable since excess capacity exists and annual maintenance can be accomplished during the two-month closure.

Results of the baseline simulation and those of the above two policies are summarized in Table III and plotted in figures 8 through 15.

Figures 9 and 11 show the impact on bay boats and offshore vessels, respectively, of closing the offshore fishing area (i.e., policy 2). Figures 13 and 15 show the impact on bay boats and offshore vessels of closing the inshore fishing area (i.e., policy 1). The even-numbered figures show shifts in yield curves and the odd-numbered figures show shifts in total value product (TVP) and total factor cost (TFC) curves for the various policies. The graphs are scaled with millions of pounds or dollars on the vertical axis and thousands of days fished on the horizontal axis. The solid lines represent the baseline and the dashed lines the shift in the curves after the policy change. The TFC curve is a long-run total cost curve since days fished is changed by varying the number of vessels in the fleet. Point 1 in each graph represents equilibrium for the baseline simulation, the two point 2s in each represent the first year impact of the policy change on revenue and cost, and point 3 is equilibrium under the new policy.

When pure rent is earned in the fishery, new capital will move in rapidly. However, when negative rents are earned, capital moves out slowly because of asset fixity. Thus, it is assumed that to achieve a new equilibrium takes 4 years when a policy creates positive rents and, under negative rents, 12 years. While this assumption is somewhat arbitrary, it is also based on past observation of expansion in the shrimp fishery and useful life of a vessel.

This analysis assumes that both bay boats and offshore vessels are owner-operated and that the crews get 20% of the revenue. For the owner/operator to maintain good crews, it is assumed that the owner/operator will absorb any losses incurred by the crew as a result of a policy change to ensure rents to the crew are not negative.

Finally, it is assumed that fishing craft and fishermen will remain idle during the seasonal closure except for the time they already shrimp in waters other than Texas. Bay boats only fish in Texas waters and do not have alternative fisheries to move into. The bay oyster season is closed and the finfish fishery would not support the shrimp boat fleet's fishing capacity. NMFS catch data shows that Texas offshore vessels catch between 11 and 19% of their harvest in

Table III.   Model Predictions under Present Conditions, Closed Offshore and Closed Inshore

Policy Alternative	Number of Full Time Equivalent Craft	Days Fished (1000)	Pounds Landed (million)	Price per Pound ($)	Total Revenue (10⁶ $)	Total Variable Costs (10⁶ $)	Total Cost (10⁶ $)	Rent (10⁶ $)	Years to Adjust	Present Value (10⁶ $)
Baseline										
Boats	500	14.7	6.81	2.80	19.05	9.98	19.05	0.00	–	–
Vessels	1169	52.6	32.13	3.97	127.66	75.73	127.66	0.00	–	–
Total			38.94							
Close Offshore										
First Year										
Boats	500	14.2	6.62	2.78	18.40	9.78	18.85	-0.45	–	–
Vessels	1169	45.4	30.72	4.06	124.53	69.01	120.94	3.59	–	–
Total			37.34							
New Equilibrium										
Boats	460	13.1	6.20	2.80	17.34	9.00	17.34	0.00	12	-2.56
Vessels	1276	49.6	32.64	4.04	131.97	75.27	131.97	0.00	4	8.49
Total			38.84							
Close Inshore										
First Year										
Boats	500	11.3	5.15	3.18	16.40	8.53	17.60	-1.20	–	–
Vessels	1169	52.6	33.02	3.43	131.07	76.45	128.39	2.68	–	–
Total			38.17							
New Equilibrium										
Boats	394	8.9	4.31	3.22	13.88	–	13.88	0.00	12	-6.93
Vessels	1261	56.8	34.78	4.04	137.83	81.77	137.83	0.00	4	6.32
Total			39.09							

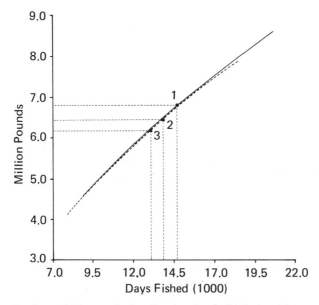

Figure 8.   Bay boat yield curves for baseline situation (solid line) and impact of closing the Texas offshore during June and July (dashed lines).

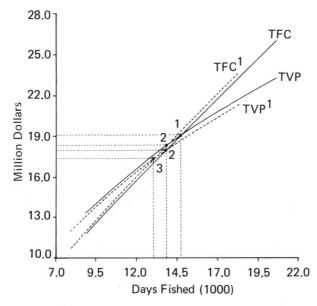

Figure 9.   Total value product and total factor cost curves of bay boats for baseline situation (solid lines) and impact of closing the Texas offshore during June and July (dashed lines).

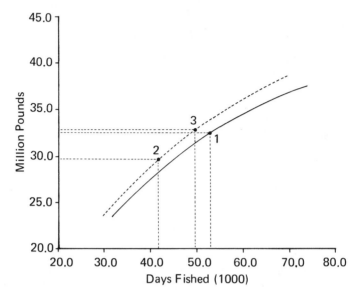

Figure 10. Offshore vessel yield curves for baseline situation (solid line) and impact of closing the Texas offshore during June and July (dashed lines).

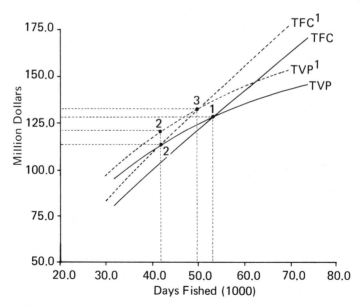

Figure 11. Total value product and total factor cost curves of offshore vessels for baseline situation (solid lines) and impact of closing the Texas offshore during the June and July (dashed lines).

Louisiana offshore waters. Although this activity may increase somewhat, is is assumed to remain constant for simplicity of analysis and because the Louisiana offshore waters will not support the entire Texas fleet during the two-month period Texas waters are closed.

Looking more closely at policy 2, it can be seen that if the decision is made to close the offshore area during June and July, the yield curve for bay boats is only slightly affected (Figure 8) but fishing effort is reduced by almost 500 days (point 1 to point 2) and landings drop by approximately 200,000 pounds during the first year. The offshore vessel yield curve (Figure 10) shifts up as expected; however, the loss in shrimp landings due to the reduction in days fished is not offset by the upward shift in the yield curve (point 1 to point 2). The simulation model predicts that first year rents to bay boat owners will decrease by $0.45 million and increase to $3.59 million for offshore vessel owners. This is shown as a movement from equilibrium at point 1 under present conditions to point 2 in Figures 9 and 11. Days fished decrease only slightly for bay boats since they depend mostly on the bays and exert little effort in the offshore area. Days fished decrease almost 22% for offshore vessels.

The revenue curve and the cost curve for offshore vessels as depicted in Figure 11 shifted up from TVP to TVP[1] and from TFC to TFC[1], respectively. The revenue curve shifted up because, for a given level of days fished, production increased and average shrimp size was slightly larger, yielding a nine cents per pound increase in average price (Table III). The cost curve increases because the number of vessels is assumed to remain fixed (assuming no alternative fishery) and because crews receive a percentage of the catch which causes variable cost to increase for a given number of days fished. Essentially, this is a new long-run cost curve, where again days fished is changed by altering the number of boats, but in this case the number of days fished per boat is reduced.

The effect on bay boats was to shift the revenue curve downward from TVP to TVP[1] and the cost curve slightly upward from TFC to TFC[1] as shown in Figure 9. Cost increased because the same number of boats are fishing fewer days per year. The revenue curve decreased because, in the offshore area during June and July, bay boats were fishing mostly for brown shrimp. By the time the season was open again in August the brown shrimp were in deeper water and inaccessible to boats.

The new equilibrium position that is achieved after all adjustments have taken place is point 3 in Figures 9 and 11. Vessels fish nearly the same number of days as before the closure; however, it takes over 9% more vessels in the industry fishing at 10% greater capacity to reach this level of days fished. Bay boats decrease days fished to 13,100 by decreasing the number of boats in the fleet by 8%. Consumers in the long run will have approximately the same amount of shrimp to eat.

Assuming it takes offshore vessels four years to reach the new equilibrium and bay boats 12 years, and assuming that adjustments are in equal increments each year, the present value of the stream of rents is – $2.56 million and $8.49 million for boats and vessels, respectively. This is calculated assuming a 3% real discount rate.

Closing the bays during the spring season (policy 1) shifts the curves somewhat differently than closing the offshore area. The yield curve for bay boats (Figure 12) shifts downward by a noticeable amount because brown shrimp have left the bays and are in deep water by the time the bays are reopened in August. The yield curve for offshore vessels (Figure 14) shifted up as expected. The TFC curve for boats increased considerably while their revenue curve has only a slight upward shift (Figure 13). The cost curve shifts up because the same number of boats are fishing fewer days per year. The revenue curve shifts up (at lower levels of days fished) because the average price received increased considerably and offset a downward shift in the production curve. In Figure 15 the revenue curve for vessels shifted up considerably, whereas the cost curve shifted up only enough to reflect increased shares going to the crew.

During the first year of the inshore closure, vessel owners will gain $2.68 million in rents at the expense of $1.20 million to the boat owners. The present value of this stream of rents would be $6.32 million for vessels and – $6.93 million for boats. Vessel owners would employ 8% more vessels in the fishery, and the effort of boats will decrease by 21%. Consumers will have the same quantity of shrimp to consume.

CONCLUSION

The goal of the Gulf Council is to manage the shrimp fishery to "attain the greatest overall benefit to the nation with particular reference to food production and recreational opportunities on the basis of maximum sustainable yield as modified by relevant economic, social or ecological factors." Under the assumptions used in this model, vessel owners would be the only ones to benefit from these policies in that they receive windfall gains, having present values of $8.49 and $6.32 million from closing the offshore and inshore, respectively. This gain comes at a cost to boatowners having a present value of $2.56 and $6.93 million, respectively. The number of vessels in the fishery increases in the long run, whereas the number of boats declines. Consumers initially have less shrimp to eat, but in the long run they would have a half million more pounds of shrimp to consume if the offshore is closed.

This analysis has only considered the impact of two proposed policies on the owners of fishing craft. It has not addressed the impact on shore

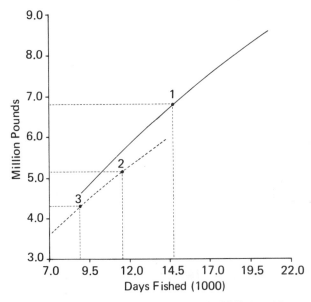

Figure 12. Bay boat yield curves for baseline situation (solid line) and impact of closing the Texas inshore during the spring season (dashed lines).

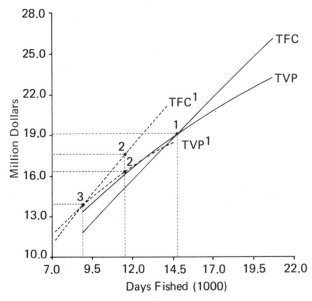

Figure 13. Total value product and total factor cost curves of bay boats for baseline situation (solid lines) and impact of closing the Texas inshore during the spring season (dashed lines).

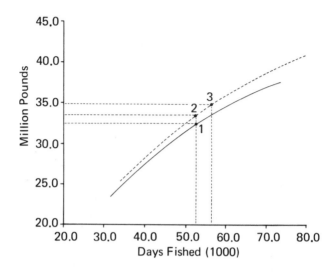

Figure 14. Offshore vessel yield curves for baseline situation (solid line) and impact of closing the Texas inshore during the spring season (dashed lines).

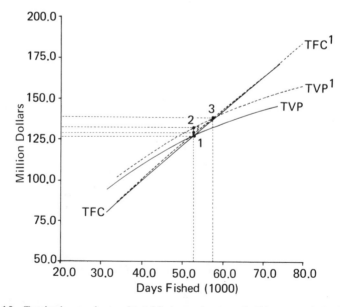

Figure 15. Total value product and total factor cost curves of offshore vessels for baseline situation (solid lines) and impact of closing the Texas inshore during the spring season (dashed lines).

facilities, fishing communities, processing plants and states neighboring Texas, which are all important considerations.

ACKNOWLEDGMENTS

Helpful comments on an earlier draft of this material were provided by Lee G. Anderson, Ron Griffin, John Nichols, and Kenneth Roberts. As a result, this manuscript has been greatly improved. Financial support during the preparation of this research was provided by the Texas Agricultural Experiment Station and the Texas A&M University Sea Grant Program. Of course, any errors remaining are solely the responsibility of the authors. This manuscript is Article No. 16495, Texas Agricultural Experiment Station.

APPENDIX

The Data

Data requirements for the simulation model are met almost entirely from secondary sources. Table IV presents a list of key parameters and data inputs, with nine dimensions varying within parentheses.

Regarding the biological parameters, sufficient information for model purposes is available in published sources. Christmas and Etzold [1979] is particularly helpful in this area, as previously noted. Other key sources are Grant and Griffin [1979] and Blomo et al. [1979]. Certainly, most biological parameter values are open to dispute, and many are in fact reported as a range of values. With this in mind, a sensitivity analysis to examine the effects of variations in key parameter values was conducted [Warren 1980]. Specific input data for key biological parameters is described below.

Phenology factor E represents time dependent recruitment rates. These are entered by month for each species and reflect seasonal trends in recruitment of organisms into the fishery [Griffin, et al. 1974]. The coefficient ICOF is a maximum monthly introduction rate for young shrimp, and is entered by species. To arrive at recruitment for a given species and month, ICOF is multiplied by the appropriate E value. The introductory coefficient is a variable for which solid estimates do not exist. In the initial phases of model tuning, ICOF is used to some extent as a tuning variable.

Boundaries between size classes are entered by species in millimeters of overall length as the parameter SL and based on Gulf of Mexico shrimp landing data [U.S. Dept. of Commerce 1963-1974]. VKIL provides a basis for manipulating minimum size limits by species, depth, and month.

Table IV.   Identification and Definition of Model Input Parameters, in Order
of Entry to GBFSM, with Dimensions Where Appropriate[a]

Parameters	Definition	Dimension
NA	Number of areas	
NC	Number of cohorts	
NSP	Number of species	
ND	Number of depths	
NVC	Number of vessel classes	
NSC	Number of shrimp size classes	
NM	Number of time periods	
NER	Time divisions, phenology factor E	
NPH	Time divisions, phenology factor GRT	
CMESH	Primary harvest lower size limit	(NSP, ND)
BMESH	Secondary harvest lower size limit	
RMESH	Auxiliary harvest lower size limit	
ETM	Conversion ratio for units in catch	
BC	Secondary harvest coefficient	
RC	Auxiliary harvest coefficient	
CF	Percentage of culls in legal catch	(NVC, ND)
C3	Linear coefficient, length/wt equation	(NSP)
C4	Power coefficient, length/wt equation	(NSP)
E	Time-dependent rate in recruitment	(NSP, NER)
ICOF	Gross recruitment rate	(NSP, NA)
ER	Movement rates (among depth, areas)	(NSP, ND, NA)
SL	Boundaries between size classes	(NSP, NSC)
VKIL	Minimum size limit	(NSP, ND, NM)
GRT	Time factors altering growth	(NSP, NPH)
NMOCF	Natural mortality rates	(NSP, ND, NSC)
FRL	Foot rope length (net size)	(NVC)
HP	Horsepower (engine size)	(NVC)
FMAX	Density factor, fishing mortality	(NSP, ND, NA)
PC	Packing charge	(NVC)
SHARE	Crews' percentage of landings	(NVC)
COST	Fishing cost per effort unit	(NVC, ND)
GCOF	Growth coefficient	(NSP)
C1	Power coefficient on HP	(NSP)
C2	Power coefficient on FRL	(NSP)
SZCOF	Minimum size shrimp move	(NSP)
CONV	Heads-on to heads-off conversion	(NSP)
MSZC	Maximum size for growth	(NSP)
USZ	Initial size for recruitment	(NSP)
DFN	Nominal days fished (effort)	(NSP, NA, ND, NVC, NM)
PMCSP	Fish (shrimp) prices	(NSP, NSC, NM)
PNUM	Initial number of organisms	(NSP, NA, ND, NC)
PSZ	Initial organism sizes	(NSP, NC)
ADSVM	Actual data (landings)	(ND, NSC, NC, NM)

[a]Adapted from Isakson et al. [1980].

Phenology factors GRT are entered by species and month, but reflect seasonal trends (if any) in growth rates. The species specific growth coefficients GCOF are multiplied by appropriate GRT values to derive growth rates for each month. Growth coefficients reported in Christmas and Etzold [1979] are used.

The natural mortality rate NMCOF is multiplied by shrimp population each week during the simulation to derive natural mortality. This parameter is set at 0.08 for both brown and white shrimp in the model. Christmas and Etzold [1979] report a wide range of values for natural mortality. The overall range includes values of from 0.02 to 0.55 for natural mortality among important shrimp species.

The density factor FMAX reflects relative density of shrimp in inshore and offshore waters, thereby directly affecting the catch per unit of fishing effort. Estimation of density factors is not a well-developed science. In view of the inexact nature of density factors, and model responsiveness to them in the inshore/offshore prediction of landings, FMAX has become an important tool for tuning the model to actual conditions.

Economic data are from a variety of sources, both secondary and primary. Specific economic parameters include vessel descriptive data which is used to derive relative fishing power. Length of foot rope of the trawl net (FRL) and engine horsepower (HP) are entered as averages for each vessel class.

Unit costs of fishing are entered into the GBFSM as the variable COST, by vessel class and depth fished. Fixed cost, FC, is entered by vessel class. These costs are estimated from a combination of secondary and primary data for bay boats, and from secondary data for Gulf vessels, as reported by Warren [1980]. Since shrimp vessels operate in waters other than Texas, their cost was adjusted to reflect this. Likewise, boats spend some time during the off-season in other kinds of fisheries and their cost was adjusted to reflect actual cost of fishing in Texas waters.

Fishing effort, in nominal days fished, is represented as the variable DFN, and is input by species, depth, vessel class and month. Estimates of effort are based on average values calculated from historical (1963-74) NMFS data.

Shrimp prices are a key input (PMCSP) and are developed by shrimp size class for each month using NMFS data (1963-74). Prices are also entered by species.

For tuning and comparative purposes, NMFS landings data for the years 1963 through 1974 are used [U.S. Department of Commerce, 1963-1974]. These data are entered by species, size class, and bay or gulf catch as the variable ADSVM.

NOTES

[1]Basically, these sections include: Section 3.2.1.2 (General Description of Fishery Effort) and Section 3.5. (Socioeconomic Characterization).

^{2}Section 3.2.1.2.

^{3}Section 3.2.1.1. or Section 3.5.13.f.

^{4}Section 8.3.

^{5}It may be argued that, since shrimp migrate toward deeper waters, bay shrimper effort occurs prior to gulf shrimper effort. Viewed in this manner one would expect y_1 to be influenced only by E_1 and y_2 to be influenced by both E_1 and E_2. When approached from this standpoint the conceptual approach will differ but the substantive conclusions are the same. However, as used here, bay and gulf shrimpers are arbitrary distinctions drawn on the basis of vessel type and the spatial location in which the majority (but not all) of their fishing effort is expended. Thus, for now the present approach is preferred.

^{6}This is somewhat analogous to Henderson and Quandt's [1971] treatment of firm profit maximization with multiple products (p. 95) and joint profit maximization for multiple firms with external effects (p. 272).

REFERENCES

1. Anderson, L. G. 1975. "Analysis of Open-Access Commercial Exploitation and Maximum Economic Yield in Biologically and Technologically Interdependent Fisheries," *J. Fish. Res. Board Can.* 32(10):1825-1842.
2. Anderson, L. G. 1977. *Economics of Fisheries Management* (Baltimore, MD: Johns Hopkins University Press).
3. Blomo, V., K. Stokes, W. Griffin, W. Grant and J. Nichols. 1978. "Bioeconomic Modeling of the Gulf Shrimp Fishery: An Application Galveston Bay and Adjacent Offshore Areas," *Southern J. Agric. Econ.* 10(1): 119-125.
4. Bromley, D. W., and R. C. Bishop. 1977. "From Economic Theory to Fishery Policy: Conceptual Problems and Management Prescriptions," in *Economic Impacts of Extended Fisheries Jurisdiction,* L. G. Anderson, Ed. (Ann Arbor, MI: Ann Arbor Science Publishers, Inc.).
5. Center for Wetland Resources. 1979. "Draft Environmental Impact Statement and Fishery Management Plan for the Shrimp Fishery of the Gulf of Mexico, United States Waters," prepared for Gulf of Mexico Fishery Management Council, Tampa, FL.
6. Christmas, J. Y., and D. J. Etzold. 1979. "The Shrimp Fishery of the Gulf of Mexico, United States: A Regional Management Plan," Gulf Coast Research Laboratory, Ocean Springs, MS.
7. Gates, J. M., and V. J. Norton. 1974. "The Benefits of Fishery Regulation: A Case Study of the New England Yellow Tail Flounder Fishery," Marine Tech. Rept. No. 21, University of Rhode Island.
8. Gordon, H. S. 1953. "An Economic Approach to the Optimum Utilization of Fisheries Resources," *J. Fish. Res. Board Can.* 10:442-457.
9. Gordon, H. S. 1954. "The Economic Theory of a Common-Property Resource: The Fishery," *J. Polit. Econ.* 62:124-142.
10. Grant, W., and W. Griffin. 1979. "A Bioeconomic Model of the Gulf of Mexico Shrimp Fishery," *Trans. Am. Fish. Soc.* 108:1-13.

11. Griffin, W., M. Cross and G. Ryan. 1974. "Seasonal and Movement Patterns in the Gulf of Mexico Shrimp Fishery," Texas Agric. Exp. Station, Texas A&M University Rept. No. 74-4.
12. Griffin, W., R. Lacewell and J. Nichols. 1976. "Optimum Effort and Rent Distribution in the Gulf of Mexico Shrimp Fishery," *Am. J. Agric. Econ.* 53:644-652.
13. Griffin, W., J. Warren and W. Grant. 1979. "A Bioeconomic Model of Fish Stock Management: The Cephalopod Fishery of Northwest Africa," United Nations CECAF/TECH Rept. 79/16, Dalsar.
14. Hannesson, R. 1978. *Economics of Fisheries* (New York: Columbia University Press).
15. Henderson, J. M., and R. E. Quandt. 1971. *Microeconomic Theory: A Mathematical Approach,* 2nd ed. (New York: McGraw-Hill Book Co.).
16. Isakson, K., W. Grant and W. Griffin. 1980. "General Bioeconomic Fisheries Simulation Model (GBFSM) User Guide," Texas Agric. Exp. Station, Texas A&M University (unpublished).
17. Johnson, D. G. 1958. "Supply Function—Some Facts and Notions," in *Agricultural Adjustment Problems in a Growing Economy* (Ames, IA: Iowa State College Press).
18. Koutsoyiannis, A. 1975. *Modern Microeconomics* (New York: John Wiley & Sons, Inc.).
19. Prochaska, F. and C. O. Andrew. 1974. "Shrimp Processing in the Southeast: Supply Problems and Structural Change," *Southern J. Agric. Econ.* 6(1):247-252.
20. Prochaska, F., and J. Cato. 1975. "Economic Growth Aspects of the Florida Shrimp Industry," *Fishing Gaz.* 92(10):18-20.
21. Scott, A. 1955. "The Fishery: The Objectives of Sole Ownership," *J. Polit. Econ.* 63:116-124.
22. Turvey, R. 1964. "Optimization and Sub-optimization in Fishery Regulation," *Am. Econ. Rev.* 54:64-76.
23. U.S. Department of Commerce. 1963-1949. Unpublished landing data. National Oceanic and Atmospheric Administration, National Marine Fisheries Service, Washington, DC.
24. Warren, J. P. 1980. "The Texas Bay Shrimp Industry: A Description and Management Model," Ph.D. Dissertation, Texas A&M Univeristy, College Station, TX.

CHAPTER 5

ECONOMIC ANALYSIS AND THE MANAGEMENT
OF ATLANTIC SURF CLAMS

Ivar E. Strand, Jr.
Department of Resource and Agricultural Economics
University of Maryland

James E. Kirkley
Northeast Fisheries Center
National Marine Fisheries Service

Kenneth E. McConnell
Department of Resource and Agricultural Economics
University of Maryland

On the surface, the management of Atlantic surf clams under FCMA appears to be a major success. The State-Federal Surf Clam Project, which preceded the Mid-Atlantic Regional Council, had established a notable record of research and policy prescriptions by the time the regional council took control. The original group had observed the depletion of numerous surf clam beds and recognized the necessity of establishing a ceiling on the harvest of surf clams [Davis et al. 1975]. The state-federal project, however, relied on individual states to enact policy recommendations, a characteristic that prevented a strong management program. The enactment of FCMA with a central decision-making authority in the council provided the additional strength needed to implement many of the management recommendations developed under the state-federal program.

The Regional Council's first Surf Clam and Ocean Quahog Fisheries Management Plan was accepted in November 1977. The plan contained objectives of rebuilding stocks so that a maximum sustainable yield (50 million pounds) could be attained, while minimizing short-term economic disruptions. A moratorium on new entry, annual and quarterly catch quotas, a limit on days and hours fished per week, restriction of fishing in areas composed of young clams, and requirements for record-keeping were all enacted to reach these goals. At the same time, the council recognized that these restrictions could force vessels into a newly developing ocean quahog fishery. They thus included provisions in the plan for quahog quotas with the possibility that other restrictions, similar to the surf clam regulations, could be imposed if new scientific evidence warranted. Since the initial plan, two amendments (September 1979, January 1980) have included provisions for an open access New England fishery and prohibition of catch after 5 PM on any day unless the vessel is permitted to fish the next day.

Although there is a divergence of opinion among the users and managers of the resource, the general consensus is that the regulations prevented a complete collapse of the fishery and has helped rebuild stocks to the point where there appears to be inadequate markets to absorb the allowable surf clam production. Figure 1 shows the trends in surf clam landings since 1950. The consensus suggests an unregulated industry would have caused higher landings in 1977 and 1978 with lower ones in the latter years. One factor not shown on this graph is a dominant 1976 age class of surf clams lying off Atlantic City. This age class could be recruited into fishery in 1981 and, by itself increase landings to a level close to the MSY level. Another indication of the "glut" of clams comes from reports of vessels not operating to land the current quota. Most vessels are operating one day per week instead of the allowable four days per week. Also, only 100 of the potential 168 licensed vessels landed surf clams during the first quarter of 1980.

Thus, the resource situation has improved to the extent that there is current pressure to remove the moratorium on vessel entry. This sentiment has been recently expressed by one Council member who stated [Mid-Atlantic Fisheries Management Council 1980] :

> If the clams and market are there and you can double the length of time you permit the present vessels to work, it would be wise to think of other people who would like to get into the fishery or change into it from their present fishery...we cannot turn our back and let a select group holding permits stay in it.

Continuation of the moratorium on entry is being debated and hence one of major provisions of the original plan may be eliminated in the near future.

The renewed debate on the moratorium raises the question that if the plan was so successful, why is there a movement to eliminate one of its major components? One possible answer is that the plan has not been as successful as previously stated and therefore needs a complete revision. A second answer is that the conditions which originally created the need for management may have changed so that the existing plan is no longer appropriate. Finally, it is possible that the proponents of lifting the moratorium do not really understand the reasoning for it and are therefore proposing a change that may have detrimental effects both to current and future users of the resource.

Whatever the correct answer, it is obvious that the management of surf clams is at a critical juncture and there appear to be several courses of action under active consideration. Three options under consideration by the council are [Mid-Atlantic Region Scientific and Statistical Committee 1980]:

1. Continuation of the moratorium on entry and maintenance of the current restrictions on areas and operations;
2. Elimination of the moratorium on new entry and maintenance of previous restrictions on areas and operations;

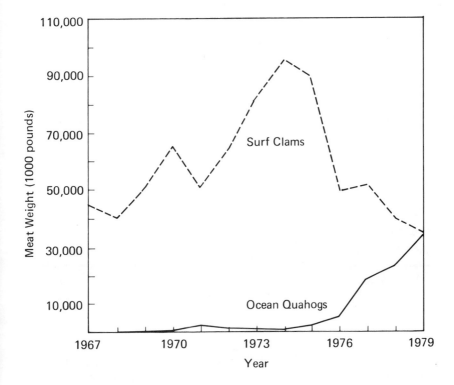

Figure 1.   Surf clam and ocean quahog catches, 1967-1979.

3.   Elimination of the moratorium and introduction of a per vessel allocation and some restriction on entry of new vessels (this might be a stock certificate program or an annual allocation per vessel). The area closures would remain but other restrictions would be eliminated.

Each of the options has economic implications for current and future users and it is the responsibility of the council to consider them. It is the purpose of this chapter to discuss the economic issues involved in the three options, the economic theory required to understand the nature of the trade-offs involved, the empirical analysis necessary to estimate the magnitudes of the trade-offs and the availability of data required to perform such analysis. Rather than attempt a discussion of all aspects of these alternatives, a review of the industry's characteristics and past literature is used to focus the paper on those issues that are of first-order economic importance. This task was greatly aided by previous work of the National Marine Fisheries Service and the regional council. We feel that their previous work contributed greatly to the management plan and are only hoping to show how it may be extended. The chapter thus follows with a description of the industry. Three aspects of the industry appear to have substantial economic importance. These are:

1.   Factor substitutability considerations: is dredge size being substituted for hours fished?
2.   Multiple species considerations: are quahogs being substituted for surf clams in production and consumption?
3.   Industry structure considerations: is the apparent concentration in the processing sector influencing its economic behavior?

The remainder of the paper is concerned with the economic trade-offs involved in these issues and the research necessary to analyze the trade-offs.

INDUSTRY BACKGROUND

The original Surf Clam and Ocean Quahog Management Plan and its amendments have a rather complete description of the surf clam and ocean quahog fishery (also see Ritchie [1977]). This section summarizes their relevant economic information and combines it with additional information from other sources.

Historical Patterns

Although there are reports of Indians roasting clams that washed up on Virginia's beaches as early as 1634 [Parker 1972], the surf clam industry began as a New England bait fishery around 1870 [Yancy and Welch 1968]. By 1940 increased demand for foodstuff led to the use of surf clams for human consumption. Two major technological advances, sand washers (1943) and hydraulic dredges (1945), created the economic impetus for an expanded industry. Surf clams provided nearly two-thirds of the entire domestic clam production by 1965 but the share has declined to about 25% now.

Before 1977 the predominant pattern in the industry was to locate a concentration or bed of surf clams and to harvest from that bed until a better alternative was found. State landings figures of New Jersey and Virginia (the two major producing states) reflect that pattern (Table I). As long as new beds were found, total landings increased (Figure 1). The most recent crisis in the industry occurred during 1975 when the harvesting of Virginia's surf clam beds began to yield substantially less output, and alternative surf clam sources were not found. The reduction in output most likely resulted in tripling in exvessel price from 14¢/lb in 1975 to 47¢/lb in 1976. The processed price response was not as high, only doubling for shucked meats, while the prices of various processed products rose by, at most, 50%. The higher prices induced a technological change that permitted the use of ocean quahogs in certain processed products (e.g., Manhattan clam chowder). Before that period, the strong flavor, dark color and expense of opening caused processors to avoid their use.

Situation Since 1977

The effectiveness of changes in the current management plan depends in part on the current status of the resource and the institutional structure of the industry. The area in which surf clams are found in greatest abundance begins in the inshore waters of Long Island and runs predominantly north-south along the East Coast in shallow waters out to a depth of about 55 meters (see Figure 2 and Ropes [1980] for further information). The current institutional setting is partly a continuation of historical evolution and partly a consequence of management restrictions. To appreciate these factors, more detail is given.

Management Restrictions

There are a number of specific restrictions imposed to assist in rebuilding the surf clam resource. These are:

1. An annual surf clam quota of 0.025 million bushels for the New England region and 1.8 million bushels for the mid-Atlantic. Ocean quahog quotas of 4 million bushels for the entire East Coast.
2. Quarterly surf clam quotas of 400,000 bushels for each of the two quarters from October through March and 500,000 per quarter for April to September.

Table I. Surf Clam Landings (1000 lb of meat) by State, 1950-1979[a]

Year	New York	New Jersey	Delaware	Maryland	Virginia	New England	Total
1950	3286	4298	—	130	—	28	7742
1951	4046	6420	—	1532	—	22	12020
1952	4138	7418	—	1089	—	3	12648
1953	3345	6578	—	2454	—	—	12377
1954	3360	6877	—	1346	—	232	11815
1955	2026	8278	—	1695	—	23	12022
1956	2368	11583	2	1850	—	123	15926
1957	1599	15224	192	934	—	4	17953
1958	429	12462	780	792	—	1	14464
1959	514	20164	1705	850	—	2	23235
1960	722	23448	478	420	—	3	25071
1961	722	26697	—	71	—	12	27502
1962	840	29830	99	75	—	10	30854
1963	974	37548	—	64	—	—	38586
1964	1218	36875	—	38	—	13	38144
1965	1505	42307	—	275	—	1	44088
1966	1840	43174	—	64	—	35	45113
1967	2305	41589	—	1149	—	16	45059
1968	3008	32181	—	5328	17	18	40552
1969	3431	36039	2757	7127	208	13	49575
1970	4182	39669	8734	13681	889	163	67318
1971	3688	28721	7694	7752	4507	173	52535
1972	2713	21332	8551	7330	23384	161	63471
1973	3319	21588	6630	7448	43323	17	82325
1974	3951	22656	5817	7448	58219	9	96078
1975	4580	35550	2315	5426	39084	16	86894
1976	3455	24378	0	5351	14064	21	49074
1977	3425	23570	0	7135	15741	—	51794
1978	—	—	—	8393	—	—	39469
1979	—	—	—	—	—	—	34912

[a]Fishery Statistics of the United States

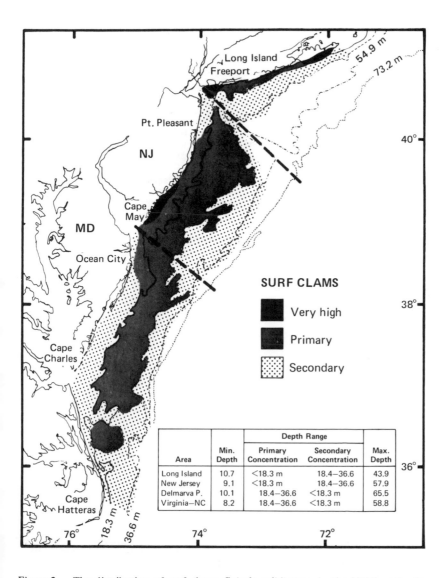

Figure 2.   The distribution of surf clams, *Spisula solidissima*, in the Middle Atlantic Bight. The categories of concentrations (very high = 5 bu or more; primary = < 5 to 1 bu; secondary = < 1 bu. Meter depths shown correspond to 10 fathoms increments. An occurrence at a minimum or maximum depth may represent only a single clam (source: Ropes [1980]).

3. The surf clam fishing week is limited to no more than four days, Monday through Thursday. To help spread the quarterly catch evenly throughout the entire quarter, each vessel is restricted to 24 hours of fishing per week at the beginning of each quarter. If the Regional Director of the National Marine Fisheries Service determines that the quarterly quota will not otherwise be harvested, the weekly hours of fishing may be increased. The Regional Director may prohibit fishing if it is likely that the quarterly quota will be exceeded. Vessels are required to stop fishing at 5:00 PM each day with the fishing week 5:00 PM Sunday-5:00 PM Thursday. In the New England Area, there are no effort restrictions unless and until half of the 25,000 bushel quota is harvested, at which time the effort restrictions operating in the mid-Atlantic area will be imposed.
4. Fishing for ocean quahogs is permitted 24 hours per day, 7 days per week. The National Marine Fisheries Service may restrict ocean quahog fishing if it is expected that the annual quota will be reached before the year's end.
5. Entry of additional vessels into the surf clam fishery in the mid-Atlantic Area is prohibited. There is no entry moratorium in the New England Area. Vessels with permits issued pursuant to the moratorium in both New England and the mid-Atlantic may fish in both areas on both quotas. Vessels entering the fishery in New England that do not meet the moratorium conditions may not fish south of the dividing line.
6. Surf clam beds may be closed to fishing if over 60% of the clams are under 4.5 inches in length and less than 15% are over 5.5 inches in length.
7. All vessels in the Fishery Conservation Zone surf clam and ocean quahog fisheries must be licensed. Fishermen and processors in both fisheries must submit reports to the National Marine Fisheries Service.

Vessel Characteristics

Vessels operating in the surf clam industry vary substantially in their characteristics. A review of Table II indicates that crew size had the least variability, varying from 2 to 7 men. Length, gross registered tonnage (GRT), horsepower and blade size have a range where the maximum value is four times the minimum. The heterogeneity combined with the knowledge that dissimilar vessels harvest similar amounts of clamming suggests a potential exists for substitution among the factors of production. The range of characteristics of the inputs appears to have varied during the period 1975 to 1978.

An important aspect of factor use is the growth in the number of larger vessels (greater than 101 GRT) from the period 1970 to 1977, the year of the moratorium on entry. From 1970 to the beginning of the moratorium, the number of large vessels rose by 47 vessels. Medium (51-100 GRT) and small vessels (less than 50 GRT) increased by only 6 and 5, respectively. A total of 60 large vessels entered the fishery in 1978. These numbers may indicate that the number of larger vessels would increase if the moratorium is lifted. However, one indication that this might not happen is suggested by the fact that 40% of the 1976 total cost of harvest for the largest class vessel was fuel. This compares with 10 and 12% for the small and medium vessel class, respectively

[Mid-Atlantic Fisheries Council 1977]. Price increases in fuels since 1976 probably have had more effect on the large vessel operation than on the smaller ones.

Another interesting aspect is that while recent surf clam harvest has been declining, there has been an upsurge in ocean quahog landings. During the year the plan was first introduced, ocean quahog production was 18,500 pounds of meat weight. Production rose to 22,900 pounds in 1978 and 34,700 pounds in 1979. The landings in 1979 were roughly equivalent to surf clam landings. The upsurge can partially be attributed to registered surf clam vessels directing effort to quahogs. In 1978 large vessels obtained 79% of the quahog revenues. Moreover, of the 153 active vessels in 1978, 21 of them accounted for 90% of the ocean quahog revenues while landing only 11% of the offshore clams. Thus, it appears a few large vessels are directing their efforts to the production of quahogs.

Processing Characteristics

Processing plants for surf clams and ocean quahogs are distributed from Maine to Virginia, with the largest concentrations in New Jersey, Maryland and Virginia. These plants process surf clams for three major products: canned chowder, canned whole and minced clams, and breaded strips. In 1977, the canned chowder market absorbed about 36% (down from 48% in 1971) of clam product, the canned whole and minced clams about 25% (down from 30% in 1971) and breaded strips about 28% (up from 9% in 1971).

Table II.   Physical Characteristics of Surf Clam Vessels, 1975 and 1978

Year		Length (feet)	Gross tonnage	Dredge length (inches)	Horse-power	Crew size
1975[a]	Minimum	37	9	34 [48][b]	60	2
	Maximum	155	386	60 [200][b]	1530	5
	Mean	70	74	49 [84][b]	265	3
1978[b]	Minimum	18	1	22	70	2
	Maximum	146	306	240[c]	1750	7
	Mean	83	110	88[d]	428	3

[a]Virginia Institute of Marine Science data.
[b]Mid-Atlantic Regional Council data.
[c]Represents double 120-in. dredges; largest single dredge was 200-in.
[d]Median was 60 in.

Although ocean quahogs cannot be used in certain of these product lines, they are being heavily substituted for surf clams in others. Evidence of this is offered in exvessel price equations estimated by the National Marine Fisheries Service. These indicate that the exvessel price of surf clams is inversely related to the harvest of ocean quahogs.

Another characteristic that is apparent within the industry is a concentration of market power in the processing sector. Again, using data gathered by NMFS, the largest four surf clam processors purchase about 75% of total industry surf clam landings. A similar concentration ratio of 75% exists for ocean quahogs. It should also be noted that there are one or two dominant firms among the top four in both industries.

A final aspect of both processing and harvesting is the ownership of vessels by the processing companies. Although there are no published reports on the vertical integration in the industry, it is common knowledge that numerous surf clam vessels are owned by processing firms. Over the past six months, the softness in the retail market has led to the processors either buying clams only from their own boats or from vessles with long-standing relationships. The market for many independents has thus been eliminated which in combination with reports that independents tend to be more efficient, leads to a concern for decreased technical efficiency in surf clam production.

MANAGEMENT ISSUES WITH ECONOMIC CONTENT

The brief sketch offered above raised several issues in the authors' minds especially in light of the current debate on the moratorium. The first was whether or not the substitution between regulated and unregulated gear would create excess capacity even if the moratorium continued. Secondly, there is reason to believe the surf clam/ocean quahog interrelationships have obscured events in the surf clam fishery to the extent that the benefits of the moratorium have not been perceived. Finally, the dominance of several firms in the processing sector raises the issue as to whether monopsony power exists in the industry and, hence, whether a moratorium or any other restricted entry strategy is socially desirable.

Substitution of Inputs

Numerous authors (e.g., Christy [1973]) have argued that restricting only certain of the inputs used for fishing will lead to expansion of the other inputs as price and resource stocks increase. Such unnecessary expansion of inputs wastes resources within the economy. In essence, the decrease in output raises prices and increases the stock density. Greater stock density creates a potential profit for the vessel owner if he can land more product. The potential profit guides him to expand production (and effort) in the only way possible, by expanding the amount of unregulated inputs he uses. In the case of surf clams, the restrictions on new entry and time fished still leave dredge size, horsepower, crew size and several other inputs unrestricted by law. The central question is whether there is sufficient substitutability among gear used for clamming to warrant expanded use of the unrestricted inputs. Whether vessel owners actually attempt to expand output is an empirical question, relating to the production function, the output price and the input costs.

Prior to the analysis of the production function and substitution issues, it is informative to provide a brief, descriptive summary of the characteristics of the vessels used in the study.[1] Table III is a summary of the vessel characteristics, which indicates the relative heterogeneity of the fleet. Most notable is the variation or range of characteristics, particularly for time fished, number of trips and landings per vessel. The total landings of the 122 vessels was 1,559,856 bushels in 1979, with most of the landings distributed among the 101- to 200-ton range (Table IV). Also shown is the expected relationships that larger vessels take more trips, fish more hours per vessel, have a larger engine and dredge, and land more per vessel. Of the 122 vessels landing surf clams in 1979, 43 vessels landed quahogs, 13 more than in 1978.

The analysis of input substitution is based on estimated cross-sectional production function for a representative vessel of this group.[2] Output was measured in bushels of surf clams landed in 1979 (LSC) and the inputs considered were gross registered tonnage (GRT), horsepower of the vessel's engine (HP), the length of the dredge blade (D) and hours fished (H). Horsepower and tonnage were highly correlated, thus only gross registered tons was included. Two alternative specifications of the production function, the Cobb-Douglas and the transcendental function, were estimated. The Cobb-Douglas has the properties of constant unitary elasticity of substitution and constant output elasticity of inputs. The transcendental, on the other hand, has nonconstant elasticity of substitution and output elasticity. Both are relatively easy to estimate.[3]

The results for the Cobb-Douglas and transcendental, respectively were[4]:

$$ln \ (LSC) = 0.112 + 0.25 \ ln \ (GRT) + 0.68 \ ln \ (D) + 1.18 \ ln \ (H) \qquad (1)$$

$$(4.84) \quad (3.16) \qquad (5.07) \qquad (21.54)$$

$$R^2 = 0.91, N = 122$$

$$ln \ (LSC) = 0.113 + 0.16 \ ln \ (GRT) + 0.72 \ ln \ (D) + 1.22 \ ln \ (H) - 0.0001 \ H \qquad (2)$$

$$(3.31) \quad (2.33) \qquad (6.85) \qquad (11.43) \qquad (4.37)$$

Table III.   Characteristics of Selected Surf Clam Vessels,[a] 1979[b]

Input	Range			Number of Vessels Exceeding Mean	Coefficient of Variation
	Minimum	Maximum	Mean		
Gross Registered Tons (GRT)	24	306	113.3	54	0.42
Horsepower (HP)	110	1,750	417.8	39	0.21
Length of Dredge Blade (D)	47 in.	240 in.	86.1 in.	41	0.37
Hours Fished (H)	8.5	1,108	494.3	59	0.61
Number of Trips	1	88	41.4	65	0.56
Landings per Trip	40	63,883	12,785	45	0.99

[a]There were 122 vessels fishing for surf clams in 1979. These data include all of them.
[b]Source: National Marine Fisheries Service, Northeast Regional Office, Gloucester, MA.

$$R^2 = 0.91, N = 122$$

where the numbers in parenthesis are t-statistics and all are significantly different from zero at the 99% level of confidence.

The first notable feature of the Cobb-Douglas production function is the apparent increasing returns to scale, suggesting that a proportionate increase in inputs will more than proportionately increase output. There are several explanations for this result. Perhaps most important is the omission of the input fuel. To expand other inputs and time, more fuel must be used. But the use of fuel is highly correlated with other inputs, so that omitting fuel will bias these coefficients upward. A second explanation is that larger vessels may fish further offshore where densities are higher. Measures of density were not available. Hence the variable GRT may proxy for stock density and bias the coefficient upward.

The omission of a variable can cause the sum of the estimated coefficients in the Cobb-Douglas production function to exceed 1 when the true value is less than or equal to 1. Suppose the true model is:

$$y = \sum_{i=1}^{n} x_i \, \beta_i + u$$

where   y = the log of output

   x_i = the log of the ith input

   n = the number of inputs

   u = the random error

$$\sum_{i=1}^{n} \beta_i = 1$$

Now suppose the estimated model is

$$y = \sum_{i=1}^{n-1} x_i \beta_i + \theta$$

The bias for each $\hat{\beta}_i$ is $E(\hat{\beta}_i) = \beta_i + \beta_n \gamma_i$ where γ_i is the coefficient of the regression of x_i on x_n. Then the sum of the expected values of the estimated coefficients is:

$$\sum_{i=1}^{n-1} E(\hat{\beta}_i) = \sum_{i=1}^{n-1} \beta_i + \beta_n \sum_{i=1}^{n-1} \gamma_i$$

$$= 1 + \beta_n \left(\sum_{i=1}^{n-1} \gamma_i - 1 \right)$$

If the sum of the γ_i's exceeds one and β_n is positive, then the estimated sum will exceed one. In many cases, it is not unreasonable to suppose that $\gamma_i = 1$, so that

$$\sum_{i=1}^{n-1} \beta_i = 1 + (n-1) \beta_n$$

which would show a substantial overestimation of scale results. We therefore caution the reader on the use of these coefficients and use them ourselves for illustration only.

The transcendental function is of particular interest because it allows for negative marginal products of an input. This is the portion of a production function where one would not expect producers to be operating. This form also allows for an approximation of an input's economic region of production when other inputs are fixed. A partial analysis suggests that the average vessel (113 GRT, 100-in. dredge) was operating in the economic region. The analysis also suggests that several vessels were operating at hours fished less than the economic range.

Table IV. Characteristics and Distribution of Landings by Tonnage Groups, 1979

Tonnage	Number of Vessels	Number of Trips	Average Number of Trips	Hours Fished	Average Hours Per Vessel	Average Horse-power	Average Dredge Size	Landings (bushels)	Average Landings	Percent of Total Landings	Cumulative Percent of Landings	Average Hours Per Trip
24-50	14	464	33	5032	359.4	193.9	62.6	32177	5869.8	5.3	5.3	10.8
51-100	47	1824	39	19647	418.0	311.4	73.7	381296	8112.7	24.4	29.7	10.8
101-150	31	1174	38	14519	468.3	395.4	84.1	338729	10926.7	21.7	51.4	12.4
151-200	26	1288	50	17342	667.0	667.9	112.1	557018	21423.8	35.7	87.1	13.5
Over 200	4	299	75	3767	941.8	1000.0	160.0	200636	50159.0	12.9	100.0	12.6

The potential for substituting dredge length (D) for either of the restricted inputs, hours fished (H) or tonnage (GRT), can be reviewed by examining the shape of isoquants and reviewing the rate of technical substitution. The isoquant shows the various possible combinations of inputs (e.g., hours fished and dredge length) that will produce a given output. The rate of technical substitution indicates the amount of one input (e.g., dredge size) that can be substituted for another input (e.g., hours fished) to maintain a given output.

Table V and Figure 3 show the combinations of dredge length and hours fished that maintain a level of output of 18,222 bushels per year and the corresponding isoquant. It shows that if a vessel's hours fished were restricted from 700 hours per year to 600, then output could be maintained by increasing the dredge length from around eight feet (96 in.) to about ten feet (120 in.). Clearly, drastic restrictions in hours fished would require more than only an increase in the dredge length. Changes in horsepower and other inputs (i.e., rerigging) would be required. An alternative way to use the isoquant is to consider the fishing hours necessary to land a given harvest if the dredge sizes were increased. Figure 3 illustrates a situation where a vessel increased the dredge size from 40 to 80 inches. For that vessel to land the same amount of clams, hours fished would have to fall by 35%, from about 1160 hours to 775 hours.

Table V.   Combinations of Hours Fished and Dredge Length for a Given Annual Landings[a] and the Corresponding Rate of Technical Substitution

Inputs		Rate of Technical Substitution $(\Delta D/\Delta H)$
Hours Fished	Dredge Length	
500	174	0.60
550	148	0.46
600	127	0.37
650	110	0.29
700[b]	97[b]	0.24[b]
750	86	0.20
800	77	0.17
850	70	0.14
900	63	0.12
950	57	0.10
1000	53	0.09
1050	48	0.08
1100	44	0.07
1150	41	0.06
1200	38	0.06

[a]Assumed tonnage of 113 tons and a fixed output of 18,222 bushels.
[b]Approximate average operational levels for 1979.

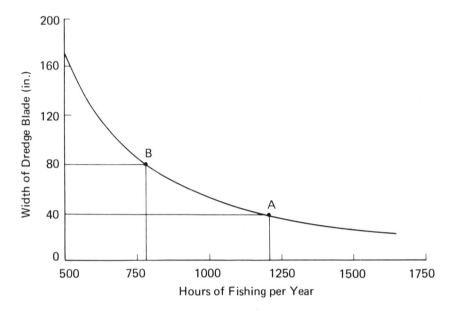

Figure 3.   Isoquant for surf clam production derived from the Cobb-Douglas function for representative vessel of 113 tons, output of 18,222.6 bushels of surf clams.

To evaluate the potential for substituting dredge length for hours fished, it would be necessary to have corresponding cost information and knowledge about the decision process within the industry. This information is currently unavailable. The National Marine Fisheries Service Regional Office is currently in the process of developing a budget simulator which would allow analysis of whether a vessel owner would increase dredge size for a situation in which prices and input costs change. We believe this is a useful project and will help in assessing management plans in the future.

Without this more detailed information, only general comments can be made about the substitutability issue. The rates of technical substitution were sufficiently low so that some substitution of dredge size for hours fished was possible. Historically, however, the industry did not initially expand dredge size. The reduction in hours fished, the seriously depleted resource base and the addition of new vessels in 1978 more than likely kept marginal costs close to prices.[5] Increasing dredge size and thus costs would likely not have been rational. However, once council discussions centered on limiting dredge size were raised, many vessel owners increased dredge size so that they would not be constrained if the council imposed restrictions.

Thus, although not properly documented, there were "wasted" expenses on excess capacity gear, i.e., dredges. This, in combination with the apparent excess vessels in the fishery since 1978, leads us to conclude that the moratorium has likely not been a deterrent to the "wastes" associated with excess capacity. Whether this will be true in the future is debatable but one would expect that as long as certain inputs are unrestricted, then the "wastes" of excess capacity will exist regardless of the moratorium. How quickly the situation will change to create interest in input expansion depends to a large degree on the surf clam/ quahog interactions. These are considered next.

Multiple Product Consideration

There is also evidence of interrelationships between surf clam and ocean quahog production and consumption. A revenue function provided in the 1979 amendment showed that each clam hour fished by a vessel grossed $220 per boat and each quahog hour fished grossed $388 per boat. Clearly surf clam vessels have opportunity costs associated with quahog production and vice versa. Previously discussed price equations appeared to link the consumption of surf clams with price of quahogs and the consumption of quahogs with the price of surf clams. (These relationships are somewhat tenuous, however, because of the potential simultaneous equation bias in the parameters.) What are the policy implications of these interrelationships?

The first observation relates to the likely consequences of surf clam production regulations on the use of the quahog resource. Limitations, such as hourly limits, constrain the surf clam operator and force the average cost of surf clam production to rise. This creates an incentive for the surf clammer to seek alternative uses of the vessel. One of the most profitable alternatives has been to harvest quahogs. Thus, the more restrictive are the surf clam regulations, the more effort is devoted to ocean quahogs and the more likely additional restrictions will be placed on them. Increased effort on quahogs will be induced whether a moratorium or stock certificates (vessel allocations) are used to manage surf clams. Without these restrictions, the incentive to harvest quahogs will be less. It might be worthwhile, therefore, to consider the quahog and the surf clam resources jointly in the discussions concerning lifting of the moratorium. One possible solution would be to create vessel allocations for *both* ocean quahogs and surf clams. Doing this would eliminate the necessity of the gear/ time restrictions that appeared so restrictive in the surf clam case. This would also placate those individuals who claimed they should have more surf clam certificates because they had been harvesting quahogs. These vessel owners would get more ocean quahog shares.

Although this may appear rational, it is not likely to be politically acceptable and the current ocean quahog regulations will probably remain in effect
for the short run. In this event, one must recognize the effort that may soon
be directed to the surf clam resource. The use of quahogs for various clam
products removed pressure on the surf clam resource in two ways: (1) it created
a market for quahogs that was profitable enough to draw vessels from surf
clam production into quahog production; (2) it also reduced the demand for
surf clams by offering a low-cost alternative product. Both effects, creating an
opportunity cost for surf clam production and lowering the demand for surf
clams, tended to remove effort from surf clams.

Unfortunately, the same two relationships are likely to be reversed and create
pressure on the surf clam resource in the near future. When the quahog resource was initially exploited, it was a virgin resource and therefore relatively
dense, causing catch per hour towed to be high. However, with exploitation,
the resource density of the quahog will fall, reducing the catch per hour towed.
Rising average costs associated with the reduction in catch per tow will lower
total harvest and raise quahog prices. These events will influence surf clam
production in two ways: (1) rising average costs would lower profitability of
quahog operations and create an incentive to move into surf clams; (2) the
rising quahog price would increase the processors' demand for surf clams, and
thus create another incentive to harvest surf clams. Additional incentives to
harvest surf clams, of course, raise fear among the managers that the current
excess capacity situation might worsen without the moratorium.

The research necessary to examine this possibility requires the biological
effects of quahog production on quahog catch per tow and the effects of
reduced catch per tow on the decision to harvest surf clams instead of quahogs.
There are a number of ways to address this including a linear programming
simulator that one could use to examine when the switch would be made
from quahogs to surf clams. This would require data on the cost of inputs,
among other things. A potential "short-cut" might be an econometric model
with the following structure:

$$X_0^d = f_0 (W_0, W_1, I) \qquad \text{(Surf clam demand)}$$

$$X_0^s = f_1 (W_0, W_1, V_0, D_0, A_0, A_1) \qquad \text{(Surf clam supply)}$$

$$X_1^d = f_2 (W_1, W_0, I) \qquad \text{(Quahog demand)}$$

$$X_1^s = f_3 (W_1, W_0, V_1, A_1, A_0) \qquad \text{(Quahog supply)}$$

$$X_i^d = X_i^s \quad i = 0, 1$$

where X_0^d, X_0^s = surf clam quantity demanded and supplied

X_1^d, X_1^s = ocean quahog quantity demanded and supplied

W_0, W_1 = exvessel prices of surf clams and ocean quahogs, respectively

I = income per capita

V_0, V_1 = input costs of surf clam and quahog harvesting, respectively

D_0 = a vector of dummy variables for binding production constraints imposed by the regulations

A_0, A_1 = measures of abundance for surf clams and quahogs, respectively

Some of these data are not available (e.g., input costs), and additional short-cuts would have to be taken. One might, for instance, use general price indices for the input costs and average catch per tow-hour for species abundance. The length of series on quahog catch would probably require a quarterly model which might offer sufficient degrees of freedom. The estimation of these equations should account for the simultaneous nature of supply and demand for surf clams and quahogs.

These analyses could be used to determine when the incentives for increased surf clam production would occur and the potential equilibrium quantities and prices. This would be useful information as then the biological model could then be consulted to determine whether the "competitive" harvest would be in excess of the harvest necessary to rebuild stocks and hence whether quotas were necessary at that point in time. Other information might be the costs that quotas impose on producers. All of this information might contribute to the argument for using vessel allocations instead of the current moratorium.

THE INDUSTRY CONCENTRATION ISSUE

The description of the industry also raised the possibility of processor oligopoly. The issues associated with this characteristic are (1) whether the processing group can, in fact, collude so as to control exvessel price and, if so, (2) what are the implications for the management of the industry.

Considerable institutional analysis of market structure (e.g., Bain [1959]) has been brought to bear on the surf clam situation [Visgilio 1973; National Marine Fisheries Service 1977]. Rather than dwell on this aspect of the structure question, we investigate the testing of monopoly behavior [Applebaum

1979]. In our case, the arguments have to be restructured for the monopsony (one buyer) instead of monopoly (one seller). Although something less concentrated than a pure monopsony occurs in the industry; the extreme is used for illustration and ease of analysis.[6]

Testing for Monopsony Power

The basic short-run monopsonist situation can be explained in a simple graph (Figure 4). (Clark and Munro [1979], however, provide a more dynamic analysis of the monopsonist processor.) In Figure 4, S represents the supply curve of the raw product X_0. The monopsonist's derived demand for the raw product

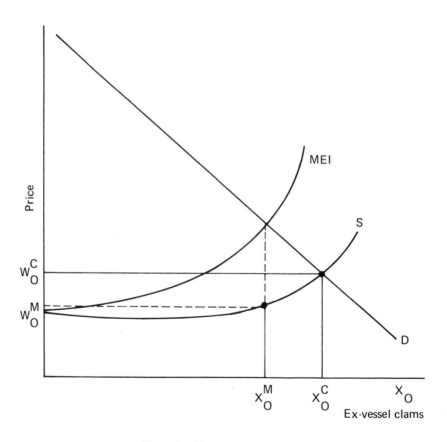

Figure 4.   Monopsony situation.

is represented by D. The marginal cost of the raw material to the processor is denoted by MC, and it diverges from the S curve because the monopsonist's cost for surf clams increases as additional clams are bought. In the presence of perfect competition, exvessel price and output would be (W_0^C, X_0^C). With a profit maximizing monopsonist, output is reduced to X_0^M and exvessel price drops to W_0^M.

Let us briefly illustrate how one would test for monopsony power. Mathematically, the previous behavior can be summarized as follows: Let X_0 and W_0 be exvessel landings and prices, respectively. Further, let the competitive exvessel firms operate so that $W_0 = \partial C (V, X_0)/\partial X_0$ where $C(V, X_0)$ is the total cost function dependent on output X_0 and input costs, V. For the monopsonist processor, the exvessel prices are, in fact, the marginal costs of vessel operations so that his raw product costs are X_0 times $\partial C (V, X_0)/\partial X_0$. Assuming the product prices are fixed at P and other processing inputs are given by X at per unit cost W, the monopsonist maximizes:

$$P \, g(X, X_0) - X_0 \ \partial C (V, X_0)/\partial X_0 - WX$$

where $g(X, X_0)$ is the production function for processed clams. One of the conditions implied by maximizing profits is that

$$P \, \partial g/\partial X_0 = W_0 + X_0 \, \partial^2 C(V, X_0)/\partial X_0^2 \qquad (3)$$

where $\partial g/\partial X_0$ can be viewed as the meat yield of clams. Thus, just as in Figure 4, the intersection of the derived demand curve $(P \, \partial g/\partial X_0)$ with the marginal expense of the raw product $(W_0 + X_0 \, \partial^2 C (V, X_0)/\partial X_0^2)$ produces maximum monopsony profit. The marginal expense of input is shown as the price (W_0) plus the additional expense of raising the price of all the clams purchased $X_0 \, \partial^2 C(V, X_0)/\partial X_0^2$.

Equation 3 offers a test for monopsony control. Using cross-sectional data, one could test whether input costs to fishermen and landings influence the difference between adjusted processed price $(P\partial g/\partial X_0)$ and exvessel prices. When output falls, one expects the difference to narrow whereas when the output rises, one expects the adjusted margin to increase. This hypothesis can be tested. If the analysis shows no significant influence, one could reject the monopsony or cartel hypothesis with some level of confidence. If not rejected, then one would be forced to consider the potential of monopsony power in surf clam production and examine the implications of that structure on management strategy.

Effects of Monopsony Power

The analysis necessary to understand the effect of monopsony power on regulation can be provided using Figure 5. The demand curve is the derived demand curve for clams by the processing sector. The open access supply curve is the long-run average cost curve of the fishery. Open access equilibrium will occur at X_0^1. The long-run marginal cost curve represents the true marginal cost of harvesting an extra unit of output including the user costs which are the present value of foregone future income arising from increased current output. The output level X_0^*, which occurs at the intersection of long-run marginal cost curve and the demand curve, is the socially optimal level of harvest because at that point the value of the last unit of harvest is equal to the true marginal cost of providing it.

It is interesting to note that in a vertically integrated harvesting industry where the single processing and harvesting entity has the same discount rate as the management unit, the uncontrolled market outcome will also be at X_0^*. This is so because the long-run marginal cost curve is the cost curve facing the integrated industry. Therefore no regulation is required.

It is more likely however, that one of the following situations is more descriptive of reality.

1.   The industry is not integrated.
2.   The monopsonist has a higher rate of time preference than the manager.
3.   The monopsonist is uncertain of its future monopsonistic power.

If the harvesting sector is regulated by an outside agency such that it must consider the full social long-run marginal costs of harvesting, then the supply curve to the monopsonist is the long-run supply curve. Therefore, for the reasons indicated in the discussion of Figure 4, the marginal cost of raw materials to the monopsonists will be as labeled. The firm will therefore produce X_0^M, which is less than the socially optimal level of output.

Returning to the case of the vertically integrated firm, if the monopsonist has a higher rate of time preference or is uncertain about its future market power, the long-run marginal cost curve it will utilize in making its output decisions will be less than the one pictured in the graph because the perceived user cost will be lower. In this situation the monopsonist will produce a level of output higher than the socially optimal one.

If the monopsonist is not fully integrated but must purchase from a regulated harvesting sector, the same type of result would follow if the regulatory device was stock certificates but the owners of these certificates had a rate of time preference higher than the management unit or if they were not sure how long they could retain the certificates. The long-run supply curve and hence the marginal cost of raw product facing the monopsonists would both then be lower than the ones pictured in the figure. As a result the output chosen by the monopsonist would be greater than X_0^M and could even be greater than X_0^*.

The conclusion is that it is difficult to determine whether the unregulated or the regulated monopsonist would achieve the proper product level unless more is known about the exact structure of the industry. The discussion about testing for monopsony, and in particular what kind of monopsony, is therefore quite relevant to the selection of alternative management plans.

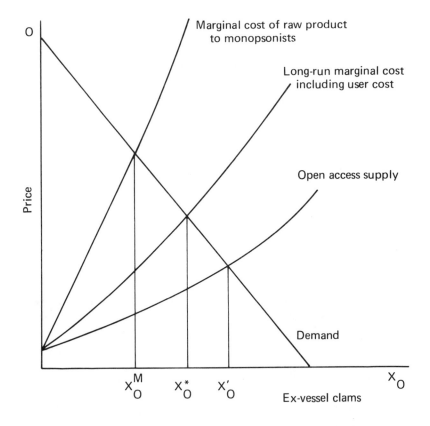

Figure 5.   Monopsony situation with regulation of the harvesting sector.

SUMMARY

The principal decision currently facing surf clam managers is whether to keep the moratorium with the current regulations or to eliminate the moratorium and impose other forms of limited entry (e.g., stock certificate or quotas per permitted vessel) or eliminate all entry restrictions. This paper presents some of the economic issues associated with those alternatives and suggests some directions for continued research.

First, it is doubtful that the moratorium has restricted new entry into the fishery. The stock was seriously depleted in 1978 and approximately 60 new vessels entered the fishery. These conditions together imply that the competitive equilibrium of vessels in the fishery was probably exceeded by 1978. Moreover, the introduction of ocean quahogs into certain of the clam markets has depressed the surf clam price and further reduced the likelihood of new vessels wishing to enter the fishery. Also, the management of surf clams may have offered a structure through which an already concentrated processing sector may have been able to reduce exvessel prices. This also would work against attracting new surf clam vessels. Finally, the recession of 1979-1980 also depressed demand for surf clams and lowered exvessel prices from their expected levels. Thus, one can reasonably argue that the moratorium has had little or no effect because the economic incentives to attract new capital have not been present.

The attention now given the moratorium by the regional council may be the first indication that the moratorium will restrain entry in the future. The promising 1976 age class lying off northern New Jersey offers one of the first positive signs associated with the management and should improve the profitability of vessel operations. That is, the denser populations will increase production per hour at sea and therefore lower costs per pound landed, causing profits to increase. Also, surf clam demand may further be enhanced if the quahog resource diminishes as the result of the recently increased production. Recovery from the current recession may be underway, offering another pressure for prices to rise. These events may eventually create a situation in which the moratorium can become effective. The moratorium alone, however, is not sufficient to avoid excess capacity and other management techniques such as vessel quotas or stock certificates should be considered as alternatives. Additional research as suggested above would be necessary to verify these assertions.

Caution must be exercised, however, in the management process. Of particular concern is a market structure that is conducive to price collusion. The arguments which are used to justify vessel quotas and stock certificates are not convincing if there is a processor cartel which is also attempting to reduce landings so that exvessel prices will be lower. In these instances, landings may be reduced to less than the efficient level.

ACKNOWLEDGMENT

We wish to thank David Keifer, Stephen Freese and Lee G. Anderson for reviewing the paper.

NOTES

[1]One could test whether the available data are consistent with the monotonic and quasiconcavity assumption of traditional theory before estimation. A useful technique is offered by Hanoch and Rothschild [1972]. To our knowledge, this procedure has only been employed once with fisheries data [Epstein 1980]. We did not attempt the test.

[2]A production function describes the technological relationship between maximum output attainable and a given set of inputs. In fisheries, certain inputs, such as weather and stock density, are exogenous to the firm, and therefore should be treated as shift parameters if data are available.

[3]A frontier function was not employed, and thus an average, rather than maximum, output is given. That is, errors were $n(0, \sigma^2)$ rather than $n(\mu_e, \sigma^2)$.

[4]Generalized least squares was used to estimate the equations because there appeared to be a relationship between hours fished and the error variance. Collinearity among variables also caused problems so that the second dredge size (D) and tonnage (GRT) terms were dropped.

[5]There is an interesting theoretical research problem of whether the individual will initially increase for unregulated gear if restrictions on other gear are imposed. It would appear that the price increases associated with lower landings would have to exceed the greater costs imposed by inefficient factor proportion to make the increase worthwhile. Existing literature does not deal with the transition phase.

[6]One must, however, recognize that the potential for price collusion or a form of purchasing cartel could easily exist, and would likely follow the same actions as a monopsonist. We therefore believe the following analysis is important, even though there is not a single processor purchaser.

REFERENCES

1. Applebaum, E. 1979. "Testing Price Taking Behavior," *J. Econometrics* 9:283-294.
2. Bain, J. S. 1959. *Industrial Organization* (New York: John Wiley & Sons, Inc.).

3. Christy, F. T. 1973. *Alternative Arrangements for Marine Fisheries: An Overview* (Washington, DC: Resources for the Future, Inc.).
4. Clark, C. W., and G. R. Munro. 1979. "Fisheries and the Processing Sector: Some Implications for Management Policy," Resources Paper No. 34, University of British Columbia, Vancouver, BC.
5. Davis, J., N. B. Theberge, M. N. Strand, N. P. Bockstael and J. Gates. 1975. "Alternative Management Schemes for the Surf Clam Fishery," SRAMSOE No. 103, Virginia Institute of Marine Science, Gloucester, VA.
6. Epstein, S. 1980. "Production Functions Associated with Atlantic Sea Scallops," University of Maryland (unpublished).
7. Hanoch, G., and M. Rothschild. 1972. "Testing the Assumptions of Production Theory: A Non-parametric Approach," *J. Polit. Econ.* 80(2):256-275.
8. Mid-Atlantic Fisheries Management Council. 1977. "Final Environmental Impact Statement/Fisheries Management Plan," Dover, DE.
9. Mid-Atlantic Fisheries Management Council. "Minutes" (August).
10. Mid-Atlantic Region Scientific and Statistical Committee. 1980. "Minutes" (October).
11. National Marine Fisheries Service. "A Description of the Surf Clam and Ocean Quahog Processing Sector, 1971-1977" (unpublished).
12. Parker, P. S. 1972. National Oceanic and Atmospheric Administration Tech. Report 364.
13. Ritchie, T. P. 1977. "A Comprehensive Review of the Commercial Clam Industries in the United States," NOAA, NMFS.
14. Ropes, J. W. 1980. "Biological and Fisheries Data on the Atlantic Surf Clam, *Spisula solidissima,*" Tech. Ser. Rept. No. 24, Northeast Fisheries Center, Woods Hole, MA.
15. Visgilio, G. R. 1973. "An Economic Evaluation of Fishery Management Alternatives: An Analysis of the Surf Clam Industry," Ph.D. Dissertation, University of Rhode Island, Kingston, RI.
16. Yancy, M., and W. R. Welch. 1968. "The Atlantic Coast Surf Clam," U.S. Fish and Wildlife Service, Circular 288.

COMMENTS–CHAPTER 5

David R. Keifer and Stephen P. Freese
Mid-Atlantic Fishery Management Council

Insofar as this paper deals primarily with issues for the next amendment to the Surf Clam and Ocean Quahog Fishery Management Plan, these comments will concentrate on those issues.

Central to the argument is the future of the moratorium on entry of vessels into the surf clam fishery. The moratorium was imposed by the original plan for one year because of (1) what was then categorized as an emergency in the fishery and (2) to acquire data on the fishery. Through the two amendments to the plan, the moratorium was extended through 1981. An emergency no longer exists in the fishery, and significant amounts of data have been gathered, primarily through the reporting systems mandated by the plan. In the original plan, the moratorium was explained as a temporary measure that could be replaced by a form of limited entry once more information became available. While the factors used to originally justify the moratorium may no longer exist, it is clear that the harvesting capacity of the fleet significantly exceeds probable quotas (and, quite likely, probable demand). Therefore, is it desirable to limit entry in some fashion to guard against additional overcapitalization?

The authors note appropriately that the moratorium was only partial in that, while it limited the number of vessels to those in the fleet or under construction or being rerigged for the fishery on November 17, 1977, it did not limit equipment. While difficult to document from available data, a significant upgrading of the capacity of the fleet occurred in 1979, in part probably in response to discussions of a freeze on dredge size and number and in part in response to a desire to maximize harvest per unit of time in response to the management regime. (Perhaps, to sharpen the analysis of the rate of technical substitution between hours fished and dredge size, 1978 vessel data should be incorporated.) It must also be noted that the 1978 "new entrants" were vessels for which construction commitments were made prior to the moratorium. Based on the 1979 race to upgrade dredges, it is highly unlikely that the industry and council would seriously consider restrictions on gear in future versions of the plan.

There are several issues relative to the structure of the industry that may be interesting from a research standpoint, but they may not be relevant from the standpoint of a fishery management plan prepared pursuant to the FCMA.

Generally, the processors do not sell a final product, and several processors may be attempting to sell product to the same buyer. Therefore, although there are only a few large processors, they may not be able to control their selling price. This is an area where additional research might be interesting, although it is far removed from FCMA considerations.

In the discussion of the possibility of processor oligopoly, the authors suggested an empirical test for the degree of monopsony power. This test requires that the demand for the various processed products is identifiable, measurable and predictable. To date, there has been very little analysis of processed product demand. Most of the economic analysis has been addressed at the processor-harvestor interface. Very little attention has been paid to the final product user-processor interface. How can we test for monopsony if we are unsure of what drives the processor? Herein lies an avenue of research where not only the important economic issue of monopsony can be explored, but also some important light may be shed on final product demand, an important element in determining the most crucial variable within a plan: optimum yield.

Whether or not monopsony exists in the industry, a primary consideration relative to management is vertical integration within the industry. To the extent that increasing shares of the quota can be harvested by vessels owned or closely associated with processors, the independent vessels will have decreasing opportunities to participate in the fishery. Available data show a decrease in the number of vessels active in the surf clam fishery. All else equal, the fewer the number of active vessels, the more time will be available (given the current regime) to the remaining vessels to harvest the quota. This situation is exacerbated by increases in efficiency (catch per unit of time), which requires still fewer vessels to harvest the quota. Any increases to the quota in the upcoming amendment would tend to compound this situation even further. This issue, therefore, gives rise to the question: Is it desirable to institute measures that would enable those who might be eliminated from the fishery to remain in the fishery somewhat longer than they otherwise would? This in turn serves as the basis for discussions of some form of allocating the quota directly to a vessel.

Two alternative responses to this problem have thus far been identified: eliminate the regulation of fishing hours and close the fishery when the quota has been harvested, or assign the quota directly to vessels based on some formula. Elimination of the regulation of fishing hours may not solve the problem since vessels could fish at a level that would satisfy the raw product needs of the several processors. Clearly, it could lead to closures in the fishery and lay-offs in the processing plants. It could also further minimize the need for independent boats, since the processor owned/controlled boats would be given preferential treatment in fulfilling raw product demand. This would in all likelihood increase the process of vertical integration.

Direct allocations to the vessels would guarantee all vessels some share of the quota. They would also eliminate the need to regulate hours, which would eliminate the inefficiencies of the current regime (equipment combinations designed to maximize catch per unit of time and relatively high fuel costs). To the extent they were transferable, they would create a "right" which could be sold, so a given fishermen could be reimbursed for leaving the fishery (assuming someone wanted to buy his share). It is unclear, what direction the establishment of these rights would influence the process of vertical integration.

It is likely that if the new amendment merely extends the current regime for several more years into the future, even more harvestors will leave the fishery. If the moratorium is lifted, or is replaced by a system that would limit the number of permits for the fishery, the effect would probably not be significantly different in the near-term future, so long as the basic regime depends on regulating fishing hours to spread the harvest throughout the quota period.

In other words, the moratorium in the original plan, coupled with the effort restrictions, was designed to minimize the impacts of the plan on participants in the fishery. As noted in the paper, it is generally felt that the plan has achieved this objective. The question for the next amendment is to determine whether additional measures should be implemented to further minimize these impacts or whether the council has gone as far as it should.

The issue of substitutability is also significant for the new amendment. Ocean quahogs are substitutable for surf clams for a portion of the market. However, quahogs cannot be substituted for surf clams in the strip market. Prior to the development of the quahog fishery, the larger surf clams were used for strips. Smaller surf clams and the portion of the larger clams left after the strips were removed were used for other products, a sector of the market now shared with quahogs. Furthermore, given the size of the ocean quahog resource, it is unlikely that the supply will be reduced in the foreseeable future, although harvesting costs for vessels using their current bases of operation will increase as the beds close to port are fished out and steaming time must be increased. To the extent that lower priced quahogs replace this share of the surf clam market, there will be a negative impact on the surf clam industry.

However, there is another problem in that many of the ocean quahog vessels are also licensed in the surf clam fishery. Therefore, they can redirect their efforts to surf clams if the cost of harvesting surf clams is less than that of harvesting ocean quahogs. While the ocean quahog resource is very large, it is distributed over a wide range. The fishery so far has been carried out in relatively confined areas off southern New Jersey and Delmarva. The surf clam resource is rebuilding in several areas, most especially off southern New Jersey around Atlantic City. It is, therefore, not unlikely that in the near future, in the absence of controls, some of the effort currently going into quahogs will be redirected to surf clams. This is of great concern to the surf clam industry since such a redirection of effort could result in the quahog vessels harvesting significant shares of the surf clam quota, possibly decreasing the supply of surf clams for the strip market. Imposition of a 5.5-in. size limit for surf clams is being proposed to decrease the chances of this happening. That size is ideal for clams for the strip market, but is quite large for surf clams that are to be used in product lines for which quahogs are currently used.

In summary, we would agree with the conclusion that entry of new vessels into the surf clam fishery in the near future is unlikely. The current management regime, based on restricting fishing hours, is a high-cost alternative and, if possible, should be replaced with a lower-cost alternative. The outcome of the upcoming amendment will be based essentially on the following questions. What is equitable to traditional participants in the fishery? Has the council done enough to minimize adverse economic impacts? Should the moratorium be replaced by some form of limited entry? Should that new form of limited entry include a direct allocation system?

CHAPTER 6

THE ECONOMICS OF SALMON MANAGEMENT UNDER THE FCMA: MUDDLING THROUGH FROM GRAVEL TO GRAVEL

R. Bruce Rettig
Agricultural and Resource Economics Department
Oregon State University

Implementation of the Fishery Conservation and Management Act (FCMA) of 1976 drastically altered the process by which Pacific salmon are managed. Concurrently, the expressed need for economic data and analyses took a quantum leap. The Pacific Fishery Management Council, the North Pacific Fishery Management Council and the National Marine Fisheries Service are particularly interested in expanding and improving the economic content of salmon management. This chapter is intended to support this effort by identification of issues in need of economic analysis and by description of some related economic literature.

The paper is divided into four major sections. The first section is a discussion of problems in identifying those issues which have economic content. These problems include the appropriate scope of management planning, the biases implicit in selection of background information, the nature of impact assessment and specific calculations of capacity and optimum yield. The second section covers methodological issues in impact assessment, while the third section details some economic research specific to impacts of regulations on particular resource uses. The final section is devoted to an important management tool: limited entry.

WHICH ISSUES HAVE ECONOMIC CONTENT?

Pacific salmon resources have traditionally been managed in the United States by the state governments. The most notable exceptions have related to (1) transboundary stock movements between the United States and Canada and between the United States and the USSR, (2) the interception of salmon by high seas trawl fleets, and (3) operation of federally constructed dams. In cases requiring federal involvement, consultation with state fishery agencies has frequently been required by legal processes. When not mandated by law, practical politics has caused federal bodies to involve states on a routine basis. Planning for Pacific salmon resources requires not only conformance with the FCMA (preparation of a fishery management plan), the National Environmental Policy Act (preparation of an environmental impact statement) and the Executive Order 12044 (preparation of a regulatory analysis), but also a large number of planning activities by state agencies, multistate groups such as the Columbia River Fisheries Council and international commissions responsible for transboundary salmon stocks. Before considering which issues have economic content, difficulties encountered in defining the scope of the regional fishery management councils' plans will be summarized.

Six species of salmon are harvested in Pacific coast waters, one of which is found only on the high seas and in Asia, but only two of which (chinook and coho) are taken in large numbers in the ocean beyond the three-mile limit. In odd-numbered years, pink salmon are caught in this zone. Pinks and the other two species form the heart of the fisheries within state jurisdictions. Thus analysis of outside-inside shares for commercial harvest of coho and chinook should include the trends and prospects for pink, sockeye and chum salmon.

Closely tied to this consideration is the sizable harvest in Washington state waters of pink and sockeye salmon migrating toward British Columbia's Fraser River. Long-standing international discussions between Canada and the United States include assessment of U.S. interception of Canadian pink and sockeye and Canadian interception of chinook and coho salmon. This assessment is, of course, an oversimplification; it ignores nonsalmon fisheries and other interception fisheries, especially the appropriate harvest of salmon that move through the U.S. fishery conservation zone (U.S. waters lying more than 3 but less than 200 miles from shore), the Alaskan panhandle and into Canadian streams to spawn. However, the point still emerges that a complete analysis of benefits and costs of joint management would require an extremely complex analysis of international fishery arrangements.

Perhaps the greatest problem in defining scope of planning comes from the concept of "gravel to gravel." Regulations derived from FCMA planning restrict ocean harvest. However, very high mortality to the salmon occurs due to inside fisheries, inside predators including resident fish predation on downstream migrants and marine mammal predation on upstream migrants, dam passage problems, and other factors. The ocean user groups want these inside mortalities documented in the belief that regulation should be applied to internal causes as well as (or rather than) ocean harvest rates.

The life history of anadromous species poses particularly difficult problems for a planning body charged with examining economic costs and benefits to alternative management measure in offshore water. The Pacific Fishery Management Council and the North Pacific Fishery Management Council are placed in the awkward position of choosing management measures applicable in the open ocean while salmon are strongly influenced by a wide range of human activity in fresh water as well as in salt water estuaries.

Salmon fry hatch from eggs which incubate in hatcheries or in stream gravel which may be located many miles from the sea. The length of residence in fresh water varies between species and among "races" of a given species, but can range up to five years. Thus, before the young salmon move into salt water, their survival will depend critically on droughts, floods, availability of food, abundance of predators, number of young salmon living in the stream, debris from logging and road construction, circumstances under which water is spilled over dams or passes through turbines in hydroelectric dams, water temperature, dissolved oxygen levels, other aspects of water quality and the speed of water courses taking the salmon to sea. All these hazards add to the mortality already due to natural predators and disease organisms.

Not only do salmon pass through a number of political jurisdictions in fresh water, but they commonly pass through several marine political jurisdictions after they are recruited into commercial and recreational fisheries. For example, Columbia River chinook salmon may pass through Alaskan, British Columbia, Washington and Oregon fisheries before returning to spawn in the waters of their birth. This transboundary harvest greatly complicates fishery management and makes the economist's task of enumerating benefits to the array of salmon groups much more difficult. The gains and losses from measures to restrict the ocean fisheries consequently cannot be identified exactly.

In addition to the numerous causes of salmon mortality in the ocean stage of its life history, a number of events other than fresh-water commercial and recreational fisheries will kill salmon before spawning can be achieved. Certain of these events are beyond human control such as the destructive residue in Washington streams which came from the volcanic eruption of Mt. St. Helens in 1980. Other events, particularly those causing deterioration in water quality and passage problems at dams are strongly influenced by human choices.

To ensure both upstream and downstream migration, significant costs are incurred. These costs consist of public and private expenditures on fishway facilities, hatchery operations and habitat maintenance as well as foregone goods and services like hydroelectric energy and irrigated farm crops. Which of these direct and indirect costs of maintaining salmon should be identified in council plans? Deciding where those who pay these costs can articulate their views and how this cost calculus is to enter FCMA analyses is extremely difficult. To date these costs have been reviewed primarily by water policy agencies, environmental quality agencies and energy agencies. Since the state fishery agencies are also active in fresh-water policy discussions, they must be the salmon advocate in these forums, then act as the sole group among the parties involved in FCMA decision-making to appreciate the concerns of loggers, power companies, irrigators and other fresh-water interests.

Of remaining considerations, two with significant economic content have been largely set aside by the council. The first is the growth of private ocean ranching. Although it falls under the jurisdiction of other forums, its output is treated by the council as part of predictions of numbers of harvestable fish. The second is what happens to salmon once the fish have been landed at the dock.

Many more issues are present, but enough have been raised to suggest the difficulty in defining the scope of fishery management planning. A rough draft of comprehensive salmon management plan was delivered to the PFMC in the fall of 1979. After many months trying to shepherd that plan into an acceptable draft for public discussion, Dr. Edward Perry, salmon coordinator for the PFMC simultaneously tendered his resignation and despaired that the comprehensive plan would never come to be. Commenting at the August 1980 PFMC meeting, Perry said, "There is now a serious question about the capability of meeting in the foreseeable future the goal established by the Council. Concepts of a comprehensive plan have been varied. Everyone has had his own views of what it should comprise. Many have visualized it as the solution to all salmon management problems."

In summary, Pacific salmon resources migrate through so many political jurisdictions, each having a major impact on the salmon life history, that planning in one jurisdiction requires a good grasp of policy issues in the other areas along with an estimate of impacts in all jurisdictions. This paper is based on this proposition and extends analysis into issues of state waters only when necessary to appreciate implications of measures currently within federal jurisdiction. The difficulties described throughout will be greatly increased if the power of the Secretary of Commerce to preempt state jurisdiction involves regional fishery management councils in additional management actions in fresh water and estuaries.

Boiler Plate

Fishery management prior to 1976 relied upon information from numerous sources. In many fisheries, plans now provide excellent summaries of "a description of the fishery, including, but not limited to, the number of vessels involved, the type and quantity of fishing gear used, the species of fish involved and their location, the cost likely to be incurred in management, actual and potential revenues from the fishery, any recreational interests in the fishery, and the nature and extent of foreign fishery and Indian treaty fishing rights, if any" as required by the FCMA. Those portions of the plan assembled to provide a descriptive background have come to be popularly known as the "boiler plate."

Salmon plans of both the Pacific Fishery Management Council and North Pacific Fishery Management Council contain little economic boiler plate. A number of reasons can be given to explain this paucity. One is that fishery agencies are unaccustomed to using economic data. Since economic knowledge was less usable, organization and display of economic data were continually put off from year to year. A second explanation is that some of the data specified in the FCMA are difficult to assemble. For example, vessels which make landings in more than one state are counted more than once if the "number of vessels involved" is calculated by adding numbers in the several states together. Having decided that this statistic was an important one, Dr. James Bray devoted a great deal of time in 1979 and 1980 to deriving the coastwide number of vessels by examination of landing receipts for California, Oregon and Washington. Whatever the rationale in the past, circumstances appear to be changing. The Pacific Fishery Management Council has made a public commitment to expand the economic description of the fishery in the 1971 amendment to the "Fishery Management Plan for the Commercial and Recreational Salmon Fisheries off the Coast of Washington, Oregon, and California Commencing in 1978."

Optimum Yield

A key requirement in the FCMA for any fishery management plan is that it shall "assess and specify the present and probable future condition of, and the maximum sustainable yield and optimum yield from, the fishery, and include a summary of the information utilized in making such specification." The concept of optimum yield can be portrayed as a far more complex concept than it needs to be. The intent in the FCMA is that planners first set a tentative goal of maximizing the physical yield from a biological resource over time without reducing the capacity of that resource to reproduce itself. Then the yield can be varied if the deviation can be proven to increase the economic or social value generated by that resource, or if the deviation is proven to generate enhanced values from ecologically related species. Special characteristics of salmon management and the life history of salmon should suggest an approach which uses a more indirect line of reasoning than that used for many other species.

"Stock of fish" was defined in the FCMA as a species, subspecies, geographical grouping or other category of fish capable of management as a unit. As an ideal standard, consider a salmon stock to be all salmon of a given species which spawn on a specific stretch of a specific stream during a specific time of the year. For salmon returning to private or public hatcheries, the hatchery site would substitute for stream location.

I define utopian escapement as that number of spawners which will maximize average annual catch. This concept is different from the popular concept of optimum escapement which I understand to be that number of spawners which fully utilize the spawning gravels, i.e., if one more salmon than "optimum" were to escape to spawn, the carrying capacity would be exceeded and the number of recruits would decline. In practice, fishery agencies make two optimum escapement calculations. What I refer to as "optimum" is used to justify agency positions in opposing habitat degradation, water removals, and so on, i.e., "optimum" escapement is what utopian escapement would be if the environment could be managed only for salmon. The second "optimum" escapement calculation, sometimes referred to as the short-run escapement goal, may be very close to what I call utopian escapement.

The sum of catches associated with utopian escapement may approximate maximum sustainable yield. However, this potential catch would be realizable only by total reliance on terminal fisheries, i.e., all salmon would have to be captured using nets, weirs, wheels or traps just downstream of the spawning grounds. As soon as fisheries are permitted in rivers, estuaries and, especially, in the ocean, the problem of mixed stock fisheries arises.

A hypothetical example may help explain the complication due to mixed stocks. Suppose two streams flow into a river. The Clear Creek stock is very large; many thousands of that stock can be harvested and still leave enough salmon to fully occupy spawning gravel in Clear Creek. The Deer Creek stock is very small; if even a hundred are caught, that stock may be threatened with extinction. Further assume that salmon caught in the river provide exciting recreational opportunities and/or are highly prized in commercial markets, while salmon caught in streams provide no angler satisfaction and are so soft and mushy that the gross commercial value is less than costs of capture and marketing. Under these assumptions, the appropriate harvest strategy requires a deliberate extinction of the Deer Creek stock. Indeed, stock is defined not stream by stream, but for the river.

The rationale for aggregating spawning groups to create stocks (in the FCMA sense of that word) is social and economic, not biological. Eventually the definition of salmon stocks along the Pacific coast should be subjected to economic analysis. With all of the problems before the regional fishery management councils, the spawning groups which have evolved by biologists' common knowledge and intuitive judgment provide a good starting point. In many cases, stocks are defined by runs—all fish of one species entering a particular river during a period of time—but some escapement goals are given for more narrowly defined groups and a number of goals are given for several rivers added together.

While the existence of mixed-stock fisheries and subsequent needs to aggregate groups of fish provide one rationale for less-than-full utilization of spawning gravels, other adjustments by biologists are also required. Downward adjustment should be made if the life history of the salmon from egg incubation to movement into the ocean poses additional carrying capacity limits. For example, if it is known that downstream migrants encounter limited food supplies, complete utilization of the spawning gravels would be wasted in extremely high natural mortality for salmon smolts.

Adjustments are required for social and economic as well as ecological reasons. This was clearly involved in the Pacific Fishery Management Council's distinction between long-term and 1980 goals in their 1980 salmon plan amendment. In the past few years, ocean harvest regulations have steadily been tightened. To have met long-term escapement goals for many salmon stocks during 1980 would have required devastating economic impacts on ocean user groups. Hence escapement goals were framed in terms of maintaining salmon stocks at some base year level. The practical judgments which led to this socioeconomic adjustment should be backed up with careful and explicit analysis.

In summary, salmon management begins with a concept of spawning escapement which would generate maximum sustainable yield. In practice, this escapement goal is adjusted to allow for ecological, social and economic reasoning. If the adjustment is made carefully and if we can assume that the surplus production is allocated in some "best" manner, the adjusted goal can legitimately be called the optimum escapement goal. If the plan can be shown as adequate to achieve the optimum escapement goals, optimum yield is any associated catch assuming economic, ecological, and social consequences of regulations were appropriately considered.

The procedure suggested is certainly not easy. In addition to the difficulties in defining stocks and considering stream, riverine and estuarine ecology, the incremental costs and benefits of ensuring up- and downstream migration should be considered. Further, the optimum escapement should be "inside escapement"—the sum of spawning escapement and estuarine and fresh-water fisheries. Consequently, standards for evaluating "inside" vs "outside" (ocean) fisheries will be discussed later in this chapter. However, management agencies have already developed certain standards for setting inside escapement goals for a number of management units. These goals can continue to be used until (and if) economic and social analysis can provide more rigorous standards.

Capacity

In most years, the capacity calculations required by the FCMA and its amendment are moot for Pacific salmon. The FCMA requires an assessment of "the capacity and the extent to which fishing vessels of the United States, on an annual basis, will harvest the optimum yield" and a later amendment added a similar requirement for processing capacity. These calculations are required, since the total allowable level of foreign fishing is equal to optimum yield minus harvesting capacity, and the joint venture allocation is the difference between domestic harvesting capacity and domestic processing capacity. On average, both domestic processing and harvesting capacity greatly exceed optimum yield. A rather special circumstance appeared for the total of all species off Alaska in 1980 when all environmental factors turned favorable simultaneously. In this case the apparent bottleneck lay in satiation of world markets, feeding back to difficulties in negotiating exvessel prices and a long strike which hurt all parties involved. However, under normal circumstances capacity both to harvest and to process salmon so greatly exceeds the available resource that this calculation becomes superfluous.

The issue of capacity, however, appears in two other contexts. First, so much excess capacity exists that the planning authorities' major work lies in determining appropriate regulations to distribute harvestable biomass among competing fishermen. Second, many Pacific coast fishing vessels have become multipurpose enterprises. Management of multipurpose vessels is difficult and has received limited analysis by economists as shown in a recent literature search by Huppert [1979]. Neglect of the impacts of management measures in one fishery on participants in other fisheries is considered but rarely quantified in current planning procedures.

Economic Impact Analysis

The key economic issues about which the Pacific Fishery Management Council needs information are (1) expected responses by fishermen to alternative regulations, and (2) ultimate economic impacts this will have on the various interest groups. Of course, some groups have more political power than others. Between council and advisory panel membership, the dominant factions are Indians, ocean commercial fishermen, ocean charter boat fishermen, recreational fishermen, inside net fishermen and fish processors. Other interests as represented by state and national fishery agencies, the Coast

Guard and a consumer representative on the advisory subpanel are less clear; they are restatements of fishing interests or an ill-defined set of goals commonly called "conservation." Before reviewing methodology to assess economic impacts on various interest groups, the next section will be devoted to special problems of economic impact assessment.

SPECIAL CONCERNS

Distribution

Many of the conflicts in salmon management arise from the need to allocate access to salmon among competing user groups. The greater the harvest by ocean (outside) fishermen, the smaller the harvest by inside fishermen. The more restricted are commercial fishermen in their access, the more salmon will be caught by sport anglers. For example, in 1979 Oregon trollers landed over 700,000 coho and over 240,000 chinook. Fearing significantly reduced naturally spawning coho stocks, the troll season was significantly reduced in 1980, and Oregon trollers subsequently landed about 380,000 coho and 180,000 chinook by early September. While a number of other conditions also changed, such as a more northerly distribution of Oregon coastal and Columbia River stocks, the jump in Oregon ocean sport harvest of coho from 176,000 coho to 305,000 coho in approximately the same number of trips must be credited partially to the commercial closure.

Other important distributional issues include court-ordered allocations between Indians and non-Indians, charter boat vs sport catch by individual anglers, and bank vs stream angling in fresh water. Conflicts might be eased by a larger number of fishing areas and a more diverse salmon population.

Economists disagree about their role, if any, in analyzing issues of income distribution and related equity issues. My own views on this issue have been significantly influenced by comments by Anthony Scott at a conference arranged by Anderson [1977] four years ago. Scott argued that the comparative advantage of economists is to identify the impacts of policy choices on resource allocation. Distribution will not be neglected because "everyone else is *already* a specialist on distribution." The standard procedure is to try to add net economic benefits by user group, geographical area, income class, age class or ethnic group, and provide such information to decision-making bodies. Economists would commonly suggest that, if a departure from policies which maximize total net economic benefits is chosen to create a "more equitable" distribution of benefits, the precise reasons for such departure be explained carefully.

The most important distributional issues related to salmon arise from special treaty rights assigned to certain Indian tribes. A number of public programs including, but not limited to, requirements governing ocean harvest rates have major economic consequences. However, the Pacific Fishery Management Council must take certain directives as given by the federal courts independent of any economic calculation. This paper follows the procedure of taking Indian/non-Indian allocations as given. However, the questions of economic consequences of alternative allocations between Indian and non-Indians and economic aspects of associated policies are certainly important and worthy of major investigation by groups outside of the regional fishery councils.

Aggregation Over Time

In the discussion of the optimum yield and optimum escapement, I argued that two escapement goals should be calculated. The first was a biological assessment of the escapement which would maximize the number of recruits into the next generation of salmon. The second was an adjustment based on ecological, economic and social criteria. When economic analysis is incorporated, the calculations will include either giving up current value of catch or incurring other costs to receive the benefits of more salmon production two or more years into the future. The process of comparing values at different points of time is not an easy one.

Standard economic reasoning would suggest that escapement is maximizing economic efficiency when the cost of sending one more fish towards its spawning environment just equals the present value of increased salmon harvest opportunities in the future. If costs are higher than the present value of future benefits, escapement should be less; if costs are less, escapement should be larger. Assuming that an estimate of eventual recruitment and harvest can be developed, how can those future quantities be converted to present value?

The first problem is to estimate future "real" prices (i.e., the change in prices not including the inflation in the general price level). To do this properly a price forecasting model is needed. Current prices can be used as a first approximation only if (1) current prices appear to be "normal," (2) supply is expected to grow "modestly," and (3) factors external to the U.S. coho and chinook salmon economy are not expected to change markedly. Very seldom will any of these three conditions hold. Even when they do, the first approximation may be off due to reasons sketched out below.

The value of recreationally and commercially caught salmon are influenced by many factors including the quantity of salmon, costs of inputs such as fuel, market conditions in beef, poultry, other fisheries and other substitute sectors, and the state of economy. For example, one could argue that coho and chinook salmon prices were unusually high in 1979 and unusually low in 1980 due to fluctuations in the factors listed above plus a number of other influences. Consequently, forecasted prices might better be based on an average of recent prices or a trend in prices over the last several years than on prices in any single year.

The second problem is to discount the future real prices to the present. The simplest way to present this argument to the public is to suggest that current value V_0 can "grow" to $V_0 (1 + r)^t$ in t years, annually compounded if r is the interest rate; hence a future value V_t is worth $V_t/(1 + r)^t$ today. Once this point is established, the appropriate discount factor, r, must be identified. Choice of the optimum social discount rate is a very complex issue. I omit a discussion of alternative points of view and suggest three approaches. First, a regional fishery management council can subjectively choose a discount rate. This rate might range anywhere from zero (the council considering itself a custodian of natural resources with as much responsibility for future generations as for the present) to the highest interest rate paid by user groups working with the council. A slight modification would be to define the discount rate implicit in recent council choices and let the council reaffirm that choice or shift it.

A more commonly recommended approach is to make computations using more than one discount rate and determine how sensitive the results are to choice of a discount rate. If the decision does depend upon the rate chosen the council could then make a subjective choice among the alternatives presented.

Finally, the council could use the long-term government bond rate as currently reported to the Water Resources Council by the Secretary of Treasury. This approach would have the merit of consistency with choice of discount factor by other government agencies. On the other hand, the argument that the government bond rate reflects a social time preference rate is muddled by market imperfections and an unknown rate of expected inflation built into the bond rate.

Uncertainty

Economists have long recognized that limited and uncertain knowledge constrains human activities in many important ways. However, many of our analytical procedures are based on a presumed ability to accurately forecast outcomes of economic activities. A recent burst of research activities generates hope that significant improvements will soon be available in economic methodology. Several economists and fishery population dynamicists have published interesting studies recently with respect to salmon. However, the discussion in this paper will be limited to certain procedures now used in benefit-cost analysis as related to salmon management tools.

A procedure which is implicit in regional fishery management council activities is to define risk-avoidance or risk-taking as an additional objective in fishery management plans. Strategies such as placing the burden of proof on movements away from maximum sustainable yield and requiring that no species be overfished (whatever that means) were inserted into the FCMA as risk-aversion strategies by Congress. Fishery councils add to this by commitments to "protect the resource, rebuild depleted stocks, meet escapement goals," etc.

When the Pacific Fishery Management Council was considering their draft anchovy plan, their plan development team presented not only expected economic values but a number of estimates of the possible variability in biomass, economic returns and other parameters. The council turned to its scientific and statistical committee to convert these complex statistics into recommendations on policy. This was rather unfortunate for two reasons. First, a number of innovative efforts by the team [Huppert et al. 1980] may have been lost in the turmoil of ongoing activities. However, some of this work has since been further refined and published [Huppert et al. 1980]. Second, I observed that one of the key differences among user groups related to risk preference. Some members of the anchovy advisory subpanel were perfectly willing to accept large year-to-year variability in economic returns if such a strategy increased expected returns. Other members of the subpanel were clearly risk-averters.

I hypothesize that one of the significant splits between commercial fishermen and scientists arises because the latter are significantly more risk averse with respect to the fishery resource in question. Fishermen who are accustomed to gambling with their lives and economic fortunes might be far more inclined to take a chance that there may be more fish available than the expected value. Techniques are available to elicit risk preferences from decision-makers, although these approaches are subject to biases identified by Tversky and Kahneman [1974]. Nonetheless, regional fishery management councils may wish to consider explicit management objectives which would lead to not only expected number of recruits into a fishery, but also standard deviations and/or other measures of variability. They could then choose to minimize risk, select specific strategies to deal with risk or choose trade-off weights between measures of risk and other management objectives.

An alternative to separating risk in an explicit management objective would be to build preference toward uncertainty into other measures. For example, the rate of discount could be increased if councils were reluctant to trade salmon today for an uncertain number of salmon tomorrow.

Another alternative would be to choose management strategies which reflect the council's view toward risk. A significant example under debate in the Pacific Fishery Management Council arises from in-season management and/or the use of quotas. Both of these tools as used in Pacific salmon fisheries are measures used to reduce risk. Simply put, a conservative quota can be set based on "worst case" assumptions and later relaxed if more salmon are observed. This strategy could assure optimal spawning escapement in most years and allow terminal fisheries to catch the surplus when there are "pleasant surprises." A liberal quota could be used instead with procedures to terminate the fishery if "points of concern" are reached. What the risk implications of this second strategy would be depends on the amount of information generated during the season and how the management agencies choose to treat that information. Given the movement by both the Pacific Fishery Management Council and North Pacific Fishery Management Council toward use of quotas in ocean salmon fisheries, more explicit analysis of risk preference is definitely in order.

ECONOMIC ACTIVITY BASED ON PACIFIC SALMON

Ocean Recreational Fishing

Fishing for coho (silver) and chinook (king) salmon in the ocean is an important Pacific coast recreational activity. In recent years, from one-third to one-half million angler days were spent fishing for salmon off the Washington coast, a like amount off Oregon and somewhat over half that rate of activity has taken place off California. Catch per person per trip was higher along Washington than Oregon which, in turn, had higher catch per angler per trip than California.

What economic value can be attached to the annual ocean angler harvest averaging in excess of a million salmon per year? Among economists, there is a consensus that sportsmen value their recreational activity above and beyond the expenditures they make to fish. Using 1974 prices, Brown et al. [1976] suggested that this net economic value from salmon and steelhead angling was at least $22 per day. In a recent study, Brown et al. [1980] approximate 1977 values at $45 per trip for Washington and $52 for Oregon. Estimates per angler day converted to 1980 dollars, using different methodology range from $23 by Crutchfield and Schelle [1978] to $156 by Mathews and Brown [1970]. That these different economists generate widely differing estimates bother resource managers searching for the only correct estimate. Despite disagreement among economists, one essential point remains: the annual value of the ocean salmon recreational fishing opportunity off the California, Oregon and Washington coasts is hundreds of millions of dollars. This amount is above and beyond the sizable expenditures already made by anglers for boats, fishing tackle, and so on.

Even if agreement could be reached on the average annual value of recreational salmon harvest, regional fishery management councils would still not know how to correctly measure the change in recreational value due to change in ocean harvest regulations. As originally pointed out by Stevens [1966] and rigorously demonstrated by Mäler [1971], the value needed must be estimated by the shift in demand for recreational angling due to the improved success rates or added fishing opportunity.

McConnell and Strand [1981] explain rigorously why changes in catch rate restrictions (bag limits) must be analyzed with different models (or rather models which are more complex) than those used to estimate impacts of trip restrictions. Crutchfield and Schelle [1978] attempted to estimate the economic consequences of a change in catch rate restrictions; they used a questionnaire in which survey respondents were asked to indicate how they would have altered their angling activities in 1977 if bag limits had been two per day rather than three. Further checks are needed on questions like this one. Of great value would be estimates using other recreational valuation methodology such as that used by Brown et al. [1980].

Estuarine and Fresh-Water Angling

Recreational valuation is needed to assess optimal escapement as well as to contrast alternative regulations. In addition to the methodological issue already raised, more work is needed to specify the role of substitutes. The question is not what the loss of value from salmon angling is but what the loss in value is if a recreationist fishes for bottomfish, trout or another species, or chooses a nonfishing recreational activity instead of salmon angling. Until such rigorous evaluation is available, some descriptive information may add to the common knowledge of the councils used to set preliminary inside escapement goals.

While more salmon are captured by anglers in the ocean than in inside waters, a great deal of participation in salmon angling takes place along stream and river banks or from small boats. An average of around 750,000 salmon are taken each year from the inside waters of California, Oregon, Idaho and Washington.

In 1977, just over 250,000 salmon were taken by anglers in Puget Sound in about 1,000,000 anglers days, 135,000 salmon were taken in 255,000 angler days inside the Strait of Juan de Fuca, while 695,000 salmon were caught in the outer waters of the strait and in the Pacific Ocean off Washington in 530,000 angler days. In 1976 with better success rates, two salmon per angler day were taken off the southern and central Washington coast, three salmon for every five angler days inside the strait and one to two salmon for every five angler days inside the sound itself.

In their study of the net economic value of sport-caught salmon in Washington in 1967, Mathews and Brown [1970] suggested that fishing days in the strait were worth about two-thirds of a fishing day in the ocean and that Puget Sound and fresh-water fishing days were half as valuable as ocean fishing days. This same order of magnitude is found in the new study by Brown et al. [1980]. While their estimate of the net economic value of a 1977 Oregon ocean salmon trip is $51.82, the net economic value of a 1977 fresh-water salmon trip is estimated to be $16.80, and a steelhead trip is valued at $23.86.

Other Recreational Values

One recreational value often ignored by economists is associated with people watching migrating salmon on their way to spawn. Recently a friend told me that one of his greatest pleasures on a boating trip in Seattle took place as he and his friends, while going through the locks which connect Puget Sound with Lake Union and Lake Washington, were able to observe salmon pass through the locks on their way to spawn.

The only economic study that I have seen which even approaches this issue is an estimation of the net economic value of visits to Bonneville Hatchery in 1974 by Larson et al. [1978]. That value was estimated to be $304,000, which was the sum of $1.19-1.25 per visit for 211,000 visitors who took trips mainly to visit the hatchery and $0.58 per visit for 319,000 visitors who dropped by on trips intended for other purposes.

Eating Salmon: Means or End?

In discussing the economic values of salmon-based recreation, I tried to establish that coho and chinook serve a wide variety of users. Now, I would like to suggest that a similar point holds for food consumption values.

How do you enjoy salmon? Broiled? Poached? Roasted? Smoked? Cured? Do you enjoy lox and bagels? Kippered salmon? Salmon as food moves through many market channels. The nature of human consumption of salmon depends greatly upon species, size of fish, gear used for capture, environmental factors which affect other quality characteristics of the fish, and an assortment of economic factors including the state of the economy, price and availability of other food items. Different consumers and purveyors of restaurant meals find different sizes, species and quality attributes preferable given the costs of making the fish available in different forms, times and places.

The consumers' surplus from salmon consumed either at home or away from home is a magnitude which has rarely been addressed. If choices are to be made resulting in allocation between recreationists and consumers and if economists agree on consumers' surplus as the appropriate measure of recreational value, more attention must be given to specifying the trade-offs with common measures of value.

Salmon as an Economic Base

One perspective on the role of salmon in the economy is its contribution to food and recreational values. A rather different perspective is the contribution of salmon to the coastal economy in terms of jobs and income opportunities. In reviewing the role of salmon in the Pacific Northwest economic base, I will not discuss public sector jobs, such as employment in fisheries agencies and research institutions, nor the rapidly growing private aquaculture firms. Nevertheless, the discussion should highlight the importance of the salmon economy.

Troll Fishery

With limited and very specific exceptions, the only legal offshore commercial salmon fishery between California and Cape Suckling in the Gulf of Alaska has been the troll fishery since the approval of the International North Pacific Fisheries Convention in 1952. Trolling is a method of dragging a number of baits or lures at desired depths behind a moving boat.

The troll fishery off California, Oregon and Washington landed an annual average of approximately 3 million chinook and coho salmon during the last decade. This landed value averaged $18 million from 1971-1975, rose sharply to over $39 million in 1976, declined slightly in 1977 and 1978, and jumped to over $48 million in 1979. In 1980 landed value was down considerably with only $21 million of landed value through mid-August.

Although the aggregate values do reflect variability in both total landings and price in the troll fishery, the impact on individual fishermen is more difficult to assess. For example, in 1976 Washington trollers fished 62,000 days and landed over $39 million in chinook and coho. Although there were 3208 vessels licensed for use, most landings were actually made by a small portion of the fleet. This finding is consistent with studies by sociologists and anthropologists which conclude that, of the many people with commercial fishing licenses, only a relatively small number are actually dependent on salmon fishing as their principal source of income.

Two methodological approaches have been employed to assess net economic returns to commercial salmon fishermen. The most acceptable to the scientist is a survey of fishermen using statistical samples. This approach has encountered violent opposition. If fishermen disagree with the results, they will refuse to to accept inference from samples as valid, argue that the scientist was innately biased and doctored the data or that systematic respondent biases caused results to be in error. Consequently, the only acceptable coverage is 100%. On the other hand, fishermen are usually suspicious of surveys and give poor response no matter what coverage is attempted by scientists.

The second methodological approach is known on the West Coast as Marine Economic Data Sheets (MEDS). This system is adapted from a teaching device used in agricultural extension programs. Individual fishermen in a particular port are identified by a local fishermen's association or a Sea Grant marine agent. Fishermen are chosen because they are known to be "good" fishermen, good businessmen and, for each group interviewed, have very similar fishing operations. The fishermen first agree upon the characteristics of the operation most common to them, then agree upon production, prices and costs. Costs and earnings data developed by this system are really devised to give other similar fishermen a frame of reference for their own financial management practices. However, even these calculations for good operations indicate quite modest returns to management and labor after subtracting all other costs from the value of landings as has been shown by Smith [1978]. Since noneconomic returns to trollers are evidently important components of their motivations, estimates of net economic benefits may be more misleading than helpful.

Two key pieces of analysis are needed to improve regional fishery management council and National Marine Fisheries Service planning and management. First, improved price forecasting is needed. Restricted fishing seasons in 1979 were somewhat offset by sharp increases in salmon prices. However, when seasons were further restricted in 1980, prices were down. Compounding this downward movement were price disagreements between fishermen and fish buyers altering the "true" starting time of the season. Second, a better understanding, if not forecasting, is needed of fishermen "switching behavior." Many salmon fishermen also fish for dungeness crab, albacore tuna, groundfish and/or other species. What causes the fishermen to switch fisheries needs to be known, both to find ways to blunt adverse impacts on fishermen of certain regulations and to allow better predictions of the response by fishermen to changes in regulations.

Net Fishery

The commercial net catch of salmon from Puget Sound and the Columbia River averaged over 5 million fish per year between 1971 and 1977. However, in more recent years, the harvest of both has been down dramatically.

In comparing economic values of net- and troll-caught salmon, the common rule of thumb is that a net-caught fish is older and heavier, but lower in quality than a troll-caught fish. Even taking into account natural mortality, the total weight of all commercially harvested salmon would be greatest if taken in terminal fisheries. Even if all society wished to do was to maximize gross revenues from all combined commercial fisheries, a variety of fisheries would probably be needed—both outside and inside.

Charter Boats

There are approximately 200 passenger-carrying vessels in Calfornia, nearly the same number in Oregon and twice that number in Washington with a large percentage of Washington's fleet located in Grays Harbor and Pacific counties on the Washington coast. Charter boats make available hundreds of jobs which strengthen the economic bases in coastal communities while offering access to fishing and a good probability of fishing success to the novice. This last effect ties charter vessels into the tourism base which is so important to the economy of the Pacific coast.

Indirect Economic Impacts

To this point, we have considered those industries which provide tens of thousands of people part- or full-time activity in landing salmon for commercial sale and consumption. In addition to these jobs, tourism and associated activities provide an economic base which triggers additional jobs in processing, distribution, retail sales, restaurants, marine supplies, and dozens of others. The appropriate procedure to consider these impacts is a matter of major disagreement among economists.

Three major efforts have recently been made to display indirect economic impacts by using interindustry models. These models summarize sales between economic sectors in a particular area and between that area and "the rest of the world." By employing certain assumptions, the models can be used to infer what sales would occur between sectors and what the total sales, jobs and income in the area would be if a basic sector were to sell more goods or services to the rest of the world. In our case, these models are used to infer the nature of decline or growth of the local economy if more outsiders arrive to participate in the sport fishery or if more salmon are sold to outsiders.

In 1978 a number of countywide input-output models were developed for the Pacific Fishery Management Council. For example, using 1977 data for the northernmost county in Oregon, commercial salmon fishermen accounted for over $10 million in sales. For every additional $16,614 in sales, an additional man-year of employment would be generated. For every dollar of troll-caught salmon sold by fishermen, $2.57 of sales would take place in the county.

In 1977, Crutchfield and Schelle [1978], working with input-output models, suggested that reduction in Washington ocean sport bag limits from 3 to 2 would lead to a drop of labor income of about $2.66 million and about 245 jobs in Grays Harbor and Pacific counties alone.

Petry et al. [1980] estimate that about 15,000 primary jobs existed in 1976 associated with sport and commercial salmon and steelhead fishing and that another 1.5 secondary jobs were created for every primary job. They also noted that these are full-time-equivalent jobs and that a much larger number of people are actually involved. Another interesting calculation by the Washington State University group is that regional income for 1977 resulting from commercial and sport fishing for salmon and steelhead originating from the Columbia River was slightly over $100 million.

The common concern among economists about indirect benefits is that they can be easily misunderstood and misused. For example, suppose more salmon were landed commercially in Westport, WA. Standard economic calculus argues that the net economic benefits are equal to the increase in landed value minus the costs of additional landings including any additional costs borne by other fishermen or the public. Part of those costs are fuel costs. Suppose the increase in fuel costs is associated with the establishment of a new marine supply outlet in Washington and that this person had just migrated north from California where his or her business had been terminated. Westport, Washington's gain might be Eureka, California's loss. The key issue is that we should not count indirect benefits if we don't know how to tabulate the indirect costs.

There may be some important exceptions to the usual rule of thumb of ignoring indirect benefits. Much commercial and charter boat salmon fishing is based in relatively small and isolated coastal communities. These communities have three major economic bases: timber, fish, and tourism. For a complex set of reasons, employment in the wood products sector is declining in many parts of the Pacific coast. Additional income loss in either or both of the other basic sectors can cause major slumps. Simultaneously switching jobs and moving to a new geographic area can be a wrenching experience. Consequently, estimates of change in a small area's income can be very useful information for informed community reaction during public hearing processes. Nonetheless, all parties should recognize that these values are different kinds of value from net economic benefits.

A SPECIAL ISSUE

Limited Entry

The Pacific salmon fisheries have long had capacity to harvest many more salmon than are available. Although early programs to limit entry into these fisheries can be traced to the nineteenth century [Fraser 1980], license limitation programs were introduced into British Columbia in 1968, Alaska in 1973, Washington in 1974 and California and Oregon in 1979. The difficulties of planning for limited entry have been avoided by regional fishery management councils by shifting responsibility for such management tools to their member states.

Opinion is divided as to the utility of the current license limitation programs. As the issues involved are reported in a number of recent publications, (see Pearse [1979] and Rettig and Ginter [1980]) and are rather complex, they will not be reviewed in depth here. However, I do have two observations before concluding this paper.

First, there is a growing concern about what limiting licenses to fish for salmon will do to other Pacific fisheries. Indeed, the concern relates to what any action taken with respect to one fishery does to other fisheries. In response to federal court actions altering the share of salmon which can be harvested by non-Indians, a decline in salmon abundance attributed to fresh-water environmental factors, reduced salmon seasons, market problems and other factors, a number of salmon trollers converted to the sablefish pot fishery. Now there are serious questions about the extent of that resource relative to growing capacity; the sablefish market has not grown as rapidly as some had expected and vessel costs have increased sharply, especially for fuel. Consequently, a fishery which was touted for growth only two years ago has become cause for concern for participants and management agencies alike.

Second, a growing number of critics are becoming disillusioned with license limitation. In part, this comes from empirical confirmation of a simple theoretical proposition. When an output results from the use of several inputs, and one of the inputs is improperly used because it is a common property resource, restricting the use of a second input does not guarantee economic efficiency. Rather, third, fourth, etc. inputs are overused. In license limitation this means that limiting the number of vessels will tend to increase investment in capital and/or increased utilization of labor on each remaining vessel. Some people who support license limitation as a fishery management tool agree with the outcome identified, but argue that the "crisis" is due to unrealistic expectations of license limitation programs which do not include specific gear reduction components and also integrate other management tools with license limitation. No matter which view is held, many fishery economists are becoming interested in searching out entirely new types of institutional arrangements.

CONCLUSIONS

The salmon plans of the Pacific Coast must include estimates of optimum yield, capacity, allowable level of foreign fishing and economic impacts of regulatory options. My analysis of optimum yield coincides with that offered in the "Preliminary Review Draft of the Comprehensive Plan for the Management of the Commercial and Recreational Salmon Fisheries Off the Coasts of California, Oregon, and Washington." Namely, "optimum yield is the average harvest of salmon realized by the aggregate of fisheries which achieves the principles of allocation and the spawning requirements for natural and artificial production." The capacity and allowable level of foreign fishing as required in the FCMA are moot, per se, since capacity is so large relative to the available resource. Nonetheless, excess capacity and the optimal management of transboundary salmon are tied into virtually every economic issue councils must face.

Economic impact analysis has two major components in the short term. First, councils should estimate the response by user groups to alternative regulations. Will reducing season length reduce fishing effort proportionately? Will a given license limitation program freeze the growth in fishing effort or even slow the growth of fishing effort below that which would be expected without the program? Second, the economic gains or losses to each user group during the current season needs to be estimated for each proposed package of regulations and this impact should be compared with any possible gains or losses due to eventual outcomes from changes in future salmon availability.

REFERENCES

1. Anadromous Salmonid Environmental Task Force. 1979. "Freshwater Habitat, Salmon Produced, and Escapements for Natural Spawning Along the Pacific Coast of the U.S.," Pacific Fishery Management Council, Portland, OR.
2. Anderson, L. G., Ed. 1977. *Economic Impacts of Extended Fisheries Management* (Ann Arbor, MI: Ann Arbor Science Publishers, Inc.).
3. Brown, W. G., D. M. Larson, R. S. Johnston and R. J. Wahle. 1976. "Improved Economic Evaluation of Commercially and Sport-Caught Salmon and Steelhead of the Columbia River," Agricultural Experiment Station Special Report 463, Oregon State University, Corvallis, OR.
4. Brown, W. G., C. Sorhus and K. C. Gibbs. 1980. "Estimated Expenditures by Sport Anglers and Net Eonomic Values of Salmon and Steelhead for Specified Fisheries in the Pacific Northwest," report to the Pacific Northwest Regional Commission by the Department of Agricultural and Resource Economics, Oregon State University, Corvallis, OR.
5. Chaney, E. and E. L. Perry. 1976. "Columbia Basin Salmon and Steelhead Analysis," Summary Report, Pacific Northwest Regional Commission, Portland, OR.
6. Chaney, E. and T. Holubetz. 1980. "Public Review Draft of a Comprehensive Plan for Production and Management of Columbia River Basin Anadromous Salmon and Steelhead," Columbia River Fisheries Council, Portland, OR.
7. Crutchfield, J. A., and G. Pontecorvo. 1969. *The Pacific Salmon Fisheries: A Study of Irrational Conservation* (Baltimore, MD: Johns Hopkins University Press).
8. Crutchfield, J. A., and K. Schelle. 1978. "An Economic Analysis of Washington Ocean Recreational Salmon Fishing with Particular Emphasis on the Role Played by the Charter Vessel Industry," Pacific Fishery Management Council, Portland, OR.
9. "Fishery Conservation and Management Act," Sec. 303(a), 90 Stat. 351 (1976).

10. Fraser, A. G. 1980. "License Limitation in British Columbia Fisheries," in *Limited Entry as a Fishery Management Tool*, R. B. Rettig and J. J. C. Ginter, Eds. (Seattle, WA: University of Washington Press).
11. Hirshleifer, J., and J. G. Riley. 1979. "The Analytics of Uncertainty and Information—An Expository Survey," *J. Econ. Lit.* 17:1375-1421.
12. Huppert, D. D. 1979. "Implications of Multipurpose Fleets and Mixed Stocks for Control Policies," *J. Fish Res. Board Can.* 36:845-854.
13. Huppert, D. D., A. D. MacCall and G. D. Stauffer. 1980. "A Review of Technical Issues in the Anchovy Management Plan," Administrative Report LJ-80-12, National Marine Fisheries Service, Southwest Fishery Center, La Jolla, CA.
14. Larkin, P. A. 1977. "Pacific Salmon," in *Fish Population Dynamics*, J. A. Gulland, Ed. (New York: John Wiley & Sons, Inc.).
15. Larson, D. M., R. J. Wahle, R. Z. Smith and W. G. Brown. 1978. "Estimated Net Economic Benefits to Visitors of Selected Columbia River Fish Hatcheries," Agricultural Experiment Station Special Report 515, Oregon State University, Corvallis, OR.
16. Lindblom, C. E., and D. K. Cohen. 1979. *Usable Knowledge: Social Science and Social Problem Solving* (New Haven, CT: Yale University Press).
17. Mäler, K.-G. 1971. "A Method of Estimating Social Benefits from Pollution Control," *Swedish J. Econ.* 73:121-133.
18. Mathews, S. B., and G. S. Brown. 1970. "Economic Evaluation of the 1967 Sport Salmon Fisheries of Washington," Technical Report No. 2, Washington Department of Fisheries, Olympia, WA.
19. McConnell, K. E., and I. E. Strand, Jr. 1981. "Some Economic Aspects of Managing Marine Recreational Fishing," Chapter 11, this volume.
20. Mishan, E. J. 1976. *Cost-Benefit Analysis* (New York: Praeger Publishers).
21. Paulik, G. J., and J. W. Greenough. 1966. "Management Analysis for a Salmon Resource System," in *System Analysis Ecology*, K. E. Watt, Ed. (New York: Academic Press, Inc.).
22. Pearse, P. H. 1979. "Symposium on Policies for Economic Rationalization of Commercial Fisheries," *J. Fish. Res. Board Can.* 36(7):711-865.
23. Petry, G. H., L. L. Blakeslee, W. R. Butcher, R. J. Fuller and S. K. Staitieh. 1980. "Pacific Northwest Salmon and Steelhead Fishery Report: The Economic and Employment Impacts of Commercial and Sport Fishing for Salmon and Steelhead in the Pacific Northwest," College of Business, Washington State University, Pullman, WA.
24. Rettig, R. B., and J. J. C. Ginter. 1980. "Limited Entry as a Fishery Management Tool," Sea Grant College Program, University of Washington, Seattle, WA.
25. Ricker, W. E. 1954. "Stock and Recruitment," *J. Fish. Res. Board Can.* 11:559-623.
26. Scott, A. 1979. "Development of Economic Theory on Fisheries Regulation," *J. Fish. Res. Board Can. 36:725-741.*
27. Smith, F. J. et al. 1978. "Socio-economics of the Idaho, Washington, Oregon, and California Coho and Chinook Salmon Industry," Final Report to the Pacific Fishery Management Council by the Department of Agriculture and Resource Economics, Oregon State University, Corvallis, OR.
28. Stevens, J. 1966. "Recreation Benefits from Water Pollution Control," *Water Resources Res.* 2:167-182.

COMMENTS–CHAPTER 6

Richard Marasco
Northwest and Alaska Fisheries Center
National Marine Fisheries Service

It has been stated that "Perhaps men and salmon cannot live together, and salmon will survive only where men cannot. Like Cousteau's splendid penguins swimming under the Antarctic ice they will abide . . . in inhospitable waters until man's day is passed" [Ellis 1977] . If there is interest in what prompted this statement, a quick examination of Rettig's paper will quench the curiosity. A multiplicity of user groups, migration across political boundaries, habitat degradation, multiple stocks and species, and marine mammal predation provide examples of problems plaguing salmon management. The enormity and complexity of any one of these problems leaves little doubt as to what led to the opening quote. Since Rettig did an effective and thorough job of articulating salmon management problems having economic content, the topic will not be addressed further. One comment, however, is in order. If policy analysis is to be effective, care must be taken in the definition of problems.

Before proceeding with the discussion of how economic analysis can be used in and integrated into fishery management plans, it is useful to discuss where fisheries scientists fit into the fishery management process. Prior to doing this, however, it is necessary to define what fishery management is all about. I would like to suggest that its purpose is to guide fisheries over some defined time horizon in a manner to either maintain or improve the well-being of the system. Once this navigational characteristic of fisheries management is recognized, the role of scientists becomes apparent. In specific, they are providers of navigational aids. Aids that are fashioned by the application of theories and techniques at their disposal to fisheries problems. The demands on scientists, their theories and techniques, can be thought of as increasing as the average size and variability of the catch increases.

The problems and characteristics of the salmon fishery discussed by Rettig suggest that the task of providing salmon managers with useful scientific information is large indeed. The complexity of the issues may require use of both conventional and unconventional approaches. Rettig indicates that salmon pass through several political jurisdictions during their cycle, with parts spend in both fresh-water and marine environments. They are, therefore, influenced by a large variety of human activities.

The multiplicity of user groups, the number of stocks and species, and migrational characteristics of salmon indicate the existence of a complex network of interactions. Successful policy analysis requires isolation of key interactions to be examined given the issue at hand. It is important to note that the complexity and number of relevant interactions will more than likely increase with the average size and variability of the catch. At this point a caution is in order. This holistic approach to the resolution of fishery problems may not produce quantifiable end products. Results more often than not, for large complex systems, will be qualitative in nature. This property should not result in discarding either the approach or the results. Attempts at the application of alternative approaches, for example, the reduction of reality into its smallest "real" entities, may prove unworkable, resulting in the conclusion that the problem is too complex for analysis.

Two final comments complete this brief discussion of approaches to fishery policy analysis. It might have been noted that minimum use was made of the terms economic analysis and economist in the preceding discussion. Policy analysis and fisheries scientists were used instead. The feeling that the key to the inclusion of relevant economic analysis into FMP is the amalgamation of economics with other fishery sciences led to this selection of terms. This is not suggesting that economists should lose their identity. What is being suggested is that there is a need for "rational creative action" by fishery scientists. Finally, I am reminded of the story of the drunk looking for a coin under the lamppost. A helpful passerby inquired—quite illogically—where the coin had been lost. Whereupon the inebriate replied that he had lost it in the park across the street but it was too dark to look for it there. Faced with the complexities of the salmon fishery, there is a real danger that policy analysts might fall into the lamppost syndrome. A serious effort should be made to avoid being too myopic.

It is necessary to reiterate that identification of important interactions is critical to successful policy analysis. In the process of isolating critical interactions, it might become apparent that costs and benefits associated with different management actions can be quantified. If this is the case, care must be taken to provide decision makers with indications of the degree of confidence that can be associated with assumption sets that enter into the B/C calculus. Frequently, price and income elasticities are used to determine how gross stock is affected by alternative management decisions. Since econometric techniques are used to estimate these elasticities, it is possible to derive probability distributions of the parameters. In other situations, only the range of values for a factor are known. This case requires that the range be subdivided into segments or subranges. After this has been accomplished each subrange or segment can be assigned a probability. Assignments can be made by (1) ranking segments on the basis of "more" or "less" likely, and (2) determining the relative magnitudes to be assigned to those likelihoods, such that the sum of the weights equal unity. This process is repeated for each factor where a formal statistical estimate of the probability distribution is unavailable. In practice, only the most important variables affecting outcomes have to be treated in a probabilistic framework. Having gone through this exercise, probabilities for different states of nature can be determined: a state of nature is defined as an event comprised of specific levels of several independent factors or variables.

As a final set in this process, a matrix can be constructed that illustrates payoffs accruing from different actions, given alternative states of nature. By presenting results in this fashion, decision-makers are made aware of the degree of confidence that the analyst associates with assumption sets utilized in the analysis.

REFERENCE

1.   Ellis, D. V. 1977. "Pacific Salmon Management for People," Western Geographical Series, Vol. 13, University of Victoria, Canada, p. 227.

CHAPTER 7

FISHERIES MANAGEMENT PROBLEMS AND RESEARCH ON FISHERIES ECONOMICS IN NORWAY AND ICELAND

Rögnvaldur Hannesson
Department of Economics
University of Bergen

In this chapter I shall attempt to give an overview of the problems confronting fisheries management in Norway and Iceland. I shall do so partly by reporting on some of the work that economists in these countries have been doing on fisheries management problems. It will not be an exhaustive catalog, however; the review is limited in scope by my knowledge of what is going on and what I find particularly interesting.

MARKET FAILURE OR MANAGEMENT FAILURE?

Despite the differences that there are between Norway and Iceland, their fisheries management problems are of a common root. In both countries the fundamental problem is overexploitation of fish stocks. This is exactly what the theory of common property resources would predict, but a further explanation is needed. The changes in the law of the sea that took place in the previous decade have meant that national jurisdiction was established over the habitat of many important fish stocks. In the case of Iceland, this happened with respect to the demersal species, cod being the most important and famous of these. Against this background it is indeed surprising that the Icelandic authorities have done so little to increase the profitability of the fisheries by restricting fishing effort. The impact thereof on the national economy would be profound, given that no less than 75% of export earnings come from fish products, and of these again more than two-thirds consist of products of demersal species.

A recent study by the Icelandic economist Árnason [1980] illustrates this well. He used a Beverton-Holt model to calculate the present value of different strategies with respect to the utilization of the Icelandic cod stock. He found that the optimal steady-state fishing effort is about 35% of the effort in 1978, with an insignificant change in sustainable yield.

The gains in terms of rent are therefore considerable, but it is worthwhile to note that they consist almost entirely of savings on alternative cost and not of increases in catches. The situation is very similar with respect to the Arcto-Norwegian cod, to which I shall return.

What could be the reason why the Icelandic authorities have done and still appear to be doing so little to change the situation? The explanation must be sought in the domain of political economy and is, undoubtedly, complex. But fundamentally I think that we are confronted with a problem of a quite general kind. Governments very often seem to be reluctant to take measures that correct market failures and increase efficiency. I suspect that the reason for this is an asymmetric distribution of gains from efficiency and gains from inefficiency. There are always some who gain from a particular kind of market failure in comparison to an uncompensated correction thereof. It is often the case that those who gain from a particular market failure are few and well organized, and that the gains accruing to each part (individual or firm) are quite considerable. On the other hand, the gains from correcting a particular market failure are distributed among consumers at large, who are seldom organized to further such interests. Furthermore the gains accruing to each individual consumer from correcting a particular market failure is likely to be rather small. There is also a problem of information; each individual will not readily be able to identify and quantify what he might gain from a more efficient exploitation of fish stocks, for example. As a result of this, governments acting in their own self interest will be tempted to cater to the interests of pressure groups at the expense of the majority. But the problem is that this is not a zero-sum game; once you pile one market failure on top of another, everyone may end up in a worse situation than if all market failures were corrected without compensation.

For Norway the situation with respect to jurisdiction is quite different. The habitat of the most important demersal stocks extends into the economic zones of other countries. The Arcto-Norwegian cod, for example, spawns in Norwegian territorial waters while the feeding areas are partly inside the Soviet economic zone. Any effective management of this stock therefore requires agreement between Norwegian and Soviet authorities. Such agreements have so far been limited to quota agreements and mesh size regulations. In countries so different economically as Norway and the Soviet Union, there is bound to be disagreement with respect to what would be a truly optimal utilization of a common fish stock. To this is added the fact that the fishing fleets of these two countries exploit predominantly different age groups of the Arcto-Norwegian cod. But even if it is highly improbable that Norway and the Soviet Union could ever agree on a "best" harvesting policy, there is little doubt that the present one is the nth best, n being a high number. Some years ago I studied the optimal exploitation of the Arcto-Norwegian cod, using a standard Beverton-Holt model [Hannesson 1978]. My conclusions were not very different from those of Ārnason. A reduction of fishing effort by 50% or more would yield a considerable benefit both for Norway and the Soviet Union, predominantly by reducing fishing costs. It ought, therefore, to be possible for both countries to agree on measures that would *improve* on the present situation.

SHORTCOMINGS OF THE STANDARD BEVERTON-HOLT MODEL

The two studies that I have mentioned so far, my own and Ārnason's, share a common method. Both are built around a standard Beverton-Holt yield model. This model is now used extensively and, one is tempted to say, has been canonized in international organizations such as the International Council for the Exploration of the Seas. I have some comments to make pertaining to this model. First, some of the inputs into the model usually reflect certain restrictive assumptions. Growth parameters, natural mortality rates, and age of maturity are usually treated as constants. There is scattered evidence, however, that we are in fact dealing with variables that respond to depletion of each particular stock. For example, the growth rate of the Arcto-Norwegian cod appears to have increased as a result of depletion and individual fish also appear to mature earlier than before. These phenomena certainly have a bearing on the economic gains of reducing the intensity of fishing. Although we do not know the magnitude of these effects, we know their directions; the gains from reducing fishing effort will appear greater than they are ever likely to be when we ignore the possible responses of natural mortality, growth and maturity to sustained exploitation.

The standard Beverton-Holt model also represents a single-species approach. Although this model can be modified to take account of interaction among species, we seldom have the quantitative knowledge to do so. But there can be no doubt that as the fishery extends to more and more interdependent species, the conclusion reached by modeling one species only can lead us seriously astray. With respect to the cod, for example, one would suspect that capelin, as a major supply of food for cod and one that has recently been sub-jected to intensive exploitation, ought to be taken into account.

Still another soft spot in our use of the Beverton-Holt model is the some-what casual treatment of cost and production relations. It is usually assumed that fishing mortality and fishing costs are directly proportional to fishing effort. But it is not always clear even what is meant by fishing effort. The economist has in mind some measure of the activities of the fishing fleet which may be related both to the production and cost, while the fisheries biologist is primarily interested in a measure which relates to the impact of fishing on the abundance of fish. A fruitful approach, I think, is to define fishing effort as the mortality generated in a fish stock of a given size and distribution. If we do so, there are two problems to be taken into account. First, fishing mortality may depend on the size of the fish stock as well as fishing effort; second, fishing vessels do more than just catch fish. I shall comment on these two points in turn. The fishing mortality generated by a given level of fishing effort may depend on the size of the exploited fish stock. It is quite possible that fish stocks do not distribute themselves more and more thinly over a given area as they are depleted, but instead occupy a progressively smaller area. This gives rise to what the biologists call Paoloheimo-Dickie effect, or diminishing returns to the fish stock as a factor of production, as the economist would phrase it. The implication of this effect is, first, that keeping stocks at high levels of abundance is less rewarding than otherwise, but extinction of fish stocks is more likely to occur as a result of unrestricted fishing. The most spectacular example of this is the virtual disappearance of the Atlanto-Scandian herring [Ulltang 1979]. This effect is probably most markedly present in pelagic stocks which are concentrated in shoals, but it may very possibly be present in demersal stocks as well. A study that I under-took of the winter cod fishery in Lofoten indicated slightly diminishing returns to fish stocks as a factor or production [Hannesson 1979, 1980a].

The second problem arising from defining fishing effort in the way I have suggested has to do with the fact that a fishing fleet engages in other activities besides catching fish. Some preliminary processing is also involved, and so are transportation between port and fishing banks and search for suitable concentration of fish. These auxiliary activities may be an important element of fishing costs, and do add considerable complications to any economic analysis. Two equal amounts of fishing effort measured as the mortality generated in a hypothetical fish stock may well be associated with different costs, because the auxiliary activities that I have just mentioned need not be of the same magnitude in both cases. For example, when fish stocks are small and catches per unit of effort are low, one expects that relatively less time will be spent on processing and transportation than on fishing proper, but more on search. No study that I know of has attempted to analyze these relations in any detail.

SECOND BEST SOLUTIONS

I indicated above that governments are not likely to have the necessary incentives to correct market failures. Indeed, what makes fisheries economics a fascinating subject, at least to me, is that on the one hand we have a classical case of market failure calling for intervention, while on the other we have government bodies that often do everything but correct such failures. A "best" world is simply not obtainable. We should then perhaps not spend too much time on deploring this fact, but seek improvements or second best solutions, given the institutional constraints. There are many examples of important theoretical and applied studies that have been carried out in this spirit. Let me take, as a point of departure, the long-term plan published by the Norwegian Ministry of Fisheries. The importance of this document lies in its being the expression of thoughts and intentions on behalf of the political authorities, rather than in being a good catalog of previous and intended measures to be taken. The plan lists the following as the highest ranking social objectives with respect to fisheries management: (1) preserve the pattern of settlements along the coast; (2) protect the fish resources; and (3) provide secure and satisfactory job opportunities. One may immediately note the absence of the following objective: efficient utilization of the fish resources, with due account taken of opportunities foregone in other industries. It is perhaps too simplistic to hope that adherence to this efficiency objective would seal the Pandora's box of conflicting objectives that this long-term plan has been found to contain. At any rate, it has been a plentiful source of inspiration for several economists working on multiple objective programming. Mathiesen at the Norwegian School of Economics and Business Administration is presently doing some very interesting theoretical and applied work on multicriteria optimizing models. His purpose is to formulate an interactive model which will enable decision-makers to find rational solutions to their management problems, given that they have vague but consistent notions of their preferences [Mathiesen 1979, 1980]. The model is being applied to the Norwegian purse seiner fleet, the objectives being maximization of a weighted sum of social and private profitability, employment and catch capacity, under a number of resource constraints. When confronted with a particular solution, the manager is supposed to be able to indicate what sort of changes in the present solution he would approve of, and by iteration the model converges to an optimal solution.

A study by Amble [1979] also should be mentioned in this context. He studied the optimal composition of a fishing fleet, given eight different goals. This multitude of goals partly reflects that his analysis was carried out for a small region; therefore tax income from fishing, for example, was one of the objectives. By varying the hierarchical structure between the different objectives, different suboptimal solutions, from which to choose the truly optimal one, were generated.

Hansen and Lensberg [1980] at the Norwegian School of Economics and Business Administration take the goal of providing job opportunities as a point of departure in a recent study. They understand this to be an expression of a coincidence of a low alternative cost of labor and restrictions on labor mobility. On this basis they set up a linear programming model in which they maximize value added in the fishery, subject to a lower limit on jobs to be provided and an upper limit on the catch quota, a lower and upper limit on profitability of operations, and political constraints on the system of subsidies. Given the objective of the exercise one would quickly guess that labor ought to be subsidized to accomplish the stated objective. However, almost everything else but labor is presently being subsidized in Norwegian fisheries; capital, fishing gear and catches are all subsidized to a varying degree. The present use of subsidies in Norwegian fisheries policy thus appears not to be tailored adequately to the problems which it is meant to solve. Hansen and Lensberg take this as being the consequence of political constraints; for some reason or another subsidization of labor is possible only to a rather low degree. But even if one takes the present subsidy rates as roughly reflecting political constraints, Hansen and Lensberg conclude that it would still be possible to obtain the employment objective by a much lower total amount of subsidies than presently is being ladled out. By increasing the subsidies of fishing gear slightly and reducing the subsidies on catches and capital, it would be possible to reduce the total amount of subsidies to 20% or less of the present level and still attain the employment objective.

THE PRESENT SYSTEM OF SUBSIDIES

Fisheries subsidies in Norway have been analyzed and criticized from still different angles. An important point of criticism concerns the fact that the purpose of the subsidies is to ensure a certain level of average income to fishermen in difficult times. The emphasis here is on the word "average," and the means by which this has been accomplished is predominantly price subsidies. From a distributional point of view this is a bit curious; if equalization of incomes is an important point of concern, price subsidies would not appear to be the most adequate instrument to use. In practice the system of subsidies is not quite as bad as it may sound, because the rate of subsidization varies between fish species and the use of the raw fish is such a way that the least profitable vessels tend to be subsidized most. Hellesøy [1980] at the University of Bergen has studied this problem.

There are two more studies dealing with the consequences of guaranteeing a certain average income to fishermen that I would like to mention. One deals with the implications of this system in a fishery with restricted entry, the other with the consequences in a free access fishery. Hellesøy [1978] studied the subsidization of the landings of the Norwegian purse seiner fleet. Entry into this fishery is now restricted, but still the present problem is one of overcapacity. A declared government policy of guaranteed income to fishermen will determine a rental value for any vessel with a license to take a certain quota of fish. Hellesøy shows that the government would be able to reduce the total amount of subsidies by buying back some fishermen's licenses at their rental value. The reason for this is increasing returns to scale at the vessel level. This phenomenon further implies that some fishermen would be interested in buying the licenses of other fishermen at their rental value, to increase to scale of their operations. This would increase the average income of those who remain in the fishery and therefore reduce the level of subsidies. A buy-back scheme and a market for licenses can therefore be considered instruments for reducing the level of subsidies. Nevertheless, neither has been put into effect.

The consequences of guaranteeing income in a free entry fishery depend on two things. First, risk will be reduced, and to the extent that fishing is more risk-prone than alternative activities, participation in the fisheries will tend to be greater than otherwise, provided that fishermen are risk averse. Secondly, the asymmetry between the incidence of profit and loss years, brought about by subsidization in loss years without offsetting taxation in profit years, will produce a ratchet effect; the incentives for exit will be weakened while entry will be encouraged. Over time participation in the fishery will increase, stocks will be depleted, and the need for subsidies will progressively increase. Brochmann [1980] at the University of Tromsø, has described how this mechanism very likely has been working in the past in the Norwegian fisheries. It has now proceeded to the point where the total amount of subsidies to fisheries in northern Norway amounts to 75% of the income of labor in fishing and fish processing.

These huge subsidies are, not surprisingly, of considerable concern to the Norwegian government. A certain amount of effort has recently been put into investigating how these might possibly be reduced without jeopardizing the most important goals pertaining to the fishing industry. It should be pointed out that the huge subsidies in the fisheries are not simply a symptom of deficient profitability in the fisheries themselves. Since the raw fish price that the processing industry can afford to pay is determined by the profitability in the industry, the subsidization of the raw fish price may just as well be a symptom of a deficient profitability in the processing industry. The reason why this could be so is the peculiar system of raw fish price setting practiced in northern Norway. A marketing board operating on behalf of fishermen has monopoly rights of selling the produce; all buyers must be authorized by the marketing organization and are subject to the minimum prices fixed by it. The minimum prices are set by negotiations between the marketing board and the buyers' organization, but, legally, the marketing board has the last word. But the marketing board cannot afford to slaughter the cow it intends to milk, so it goes to the government asking for subsidies, if it finds out that the prices the buyers can afford to pay are too low to give the fishermen an acceptable income.

The government and the fishermen's organizations seem to have had some doubts about how successful the marketing board has been in milking profits from the processing industry without putting its existence in jeopardy. I investigated this and came to the conclusion that there is very little additional money to be squeezed from the processing industry. One is forced to conclude that fish processing, freezing in particular, is not a very profitable industry at the Norwegian level of wages, particularly when raw fish is scarce and its price high [Hannesson 1980b].

As an aside to the above one might ask if this marketing arrangement is compatible with efficiency. The answer is that it will generally not be so; the fish marketing board may be regarded as a monopsonist which hires processing capacity from the processing industry. If the marginal cost curve of the industry is rising, the level of the raw fish price will determine the break-even quantity of the processing industry. The marginal factor cost of the fish marketing board will rise even faster than the marginal cost of the processing industry, and so the marketing board will set a higher price of raw fish and hire less processing capacity than is socially optimal.

CONCLUSION

I have tried to describe fisheries management problems in Norway and Iceland, and the work that economists are doing on fisheries in these countries. To summarize, much theoretical and applied work remains to be done. The most demanding areas theoretically are that of multispecies fisheries, and to understand better the motivating forces behind regulatory authorities. The fact that they often act against what economists would advise has, in my view, more to do with lack of the necessary incentives than with absence of economic advice or imperfect information. Empirically there is much that economists could do to help regulators better attain the goals that they have set themselves, regardless of whether these goals make good economic sense.

REFERENCES

1. Amble, A. 1979. "Multi-Objective Optimization of a Local Fishing Fleet— A Goal Programming Approach," paper presented at the NATO Symposium on Applied Operations Research in Fishing, Trondheim, Norway, August 14-17, 1979.
2. Árnason, R. 1980. "Tímatengd fiskihagfræði og hagkvæmasta nýting íslenzka porsktofnsins," *Fjármálatidindi* (January-April).
3. Brochmann, B. S. 1980. "Virkninger på lang sikt av statsstøtte til fiskeriene," University of Tromsø.
4. Hannesson, R. 1978. "Trålfiske eller skreifiske? Om optimal beskatning av den norsk-arktiske torsk." Dept. of Economics, University of Bergen, Economic Papers No. 12.
5. Hannesson, R. 1979. "The Bioeconomic Production Function in Fisheries: A Theoretical and Empirical Analysis," Dept. of Economics, University of Bergen, Norway.
6. Hannesson, R. 1980a. "Frontier Production Functions in Some Norwegian Fisheries," Dept. of Economics, University of Bergen, Norway.
7. Hannesson, R. 1980b. "Om Norges Råfisklags nettopriser," Rapport avgitt til et utvalg for utredning av fiskesalgslagenes prispolitikk, Department of Economics, University of Bergen.
8. Hansen, T., and T. Lensberg. 1980. "The Problem of Regional Unemployment—Second Best Solutions When Wage Rates are Given and There are Constraints on Subsidies," Norwegian School of Economics and Business Administration, Discussion Paper No. 13.
9. Hellesøy, A. 1980. "Prisstøttens inntektsfordelingsvirkninger i fiskerinæringen 1976-77," Department of Economics, University of Bergen.
10. Hellesøy, A. 1978. "Subsidier og konsesjoner i ringnotfisket," Dept. of Economics, University of Bergen, Norway, Economic Paper No. 15.
11. Mathiesen, L. 1979. "A Multi-Criteria Model for Assessing Industrial Structure in the Norwegian Fish Meal Industry," Center for Applied Research, Norwegian School of Economics and Business Administration, Working Paper No. 5.
12. Mathiesen, L. 1980. "A Multi-Criteria Model with Stochastic Coefficients," Center for Applied Research, Norwegian School of Economics and Business Administration," Working Paper No. 6.
13. Norwegian Ministry of Fisheries. 1977. "Langtidsplan for fiskenæringen," Oslo, Norway.
14. Ulltang, Ø. 1979. "Factors of Pelagic Fish Stocks Which Affect Their Reaction to Exploitation and Require a New Approach to Their Assessment and Management," Institute of Marine Research, Bergen, Norway.

COMMENT–CHAPTER 7

Fred Olson
National Marine Fisheries Service
International Fisheries Development and
Services Division

It is interesting to note that Dr. Hannesson finds some of the same problems in Norway and Iceland that we have in North America–overexploitation of fish stocks and shortcomings of the standard Beverton-Holt model–and because of the solutions they have tried.

The problems associated with the Arcto-Norwegian cod, which is within both the Norwegian and Soviet zones, are interesting because there are many other stocks that cross two or more zones and therefore require joint management. Even when the two countries are as similar as Canada and the United States there can be disagreements in how the joint stocks should be managed because of different discount rates or because the secondary benefits on other species may affect each country differently.

The Beverton-Holt model is an imperfect representation of the real world. Growth rates are a function of density. This has been clearly demonstrated in Pacific salmon. In the marine area we must use a multispecies approach in order to determine how to make the first best use of our marine fishery resources rather than the present use which is the nth best solution. In this regard Hannesson's report of Hansen and Lensberg of maximizing value added subject to a lower limit on jobs, an upper limit or catch quotas, a lower and upper bounds on profits and an upper limit on subsidies is very interesting. In the first place, value added is the relevant measure to consider [Pontecorvo et al. 1980]. In the second place, the constraints can all be identified in the biological, political or economic arena. If you consider a royalty on landings then you can remove the constraint of an upper limit on profits because royalties can be increased to any level to keep profits at a maximum.

Hannesson also had an interesting discussion on subsidies. He indicated when there are increasing returns to scale then a buy-back program would reduce subsidies. I feel that Norway needs to take Sinclair's advice of limiting entry before doing anything else in helping fisheries.

Economists on both sides of the ocean need to look at maximizing the value added by a fleet or from a biomass and help define and articulate the theory. This activity would help define deficiencies in the data.

If you define subsidies as the net amount of money transferred to the fishing industry, the upper limit of subsidies may not be limiting. This is why I maintain that management and development are closely related.

Limited entry creates an excess cash flow that goes somewhere. It can be drained off as a royalty on landings; it can be used to increase revenue from a public resource; it can be transferred to an unprofitable fishery thereby creating more jobs, growth, development or value added by the fishing industry; or it can be used by fishermen for retirement, disability, health benefits, research on productivity increasing activities, etc. If this is not done this cash flow becomes capitalized into the right that goes along with this limited entry or vessel or enterprise quota.

A royalty would clearly reduce the incentive for overcapitalization. In fact, the level of the royalty could eliminate the capitalization of future returns above all other costs. It should not, however, be used by itself to govern the growth of fishing effort because this will keep the fishermen in the same poverty that existed before limited entry.

As economists we also should not be making political assumptions that a royalty could not be high enough in lucrative fisheries, like the offshore scallops, to prevent overcapitalization. The political feasibility may well depend on the uses made of the royalties. If they went back to the same fishermen in alternative developing fisheries, applied research or other direct benefits to fishermen, high roylaties may well be politically feasible.

Hannesson mentioned joint stocks. Two other international aspects of fisheries managment include the highly migratory species under international control—tuna, fur seals, whales—and fish caught in the national zone of one country and consumed in another country. Who catches and consumes the fish may not necessarily be the group who benefits from the fishery resources. In the international field this depends upon the foreign fishing regulations, the bycatch limits, the time limit on the allocations which could vary from one month duration to as long as five years. Another area of interest is managing highly fluctuating stocks and how these relate to long distance high seas fleets.

REFERENCE

1. Pontecorvo, G., M. Wilkinson, R. Anderson and M. Holdowsky. 1980. "Contribution of the Ocean Sector to the United States Economy," *Science* 208:1000-1006.

CHAPTER 8

ECONOMIC ANALYSIS AND
CANADIAN FISHERIES MANAGEMENT

C. L. Mitchell

Economic Research
Department of Fisheries and Oceans
Canada

Fisheries economics in Canada is going through a particularly interesting phase with respect to its relevance and use in the management of Canada's fisheries resources. This phase harks back to the establishment of the 200-mile economic zone for Canada's fisheries, which gave Canada management responsibility for the resources within this area. Prior to this, ICNAF, the international body for management, was not really concerned with the economic, but primarily with the biological (conservation) aspects of management.

With Canada taking over management in the 200-mile zone, "best use" became the guiding principle [Environment Canada 1976]. This principle was defined as "the sum of net social benefits (personal income, occupational opportunity, consumer satisfaction and so on) derived from the fisheries and the industries linked to them." In effect, it is an attempt to manage exploitation based on both biological and economic considerations. This chapter will endeavor to examine the evolution of the approach since it has been and will continue to be an interesting period for fisheries economics.

The chapter will examine the following:

1. Canada's fishing industry: an overview;
2. major management issues in Canada's fisheries;
3. the contribution of economics to fisheries management in Canada; and
4. new approaches in fisheries economics.

CANADA'S FISHERIES: AN OVERVIEW

Fisheries is an important industry to Canada and of special importance to the Atlantic and Pacific regional economies. The industry consists of two major subsectors: (1) primary fishing, and (2) the fish processing sector together with allied distributional activities. The structure of the industry differs between the major regions based on differences in resource availability, location, seasonality, management strategy and general economic conditions. The Atlantic coast industry is more diversified with distinct inshore (small boats, seasonal fishing, small plants) and offshore (large vessels, full year operations, large plants) fisheries. The Pacific coast fisheries has no distincct inshore-offshore orientation but there is a higher degree of concentration in both primary and secondary activities of the industry.

Growth in output in Canada's fisheries for the period 1978-1979 is shown in Table I. In 1979, primary fisheries produced 1.4 million metric tons, with a landed value of $873 million. Of this, 1217 metric tons with a landed value of $479 million were landed on the Atlantic coast and 116 metric tons valued at $332 million were landed on the Pacific coast. The secondary manufacturing sector produced fisheries products valued at over $1.6 billion, of which $1 billion were produced on the Atlantic coast and $562 million on the Pacific coast.

Because of common property and free entry into fisheries, primary fisheries activities are usually associated with excessive inputs of capital and labor. In the secondary manufacturing sector there is also a tendency for this to occur because of seasonality and because the capital costs associated with entry are not high. For these reasons, Canada's fishing industry during the 1960s and early 1970s, when free entry conditions were prevalent, was characterized by surplus capacity in the fleet and processing plants leading to relatively low returns in both. Factor inputs, i.e., labor and capital, in the industry for 1978 are shown in Table II.

In 1978 about 73,000 fishermen were engaged in Canada's primary fisheries of which 48,000 were in the Atlantic fisheries, 17,000 in the Pacific and 8,000 in the inland fisheries. The average gross value of output per fisherman ranged from $9600 in the Atlantic to $15,000 in the Pacific. From these, average net per capita earnings was estimated at about $4800 for the Atlantic coast in comparison with $8800 for the Pacific coast. There are great ranges in incomes from fishing, depending on resources exploited, time spent fishing and skill required. Some incomes are in the $30,000-40,000 range in both the Atlantic and Pacific coast fisheries. However, the majority of fishermen (about 92%) are employed in fishing for less than six months during the year. In many remote communities, alternative incomes and employment opportunities are few. As a result of this, many fishermen have had to depend to a great extent on unemployment insurance benefits to supplement their income and on government subsidies to finance fishing investments.

Table I.   Canadian Fisheries Landings and Market Values (1968-1979)[a]

Year	Atlantic			Pacific			Total		
	Vol. of Landings (1000 metric tons)	Value of Landings ($ million)	Market Value ($ million)	Vol. of Landings (1000 metric tons)	Value of Landings ($ million)	Market Value ($ million)	Vol. of Landings (1000 metric tons)	Value of Landings ($ million)	Market Value ($ million)
68	1267.5	115.7	240.4	131.1	57.4	123.9	1450.8	186.1	384.1
69	1207.5	120.7	271.0	88.4	47.4	87.9	1350.4	183.8	381.9
70	1174.0	131.4	277.8	117.0	60.3	123.3	1333.9	204.9	426.0
71	1094.7	133.3	316.4	113.4	58.6	120.2	1249.6	205.0	461.8
72	931.2	145.1	354.7	162.3	75.1	159.1	1136.0	236.0	545.4
73	888.5	171.1	462.7	183.8	130.4	285.0	1117.8	320.6	786.2
74	781.0	171.6	422.7	141.1	101.0	220.5	969.1	290.8	680.4
75	805.3	190.8	483.5	133.0	79.7	167.0	980.8	291.4	694.3
76	880.9	224.1	625.8	180.9	141.8	297.6	1101.5	390.0	972.7
77	1003.1	288.3	750.2	204.4	167.9	364.8	1254.7	487.2	1175.0
78	1153.2	416.0	973.1	198.7	252.2	517.6	1399.5	701.1	1549.5
79[b]	1216.9	497.5	1005.7	155.6	332.5	561.7	1421.6	873.2	1567.4

[a]Source: DFO, Annual Statistical Review of Canadian Fisheries.
[b]Preliminary.

Table II.   Factor Inputs, Canada's Fishing Industry (1978)[a]

	Atlantic	Pacific	Total[b]
Primary Industry			
Number of Fishermen	48,496	16,785	73,572
Gross Value of Output per Fisherman ($)	8,578	15,025	9,530
Number of Vessels and Boats	30,728	7,264	39,751
Value of Vessels and Boats (10^3 $)	495,506	368,489	876,475
Secondary Industry			
Number of Plants	601	120	854
Estimated Value of Plants (10^3 $)	315,016	165,959	512,220
Number of Workers	24,000	4,200	29,349
Average Income per Worker ($)	13,872	18,621	16,000

[a]Source: Mitchell (1980b).
[b]Inland fisheries included.

In the secondary or manufacturing sector of the industry, there are about 900 plants in operation employing about 29,000 workers. The economic performance of Canada's fish processing industry is dependent on a number of factors, the most important of which are its structure (including vertical integration) and location in terms of resources and markets. Virtually all of these differ between regions. In general, however, the industry is characterized by considerable horizontal integration and also vertical integration of large vessels and plants. The operations of the medium and small plants tend to be more affected by seasonal variations in fish availability than the large plants with more diversified operations and a fleet to take care of some of their needs.

MAJOR MANAGEMENT ISSUES–CANADA'S FISHERIES

In general, the major management concerns of commercial fisheries can be classified as (1) resource management, i.e., controlling and allocating exploitation, thereby protecting stocks and affecting economic returns; and (2) fisheries development, i.e., bringing about growth and development in both the primary and secondary manufacturing sectors and ensuring that the industry, through linkage effects, would make a maximum contribution to the regional economy. Concentration will be primarily on the former, since management responsibility of the Department of Fisheries and Oceans is mainly with this, and it is also the concern which has predominated in fisheries economics.

The major management problem in Canada's fisheries has been the excessive inputs of labor and capital relative to resource availability. However, the magnitude and extent of this and measures for its solution vary depending on differences in resource availability, location and seasonality; the region where the fishery is situated, particularly the growth and employment experience of the region;[1] and the traditional approaches of management in the region. The major management issues will therefore be discussed separately for the Atlantic and Pacific fisheries.

The Atlantic Fisheries

The structure of the primary fisheries on this coast has been characterized by its inshore-offshore orientation, with a great diversity of fish species exploited in both of these.

The offshore sector, which employs about 10-12% of the fishermen, is an international fishery which only came under Canadian control and jurisdiction in 1977.[2] Canadian offshore fishing operations are mainly for groundfish, utilizing mainly wet fish trawlers (stern and side), draggers and longliners. There are also operations for pelagic species, utilizing seiners and midwater (stern) trawlers; and also for mollusks and crustaceans (scallops, lobster, crab and shrimp). All these vessels (generally over 50 gross tons with 60% over 100 gross tons) are capital-intensive, require skilled crews and operate out of relatively large ports in the Atlantic provinces and Quebec.

Inshore operations are usually conducted within the territorial limits along the coast. The major characteristics of this fishery are labor intensity, seasonality and the predominance of two fisheries (1) lobster and (2) cod. Inshore fishermen have been and remain the mainstay of Canada's Atlantic coast fisheries, many living in tiny settlements scattered along the coast. Their fishing operations are confined to the period from May to September because the vessels and boats used are small, making winter operations hazardous, particularly in the more exposed areas on the coast. By the same token resource availability is higher in those months: groundfish and pelagic resources such as cod, herring and capelin migrate from offshore into inshore waters during the late spring and early summer months and move out again during the fall and winter. (The inshore lobster fisheries is also seasonal but this is due to resource availability and fishing area restrictions.)

The Atlantic coast fisheries were free entry fisheries up to the mid-1970s with regulations pertaining mainly to conservation, i.e., gear and mesh size limitations, closed seasons and areas. The experience of these fisheries revealed that uncontrolled exploitation leads, as indicated in the theory [Gordon 1953] to (1) biological overfishing—which became evident in the early 1970s; and (2) to economic overfishing by 1974 in the important offshore groundfish fisheries and even earlier in other fisheries. Other problems include inshore-offshore conflicts, competition for the resources from various fleet segments and heavy levels of unemployment in the region, all of which serve to indicate the complexities faced by fisheries management on this coast.

Pacific Coast Fisheries

Canada's Pacific coast fisheries are conducted within the 200-mile limit. Because of a narrow continental shelf, fishing operations, however, take place within a 50-mile coastal zone. The fishery is an inshore or nearshore fishery with no distinct inshore-offshore structure.

The Pacific coast primary fisheries is dominated by three major species: salmon, herring and halibut (fished off Alaska), but there are also a large number of other species, mainly groundfish and mollusks and crustaceans. During the period 1968-1979 landings of all sea products fluctuated, but were in excess of 300 million pounds, of which 47% was salmon. There was a decline in 1970 in the halibut fishery; a recovery in the herring fishery in 1972, which had been closed down completely in the 1960s; an increase in the groundfish fishery; and relative stability in shell fish as a class during this period.

In comparison with the Atlantic coast industry, the Pacific coast industry has been a highly regulated one. In 1969 license limitation was introduced in the salmon industry and license fees were charged. This was accompanied by a buy-back program to encourage fishermen to leave the industry. Transfer-ability of licenses was permitted, thereby creating a license market and a means of regulating exit and entry into the industry. A reopening of the herring fishery for roe exploitation was based on a whole array of management measures which included license limitation, high fees for these licenses, and closed seasons. Despite these measures, the Pacific coast industry has been problematic from an economic standpoint.

The major economic problems again stemmed from an inadequate control over fishing effort relative to resources leading to excessive inputs of fishing effort and to overcapitalization of the fleets exploiting them.[3] Sinclair [1979] produced a report which represented an extensive review of economic conditions in the Pacific coast fishery. This is a classic work in terms of indicating the problems of fisheries management and in advocating economic solutions. His main findings will be summarized in the next section.

THE CONTRIBUTION OF ECONOMICS
TO CANADIAN FISHERIES MANAGEMENT

Fisheries economics has been making an increasing contribution to the management of Canda's fisheries. This contribution has manifested itself primarily in: (1) the introduction of limited entry programs which now cover virtually all fisheries; and (2) the acceptance in principle of cost recovery for enhancement programs. But, perhaps the most significant has been the articulation of the "best use" principle based on biological, social and economic objectives. Although this principle can be considered more philosophic than operational, it is significant in that acceptance brings fisheries management into the multidisciplinary realm where it really belongs.

Introduction of Limited Entry

Fisheries economic theory since Gordon [1953] has been consistent on the point that common property and free entry into the industry result in an equilibrium level of exploitation characterized by both biological and economic overfishing. Because the common property feature was seen as the main culprit, the economic prescription for curing this problem was through sole ownership [Scott 1955] since the sole owner would be able to control effort at economically desirable levels. Sole ownership rights could be exercised by the state. This economic solution has been neither easy to accept, nor apply in either national or international fisheries. Fortunately in Canada, a conjuncture of favorable circumstances made limited entry possible.

As pointed out earlier, prior to the mid-1970s fisheries management in Canada was primarily concerned with biological conservation of resources. The exception to this was on the Pacific coast, where a license limitation was instituted in 1969 for the salmon fishery which had both biological and economic objectives [Pearse and Wilen 1979]. However, on the Atlantic coast overexploitation of the abundant fisheries resources of the northwest Atlantic became evident in the early 1970s when increased international effort resulted in declining landings. ICNAF began to increase its quota controls (first introduced in 1969) in number and stringency. Canada, having the biggest stake in the fisheries directly off her coast, was particularly hard hit by reduced quotas since her industry had expanded its fleet and plant capacity considerably during the 1960s. As a result of the imbalance between resource availability and existing capacity, an economic crisis exacerbated by inflationary pressures and the oil crisis began to develop in the industry by 1974. The Minister at the time, Jack Davis, introduced a vessel licensing policy in 1974 whereby a moratorium was declared on the number of vessels in an attempt to bring fishing capability more in line with resource availability.

Despite this measure, economic conditions worsened. Government finally had to assist the industry through a temporary assistance program (TAP), which provided financial assistance at both the primary and secondary levels. This program was preceded by extensive economic studies on the state of the industry which advocated certain economic presciptions. The most significant aspect of the crisis, however, was that government, after expending considerable sums of money, became committed to the economic viability of the industry over the longer term. This commitment which necessitated the articulation of the "best use" management principle in 1976 could only imply an increased role for fisheries economics in management. It was just in time for the establishment of the 200-mile limit which gave Canada the necessary control for more effective management.

With the 200-mile limit, limited entry became a fact of life in Canada's fisheries. License limitation was applied in most fisheries, certainly the important ones, in both the Atlantic and Pacific. The only major exception for some years was the inshore groundfish fisheries on the Atlantic coast where the majority of fishermen operate. However, even in this fishery, free entry is now possible only in the northeast coast of Newfoundland, where because of northern cod, resource availability is not considered a problem.

In Canada, it has been demonstrated that in just about every fishery where license limitation or control has been exercised (i.e., the offshore scallop, lobster, crab and shrimp fisheries on the Atlantic coast) economic benefits have followed. With increasing resource availability, the offshore groundfish fishery too should also be a profitable one. On the Pacific coast license limitation increased incomes and returns in the salmon and herring fisheries but there were serious problems despite this measure. The Pacific coast experience is extremely important, however, because it is indicative of the problems which can emanate from limited entry.

Problems of Limited Entry: The Sinclair Report

Sinclair examined the economic and managerial problems of the British Columbia fisheries. He concluded that the limited entry program introduced in 1969 in the salmon fishery: (1) did not reduce fishing effort or catching power; (2) did not reduce excess capitalization; (3) increased incomes somewhat, but rising prices played a significant role here; and (4) permitted government to attain only a minimal amount of rent through license fees. In the herring fishery the same findings were pertinent. Here, a high license fee did not result in reducing effort, which had in fact increased. For the other fisheries, not subject to license limitation or effective entry control measures, economic returns were adversely affected by their absence, and Canadians on the whole did not get returns from them in the form of rent. In short, Sinclair indicated that license limitation alone is an inadequate tool to achieve the economic optimum or "best use" of fisheries resources. However, he stressed that every fishery should be under effort control. In other words, this is a necessary, although not sufficient condition for viable fisheries.

To correct the problems identified above, the report recommended:

1. that entry to all fisheries be limited; and
2. that over-capitalization be controlled by (1) increased fishing vessel license fees, (2) implementation of a royalty on landings, and (3) implementing a buy-back program to reduce total fleet size.[4]

The Department of Fisheries and Oceans is still wrestling with Sinclair's proposals, hence we shall come back to them in the section on new approaches. However, it marks a milestone in the approach to Canadian fisheries management. Another new concept to fisheries, that of cost recovery, was also introduced on the Pacific coast.

Cost Recovery

The Salmon Enhancement Program on the Pacific coast is a major program which endeavors to about double the production or landings of salmon by the 1990s. To do so, an extensive enhancement program was devised which involves considerable government funds over the period. To justify the program, the Treasury Board demanded a benefit-cost analysis, plus a commitment to cost recovery from the major beneficiaries, the fishermen [Pepper 1979]. Although the cost recovery mechanism has still not been introduced, the acceptance by government of the principle of cost recovery for programs such as these, has to be considered another example of the application of economic analysis and its tools in fisheries management.

NEW APPROACHES TO FISHERIES ECONOMICS

The role of economics in fisheries management depends to a great extent on its success in (1) improving management measures, (2) increasing efficiency in the industry, and (3) satisfying the needs of fishermen and the general public. It is doubtful if all three of these can be accomplished simultaneously. However, there are important lessons to be learned from the Canadian experience.

The Canadian experience has shown that license limitation by itself does not solve all the problems from an economic efficiency standpoint. The destructive competitive tendencies which are an unavoidable consequence of fish stocks being treated as common property remain, in that ways and means will be found to circumvent the limitation by number and even by size of vessels through the use of more capital-intensive methods. In other words, with license limitation alone, the tendency for the dissipation of these rents remains with all its implication for economic efficiency.

Another problem which has emerged from license limitation is that fishermen who are most vociferous against its introduction become firm adherents of it once its economic effects become apparent. License limitation has created many wealthy fishermen in some fisheries since the rents accrue to them because of low and nominal license fees. They are anxious to keep it that way by excluding or making it difficult for new entrants. Yet, decisions may have to be made about either (1) capturing some of the rents or (2) allowing new entrants into the fishery.

The major problems, after the imposition of license control, pertain to: (1) allocating and distribution of fisheries resources between fleet segments; and (2) bringing about a more efficient combination of factor inputs in the various fisheries. In short, fisheries economics has to be more concerned with *equity* and *efficiency*. As mentioned earlier, Sinclair [1979] urged (1) higher license fees, and (2) the introduction of royalties or landings charges. To these can be added (3) the introduction of property or usufructuary rights through enterprise quotas. Short comments will be made of the last two measures which are certainly the most interesting from the standpoint of fisheries economics.

Introduction of Royalties or Landings Charges

The royalty or landing charge approach is considered by Sinclair [1979] as one which would (1) act as a governor of the rate of growth of fishing effort and would reduce the incentive for over-capitalization; and (2) act as a means of increasing government revenues by recovering resource rent thereby providing payment to the owners of the resource, the people of Canada. Depending on the elasticity of fishing effort, a royalty may not be effective as an effort control measure. For example, McGaw [1979] showed that for a lucrative fishery such as the offshore scallop fishery, the royalty would have to be so high to control effort that it would not be politically feasible to apply. However, this measure could be effective in controlling effort and dampening overcapitalization in less lucrative fisheries.

The main purpose of a royalty, however, could be to capture resource rent. In the number of Canadian fisheries now enjoying considerable rents as a result of license limitation, decisions will have to be made as to whether these should be captured by or shared with government or whether they should be distributed more widely by allowing more fishermen in. Certainly on the Atlantic coast, because of the regional unemployment situation there, to increase employment might hold sway over the generation of revenues for government.

Although the royalty is a much debated measure in Canada, there is no doubt it is a powerful economic management tool. As such, it cannot be ignored for long, especially if problems of the surplus and inefficient use of capital persist. Another powerful tool, considered by some economists as the best solution yet to the problems of fisheries exploitation, is the establishment of property or usufructuary rights.

Establishment of Property Rights

Since common property is one of the major obstacles to economically inefficient fisheries exploitation an interest is now developing in academia [Moloney and Pearse 1979] and in government [Grinnell 1978, 1980; Department of Fisheries and Oceans 1979] circles in establishing individual vessel or enterprise quotas as a means of correcting for it. The economic rationale advanced is that this would permit fishermen to make rational decisions of how best to take their quotas in much the same way the farmer determines the best combination of labor and capital to exploit his land. Individual vessel or enterprise quotas have many advantages from a management standpoint. These are as follows:

1. They are a means of ensuring that catches remain within biologically acceptable levels.
2. They provide operational flexibility to fishermen since they determine the best way to catch their quota—in this "milieu" over-capitalization will be soon rationalized.
3. They can be marketable, thereby providing an endowment to fishermen if and when they decide to withdraw from the fishery.
4. They are a means of collecting management fees.

An individual vessel and enterprise quota system, accompanied by a free market for these quotas, once established can be a strong self-regulatory mechanism for fisheries exploitation [Mitchell 1980] and hold the greatest promise for achieving economic efficiency in fisheries. They have, without the free market or transferability aspect, already proved their worth in Canada in the Bay of Fundy herring fishery. It is not possible to go into detail about this experience except to say that it proved that individual vessel quotas can be administratively feasible, acceptable and popular with fishermen, achieve greater efficiency in production, and bring about a more equitable distribution of incomes and returns.

CONCLUSION

Economic analysis has been playing an increasing role in Canadian fisheries management. This is because fisheries problems although due to biological factors are largely socioeconomic in nature. As a result, biological measures alone are incapable of solving them and it is now recognized that a bioeconomic approach is necessary for fisheries management. The job of fisheries management can be put in the following manner: to maximize socioeconomic returns to society subject to both biological (the resource) and economic constraints (labor and capital). This is consistent with the "best use" principle, the management principle for Canada [Mitchell 1979].

The contribution of economic analysis to fisheries management has been in (1) introducing license limitation as a means of controlling fishing effort, and (2) having the principle of cost recovery accepted. License limitation, however, despite proving its capability of increasing incomes and returns, has brought to the fore new problems. These are associated with concerns about allocation, economic efficiency, equity, distribution and public revenue generation. New measures are being advocated to increase efficiency and public revenues through taxation, and by the introduction of property rights through individual vessel or enterprise quotas. The success of the latter in the Bay of Fundy herring fishery augurs well for its introduction in other fisheries.

DISCLAIMER

The ideas expressed do not express the views of the Department of Fisheries and Oceans, but only those of the author. He would like to acknowledge helpful comments and criticisms from T. Peart, H. R. Grinnell and W. C. MacKenzie.

NOTES

[1]For example, because the Pacific coast fishery is situated in British Columbia, a province which has been experiencing steady growth with increasing employment opportunities, there is a difference in approach to fisheries management there than on the Atlantic coast, where most of the provinces are "have nots" with higher levels of unemployment than the Canadian average.

[2]As a result, Canada now has the management responsibility to (1) establish overall quotas (TAC) for this area; (2) allocate these between the Canadian fleet, based on its catching capacity and needs of its coastal community, with surpluses allocated to foreign fleets; and (3) collect revenues from these fleets.

[3]In fact, on the Atlantic coast low incomes to the majority of fishermen have been the major problem, whereas on the Pacific coast excess capital or "capital stuffing" in vessels and boats has been more problematic.

[4]Sinclair indicated the nontransferability can no longer be used to accomplish that end. Transferability, and the attendant major investment related to license value, is now firmly entrenched in the salmon industry.

REFERENCES

1. Department of Fisheries and Oceans. 1979. "Canada's East Fleet Development to 1985," Ottawa, Ontario (unpublished).

2. Department of Fisheries and Oceans. 1980. "Annual Statistical Review of Canadian Fisheries," Ottawa, Ontario.
3. Environment Canada. 1976. "Policy for Canada's Commercial Fisheries," Ottawa, Ontario.
4. Gordon, H. S. 1953. "An Economic Approach to the Optimum Utilization of Fishery Resources," *J. Fish. Res. Board Can.* Vol. 10.
5. Grinnell, H.R. 1978. "A New Approach to Allocating Fisheries Resources," Department of Fisheries and Oceans, Ottawa, Ontario.
6. Grinnell, H. R. 1980. "Resource Supply Allocation: An Examination of a New System of Fisheries Management Involving Transferable Enterprise Quotas and Open Access Buffer Supplies," Department of Fisheries and Oceans, Ottawa, Ontario.
7. McGaw, R. L. 1979. "Bioeconomic Models of the Georges Bank Scallop Fishery," Department of Fisheries and Oceans, Ottawa, Ontario.
8. Mitchell, C. L. 1979. "Bio-economics of Commercial Fisheries Management," *J. Fish. Res. Board Can.* 36(6).
9. Mitchell, C. L. 1980a. "Towards a Self-Regulatory Strategy for Fisheries Development: Canada's Atlantic Coast Fisheries," paper presented at the Atlantic Canadian Economics Association Conference, Acadia University, Nova Scotia.
10. Mitchell, C. L. 1980b. "Canada's Fishing Industry: A Sectoral Analysis," Department of Fisheries and Oceans, Ottawa, Ontario.
11. Moloney, D. G., and P. H. Pearse. 1979. "Quantitative Rights as an Instrument for Regulating Commercial Fisheries," *J. Fish. Res. Board Can.* Vol. 36.
12. Pearse, P. H., and J. E. Wilen. 1979. "Impact of Canada's Pacific Salmon Fleet Control Program," *J. Fish. Res. Board Can.* Vol. 36.
13. Pepper, D. A. 1979. "Public Expenditure and Cost-Recovery in Fisheries: Modelling the B.C. Salmon Industry for Policy Analysis and Government Investment Decisions," paper presented at the NATO symposium on Applied Operations Research in Fisheries, Trondheim, Norway.
14. Scott, A. D. 1955. "The Fishery, the Objectives of Sole Ownership," *J. Polit. Econ.* Vol. 63.
15. Sinclair, S. 1979. "A Licensing and Fee System for the Coastal Fisheries of British Columbia," Department of Fisheries and Oceans, Vancouver, BC.

COMMENT–CHAPTER 8

Fred L. Olson

National Marine Fisheries Service
International Fisheries Development
and Services Division

Mitchell has presented an excellent overview of economics and Canadian fisheries management, where he defined resource management and fisheries development as the major management issues. He defines resource management as controlling and allocating exploitation so as to protect stocks and not adversely affect economic returns and defines fisheries development as bringing about growth and development.

Historically, Canada has taken a regulated approach in its Pacific fisheries and a free entry approach in its Atlantic fisheries with different problems arising because of its different approaches.

The last two sections of Mitchell's paper are the most interesting. He states that the introduction of limited entry and the acceptance of cost recovery for enhancement are direct contributions of economics to Canadian fisheries management. This is interesting because over a decade ago in the Bureau of Commercial Fisheries (predecessor to the National Marine Fisheries Service) the term "limited entry" could not be discussed above the level of a whisper in staff meetings even though economists were present for nearly 10 years. The United States still does not accept the principle of cost recovery for essentially enhancement programs because Congress does not allow the charging of domestic fees except to recover the administrative costs of issuing permits. However, the United States should also seriously consider the cost recovery mechanism of the U.S. salmon enhancement program.

It is important to emphasize that the Sinclair report on limited entry stressed that limited entry is a necessary, though not sufficient, condition for viable fisheries. The report also recommended that overcapitalization be controlled by increased fishing vessel license fees, a royalty on landings and a buy-back program since transferability is firmly entrenched in the salmon industry. The concept of a royalty on landings is a very useful one from the fishermen's point of view because it reduces their financial risks and cash flow problems— they have no financial obligations until they have production.

The establishment of property rights, which recently has been done in the Bay of Fundy herring fishery with individual vessel or enterprise quotas, raises more issues. Mitchell indicates that the individual vessel or enterprise quotas are administratively feasible, acceptable and popular, cause greater efficiency, and bring about a more equitable distribution of incomes and returns. I find no problem with the first two—administratively feasible, acceptable and popular. The advantage of greater efficiency needs to be made in relation to an alternative institution. There would be greater efficiency relative to no limited entry but compared to vessel or effort control there is no clear indication of greater efficiency.

If there were greater efficiency, the issue then becomes who benefits from the greater efficiency. The consumer does not benefit because there is no additional production. With the same production, producer and consumer prices remain the same. With greater efficiency, however, the costs of production are lower and therefore the producer or fishermen benefit. If these quotas are marketable, the current generation of fishermen reap the present value of all future benefits that would accrue to all future generations of fishermen in this fishery. While it would improve the current fishermen's incomes compared with nonfishermen, there is no indication of a better distribution of income among fishermen of the same generation, or that improving the income of current fishermen at the expense of future generations of fishermen is an overall improvement for society.

Ten years from now we could have a Sinclair report finding the same problems as he found in the Pacific fisheries. Time will tell whether the introduction of property rights through individual vessel or enterprise quotas are successful in the Bay of Fundy herring fishery. The problem in the Pacific fishery was not limited effort but the establishment of transferable property rights in the licensing scheme of limited entry. In the Bay of Fundy, Canada is again establishing a transferable property right, only this time by an individual vessel or enterprise quota. In both fisheries a nontransferable system could have been established that would have eliminated the problems identified in the Pacific fishery, and that I predict will arise in the Bay of Fundy herring fishery.

CHAPTER 9

IMPLEMENTING MULTIOBJECTIVE MANAGEMENT OF COMMERCIAL FISHERIES: A STRATEGY FOR POLICY-RELEVANT RESEARCH

Richard C. Bishop

Department of Agricultural Economics
University of Wisconsin

Daniel W. Bromley

Department of Agricultural Economics
University of Wisconsin

Steve Langdon

Department of Anthropology
University of Alaska

The Fishery Conservation and Management Act (FCMA) of 1976 established a number of regional councils whose general charge is to formulate fishery management plans in recognition of the many disparate objectives which bear on collective action taken in the fisheries. Several conditions preceded the act which made improved management of utmost concern. Among these were: (1) declining physical productivity in many fisheries; (2) increasing recognition of the economic, social and biological implications of open access; (3) the persistence of low incomes in some fisheries; (4) expanded efforts to increase high-protein food supplies; and (5) continued heavy fishing by foreign fleets in certain areas considered "ours."

The composition of the councils has virtually assured the formulation of management plans based on a set of criteria that goes beyond simplistic motions of maximum sustainable yield (MSY) and maximum economic yield

(MEY). Indeed, broader considerations are called for in the act—with economic wellbeing of both commercial and recreational fishermen, as well as the local and regional economies receiving prominent mention.

We have argued elsewhere—on theoretical as well as practical grounds—that multiobjective evaluation of fishery management plans is called for [Bishop 1973, 1975; Bromley and Bishop 1977; Bromley 1977]. Those arguments will only be mentioned briefly here. Instead, the actual issues surrounding transfer of entry permits in the Alaskan salmon and herring fisheries will be used to illustrate the noncomplementary objectives among the various interest groups that impinge on fishery policy. While the Alaskan situation is rather unique, we consider it indicative of the larger problems of fisheries management in general.

One might enquire as to why there is such a dearth of applications of multiobjective analysis to fisheries decisions, but such a query would take us beyond the scope of this chapter. Whatever the reasons, it is surely not because there are no models on which to draw. Indeed, the literature on decision analysis is growing at a rapid pace. But there have been no applications to fishery management problems that we can find. Hence, our primary purpose here is to illustrate how one would undertake such a study in the Alaskan setting.

The chapter will proceed in the following manner. We will discuss the problems of fishery management from the broader social perspective. Following that, we will look at fishery management as a scientific problem. Next, we will introduce a research strategy employing multiobjective decision analysis. This section will present both the conceptually ideal approach to decision analysis using multiobjective techniques, as well as a more operational approach which could be implemented in most fishery settings. Then, we will offer a brief discussion of several applications of multiobjective decision models in other problem settings. This treatment is intended to illustrate the practical applicability of such models. We will conclude with some general statements concerning public choice in the face of conflicting objectives.

THE SOCIAL PROBLEM

Current public policy issues involving the Alaska limited-entry program vividly illustrate the need for a multiobjective decision framework. In 1973, the Alaska legislature passed AS 16.43 which authorized limited entry into the commercial fisheries under its jurisdiction. This bill, and a state constitutional amendment which preceded it, laid the groundwork for a radical departure from the traditional system of open-access fishing. Under open access any Alaskan or citizen of another state could fish in Alaskan waters provided only that he or she could muster the capital and know-how to do so.

The goal of AS 16.43 is "to promote the conservation and sustained yield management of Alaska's fishery resource and the economic health and stability of commercial fishing in Alaska by regulating and controlling entry into commercial fisheries in the public interest and without unjust discrimination." The Alaska Commercial Fisheries Entry Commission was empowered to designate limited entry fisheries where only those holding entry permits could fish.[1]

The first major fisheries to come under limited entry were those for salmon and herring. Beginning in 1975, permits were issued for all types of commercial salmon fishing except unpowered trolling. All permits relate to specific gear types including power trolling, drift gill nets, set gill nets, purse seines, beach seines and fishwheels. These entry permits are only valid for one of 14 regions stretching from southeastern Alaska to the upper Yukon region, except for power trolling permits, which apply statewide. Based on historical participation and economic dependence on fishing, 9861 permanent salmon fishing permits have been issued [Langdon 1980]. An additional 450 permanent permits for herring have been issued, and the state has recently decided to extend limited entry to unpowered salmon trolling. Limited entry may soon be instituted in several other fisheries as well.

Given the economic importance of fishing in general and salmon fishing in particular throughout Alaska,[2] it is not surprising that the limited-entry program has been controversial. Numerous court battles have been and continue to be waged. A referendum to abolish limited entry was voted on in 1976. Still, the program has survived, and is well entrenched socially and politically, although it is still not totally free from judicial and legislative battles. Any basic policy change leaves numerous smaller issues to be resolved, and limited entry in Alaska is no exception. Such issues can be very important to some communities and certain segments of the population. One such issue in Alaska relates to the process by which some fishermen exit and others enter the salmon and herring fisheries. Under the current system, an exiting fisherman can transfer his/her permit to another who can display "present ability to participate actively in the fishery." The only other qualifications established by the state are that the transferee not be a corporation and not already hold a permit in that particular fishery. Interestingly, the market for permits has been a brisk one. Since 1975-1976 when most of them were issued, 36.5% of all the salmon permits have been transferred at least once [Langdon 1980]. All of these transfers have been between individuals, since Alaska currently does not have a "buy back" program. Furthermore, in many cases, the amount of money involved has been substantial. Transactions with tens of thousands of dollars changing hands are common, and instances where individual permits sold for over $100,000 have occurred. Some Alaskans are now asking whether this is a desirable state of affairs. Is it fair that initial participants who obtained free permits to use a public resource should now be receiving windfall gains at the expense of new entrants? Will open-market transfer of permits lead to increases in nonresident participation at the expense of Alaska residents? If so, what will be the effects on income and employment in Alaska? Are younger people going to find it difficult to get into fishing because of large capital requirements for entry permits as well as vessel, gear and shore facilities? Will free transfer of permits lead to erosion of the economic base of rural coastal communities? How will emerging transfer patterns affect other fisheries? Will excluded fishermen create problems in unrestricted fisheries?

Langdon [1980] has recently completed a study of transfers of salmon per-permits. Statewide there has been a slight *increase* in the number of resident permittees relative to nonresidents. However, a detailed analysis of transfer patterns showed that nonresidents have increased their share of the permits in the more productive fisheries so that their share of the net profits from salmon fishing has increased slightly. Much more striking, however, has been the transfer patterns among Alaska residents. To quote Langdon (p. 28), "There has been a clear and escalating trend since 1976 for rural residents to lose permits, particularly rural locals. There is likewise a clear and escalating trend for urban nonlocals to gain permits." He estimated that Alaskan rural locals earned $2 million (7.7%) less in annual earnings than they would have earned if the allocation of permits among groups had been constant since 1976. This trend appears to be closely related to poor access to capital markets among rural residents.

Further support for the conclusion that limited entry may be leading to adverse impacts on rural communities comes from Koslow's [1979] study of the Bristol Bay salmon fisheries. According to this study, local residents believe that they were unjustly treated in the initial allocation of permits. Poor fishing during the years just prior to permit issuance led many traditional fishermen to seek alternative employment, yet participation during those years was an important part of the criteria for receiving an initial permit. Now access to permits requires substantial capital which is often difficult to obtain. Thus, about 40% of local residents (who are largely native Alaskans) believe that their incomes are substantially below levels that could have been attained without limited entry. Koslow concluded: "The present limited entry policy is seriously limiting access for many Bristol Bay residents to the area's primary economic resource. This unintended consequence of present policy has serious implications to already-marginal village economies" (p. iv).

Beyond the evolving impacts of market transfers on the economic well being of rural communities, some find it objectionable that many initial participants have received (or will receive) windfall gains; future rents are being capitalized into permit values. This means that later entrants will have to pay the present values of future resource rents to exiting fishermen. One view is that more of these rents should go to the state since the resource is public property. Others argue that more of the rent should go to those who actually catch the fish rather than being committed to paying off the former owners of the permits. Furthermore, economic power of processors over individual fishermen has been considered a serious problem for many years. There is some concern that additional capital requirements associated with entry permits may give processors an additional source of leverage to exploit individual fishermen. Langdon [1980] surveyed various possible sources of finance for permit purchase. Processors financed 13% of the loans that were reported in the survey responses, and Langdon suspects that the actual percentage is much higher since the processor response rate was relatively low compared to banks and credit associations.

Still another dimension of the problem may develop in the Alaska Supreme Court. While the court upheld the limited-entry legislation in the particular case of interest here, Senior Justice Dimond used the case to voice concerns about the transferability provision. First, transferability was leading to exclusion of the poor from access to a public resource in favor of the well-to-do, a situation that the justice viewed as discriminatory. Secondly, while hardship was considered in the initial allocation of the permits, it is not considered in transferring them. Again, unjust discrimination may be present. These two points raise the possibility that the entire limited-entry program could be struck down because of the transfer mechanism.

But what should be done about these problems? Several alternatives have been suggested. One approach would be to make permits nontransferable. An apprenticeship program could be initiated, and when a fisherman exits the permit could be reallocated to a person who has fulfilled the apprenticeship requirements. If there were more qualified applicants than availalbe permits, a first-come-first-served system or lottery could be instituted. Another approach would be to maintain transferability through the market but also initiate a special subsidized loan program for rural Alaskans. In a broader context, those who believe that initial participants are making unfair gains at the expense of new entrants are suggesting that stiff taxes be levied on permits at the time of transfer, or that the state set permit prices based on earnings potential.

From the foregoing, it is clear that Alaska confronts a multiobjective decision problem. The system by which entry permits are transferred may affect: (1) the distribution of resource rents among various groups within the fisheries and between individuals and the state; (2) the economic viability of coastal communities; (3) the status of fish stocks and hence fishermen outside the limited entry fisheries; (4) the degree of dependence of fishermen on processors; and (5) other economic and social parameters which impinge on the achievement of many social objectives. This, then, brings us to the scientific problem: no multiobjective decision framework has yet been developed to deal with such fishery management problems.

THE SCIENTIFIC PROBLEM

The first scientists to take an interest in fisheries management were mostly biologists. The problem of yields from several fisheries falling far below historical levels became a matter of some concern during the first half of the twentieth century. The biologists who responded naturally thought in terms of restoring biological productivity to former levels. Certainly, they would admit that society might have other goals with regard to fishery management, but their thinking was heavily oriented toward a single goal: maximization of the sustained output of fish (MSY).

Economists did not enter the fisheries policy arena in significant numbers until the early 1950s. The seminal article by Gordon [1954] focused on the fishery as a "common property" resource. After 25 years a large literature has accumulated on this topic.[3] The central argument is that, like any other scarce natural resource, a valuable but limited fish population is capable of earning a rent. This scarcity rent, when maximized in present value terms, indicates that an economically efficient amount of capital and labor is being allocated to fishing compared to other economic activities. However, fisheries have traditionally been managed as open-access resources, meaning that a large number of potential fishermen can enter and fish as much as they want without any restrictions. Thus, if existing fishermen are earning any scarcity rents, this will only serve to encourage them to expand their level of fishing to capture a larger share of the rents. Furthermore, others who have not previously participated in the fishery in question will notice that extra money can be made there and will be enticed to enter. The result is that fishing effort will tend to expand until all rents disappear. Rent dissipation signals that excess capital and labor have been allocated to fishing compared to other pursuits. In other words, the efficiency of the economy could be improved by reallocating labor and capital to other sectors of the economy. Open access may also have dire impacts on the fishery resource itself since excess labor and capital may lead to over exploitation in a fashion described by Hardin [1968] as "the tragedy of the commons."

Interestingly, from the economist's point of view, traditional biological approaches to fishery management only tend to exacerbate economic inefficiency. If, for example, a closed season is implemented, the fishermen will tend to allocate even more capital and labor to fishing in order to catch as large a share of the total harvest as possible before the season closes. As all fishermen follow this course, the fishery may become even more inefficient than it was prior to management. Thus the economists suggested that the biologist's goal of maximum sustainable yield be replaced with the single objective of maximum economic efficiency.

To achieve this economic goal, economists devised the idea of limiting entry. Limited entry is any form of fishery regulation which will improve economic efficiency by restricting capital and labor in fishing compared to a regime of open access. Alaska's current permit system exemplifies one form of limited entry. Other approaches include taxes on catch or inputs to discourage excessive fishing and the assignment of annual or permanent catch quotas to a fixed number of individual fishermen. Under the latter system each fisherman would have an economic incentive to minimize the cost of capital and labor used in catching the quota, thus helping to achieve economic efficiency.

Limited entry management has been advocated in several studies of actual fisheries, including a widely cited study of the Pacific salmon fisheries by Crutchfield and Pontecorvo [1960]. They estimated that a limited entry program could eliminate excess capacity while maintaining the annual catch and save $50 million annually, with 40% of this total attributable to Alaska alone.

The heavy emphasis on the efficiency goal in most of the economics literature has been challenged by both economists [Arnold and Bromley 1970; Ciriacy-Wantrup 1971; Bishop 1973, 1975; Bromley and Bishop 1977; Bromley 1977] and by other social scientists [Orbach 1978; Cicin-Sain 1978; Langdon 1978]. Usually, these criticisms of the standard economic approach have not been opposed to limited entry per se. Rather, the concern has been that efficiency is not the only social goal in fishery management and may be less important than other social goals. A given limited entry program may be desirable or undesirable depending on how its specific provisions affect various fishermen and consumer groups. Alternative fishery management proposals, including various possible limited entry schemes, should be considered in a framework including multiobjectives.

Having said this, however, it is also noteworthy that little has been done to develop such a framework. While a number of additional possible social goals have been mentioned in the writings of those who criticize the single-objective approach, integrated multiobjective decision-making techniques have not been applied to fisheries management issues. Furthermore, a wealth of material exists to draw on in this regard. The techniques now available for the solution of multiobjective problems include goal programming, conjunctive and disjunctive constraint methods, the lexicographic approach, constrainted optimization, and the surrogate-worth approach [Keeney and Raiffa 1976; Bell et al. 1977; Sfeir-Younis and Bromley 1977; McKenna 1980].[4]

The nature of the choice problem in the Alaskan fisheries is such that the preferences of the various interest groups must be given effect. While the concept of a "decision-maker" is to be applied rather generally, it is a fact that the preferences of interested parties will be weighed in the political process.

The approach to be suggested here will formalize the process of integrating these preferences. This requirement implies, therefore, that one of the approaches which relies on prior preference specification be utilized. Hence, it will be necessary to choose from among: (1) constrained optimization; (2) goal programming; and (3) utility function analysis.

Constrained optimization allows one to maximize a single-attribute objective function. One overriding objective is agreed upon, and maximized subject to the attainment of the others as constraints. Because there is no dominant objective in the Alaskan situation, this approach is less relevant here.

Goal programming is a possible candidate, and in fact has been applied to a wide variety of multiobjective choice problems [Sfeir-Younis and Bromley 1977]. Here, the problem is to select that feasible activity (or vector of feasible activities) which minimizes the weighted deviation from the decision-makers' prespecified targets (goals). After the appropriate framework is specified, the decision-maker(s) must specify the target levels for an ideal outcome. Then, linear weights are attached to the positive and negative deviations from these targets. The solution involves selecting the activities which minimize this weighted sum of the deviations. Goal programming is useful under a rather restricted set of assumptions, and where the decision-maker is able to develop a reasonable set of target attributes. For fisheries decision problems it is hypothesized that goal programming will be less useful than utility function analysis. When there are no targets other than the highest possible level of the various objectives, goal programming degenerates into linear additive multiattribute utility analysis.

Fishery management problems such as those in the Alaskan salmon fisheries involve the selection of a subset of a larger set of activities, where those activities are alternative ways to enhance fisheries objectives. When the possible activities are *interdependent*, then we have a situation which involves *portfolio analysis*. When portfolio analysis is carried out with multiobjectives, we have a problem in *portfolio multiattribute utility analysis*. This is the approach which we advocate for the Alaskan entry-permit transfer problem.[5] The difference between a portfolio problem and a simple multiattribute problem can be illustrated with reference to meal choice from a three-part menu. Imagine a menu containing four selections each of: (1) appetizers; (2) entrees; and (3) desserts. A child would likely make independent choices from the three categories, treating each subsequent choice as an independent of the previous choice. A gourmet, on the other hand, could be expected to recognize the interdependence of the choices, and to select the combination (portfolio) which maximizes utility. For the gourmet, this interdependence means that there are really 64 possible meals (portfolios). Similarly a portfolio concept is needed for the Alaskan problem because of the interrelatedness of the choice. For example, an apprenticeship requirement might well affect the cost of, need for, and impact of a subsidized loan program.

We now turn to a detailed research strategy which would involve the appli-cation of portfolio multiattribute utility analysis to the Alaskan problem.

A MULTIOBJECTIVE FISHERY MANAGEMENT STUDY

Application of multiattribute utility analysis to a fishery management prob-lem would follow five steps: (1) choosing objectives and attributes; (2) defining activities and alternatives; (3) developing a decision matrix; (4) holding a multiobjective decision workshop; and (5) optimizing the system. The Alaskan situation will illustrate how each step might be accomplished.

Choosing Objectives and Attributes

At the broadest level the goal of public policy in our case study might be described as simply to improve the Alaska fisheries. The goal stands at the top of the pyramid in Figure 1. At the next lower level, more specific "objectives" have been defined. The purpose of objectives is to specify the various dimen-sions of the broader goal without attempting yet to specify how attainment might be measured.

Our tentative list of objectives in Figure 1 is an attempt to capture the objec-tives of the various groups that are concerned about entry permit transfers. For example, the objective "equitable distribution of rents" is designed to represent concerns about windfall gains to current permittees *and* concerns of current permittees about the value of their permits as assets. Particularly for the person who has recently paid tens of thousands of dollars for a permit, the prospect that the state might suddenly declare them nontransferable is a threat; and this aspect (among many others) needs to be considered in the de-cision process. In the case of "orderly entry and exit," one fact of economic life is that over time some people will want to leave particular fisheries; and others may want to enter. A system of transfer, which, for instance, encourages people to hold permits they are not using would thwart this objective. Similar remarks could be made about the other objectives shown in the figure.

The tentativeness of this list also deserves emphasis. One important early step would be to refine it. Personal interviews with leaders of both resident and nonresident fishermen's organizations, federal and state officials, representa-tives of native Alaskan organizations, and other people would serve as a basis for adding objectives to the list and eliminating those that seem to be unim-portant. In addition, these personal interviews would gather information to help define alternatives and activities (step 2), discover sources of data for the decision matrix (step 3) and choose participants for the workshop (step 4). Once the list of objectives has been finalized, the attributes must be designed. Here the challenge is to define quantifiable variables that express the degree

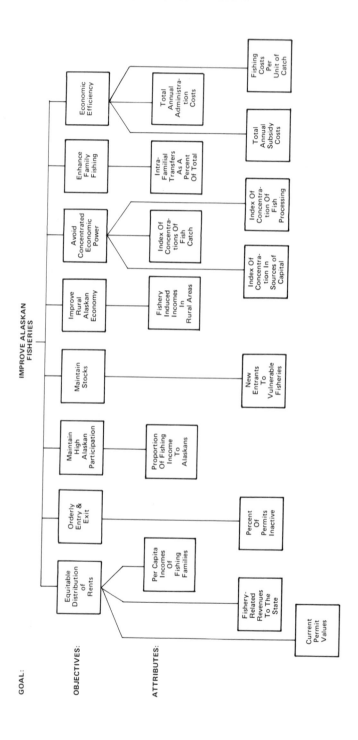

Figure 1.   Goal, objectives and attributes for Alaskan fisheries.

to which each objective would be achieved. While some attributes might involve monetary measures, examination of Figure 1 will illustrate that nonmonetary measures are also important.

At this point, we can begin to state the multiattribute utility model in more formal terms. The end result of the first step would be a set of quantifiable attributes, X. Let x_j symbolize the level of attainment of the jth attribute within that set, $j = 1, 2, \ldots, m$. For example, from Figure 1, x_1 could be the market value of all permits, x_4, the percentage of permits inactive, and so on.

Definition of Activities and Alternatives

Activities are individual programs or policies, while alternative "portfolios" are comprised of various combinations of activities. A list of activities for the case in point includes:

1. establish low interest loans to fishermen;
2. fund apprenticeship program;
3. place tax on permits at time of transfer;
4. make permits nontransferable;
5. set annual renewal fee for permits;
6. establish annual auctions for individual harvest quotas similar to public timber sales;
7. establish permit buy-back program;
8. limit entry to substitute fisheries;
9. establish program of loans to rural coastal businesses; and
10. fund rural development grants to communities.

A portfolio could include any compatible combination of these activities. The goal of the study would be to establish an "optimal" portfolio (step 5).

In formal terms, let A equal the set of activities, with A_i symbolizing individual activities, $i = 1, 2, \ldots, m$. From the above list, A_1 might be establishment of a low interest loan program. Units to measure the extent of each activity would have to be carefully defined. For example, $A_1 = 1$ might symbolize a $1 million loan program, $A_1 = 2$, a $2 million program, and so on. In special cases, activities may be more appropriately described in binary terms. If A_4 is "make permits nontransferable," then it could take on values of unity and zero only. Portfolios are then simply vectors of activity levels, $A^k = (A_1^k, A_2^k, \ldots, A_m^k)$, where A_i^k is the level of the ith activity in the kth portfolio. The incompatability of activities (e.g., establishment of low interest loans would be useless if permits are made nontransferable) would be built into the model through formal constraints.

Develop Decision Matrix

The contribution of a unit of activity A_i to an attribute X_j is denoted by x_{ij} for all $i = 1, \ldots, m$, and for all $j = 1, \ldots, n$. The resulting m x n matrix will be termed the "decision matrix" since it displays the implications of choosing a unit of each possible activity for the attainment of each attribute. For the kth portfolio, the level of attainment of the jth attribute is given by x_j^k, where

$$x_j^k = \sum_{i=1}^{m} A_i^k \, x_{ij}$$

For such a portfolio, a vector of consequences, $x^k = (x_1^k, x_2^k, \ldots, x_n^k)$, can be found by the matrix multiplication

$$x^k = A^k \, [x_{ij}]$$

where $[x_{ij}]$ symbolizes the decision matrix.

Data for the matrix could be drawn from a number of sources. For instance, in the Alaska case, much of the data on permit ownership, recent transfer patterns, sources of finance for permit purchases, and the like from the Langdon [1980] study could be used. Basic data on the role of fishing in Alaskan regional economies has been accumulated by Rogers and Kreinheder [1980]. Additional secondary data sources could include the organizations and agencies contacted during the interview process described above. For example, the costs of administering a subsidized loan program would have to be estimated. Here, experience with Alaska's vessel loan program, which is administered by State Division of Business Loans, would be useful.

The principal primary data source could be a random sample of, say, 1000 commercial salmon fishermen to be surveyed by mail. The survey could be designed to provide data to fill cells in the matrix. Some examples will illustrate. One objective (Figure 1) relates to the effects of alternative policies on continuity of family fishing operations between generations. Langdon [1980] has determined that since 1976, 23.2% of all transfers have been between people with the same last name. The mail survey can help determine how many intrafamilial transfers are likely to occur under alternative systems. Another tentative objective is to maintain a wide dispersion of economic power. In a random sample of 1000 permittees there should be at least 300 individuals who were not original holders of entry permits. Thus, it would be possible to determine the sources of funds for a substantial cross section of permit holders. A second goal of the mail survey would be to obtain data on the attitudes of current permittees toward alternative methods of allocating permits. These attitude measures could be used in the multiobjective decision analysis (step 4).

Another task relating to the decision matrix is to establish additional constraints. Governmental budget constraints would be constructed at this stage.

Perhaps it would become apparent that certain technically feasible activity levels would be infeasible politically. Other constraints on the feasible set of portfolios would be added.

The decision matrix and constraints are then used to define minimal and maximal levels of attainment for each attribute. For example, across the full range of feasible portfolios, there would be some maximal level of attainable Alaskan participation and some minimal level. Let x_j^{min} and x_j^{max} be the minimum and maximum for the jth attribute and $U_j(x_j)$ be the "single-attribute utility function" for the jth attribute. Then the jth utility function is scaled such that

$$U_j (x_j^{max}) = 1$$

$$U_j (x_j^{min}) = 0$$

An as yet unresolved issue in the literature is whether or not the $U_j (x_j)$ functions can be linear. Keeney and Raiffa [1976] prefer curvilinear relationships, while Edwards [1976] argues that linear functions are "good enough" for the bulk of applied work. If nonlinear functions appeared to be necessary to reflect diminishing returns to attribute attainment, such functions would be approximated with linear segments for purposes of linear programming (step 5, below).

Multiobjective Decision Workshop

This would involve a meeting of approximately 15 people to participate in a multiobjective decision workshop. The individuals could be chosen based on the personal interviews described above to represent a cross section of the groups and agencies with interests in Alaskan fisheries management.

The first stage of the workshop would involve identification of constraint attributes. It is often possible to obtain agreement among diverse parties that certain objectives will be satisfied by reaching some minimal level of achievement. In this way some of the objectives are shifted to the constraint set. An example might be some fraction of the permits remaining in the hands of native Alaskans. If the jth attribute turns out to be a constraint attribute at some minimal level $\bar{x}_j$, then a constraint $x_j \geqslant \bar{x}_j$ is added to the constraints in the model, and it becomes unnecessary to consider that particular attribute when developing utility weights.

Attributes which cannot be converted to constraint attributes must be assigned weights. Again the linear form is to be strongly preferred, if it can be justified. Letting $U(A)$ symbolize the multiattribute utility function and assuming linearity,

$$U(A) = \sum_{j=1}^{n} W_j \, U_j(x_j) = \sum_{j=1}^{n} W_j \, U_j(\sum_{i=1}^{n} A_j x_{ij})$$

where W_j is the weight assigned to the jth single attribute utility level. This function or possibly its nonlinear counterpart is the objective function for the multiattribute utility model.

The workshop would play two important roles here: (1) testing the linearity assumption and (2) developing the weights. The linearity assumption holds if and only if "mutual preference independence" exists. Drawing on Keeney and Raiffa [1976]: "If every *pair* of attributes is preferentially independent of its complementary set, then the attributes are mutually preferentially independent." In practice, the test would be conducted as follows. Suppose that x_1' and x_1'' are two attainment levels for x_1, and that x_3' and x_3'' are two attainment levels for x_3. Suppose workshop participants prefer (x_1', x_3') to (x_1'', x_3''), given that $X_2, X_4, \ldots, X_n$ are at their worst possible levels. Next respondents would be asked if their preferred pair would change assuming that $X_2, X_4, \ldots, X_n$ are at their best levels. New levels of X_1 and X_3 are chosen, and the process is repeated. If, after repetitions across a broad range of values of X_1 and X_3, it was clear that participant preferences do not depend on whether other attributes are at their best or worst levels, then the mutual preference independence assumption is justified for X_1 and X_3. Other pairs of attributes would have to be tested in a similar way. If mutual preference independence is supported by these tests, the linear form of U(A) would be used. If not, it might still be necessary to proceed with a linear form, but a careful eye would have to be kept on the potential biases. Approximation of nonlinear functions with linear segments might be a necessary compromise.

Development of the weights themselves might involve one of several approaches. In one possible scenario, the workshop participants could be asked independently to rank the major attributes in order of their importance. This is not their ranking in terms of overall social desirability but rather desirability within the choice set. That is, the highest ranked attribute is the one which, when moved from its lowest possible level to its highest possible level, creates the most subjective utility for the interest group. For instance rural employment may be a very important objective in the broader context of Alaska's salmon fisheries, but if it is discovered that there is little difference among the possible management alternatives with respect to rural employment this objective may turn out to be of quite low importance *in the context of fishery policy* for Alaska.

These independent weightings would then be reconciled through second (and perhaps other) iterations until a consistent ranking of attributes is found for the various interest groups. Finally, the lowest ranking attribute would be assigned an arbitrary number (such as 10) while the higher ranking ones would be assigned relatively higher weights through a process of reconciling differences when and if they exist. These weights would be normalized to some value (such as 100).

It should be noted that to call U(A) "utility" in the present case is probably inconsistent with the economist's usual use of the term. The workshop would tend to elicit strategic behavior and political bargaining from participants rather than behavior fully reflecting their true preferences. Nor can U(A) be interpreted as a "social welfare function." The weights, W_j, would reflect the composition of the workshop participants. Changing this composition would change the weights, leaving us in the longstanding economic quandary of having no basis to choose from among an infinite number of potential optima. However, the weights would still fulfill the more limited goal of searching out potential compromises which meet the objectives of diverse groups.

Optimization of the System

The final step is to determine an optimal portfolio. Provided that linearity assumptions hold to a sufficient degree of approximation, linear programming would be applied. The multiattribute utility function, U(A) as defined above, would be maximized subject to budget, attribute and imcompatible activity constraints, and any other constraints that appear necessary from the decision matrix analysis or the workshop. Sensitivity analyses would also be performed to test the robustness of the optimal portfolio. Results of the exercise would then be carefully analyzed and described in terms accessible to public decision-makers and citizens.

At this point two important questions could be asked. One would be whether such a research plan is really feasible. Another relates to the large amounts of time and money involved in the type of study we have just advocated. If time and/or money are short, what alternatives exist to reduce the size of multiobjective studies? Before drawing some final conclusions, we will address these questions.

ARE MULTIOBJECTIVE STUDIES FEASIBLE?

The plan we have just advocated is not a typical economic approach to fisheries issues. Fisheries management problems are frequently complex and controversial, and yet we are convinced that multiobjective analyses can succeed in developing results that will add a new dimension to the scientific basis for fisheries management. To gain an appreciation for the potential of these analytical techniques, we will briefly summarize two actual studies, one involving negotiation of an international oil tanker agreement and the other, the location of a power plant in the Pacific Northwest. These particular studies were chosen because they involve issues which are at least as complex and controversial as most fishery management issues. Moreover, they share methodological similarities with the plan which has just been described.

Ulvia and Snider [1980] summarize a study which preceded international negotiating sessions for a treaty setting oil tanker standards. The negotiations were convened in February 1978 by the United Nations Intergovernmental Maritime Consultative Organization. The problem faced by the analyst was to help the U.S. delegation prepare to deal with a number of complex and technically difficult issues.

First, a set of "attributes" was developed. These included the amount of oil (in metric tons) discharged per year into the world's oceans; oil discharged within 50 miles of the coasts of the countries involved in the negotiations; deaths, injuries and property damage reductions attainable through alternative regulations; costs of implementation; enforceability; and others. Rather than individual activities, this study considered four fully defined alternatives (comparable to our "portfolios") including the status quo under current maritime treaties and laws, an alternative dubbed the "U.S. proposal" and two other alternatives. In the decision matrix, the effects of alternatives on attributes were expressed on scales from 0 (worst level of attainment) to 100 (best level of attainment). In some cases, submodels were constructed to help calculate these effects.

Two different approaches were used to develop the utility weight for each attribute. To help U.S. negotiators anticipate the course that the actual negotiations might take, U.S. Coast Guard personnel who had been involved in several similar negotiations engaged in role playing to simulate the views that each of the 50 or 60 countries might express. This resulted in rankings of the alternatives for each country which could be easily revised as the respondents learned more about the positions of the various countries. Secondly, in order to better understand which alternative the United States should support and to what extent, the analysts solicited weights from various interest groups within the United States. No attempt was made formally to combine weights assigned by the different groups. Instead, members of the negotiating team informally synthesized the weights used in the analysis from the responses of the various groups based on their views of U.S. interests. One result of the analysis was a comparison of how the United States and other countries would rank the alternatives.

The ultimate outcomes of this exercise were impressive. Through the process of developing the model and analyzing the results, the U.S. delegates were able to formulate a new alternative that was very close to the one finally adopted. They were also able to conceptualize actions that the United States could take unilaterally if the negotiations should break down. This led to a minimum set of requirements for the United States without which unilateral action would have been preferred. (This was not actually used since the negotiations succeeded.) Furthermore, working with the model helped the negotiators formulate the communication approaches used with U.S. interest groups to help achieve Congressional approval of the agreement.

The nuclear power plant siting analysis was reported by Keeney and Nair [1977]. It involved new sites for the Washington Public Power Supply System (WPPSS), a joint operating agency consisting of 21 publicly owned utilities in the state of Washington. To quote Keeney and Nair: "The objective was to recommend sites having a high likelihood for successful licensing and would be suitable for the detailed site specific studies necessary to select finally a single nuclear plant site" (p. 223). The area addressed by the investigation included all of Washington and portions of Oregon and Idaho.

The activities in this study involved location of a 3000-MW nuclear plant at alternative sites. Sites in the study area were screened on the basis of criteria relating to health and safety, environmental effects, system cost and reliability, and the like. Nine sites were identified. Detailed descriptions of the sites plus information gained in the screening process helped the analysts to develop about 30 potential objectives with associated attributes. This list was reduced through an evolutionary process based on increasingly detailed information about the sites, the extent to which the impacts varied from site to site (impacts that are nearly the same at all sites could be ignored), and probabilities of the impacts. Some of the attributes used in the study were objective (for example, cost in dollars) while others were subjective (such as socioeconomic effects). In power plant siting, uncertainty is an important consideration. This meant that, in completing the decision matrix, considerable attention had to be given to the probabilities of various effects.

The utility function developed for this study was based on the views of a team of experts. However, in the conclusions of the study Keeney and Nair recommend additional research to include preferences and judgments of WPPSS members and the general public in the ranking process. Based on the preferences and judgments of the experts, the research resulted in a ranking of the alternative sites based on expected utility. Three sites were identified as the most promising for more detailed, site specific study. The authors do not indicate whether WPPSS implemented their recommendations.

The point to be drawn from these case studies is that multiobjective decision techniques have been successfully applied to other difficult decision problems. There seems little reason to suppose that they could not also be applied in fisheries management. Before concluding the paper with an overview of what such analyses would offer decision-makers, we want to focus for a moment on the question of whether simpler methods could be devised for the entry permit transfer problem.

POSSIBLE METHODS TO REDUCE TIME AND COSTS

Managers dealing with resources on a daily basis would normally have a fairly well developed sense of the social objectives relevant to a given fisheries management issue. With the help of a decision analyst, it should be possible to articulate these objectives to a satisfactory degree without extensive personal interviews. Attributes and activities could be defined in ways that are explicitly designed to use secondary data to a maximum degree.

The problem of how much primary data to gather is similar to that faced by a survey researcher who is faced with choosing how large a sample to draw. Other things being equal, the larger the sample, the better. Likewise, in economic analysis, the better and more detailed the data going into the decision matrix, the more reliable and insightful the results will be. However, just as cost often dictates sample size, it also affects how much primary data can be gathered. In the extreme it may be feasible to get by with secondary data plus subjective judgments regarding the magnitudes of some impacts. Such subjective judgments were used, for example, in the power plant siting study. Ideally, we believe that fishermen's groups and other interests should be contacted directly in formulating utility-weights. However, as we saw in both the oil tanker agreement and the power plant siting cases, this is not always feasible. Panels of carefully chosen experts, role playing and other such techniques can still provide useful insights.

As experience with multiobjective techniques grows and applications to fisheries problems are completed, many additional ideas for saving time and money should be obtained.

MULTIOBJECTIVE STUDIES AND PUBLIC DECISIONS

In addition to the two applications outlined above, multiobjective techniques have been applied to such disparate activities as career search, location of the Mexico City airport, busing programs and corporate personnel policies. The reasons are quite simple—few choices are so easy that all dimensions can be reduced to a single objective.

We do not wish to minimize the problems involved in applying multiobjective techniques to fisheries decisions. Very real research problems will arise in efforts to: (1) choose the appropriate management objectives; (2) determine the correct functional relationship between possible management activities and their corresponding attributes; and (3) conduct successful workshops.

The first difficulty can be minimized through the involvement of knowledgeable persons early in the process. The second problem can only be overcome through sophisticated empirical studies. Of course, there will be an important role for experience and "hunches" in several of the areas. Regarding the workshops, it must be borne in mind that the essence of multiattribute techniques is to search for agreement on preferences rather than on activities. Put in more conventional language, we want to seek agreement on ends while ignoring means. This is not to imply that means (activities) are irrelevant. But interest groups usually have a history of advocating specific means (pet "projects"), and failing to search for areas where agreement on goals and objectives is obvious. The meeting–to be successful–would need to deflect these traditional fights over means toward constructive discussions concerning objectives and the contributions of certain activities (means) to the attainment of the agreed-on objectives. Not having tried this yet, we are unable to offer first-hand experience that it will work.

Nevertheless, successes in nonfishery applications are encouraging. Let us conclude this paper by suggesting what multiobjective fishery studies could contribute to the public decision process that current, single objective biological and economic studies have left undone. First, the exercise of formulating decision matrices would provide a more systematic evaluation of how a larger set of objectives would be impacted by alternative policies. Single-objective studies pay little or no attention to these broader issues. Second, utility analyses should point to ways that compromises between diverse interests may be reached. In so doing, multiobjective studies would, it is hoped, reduce the transactions costs of resolving fishing issues. Third, in some cases, "ends-oriented" multiobjective studies may help to uncover previously unrecognized management strategies (portfolios) which better serve the needs of various groups than the strategies which are normally obtained from "means-oriented" political debates. In these and perhaps other ways, the kind of studies advocated here would add a new dimension to the scientific basis for fishery management.

Earlier efforts to move fishery management beyond concentration on the single objective of economic efficiency have usually ended up focusing on efficiency *and* distributional aspects–but still primarily concerned with fishermen. This preoccupation with allocation and distribution derives largely from our economic orthodoxy. However, as indicated in Figure 1, there are a number of objectives which are not related to efficiency or equity as we define those terms. The time has long since passed when serious people need to spend much time arguing about the relevance of multiobjective management. The responsibility is now rather straightforward–go out and do it.

ACKNOWLEDGMENTS

This paper is a contribution from the College of Agricultural and Life Sciences, University of Wisconsin, Madison, and from the University of Alaska, Anchorage. The authors are grateful to Suzanne Holt for several very helpful comments on an earlier draft.

NOTES

[1]These permits have a number of unique features. Corporations are expressly forbidden to own permits. No individual may own more than one permit in any fishery. Permits confer rights to fish indefinitely subject to regulations administered by the Alaska Department of Fish and Game. They also may be freely transferred to other qualified fishermen either by gift or sale and they cannot be leased, mortgaged or foreclosed on.

[2]The dockside value of fish landed in Alaskan ports in 1978 was $438 million [U.S. Department of Commerce 1979]. In relative terms, one out of five or six employed Alaskans as well as many nonresidents are employed in fishing related occupations during the summer months, making it Alaska's largest natural resource-related employer. Among resource-related industries, only oil adds more to gross state product [Weeden 1978]. Fishing is of particular importance to hundreds of rural coastline communities [Rogers and Kreinheder 1980].

[3]For instance: Agnello and Donnelley [1976]; Anderson [1975, 1976, 1977a, b]; Bell [1972, 1978]; Christy and Scott [1965]; Clark [1976]; Crutchfield [1956, 1961, 1962, 1964]; Crutchfield and Pontecorvo [1969]; Crutchfield and Zellner [1962]; Scott [1955]; Smith [1968, 1969].

[4]For other sources see: Charnes et al. [1968]; Cochrane and Zeleny [1973]; Cohon and Marks [1975]; Easton [1973]; Fishburn [1970]; Haimes et al. [1975]; Lee [1972]; and MacCrimmon [1973].

[5]A recent application of portfolio multiattribute utility analysis under the supervision of Bromley is found in Feldman [1979].

REFERENCES

1. Agnello, R. J., and L. P. Donnelly. 1976. "Externalities and Property Rights in the Fisheries," *Land Econ.* 52:518-529.
2. Anderson, L. G. 1975. "Analysis of Commercial Exploitation and Maximum Economic Yield in Biologically and Technologically Interdependent Fisheries," *J. Fish. Res. Board Can.* 32:1825-1842.
3. Anderson, L. G. 1976. "The Relationship Between Firm and Fishery in Common Property Fisheries," *Land Econ.* 52:179-191.
4. Anderson, L. G. 1977a. *The Economics of Fisheries Management* (Baltimore, MD: The Johns Hopkins University Press).
5. Anderson, L. G., Ed. 1977b. *Economic Impacts of Extended Fisheries Jurisdiction* (Ann Arbor, MI: Ann Arbor Science Publishers, Inc.).
6. Arnold, V. L., and D. W. Bromley. 1970. "Social Goal, Problem Perception and Public Intervention: The Fishery," *San Diego Law Rev.* 7:469-487.
7. Bell, D. E., R. L. Keeney and H. Raiffa, Eds. 1977. *Conflicting Objectives in Decisions* (New York: John Wiley and Sons, Inc.).
8. Bell, F. W. 1972. "Technological Externalities and Common Property Resources: An Empirical Study of the U.S. Lobster Fishery," *J. Polit. Econ.* 80:148-153.
9. Bell, F. W. 1978. *Food from the Sea: The Economics of Ocean Fisheries* (Boulder, CO: Westview Press).

10. Bishop, R. C. 1973. "Limitation of Entry in the United States Fishing Industry: An Economic Appraisal of a Proposed Policy," *Land Econ.* 49:381-390.
11. Bishop, R. C. 1975. "Limitation of Entry in the United States Fishing Industry: A Reply," *Land Econ.* 51:182-185.
12. Bromley, D. W. 1977. "Distributional Implications of the Extended Economic Zone," *Am. J. Agric. Econ.* 59:887-892.
13. Bromley, D. W., and R. C. Bishop. 1977. "From Economic Theory to Fisheries Policy: Conceptual Problems and Management Prescriptions," in *Economic Impacts of Extended Fisheries Jurisdiction*, L. G. Anderson, Ed. (Ann Arbor, MI: Ann Arbor Science Publishers, Inc.).
14. Charnes, A., W. W. Cooper, D. B. Learner and E. F. Snow. 1968. "Note on an Application of a Goal Programming Model for Media Planning," *Management Sci.* 14:431-436.
15. Christy, F. T., Jr., and A. Scott. 1965. *The Commonwealth in Ocean Fisheries* (Baltimore, MD: The Johns Hopkins University Press).
16. Cicin-Sain, B. 1978. "Evaluative Criteria in Making Limited Entry Decisions: An Overview," paper presented at the National Workshop on Limitation of Entry into the Fisheries, Institute of Marine Studies, University of Washington, May 15-18, 1978.
17. Ciriacy-Wantrup, S. V. 1971. "The Economics of Environmental Policy," *Land Econ.* 47:36-45.
18. Clark, C. W. 1976. *Mathematical Bioeconomics: The Optimal Management of Renewable Resources* (New York: John Wiley and Sons, Inc.).
19. Cochrane, J. L., and M. Zeleny, Eds. 1973. *Multiple Criteria Decision Making* (Columbia, SC: University of South Carolina Press).
20. Cohon, J. L., and D. H. Marks. 1975. "A Review and Evaluation of Multiobjective Programming Techniques," *Water Resources Res.* Vol. 11.
21. Crutchfield, J. A. 1956. "Common Property Resources and Factor Allocation," *Can. J. Econ. Polit. Sci.* 22:292-300.
22. Crutchfield, J. A. 1961. "An Economic Evaluation of Alternative Methods of Fishery Regulation," *J. Law Econ.* 4:131-143.
23. Crutchfield, J. A. 1962. "Valuation of Fishery Resources," *Land Econ.* 38:145-154.
24. Crutchfield, J. A. 1964. "The Marine Fisheries: A Problem in International Cooperation," *Am. Econ. Rev.* 54:207-218.
25. Crutchfield, J. A., and A. Zellner. 1962. "Economic Aspects of the Pacific Halibut Fishery," *Fish. Ind. Res.* 1:1-173.
26. Crutchfield, J. A., and G. Pontecorvo. 1969. *The Pacific Salmon Fisheries* (Baltimore, MD: The Johns Hopkins University Press).
27. Easton, A. 1973. *Complex Managerial Decisions Involving Multiple Objectives* (New York: John Wiley and Sons, Inc.).
28. Edwards, W. 1976. *How to Use Multiattribute Utility Measurement for Social Decision-Making* (Los Angeles, CA: Social Science Research Institute).
29. Feldman, M. L. 1979. "Portfolio Multi-Attribute Utility Analysis: An Application to the 1979 Wisconsin State Energy Plan," Ph.D. Dissertation, Department of Agricultural Economics, University of Wisconsin—Madison.
30. Fishburn, P. 1970. *Utility Theory for Decision Making* (New York: John Wiley and Sons, Inc.).
31. Gordon, H. S. 1954. "The Economic Theory of a Common Property Resource: The Fishery," *J. Polit. Econ.* 62:124-142.

32. Haimes, Y. Y., W. A. Hall and H. T. Freedman. 1975. *Multiobjective Optimization in Water Resource Systems* (New York: Elsvier).
33. Hardin, G. 1968. "The Tragedy of the Commons," *Science* 162:1243-1248.
34. Keeney, R. L., and H. Raiffa. 1976. *Decisions with Multiple Objectives* (New York: John Wiley and Sons, Inc.).
35. Keeney, R. L., and K. Nair. 1977. "Nuclear Siting Using Decision Analysis," *Energy Policy* 5:223-231.
36. Koslow, J. A. 1979. "Limited Entry Policy and the Bristol Bay, Alaska Salmon Fishermen," report to the Alaska State Legislature.
37. Langdon, S. 1978. "Managing Modernization: A Critique of the Formalist Approaches to the Pacific Salmon Fisheries," paper presented at the Symposium on Modernization in Fishing Industries and Communities, East Carolina University, April 27-29, 1978.
38. Langdon, S. 1980. "Transfer Patterns in Alaskan Limited Entry Fisheries," Report for the Limited Entry Study Group of the Alaska State Legislature.
39. Lee, S. M. 1972. *Goal Programming for Decision Analysis* (Philadelphia, PA: Auerbach Publishing Co.).
40. MacCrimmon, K. R. 1973. "An Overview of Multiple Objective Decision Making," in *Multiple Criteria Decision Making*, J. L. Cochrane and M. Zeleny, Eds. (Columbia, SC: University of South Carolina Press).
41. McKenna, C. 1980. *Quantitative Methods for Public Decision Making* (New York: McGraw-Hill Book Co.).
42. Orbach, M. K. 1978. "Social and Cultural Aspects of Limited Entry," paper presented at the National Workshop on Limitation of Entry into the Fisheries, Institute of Marine Studies, University of Washington, May 15-18, 1978.
43. Rogers, G. W., and J. Kreinheder. 1980. "Socioeconomic Analysis for Fishery Areas and Census Division," report to the Limited Entry Study Committee of the Alaska State Legislature.
44. Scott, A. C. 1955. "The Fishery: The Objective of Sole Ownership," *J. Polit. Econ.* 63:116-124.
45. Sfeir-Younis, A., and D. W. Bromley. 1977. *Decision Making in Developing Countries: Multiobjective Formulation and Evaluation Methods* (New York: Praeger Publishers, Inc.).
46. Smith, V. L. 1968. "Economics of Production from Natural Resources," *Am. Econ. Rev.* 58:409-431.
47. Smith, V. L. 1969. "On Models of Commercial Fishing," *J. Polit. Econ.* 77: 181-198.
48. U.S. Department of Commerce. 1979. "Fisheries Statistics of the United States, 1978," Current Fisheries Statistics No. 7800, Washington, D. C.
49. Ulvia, J. W., and W. D. Snider. 1980. "Negotiation of International Oil Tanker Standards: An Application of Multiattribute Value Theory," *Operations Res.* 28:81-96.
50. Weeden, R. B. 1978. *Alaska: Promises to Keep* (Boston, MA: Houghton and Mifflin Co.).

COMMENT–CHAPTER 9

Suzanne Holt
   University of California
   Santa Cruz

Decision analysis has emerged in the last 15 years as an interdisciplinary field linking the concerns and methods of operations researchers, management scientists, engineers, political scientists and economists. For both public and private policy choices, researchers in the field have developed the "science" of decision-making, with methodologies such as goal programming and specific forms of utility analysis. However, applications of these methodologies to the formulation of public policies have been limited, for a variety of reasons. The chapter by Bishop et al. is intended to initiate such applications in the field of fisheries management, using the methodology of portfolio multiattribute utility analysis (PMUA). The methodology is particularly well-suited to the multiple objectives of fishery management plans (FMP) mandated by the Fishery Conservation and Management Act of 1976 and to the interdependence of different policies designed to meet the different objectives. The authors illustrate the procedure by which PMUA might be implemented by focusing on the design of an optimal transfer program for fishing permits in Alaska. In the process, their discussion demonstrates many of the economic strengths and limitations of decision analysis. It is to these strengths and limitations that the following comments are addressed.

The value of decision analysis lies in recognizing its appropriate application and realizing the economies that it can bring to public choice processes. The nature of decision analysis is prescriptive rather than descriptive. It is not designed to describe how people think about complex real-world problems but how concerned individuals and groups might systematically address such problems. Decision analysis cannot "methodologize" or objectify the inherently political process of public policy development. That process involves a number of interest groups (including policymakers and scientists) with imperfect information and less than accurate perceptions. These groups deal in shorthand fashion with complex issues, and strategize with and against each other, all within institutional structures which may not facilitate consensus or compromise. In contrast, decision analysis imposes an analytic construct of rational, systematic impact and value assessment on decision-makers. Inherently therefore, the analytic constructs impose practical difficulties and restrictive assumptions on the choice process. It is important to recognize these limitations.

The authors address two of the practical difficulties of PMUA (1) the tradeoff between gathering extensive primary data vs relying on secondary data and subjective judgment in identifying attributes and policies, and in formulating decision matrices; and (2) the tradeoff between using interest group representatives vs experts in the utility weighting workshop. The data and judgment problem of identifying policy impacts for the decision matrix deserves further attention. A sizable amount of behavioral modelling is required to anticipate the reactions of different actors in a fishery system to predominantly new policy portfolios. Inherent in the modelling will be various behavioral assumptions whose realism cannot be judged until after policies take effect. Consequently, the decision matrix must be largely the product of educated "guesstimates." This raises the question of what is the appropriate amount of effort to allocate to this portion of the decision analysis. In addition, individual policy impacts are stochastic rather than deterministic. The measurement of attributes will therefore involve joint probability distributions, threatening to make the decision matrix look like a mountain of conflicting information. Third, the resistance which interest group representatives might demonstrate in workshops to taking policy impacts as given should not be underestimated. Finally, it is not clear that a reconciliation process exists through which iterations of the workshop weighting process will converge to a single set of weights. The strategic behavior of workshop participants may not possess an equilibrium.

Decision analysis is further limited by restrictive assumptions. PMUA in particular is set up as a linear programming problem. Both policies and attributes are assumed to have additive separable effects on attributes and utilities, respectively. For the case of policies, it is not clear that a combination of policies has the same effect on attributes as the combined effects of individual policies. Implicit in the assumption is a certain linearity in the behavioral responses of actors in the system. When policies are discrete (e.g., the authors' transferable/nontransferable fishing permits), behavioral responses to combinations of policies are more likely to be characterized by thresholds. At the utility level, additive separability in the contributions of attributes to utility occurs if and only if participants demonstrate mutual preference independence across pairs of attributes. These limitations to PMUA appear significant. However, a case can be made that PMUA, and decision analysis in general, brings sizable economies to the public decision-making process, economies which render the limitations less significant.

One could argue that the real value of PMUA applications lie not in their optimal policy portfolio determination, but in their ability to delineate politically successful, better informed strategies for decision-makers. By systematically modelling expected policy impacts and values of various interest groups, it is possible to reduce substantially the resources devoted to gathering information, designing and implementing any aspect of public policy. Policy costs include not just the opportunity costs imposed by the decision, but also the costs of coming to a decision (public policy transactions costs).

An example of the ability of PMUA to reduce transactions costs is described by Ulvia and Snider [1980] in the preparations undertaken by the U.S. delegation negotiating U.N. international oil tanker standards in 1978. (This case is cited by the authors, but is insufficiently stressed.) Policy analysts helped the delegation prepare for the negotiations by playing a PMUA "game." Participants in previous negotiations simulated the views of other countries as well as the views of domestic interest groups. Three major benefits came from the game (1) the delegation developed a policy portfolio close to the tanker standards actually adopted; (2) they identified the conditions under which noncooperation was preferred; and (3) they developed interest group communications approaches to facilitate Congressional approval. These successful applications demonstrate that PMUA can provide valuable information about the likely outcomes of negotiations, can delimit the minimally acceptable policy changes from the status quo for different interest groups, and can substantially reduce the conflict in real-world public policy decision processes. The value of the PMUA "game" lies not in its particular content nor even in the optimal policy portfolio derived, but rather in its ability to narrow the variety of possible policies to the admissible or feasible set—to those policies which can be judged socially, politically and economically acceptable or satisfying. In this light, the limitations enumerated above are likely insignificant.

The power of PMUA to reduce conflict and to promote compromise is beneficial to any resource policy formulation process. For fishery management plans, PMUA can provide a partial shortcut through the decision-making process by systematically assessing policy impacts and attribute utility-values and by encouraging cooperative behavior. FMP are the outcome of a compromise-building process. However, while this process was legislatively designed to encourage participation of affected interest groups, relatively little attention was given to minimizing transactions costs. Consequently, transaction costs have often been a sizable portion of the public policy costs of FMP.

These transaction costs are frequently the result of institutional obstacles to compromise. For example, the FMP development team is assisted by an advisory panel of key interest group representatives. While the panel often wishes to formulate a consensus set of policies, the FMP process generally requires them to step back and simply inform the team and the regional fishery management council of their separate opinions. This restricted form of participation can be particularly frustrating, and inhibiting to future participation. When teams do not pay sufficient attention to the interests of panel members, those members are encouraged to withhold information and to strategize against the plan.

As a second example, practically every stage of the FMP process includes public hearings. However, public hearings are generally adversarial in nature, encouraging criticism rather than compromise, and exaggeration rather than accuracy. Finally, the FMP process generally involves distinct sets of actors at different stages. Consequently, compromises made at an early stage may be overturned at a later stage.

Were PMUA to be applied to any policy issue in the FMP process, it is likely that the resulting information would reduce the costs of making the real policy choice. Potential economic gains from less costly decisions and from institutional redesign make PMUA particularly attractive. Hopefully, the paper will encourage its application to assist the design of FMP and other resource management programs.

REFERENCE

1.   Ulvia, J. W., and W. D. Snider. 1980. "Negotiation of International Oil Tanker Standards: An Application of Multiattribute Value Theory," *Operations Res.* 28:81-96.

CHAPTER 10

INTERTEMPORAL ISSUES AND ECONOMIC ANALYSIS IN FISHERY MANAGEMENT UNDER THE FISHERY CONSERVATION AND MANAGEMENT ACT OF 1976

D. H. Wang
   New England Fishery Management Council

J. J. Mueller
   Northeast Regional Office
   National Marine Fisheries Service

The United States extended its jurisdiction over the living resources up to 200 miles off its coasts with the enactment of the Fishery Conservation and Management Act (FCMA) [1976]. The principal goal under the act is the conservation and management of the fishery resources within the 200-mile limit. To achieve this goal the regional fishery management councils which were established under the act have been assigned the responsibility for preparing, monitoring and revising fishery management plans for the marine resources in varying states of commercial and/or recreational development.

In the preparation and revision of the fishery management plans, the councils must meet certain national standards which are mandated by the act. The councils must also specify several required provisions and have an option to address other discretionary provisions. Among the required provisions is the requirement to assess and specify the optimal yield (OY) from the fishery. The OY is defined as the yield from the fishery which will provide the greatest overall benefit to the nation.

Along with the national standards requirements and the required and discretionary provisions, the councils must identify the problems in the fishery and propose a plan to solve the problems. Some of these problems can easily be identified, and are frequently related to the problem of overfishing a fish stock. Therefore, councils often propose to restore and/or maintain the fish stocks falling under the purview of the management plan.

When the restoration of a stock is proposed, several issues have to be addressed, since the restoration cannot normally be achieved in a single year. These include the proposed rate of stock restoration, the desired level of the stocks at the end of the planning period and the length of the planning period. Thus, a long-term plan for stock rebuilding raises the issue of the appropriate intertemporal levels of the optimal yield to generate the greatest benefit to the nation over time. The determination of the intertemporal levels of OY under a long-term plan is an optimal intertemporal allocation problem.

A council's decision to manage a fishery in an optimal fashion within an intertemporal allocation context is based on the premise that the necessary scientific data, including biological and economic data, are available. Unfortunately, this premise is generally not realistic, and, consequently, creates problems for economic analyses. The proper approach in conducting economic research for an intertemporal allocation problem is a maximization modeling approach which, in the case of fisheries, requires the necessary biological catch/stock/recruitment relationship, as well as certain economic inputs. However, such a biological relationship in most fisheries generally cannot be specified or identified, and some economic information may not be available. As a result, the maximization modeling approach for the economic analysis cannot appropriately be adopted, and a "fallback approach" is usually applied instead. The next section describes the maximization modelling and fallback approaches, and outlines their distinctions. Two empirical approaches adopted in the New England Council's FMP are presented in the third section to show the deviation from the ideal approach.

ECONOMIC ANALYSIS

Ideally Active Economic Analysis

As indicated above, scientific knowledge plays a crucial role in the determination of approaches to be used in addressing the intertemporal allocation issue. Clearly, knowledge of fish stock population dynamics is a fundamental element to this determination. The reason is that the catch/stock/recruitment relationships demonstrate the impact of management strategies (e.g., control on OY over time) on the stream of stock sizes through time.

Biological stock dynamics could perhaps demonstrate that (1) the catch levels in a time stream are dependent on each other if the levels of beginning and ending stock are fixed, and (2) that the catch streams and stock size streams interact, and are mutually and simultaneously determined. There is no doubt that environmental factors introduce a considerable amount of randomness into the process. However if a catch/stock/recruitment relationship appears to be operative in a fishery, then policy instruments (i.e., management strategies) affecting any catch level in the stream will simultaneously affect the entire catch stream and its related stock stream as well. Similarly, a policy decision to change a desired level of stock size in the same period affects the related catch stream and the stock stream as well. This implies then that to satisfactorily address the intertemporal allocation of catches, a maximization modeling would be the most appropriate approach. The following discussion is devoted to an elaboration of the general notions of such an approach.

For the purpose of elaboration, it is assumed that a management authority decides to restore a fish stock from the beginning level (BL) at time t to a target level (BT) at time t + n (i.e., n periods) and the management objective is to maximize the present value of consumer and producer surplus (W) over the plan periods. Then, with a specified biological transition equation, a mathematical programming model reflecting the notions of optimal intertemporal allocation can be formulated for the determination of the appropriate intertemporal allocation of catches to maximize the objective function, as indicated:

$$\text{MAX} \quad W = \sum_{t-1}^{n} B_t \int_0^{Q_{tk}} [P_{dt} - P_{st}] \, dQ \qquad (1)$$

where
C_1 = a biological transition equation (i.e., a catch/stock/recruitment relationship)

C_2 = BS_1 = BL, BS_n = BT

C_3 = national standard constraints

C_4 = political constraints

C_5 = sociological constraints, etc.

W = present value of summation of consumer and producer surplus over n periods

B_t = discount factor to t period

Q_{tk} = market equilibrium quantity at t

P_{dt} = price expressed as a function of quantities in t

P_{st} = cost expressed as a function of quantities in t

The function of the economic analysis in the process of management strategy selection can be demonstrated as follows. A useful first step is to provide the unconstrained optimal management strategy by generating the solution to Equation 1 with constraints C_1 and C_2. The solution consists of one maximum W, say W_1, a catch stream, a, and its corresponding stock stream S_1 as indicated in Figures 1 and 2. The catch stream, a, is the optimal catch stream in a set of all alternatives, denoted as A in Figure 3.

This unconstrained optimal catch stream as a management strategy is then judged in terms of the acceptability with respect to various other concerns. It would be selected as a management strategy if it is acceptable in regard to other issues, such as one of the national standards. If not, an additional step should be taken. Suppose, it is judged that the stock size at some t_i is too low to meet the requirement of the national standards. Therefore, the "a" catch stream is not an acceptable solution, since it falls within a subset of alternatives unacceptable to the national standards, denoted as N in Figure 3.

The next step is to search for an optimal solution which would meet the national standards along with constraints, C_1 and C_2. This is equivalent to imposing the national standards as a extra constraint set (C_3) to the solution of Equation 1.

Assume that the optimal solution for Equation 1 under the enlarged set of constraints is the catch stream, b, the corresponding stock stream, S_2, (as shown in Figures 1, 2 and 3) as well as a net present value of surplus equal to W_2. Again, this catch stream as a management strategy, has to be evaluated for its acceptability, and a decision must be made if further analysis is required. It could be assumed that for political reasons the "b" stream is not acceptable because the catch level at t_m is too low to be acceptable to the fishing industry because of the cashflow problems it would involve.

The third step is to impose an additional constraint (C_4) representing political considerations to the solution of Equation 1. The constraints are now C_1, C_2, C_3 and C_4. Assume that the optimal solution to Equation 1 under this new set of constraints is the catch stream C, and the stock stream, S_3, as indicated in Figures 1, 2 and 3. Acceptability of this catch stream is then evaluated. Perhaps this is unacceptable for "sociological reasons," and another consideration and iteration must be undertaken, resulting in solution "d" being generated.

It should be stressed that the solutions (i.e., management harvest strategies) a, b, c and d, are all optimal management strategies since they generated the maximum consumer and producer surplus under different sets of constraints. However, the "d" management harvest strategy maximizes the surplus while satisfying the national standards, political and social concerns. Therefore, the "d" management strategy could be presented to decision-makers as an intertemporal management strategy along with the a, b and c strategies to allow the proper evaluation of the trade-offs between these strategies. The economic

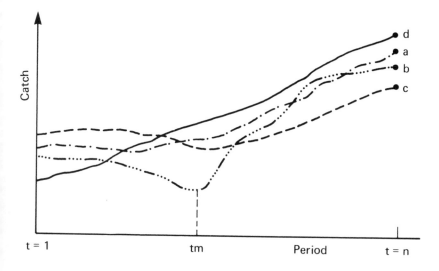

Figure 1. Catch streams.

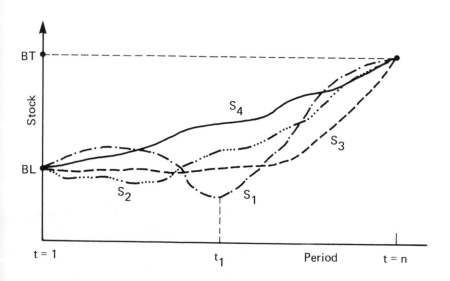

Figure 2. Stock streams.

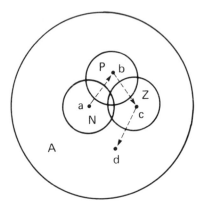

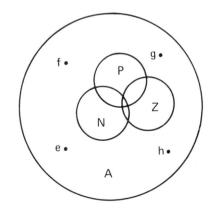

$$F = A - (N \cup P \cup Z); \ e \in F, f \in F,$$
$$g \in F, \text{ and } h \in F$$

Figure 3.   Solutions under ideal
approaches.

Figure 4.   Solution set under fallback
approaches.

impacts on the various user groups of the resources should also be generated for decision-making information.

It must be acknowledged that to use this type of mathematical programming approach the following assumptions must hold: (1) all the necessary scientific data are available and reflected in the model; (2) the objective function, the present value of consumer and producer surplus, is a direct measurement of the management objective; and (3) the objective to be achieved can be measured. This kind of analysis is considered as an "active" approach, since it could actively influence or guide management decisions by providing the necessary economic and biological information to decision-makers at the right time for the right issue.

Fallback Passive Economic Analysis

As stated previously, the ideal approach requires considerable scientific data on the fishery in question. Unfortunately such data are not always available. For example, the fish stock transition equation (i.e., catch/stock/ recruitment relationship) is not available for most fisheries under management or under consideration for management. The necessary economic inputs to the model are not always available for many fisheries either. As a result, a model of the kind elaborated above cannot be always successfully formulated. In such a case, a fallback approach is usually adopted instead. One fallback approach that can be adopted is to evaluate a set of predetermined catch streams. This approach prespecifies a set of catch streams, and then economic evaluation of its effects is performed. Presumably the set of alternatives has been generated in light of the national standards, political concerns and sociological considerations.

To demonstrate this approach consider the same management problem: stock restoration is desired with an objective of maximizing consumer and producer surpluses over a period of fish stock rebuilding. Unfortunately under this approach, the extent to which the consumer and producer surpluses is actually maximized is unknown since there is no way to generate the maximum surplus. Under this fallback approach, the analysis starts with the matrix of all alternatives, A, and the subset of alternatives unacceptable to the national standards, political concern and social considerations, defined as N, P and Z, respectively. The feasible set of alternatives is defined as F where F is the difference between A and the union of sets N, P and Z[1] (Figure 4).

Facing the feasible set, F, with no knowledge of "d," which is the optimal solution under the active approach for the same constraints, the fishery managers (presumably with scientific judgment) select several catch streams (within F) and identify the related stock streams. These selected streams are denoted as e, f, g and h, as shown in Figure 4. Then the levels of consumer and producer surpluses under these catch streams are estimated, and the biological and economic impacts are also analyzed. Finally, a choice of optimal path is made on these economic and biological analyses.

The economic analysis under this fallback approach merely evaluates the predetermined alternatives, and generates economic impacts of the alternatives which are of secondary importance to decision-making. This fallback approach is therefore regarded as a passive approach in the sense that the economic analysis under this approach is undertaken in response to the request for necessary economic impacts; however, it cannot guarantee that the optimum strategy is selected.

The ability of these two approaches, namely the ideal and the fallback approaches for evaluating the intertemporal management issues, is further summarized in Table I according to (1) the requirement of sufficient biological and economic data; (2) optimality in the achievement of management objectives and goals; (3) the extent to which the analysis influences the management decisions; (4) the amount of subjective opinion into decisions; and (5) the activeness of the analysis in the process of management decisions.

NEW ENGLAND INTERTEMPORAL ANALYSIS

In this section, two examples of our experience in attempting to conduct intertemporal management analysis are presented with respect to the sea scallop and the groundfish fisheries.

Table I.   Summary of Approach Comparison

Category	Ideal Approach	Fallback Approach
Requirement of sufficient biological and economic data	Extremely high	Moderate
Optimality in achievement of the management objectives and goals	Yes	No
Extent to which the analysis influence decision	High	Moderate
Subjective opinion into decisions	Low	High
Activeness of the analysis in the process of management decisions	Active	Passive

Atlantic Sea Scallop Management

The New England Council, in consultation with the Mid-Atlantic and South Atlantic Councils, decided to develop a management plan for the sea scallop *(Placopecten magellanicus)* fishery resources in the waters off the northeast coast of the United States. There are three major concerns for the fisheries: (1) the instability of the sea scallop stocks; (2) the ability of these resources to support the current level of effort; and (3) the danger of overexploitation in light of anticipated increases in demand [New England Fishery Management Council, 1980b].

With these concerns, an understanding of the management institution, and the social and political framework, the council established the following management objective for the Atlantic sea scallop plan [Wang et al. 1980]:

> The broad long-term objective for management of the Atlantic sea scallop resources shall be to maximize over time the joint social and economic benefits from harvesting and use of the resources. In support of this broad objective the following considerations shall enter:
>
> a) Restoration of the adult stocks in terms of their abundances and age distribution can be expected to reduce the year to year fluctuations in stock abundance caused by variation in recruitment.
> b) Enhancement of the yield per recruit for each stock.

c) Evaluation of the impact of the plan provisions on research, plan development, and enforcement costs.
d) Minimization of adverse environmental impacts on stock levels and utilization.

In this set of management objectives, the intertemporal allocation issues are clearly defined since the council explicitly expressed "long-term" and "over-time" as the dimensions of this plan. The management issue is obviously an intertemporal optimal issue because (1) the plan calls for the maximization of benefits over time and (2) a restoration of the adult stocks is proposed as well. The ideal technical approach for addressing these management objectives and issues would be similar to that approach elaborated above. However, due to the lack of understanding the catch/stock/recruitment relationship for sea scallops, it was decided that management strategies for sea scallops affecting catch streams would not be evaluated within this framework. Therefore a fallback approach was adopted. In this particular fallback approach, a matrix of management strategies, which was narrowed down in view of national standards requirements and political and social concerns, has been specified for further biological and economic analyses. These strategies involved various meat counts and effort controls. The strategy matrix is presented in Table II. Thus, the economic analysis became one of evaluating the relative merits of these strategies at the steady state biological equilibria,[2] and addressing the short-term impacts of these strategies for 1980-1981. This fallback economic analysis is outlined in the following sections.

Economic Analyses of Long-Term Management[3]

The long-term economic analysis emphasized the comparison of the economic consequences of the 12 management strategy scenarios at their long-term biological equilibrium conditions. The long-term equilibrium conditions in sea

Table II.   Strategy Matrix—Effort Control Specification

	No Management Control (i.e. at historical average); 7001 USA std. d. f.	Control at 4350 USA std. d. f.	Control at 3292 USA std. d. f.
60 Meats	SS1	SS2	SS3
40 Meats	SS4	SS5	SS6
30 Meats	SS7	SS8	SS9
25 Meats	SS10	SS11	SS12

scallops, however, are not steady due to the 16-year cycle in the population dynamics of the resource. Therefore, to evaluate properly the economic implications of these strategies at their long-term equilibria, a 16-year period has been used as a common basis for the evaluation of these hypothetical meat count and effort control strategies. The biological model used to generate the strategies is presented in the Appendix.

The economic analysis emphasized the comparison of the economic consequences of the 12 management strategy scenarios at the long-term biological equilibrium conditions. The economic implications of these equilibrium conditions under these strategy scenarios are different from those of a complete long-run evaluation, where all multiperiod management decisions are involved. The difference is that this analysis concentrated merely on the equilibrium conditions themselves, and ignored the transition conditions, whereas the latter analysis for long-run management decisions would include the equilibrium conditions and the transition states as well.

The results were expressed in terms of the differences in the outcome of each strategy relative to prespecified economic criteria (i.e., price, employment, revenue, impact on regional income and consumer surplus). The expression of these differences provided relative comparisons between these scenarios for the decision-makers without knowing the absolute values, which may be considered of secondary importance. In this analysis, strategy scenario one (SS1), which is a combination of 70 meat count and no mangement control on effort levels, was chosen as a common base for strategy comparison. The methodology used for the analysis is presented below.

Changes in Prices. Changes in prices between strategy scenarios M and N (i.e., scenario N is the base scenario) can be expressed as follows:

$$PE^{mn}_i = a \, (Q^m_i - Q^n_i) \tag{2}$$

$$PW^{mn}_i = b \, (Q^m_i - Q^n_i) \tag{3}$$

$$PR^{mn}_i = c \, (Q^m_i - Q^n_i) \tag{4}$$

where PE^{mn}_i = change in exvessel price (cents) from a change from senario N to scenario M in year i.

PW^{mn}_i = change in wholesale price (cents) from scenario N to scenario M in year i

PR^{mn}_i = change in retail price (cents) from scenario N to scenario M in year i

Q_i^m = catch (1000 lb) under option M in year i

Q_i^n = catch (1000 lb) under option N in year i

a,b,c = the slopes of the price equations for exvessel, wholesale and retail markets, respectively

Changes in Employment. Changes in employment in the fresh and frozen sea scallop processing sectors resulting from a change from scenario N to scenario M are expressed as follows:

$$EMH_i^{mn} = e\,(Q_i^m - Q_i^n) \qquad (5)$$

$$EMN_i^{mn} = f\,(Q_i^m - Q_i^n) \qquad (6)$$

where EMH_i^{mn} = change in employment (man-years) in fresh sea scallop processing from a change scenario N to scenario M in year i

EMN_i^{mn} = change in employment (man-years) in frozen sea scallop processing from scenario N to scenario M in year i

e, f = the production-employment coefficients for fresh and frozen processing, respectively

Producer Revenues. The change in the fishing revenues of harvesters from a change from scenario N to scenario M is derived as follows:

$$R_i^{mn} = PE_i^m Q_i^m - PE_i^n Q_i^n = (Q_i^m - Q_i^n)\,(-aQ_i^m + PE_i^n) \qquad (7)$$

where R_i^{mn} = change in harvesting revenues from a change from scenario N to scenario M in year i

PE_i^m = exvessel price under scenario M in year i

PE_i^n = exvessel price under scenario N in year i

The present value of these revenues, in relation to the first year of the long-run equilibrium cycle, is expressed as follows:

$$PVR^{mn} = \sum_{i=1}^{16} \frac{R_i^{mn}}{(1+r)^i} \qquad (8)$$

where PVR^{mn} = change in present value in the first year of the cycle from change from scenario N to scenario M

r   = discount rate

New England Regional Economic Impacts. New England regional economic impact is the impact on regional income resulting from a change in scenario, and is indicated as follows:

$$RI^{mn}_i = R^{mn}_i K \qquad (9)$$

where RI^{mn}_i = change in impact on regional income from change from scenario N to scenario M in year i

K   = income multiplier of fishing sector to the regional economy.

The present value of a change in the impacts on regional income in the first year of the cycle is expressed as follows:

$$PVRI^{mn} = \sum_{i=1}^{16} \frac{RI^{mn}_i}{(1+r)^i} \qquad (10)$$

where $PVRI^{mn}$ = change in present value of the impacts on regional income from change from scenario N to scenario M

Consumer Surplus. Annual changes in consumer surplus resulting from a change from scenario N to scenario M are presented as follows (a linear demand function is assumed):

$$CS^{mn}_i = [(Q^m_i + Q^n_i) \cdot PR^{mn}_i]/2 \qquad (11)$$

where CS^{mn}_i = change in consumer surplus from change from scenario N to scenario M in year i

The present value of the changes in consumer surplus in the first year of the cycle moving from scenario N to scenario M is indicated as follows:

$$PVCR^{mn} = \sum_{i=1}^{16} \frac{CS^{mn}_i}{(1+r)^i} \qquad (12)$$

where $PVCR^{mn}$ = present value of the change in consumer surplus in the first year of the cycle from a change from scenario N to scenario M

It should be noted that Equations 2 through 12 will be used to estimate the quantitative values of the specified economic variables. As long as the catch streams (Qs), the price and employment coefficients (a, b, c, e, f), the discount rate (r), and the regional impact multiplier (k) are known, all variables can be estimated except R_i^{mn} in Equation 7, which requires additional data on PE_i^n. The coefficients are from the economic analysis undertaken by the council staff economists and their values are as follows:

$$a = -0.002047$$
$$b = -0.002150$$
$$c = -0.00311$$
$$e =\ \ 0.0337088$$
$$f =\ \ 0.0102592$$

The discount rate (r) and regional multiplier (k) are adopted from Rorholm et al. [1965], and are equal to 7-1/8% and 2.96, respectively. The procedures used to generate the above parameter estimates and the results of the analysis are detailed in New England Fishery Management Council [1980b] and Wang et al. [1980].

Economic Short-Term Impact Analysis

The short-term economic impact analysis is limited to a period from 1980 to 1981, since the long-term projections of biological abundance are believed to be imprecise and uncertain. This economic analysis is conducted as a comparison of two strategy scenario groups with a base case. This base case is a group of scenarios for no effort control (i.e., S1, S4, S7, S10) of various meat counts, which was chosen due to a lack of data on meat count composition of landings and a lack of understanding of the impacts of various meat count measures. Thereby, the 1980-1981 forecasts under no effort control generated with the econometric model provided in Wang et al. [1980] are suggested as the base case.

The two strategy scenario groups with differing levels of effort control to be compared are (1) an overall limit of 7500 U.S. standard days fished (i.e., S2, S5, S8, and S11); (2) an overall limit of 5676 U.S. standard days fished (i.e., S3, S6, S9, S12). The 1980-1981 forecasts under these different levels of effort controls with the same econometric model are used to compare with the base forecasts. The findings of these analyses are detailed in the above-cited references.

Atlantic Groundfish Management

The Atlantic groundfish fisheries for cod, haddock and yellowtail flounder have been managed for the past three years by a plan that was originally recommended by the New England Fishery Management Council and was implemented by the Secretary of Commerce in March 1977 [U.S. Department of Commerce 1977]. The major elements of the plan included an OY specification, quota regulations and trip/week vessel catch limits by species. The plan, which failed to specify explicitly the management objectives, must be considered as a monitoring management plan. Therefore, the intertemporal management issues did not arise as management issues.

The Atlantic Groundfish Plan, according to the council's judgment, has not been a success. The council, therefore, made a further management decision: while allowing the plan to continue in effect, the council decided to develop an Interim Groundfish Plan and a more comprehensive Atlantic Demersal Finfish (ADF) Plan. The Interim Groundfish Plan is necessary, since it is believed that the ADF will not be ready for implementation for some time. Therefore, in addition to the extant groundfish plan, there are two other groundfish plans under preparation by the New England Council.

The Interim Groundfish Plan is supposed to be a temporary one with a set of clearly defined, but limited objectives. These are:

1. enhancement of spawning activities;
2. reduction of the risk of recruitment overfishing of cod, haddock and yellowtail flounder; and
3. acquisition of reliable data, in support of the development of the ADF FMP, on normal fishing patterns of the industry and biological attributes of stocks as may be determined from commercial activities.

The plan is clearly short-term in nature and does not explicitly address the intertemporal issues in its management.

However, in recognition of the need for a comprehensive plan, the council has adopted the following set of management objectives for its Atlantic Demersal Finfish Plan [Marchesseault et al. 1979] :

> Recognizing that management of demersal finfish impacts on benefits and costs in the utilization of other species, the overall objective of the plan shall be to manage the demersal finfish fishery in a manner which will generate over the period of the plan the greatest possible joint economic and social net benefits from the harvesting and utilization of the overall fishery resource.

Subobjectives/considerations were:

1. prevention of abrupt changes in the relative shares of domestic user-groups in the resource;
2. freedom of decision-making and choice for individual participants in the fishery should be maintained to the greatest possible extent;
3. inducement of diversification in the groundfish fishery toward increased utilization of species other than cod, haddock and yellowtail;
4. minimization of management regulations, subject to attainment of the overall objective;

5. minimization of enforcement costs, subject to attainment of the overall objective; and

6. provision for accurate and consistent economic, social and biological data required to monitor effectively and assess the performance of the fishery relative to the overall objective.

The overall objective clearly implies that, among many others, a multiple-year planning period is required so as to make a determination, within the framework of the plan, of how alternative harvesting levels in the immediate future affect the amounts available for later years.

In short, the selection of a management strategy for the New England groundfish fishery involves the finding of the optimum distribution of harvests (benefits) over the plan period. Optimum in this context is defined by the overall objective of the plan, i.e., the generation over the plan period of the greatest possible joint benefits from the harvesting and utilization of the groundfish resource. So here again, the task is to develop a model similar to that specified above.

Based on this judgment, the following model is currently under consideration for adoption as one that appears to capture many of the desirable features as specified previously.

Decision Model[4]

The process of identifying a large number of individual management strategies relative to annual species TAC over a multiple-year plan period and of assessing their impacts to find the optimum strategy can be lengthy and difficult. Further, the feasibility and usefulness in pursuing this avenue is limited by our ability to effectively discriminate between individual stages based on their predicted impacts in future time periods on stock size. To effectively shorten the search process, a mathematical programming method may be employed. The objective function of the model is:

$$\text{Max } Z = \sum_i \sum_j \sum_t B_t \cdot X_{ijt} \cdot (P_{it} - C_{it}) \qquad (13)$$

where

Z = present value of total net income to the fishing industry over the planning period

B_t = the discount rate used to adjust future benefits to present value equivalents

X_{ijt} = pounds of species i in area j landed in a directed fishery for that species during period t

P_{it} = revenue realized per pound of species i landed in a directed fishery for species i during period t (includes the values of the by-catch)

C_{it} = cost incurred per pound of species i landed in a directed fishery for species i during the period t (including the cost associated with capturing the by-catch)

Equation 13 is the objective function to be maximized. It shows the number of pounds of each species that should be caught in a directed fishery in each area over time in order to maximize the present value of net income, consistent with the biologic constraints listed below.

It should be noted that an additional subscript could be added to X_{ijt} that would reference a particular year classes of the species. This problem is not addressed in the current formulation. Further, for purpose of simplicity, it is assumed that $j = 1$, i.e., that there is only one relevant area and subscript j is dropped from further specifications. Other "activities" that are discussed below, namely G_{mt}, SS_{mt}, N_{mt}, REC_{mt}, are also included implicitly in the objective function. However, they have a zero price. A series of biological constraints are presented below that constrain the solution to Equation 13.

Initial Stock Size. To initiate the model it is necessary to initialize the relevant stock size of each species. This is simply accomplished by

$$SS_{mt} = BEGS_{m1} \quad \text{for t = 1 for all m} \tag{14}$$

where SS_{mt} = stock size of species m at beginning of the first period

   $BEGS_{m1}$ = initial stock size

Intermediate Stock Sizes. It is assumed that it is undesirable to allow the stock sizes of the species to fall below certain levels so as to potentially jeopardize recruitment. To achieve this, the following is formulated.

$$SS_{mt} \geqslant IS_{min} \quad \text{for t = 1} \tag{15}$$

where IS_{min} = minimum intermediate stock size level

Ending Stock Size. It is assumed that there is a minimum ending stock size that the New England Council wishes to achieve. The advantage of using this model is that it could enable the council to evaluate trade-offs between ending stock sizes and intermediate period incomes. It will also assist the council in evaluating whether or not certain stock size goals for groups of species are incompatible. This constraint is simply:

$$SS_{mt} \geqslant FSS_{mt} \tag{16}$$

where FSS_{mt} = minimum acceptable stock for species m at the end of the planning period

Specific Period Catch. The total catch of any species that occurs during any period is the sum of the directed catch of the subject species and the by-catch of the species that occurs in other directed fisheries. To reflect this, the following constraint is formulated:

$$\sum_i A_{mit} \cdot X_{it} - T_{mt} = 0 \tag{17}$$

where A_{mit} = number of pounds of species m caught per pound of species i in a directed fishery for species i during period t (it is assumed that these A_{mit} are the same for all vessel categories)

       T_{mt} = total catch of species m that occurs during period t associated with directed fisheries X_{it} (this includes the directed catch when i = m, and the by-catch when i ≠ m)

Stock Transition Phase. To incorporate the period to period changes in stock sizes, it is necessary to incorporate natural mortality, growth and recruitment in addition to the catch.

These relationships are contained in the formulation below. It is assumed that natural mortality and growth that occur during the period are proportional to the stock size at the beginning of the period. This equation then, is:

$$SS_{mt} - n_{mt} \cdot NM_{mt} + g_{mt} \cdot G_{mt} + r_{mt} \cdot REC_{mt} - TC_{mt} - SS_{mt+1} = 0 \tag{18}$$

where NM_{mt} = natural mortality that occurs to stock m during period t

       G_{mt} = growth in stock m during period t

       REC_{mt} = recruitment to stock m that occurs during period t

       SS_{mt+1} = beginning stock size for stock m for the next period

       n_{mt}, g_{mt}, r_{mt} = proportionality coefficients for natural mortality, growth and recruitment, respectively

The determinants of recruitment, growth and natural mortality in any particular period are, no doubt, a complex matter. The alternative of assuming that they are stochastic may be the most realistic and if a deterministic specification appears inappropriate the model will be restructured accordingly. In this formulation it is assumed that natural mortality and growth are proportional to stock sizes at the beginning of the period. To force such proportionality into the stock transition equation, the following equations are necessary:

$$SS_{mt} - NM_{mt} = 0 \tag{19}$$

$$SS_{mt} - G_{mt} = 0 \qquad (20)$$

Recruitment of a particular species is assumed to be a function of the stock sizes of numerous species lagged several time periods. In general, the constraint would appear as:

$$\sum_{n, m} REC_{mt - n} \cdot SS_{mt - n} - REC_{mt} = 0 \qquad (21)$$

where the appropriate n's will be statistically determined. The $REC_{mt - n}$ are the coefficients that relate changes in various lagged stock sizes to changes in recruitment. These coefficients would be estimated using various regression techniques.

Minimum Income or Cash Flow Constraint. While it may be certainly desirable to rebuild the stocks at particular rates so as to maximize the present value of net income during the period, it has to be recognized that there is a minimum cash flow that the industry requires during any particular time period so as to cover its fixed charges, i.e., mortgage payments. To reflect this, the following constraint was formulated:

$$\sum_{i} (P_{it} - C_{it}) X_{it} - CMIN_t \geq 0 \qquad (22)$$

where $CMIN_t$ is the minimum cash flow required during period t.

Data Requirement and Availability

The groundfish management objectives adopted by the council explicitly call for the incorporation of *species interdependence* considerations in the identification and evaluation of strategies [Marchesseault et al. 1979]. Various forms of such interdependence result from resource and market characteristics. Among these are:

1. biological links: predator/prey relations and stock recruitment relationships across species;
2. substitutions among species in the market place, with the implication that the price of species A is dependent partially on the price/landings of species B;
3. substitution of species as inputs into the production of a landing, i.e., the price of species A relative to species B may impact on the fishermen's decision to direct effort towards any one of the species; and
4. joint harvesting relationship, by-catch ratios, in the harvesting sector, i.e., for some combination of species the joint probability of capture in a certain area, by a certain gear type at a certain time of the year may be very high.

The model above attempts to reflect these interdependencies. Our knowledge of and ability to measure the above aspects of interdependencies is limited. Research efforts on predator/prey relations and interspecies stock recruitment relationships are progressing, but have previously not been modeled. Similarly, fishermen's supply behavior in response to relative prices and harvesting costs of alternative species or species mixes has not been modeled empirically. Given the state of the art and availability of data it would appear, however, that substitution among species in the market place and the by-catch or joint catch aspects are dimensions of the species interdependence that at this time could be incorporated in a decision model.

An important prerequisite for the determination of the optimal annual species TAC is an ability to predict recruitment and growth in major fish stocks over a plan period. Appropriate methods appear to be available for incorporating in a formal decision framework expected recruitment and growth to individual major fish stocks over the next several years. Thus the elements of this general model formulated above are being developed by New England Council and NMFS staff.

SUMMARY AND CONCLUSION

On the enactment of the Fishery Conservation and Management Act in 1977, the Regional Fishery Management Councils were assigned the responsibility for preparing, monitoring and revising fishery management plans. In the process of management plan preparation, it became apparent that an issue in fishery management is an optimal intertemporal allocation issue and should be addressed with a maximization modeling approach.

A fishery council's decision to manage a fishery in an optimal fashion with regard to the intertemporal issue is based on the premise that the necessary scientific data, including biological and economic data are available. Unfortunately this premise is not always realistic and consequently creates problems for conducting the economic analyses in the appropriate framework. Frequently the necessary biological relationships cannot be specified or identified, and economic information may not be available. As a result, the maximization modeling approach cannot be appropriately adopted for conducting the analysis of the intertemporal fishery management issue and a fallback approach is usually applied instead.

The maximization modeling approach is considered as an ideal active approach in the sense that (1) all necessary scientific data are available; (2) the objective function (e.g., consumer and producer surplus) measures the achievement of the management objective; and (3) the model is capable of identifying an optimal strategy for meeting the objective.

Unlike the ideal active approach, economic analysis under the fallback approach merely evaluates the predetermined alternatives. There is no guarantee that the optimal strategy will be selected.

Along with the above general discussion on the ideal active approach and the fallback passive approach, two examples of ongoing work in New England were presented: sea scallop management and groundfish fishery management. The approach adopted in the sea scallop management is in the category of the fallback passive approach, whereas the approach proposed to be used in the groundfish management is reflective of the ideal active approach. These two examples attempt to demonstrate why appropriate economic analysis is often constrained due to the unavailability of scientific data. Consequently it is important for biologists and economists to work together in order to provide the necessary scientific data for intertemporal issues, so that they can be handled satisfactorily with the ideal active approach.

ACKNOWLEDGMENT

The authors acknowledge the assistance of New England Fishery Management Council staff biologist, Howard Russell, on the understanding of his model.

APPENDIX: BIOLOGICAL MODEL
FOR LONG-TERM EQUILIBRIUM CATCH

In the context of a long-term equilibrium, total yield may be calculated from the Beverton-Holt function:

$$Y = FRe^{-M(t\rho' - t\rho)}W_\infty \sum_{n=0}^{3} \frac{U_n e^{-nK(t\rho' - t_0)}}{F + M - nK}$$

at a desired level of fishing mortality, F, given an estimate of the number of recruits, R, the age at first capture, $t\rho'$ (assumed equivalent to the age at the cull size), $t\rho$ (assumed as $t\rho$ = 2.0 years), and the values of the von Bertalanffy growth parameters. For Georges Bank sea scallops, these are:

W_∞ = 53,637 g

K = 0.3374

t_0 = 1.4544 yr

M = 0.10

It is, therefore, noted that $t\acute{p}$ is changed in response to changes in the meat count straegy. The recruitment (R) is estimated in response to catch per unit effort (CPUE) and fishing mortality rate (F) in a simulation of the historical fishery. The average level of recruitment from the historic fishery (over a 16-year resource cycle), assumed to represent future average recruitment, was then applied to the Beverton-Holt equation, with a range of constant fishing mortality rates, to estimate the equilibrium yield at the corresponding levels of fishing effort.

NOTES

[1]It should be noted that the sets N, P and Z can be disproportionated to those in Figure 2, due to possible overemphasis of the concern represented by these sets.

[2]Since the knowledge of the stock dynamics was limited, it was not possible to specify the stock or catch streams accurately during the period of transition to the biological long-term equilibrium.

[3]This section is summarized from Wang et al. [1980].

[4]This model is based on and expanded from Mueller et al. [1979].

REFERENCES

1. Fishery Conservation and Management Act of 1976, Public Law 94-265.
2. Marchesseault, G., R. Ruais and D. H. Wang. 1979. "History and Status of the Atlantic Demersal Finfish Fishery Management Plan," report to Northeast Fishery Management Task Force.
3. Mueller, J. J., L. Vidaeur and J. Kirkley. 1979. "A Linear Programming Model for Evaluating Alternative Intertemporal Harvest Strategies in a Multiple Species Fishery," NATO Symposium on Applied Operation Research in Fishing, Vol. 1, pp. 469-483.
4. New England Fishery Management Council. 1980a. "Summary of the Interim Groundfish Plan," prepared for public hearings, July 1980.
5. New England Fishery Management Council. 1980b. "Fishery Management Plan and Regulatory Analysis for Atlantic Sea Scallops *(Placopecten magellanicus)*."
6. Rorholm, N., H. C. Lampe, N. Marshall and J. F. Farrell. 1965. "Economic Impact of Marine Oriented Activities—A Study of Southern New England Marine Region," Agricultural Experiment Station Bull. No. 396, University of Rhode Island.
7. U.S. Department of Commerce. 1977. "Atlantic Groundfish Plan: Notice of Approval, Implementation and Emergency Regulation," *Federal Register* (March 14).
8. Wang, D. H., L. Goodreau and J. J. Mueller. 1980. "Economics of Atlantic Sea Scallops Fisheries," Research Document 80SC 10.1, New England Fishery Management Council.

CHAPTER 11

SOME ECONOMIC ASPECTS OF MANAGING MARINE RECREATIONAL FISHING

Kenneth E. McConnell
   Department of Agricultural and
      Resource Economics
   University of Maryland

Ivar E. Strand, Jr.
   Department of Agricultural and
      Resource Economics
   University of Maryland

When formal authority to manage recreational fisheries in marine waters was granted by the Fisheries Conservation and Management Act (FCMA) of 1976, the United States had almost no experience in the management of marine recreational fisheries. Naturally enough, there was little data to support management, and not much understanding of the institutions and people to be managed. Nevertheless the FCMA properly recognized that if the ultimate use of scarce fish stocks is the satisfaction of human wants, then recreational use of the fish stocks deserves equal consideration along with commercial use.

Since the FCMA was enacted, management plans have been written for several species important to recreational anglers. Pacific salmon, Atlantic mackerel, grouper-snapper fisheries of the South Atlantic and Gulf, and Atlantic billfish are some of the fisheries covered by management plans. On the whole, marine sportfishing seems large in terms of the number of participants, about 9 million anglers in 1970 [U.S. Department of Commerce 1973], and large in terms of the catch, about 800,000 tons in 1970. Nevertheless, most management activity has been devoted to commercial fisheries.

Marine fishery managers have made few attempts to regulate recreational fishing, despite its rather large size. A brief explanation of this phenomenon serves as an introduction to recreational fishing. First and most important is the institutional and historical setting which provided data and experts on commercial fisheries long before the majority of people had enough leisure time to do substantial sportfishing. The inertia of several centuries is strong and the impetus created by the FCMA will take a long time to gain momentum. Second, most recreational fishing takes place within three miles of the shore and thus outside the hegemony of regional councils. Being predominantly inside three miles, marine sportfishing is not only outside the authority of regional councils, but it tends not to compete with the more important commercial species which are clearly offshore. Third, to the extent that economic factors guide management actions, the economic benefits to sport anglers are not highly visible. The benefits to sport anglers are measured by their willingness to pay for the right to fish. This concept is not only abstract, but can be assumed to be high or low, depending on one's proclivities, because there are no readily available market figures to disprove any assertions about benefits. Thus, given the proclivity to deal with commercial fisheries, it is only natural that the economic value of recreational fisheries would be assumed small. Fourth, and sensibly, even if the above impetus to ignore sportfisheries were absent, the task of managing a diverse set of people and institutions such as sportfishing is difficult, and requires substantial resources. Despite the evidence from economic theory that unregulated sportfishing is inefficient, one would think that the consideration of management costs would create a prima facie case for not managing sportfisheries until substantial evidence suggests that the benefits would outweigh the costs.

Because of the distribution of catch and trips among fishing sites and anglers of differing abilities, regulation of recreational fishing must make the tradeoff between high enforcement costs and substantial distributional consequences. Marine sportfishing in Rhode Island serves as an example. Most of the fish are caught by anglers fishing from private boats (80% in 1978). Only 50% of the trips are from private boats. Almost 50% of trips are taken from shore but only about 20% of the fish are caught there. This is an additional extreme distribution of catch among fishermen on any particular day. About 60% of angling trips at any time and place are unsuccessful in that they catch no fish. Thus a relatively small number of trips on private boats tends to account for a large proportion of total catch.[1] Regulation directed to reduce the total catch can be relatively cheap if it concentrates on anlging from boats. However, such regulations will cause a small proportion of anglers to absorb the total cost of the regulation. This example illustrates the trade off between the expenses of management and the distribution consequence of management for recreational fishing.

While the short-run experience of the FCMA with sportfishing is limited, it may be quite different in the long run. The long-run value of fish stocks in commercial and recreational use depends on the demand for the final product of each use. For recreational activity, the final product is the use of the fish stocks combined with scarce leisure time to provide satisfaction. For commercial use, the final product is fish as an item for consumption. The relative value of fish in commercial or recreational use depends on the development of substitutes for each. The economic value of the opportunity to fish recreationally depends on the availability of substitutes such as freshwater fishing, camping, hunting and other activities combining the use of natural resources and leisure time. The economic value of consuming fish depends on the price of food substitutes such as beef, chicken, poultry and cheese. It seems likely that technical change, the increasingly efficient use of given levels of resources, will affect substitutes of commercial use of fish more than the recreational use. (This thesis is developed at greater length in Krutilla and Fisher [1975].) Technical change in agriculture, the use of greater mechanization, and better fertilizers and pesticides, can have the impact of reducing the relative market price of substitutes for the commercial use of fish. For example, the development of more mechanized methods for raising poultry can lower the relative price of poultry products, which are good substitutes for fish.

However, technical change is biased toward substitutes for commercial fish. The substitutes for marine recreational fishing are other natural environments. To lower the cost of natural environments means to provide more and easier access to the users. Such changes are unlikely because the supply of natural environments cannot be increased in the relevant time period. For example, a plausible substitute for marine sportfishing is freshwater fishing. Yet society's ability to increase the number of lakes and streams for freshwater fishing is quite limited. Indeed, it seems likely that the substitutes for marine recreational fishing will decline because of the increasing value of these resources for various commercial uses and because of the cumulative pollution which results from continued economic growth. The consequence of the biased technical change is that the value of using fish stocks for recreational purposes is likely to increase relative to their value in commercial use. The observed phenomenon will be an increase in recreational fishing demand relative to commercial fishing demand.

The purpose of this chapter is to elucidate some basic relationships important to the long-run management of sportfisheries. First, the relationships required by optimal management are developed. Second, the economic costs of various approaches to regulating sportfishing catch are demonstrated. Third, an example of the costs of regulating a recreational fishery is given.

Throughout this chapter it is assumed that the goal of managing recreational fisheries is to make the anglers themselves better off. It is therefore assumed that making anglers' surplus large means making them better off. No attempt is made to deal with the important issue of the economic impact of sportfishing on suppliers such as bait stores, charter boats, tackle shops and other supporting activities. Impact analysis is important, but such analysis should be undertaken subsequent to obtaining a good understanding of the simple analytics of what makes anglers better off. In addition to ignoring the various aspects of impact analysis, the paper does not deal with the dynamic issues of the age distribution of the fish stocks nor with the problems associated with deviating from equilibrium paths for recreational fisheries.

SOME BASIC RELATIONSHIPS FOR SPORTFISHING

Suppose that anglers choose the level of their fishing effort depending on the expected catch per trip, h, and their costs per trip, c. Measure their level of effort in trips of fixed length (say one day), which will be called x. Then the demand curve for a representation angler is given by $x = g(c, h)$, where c is the cost per trip and h measures the expected catch per trip. The cost per trip is made up of variable expenses such as travel cost, bait cost, tolls, parking fees, charter prices and the opportunity cost of the angler's time. The catch per trip (or per day) may be considered synonymous with the angler's success, bag or daily catch. By specifying the demand function as depending only on the catch per trip and the cost per trip, we are not suggesting that other factors, such as the size and composition of catch, the gaming nature of the species caught, income, and the desire to be outdoors, are not important. This chapter, however, deals with the management of fish stocks, and to the extent that other variables are uncorrelated with catch rates, costs and fish stock densities, they can be ignored.[2]

It is generally more convenient to deal with the inverse demand function given by $c = f(x, h)$ where $f(x, h)$ may be considered the marginal value function. If the catch rate is x_0 and the cost per trip is c_0, in terms of Figure 1, the net willingness to pay for the representative angler is represented by the area Ac_0c^*. It is the area above the cost line c_0A and under the demand curve $f(x, h)$. Mathematically, it is

$$\int_0^{x_0} f(x, h_0)dx - x_0 c_0$$

What happens if h increases? The angler will increase days fished to x_1, and he will be willing to pay the amount

$$\int_0^{x_1} f(x, h_1)dx - x_1 c_0$$

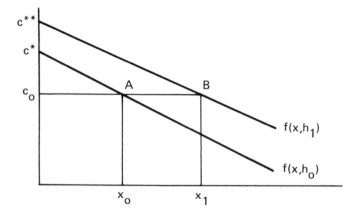

Figure 1.   Effect of catch rate on marginal value of a fishing trip.

It is area $c_o c^{**}B$ in Figure 1. If we subtract what he will pay when the catch rate is h_1 from what he will pay when the catch rate is h_o, we find the incremental value of the catch rate, which should play a central role in management. In Figure 1, the difference in willingness to pay for the right to access with a catch rate of h_1 and right to access with a catch rate of h_o is $c^{**}Bc_o - c^*Ac_o$, which equals the strip $c^*c^{**}AB$.

Suppose there are n identical anglers with x trips per angler, and h fish per trip. The total willingness to pay for the right to access for a given species is

$$n[\int_0^x f(z, h)dz - xc]$$

Suppose that the anglers are identical not only today, but that they remain so through time with their number constant. The total value, B, of the right to access for this year, for next year discounted and as far in the future as we want to go is given by

$$B = \int_0^T n[\int_0^x f(z, h)dz - xc]e^{-rt}dt \qquad (1)$$

where r is the rate at which benefits are discounted over time, and T is the length of planning period.

Fishery policy is introduced analytically by determining the controllable variables that influence B in Equation 1. Increasing n, the number of anglers, or h, the catch per trip, will increase B. Decreasing x for a given h and c will reduce B. However, none of these direct controls can be exercised without affecting the total catch by anglers. The total catch per period of time (year) is

$$C = nxh = \text{number of anglers} \times \text{trips per angler} \times \text{catch per trip} \qquad (2)$$

Individuals behave as if they have no impact on total catch. For management, the relationship between B and C (benefit and catch) is crucial, for if additional sportfishing has no impact on catch, then authorities, by maximizing B and ignoring C, would achieve the same allocation of catch and efforts as would individual anglers acting unconstrained in their own self-interest.

The direct controls on benefits and catch are the number of trips per angler, x, the number of anglers, n, and the catch per angler, h. Indirect controls could be introduced with license fees that affect the cost of sportfishing, c. An annual fee, of course, would not affect c (cost per trip) but would influence the annual costs of trips. By imposing an annual fee, one expects that the number of anglers, n, would be decreased but the trips per person and harvest rate would remain the same. A license fee per trip (i.e., daily license) would presumably influence both the number of anglers and the number of trips per year. The catch rate would depend on the relationships between fishing success and stock density and the relationship between stock density and catch rate (see below). A fee for catch appears out of the question because of the enforcement expense.

Fishery management policy, of course, is usually concerned with maintaining a density of fish which, in some manner, benefits the resource users.[3] A variable for stock density in year t, S(t), is introduced and could be in practice measured as the stock's biomass, number of fish, or any other appropriately specified unit. Benefits from fishery management accrue when the density is increased and catch per trip rises. Thus h is a function of S: $h = h(S)$[4]. If there are more fish about, they will on average be easier to catch for the representative angler, so that $h'(S) > 0$.

The fish stock as a variable provides two links. It is the dynamic link in the relationships between the benefits of fishing today versus the benefits of fishing tomorrow. It is the static link providing competition between commercial and sportfishermen. The impact of changes in stock density on recreational and commercial catch provides a measure of the severity of competition between the two sectors.

The dynamic elements of fishing are important for fishery policy, as Clark [1977] emphasized. With regard for Clark but with an eye on the realities of management, we will introduce and then suppress the dynamic notions of recreational fishing. Accordingly, suppose that S grows according to the biological relationship $S(t + 1) = S(t) + g(S(t))$ when there is no fishing.

Assume that the biomass growth function g(S) is concave with an S* such that g'(S*) = 0. Suppose that fishery managers find themselves with a sportfishery which they expect not to change for the foreseeable future. What levels of stock density and effort maximize the present discounted value of benefits to this fishery under the assumption that the chosen levels of density and effort repeat themselves indefinitely?[5]

If S(t + 1) = S(t) + g(S(t)) is the biological growth function with no harvest, then the introduction of fishing effort into the biomass relation requires that we subtract catch from this year's growth to give us next year's stock:

$$S(t + 1) = S(t) + g(S(t)) - nxh(S) \tag{3}$$

The level of fish stock and fishing effort are chosen to repeat themselves year after year, so that S(t + 1) = S(t). The amount harvested, nxh(S), must equal the annual surplus g(S). In the optimum steady state solution the fish stock is going to have an important value per unit, called user cost and denoted λ. The mathematical value of λ comes from its service as a Lagrangian multiplier in the surplus equals catch constraint. The substance of the value of the user cost is that having more fish in the ocean makes fish easier to catch, and this increased fish density can be given a monetary value as shown below. The annual (or rental) value of the resource stock is $r\lambda S$, where r is the discount rate. As Burt and Cummings [1977] show, the steady-state maximization problem which yields the same solution as a dynamic problem which settles down to an equilibrium is given by the problem: maximize the Lagrangian expression

$$L = n[\int_{o}^{x} f(z, h(S))dz - xc] - \lambda rS - \lambda[nxh(S) - g(S)] \tag{4}$$

We take it as a given that it is not possible to manage any fishery by controlling fish stock only. Hence this expression is optimized with respect to fishing trips (x) and stock (S). The optimal values of x and S are the ones which satisfy the conditions:

$$\frac{\partial L}{\partial x} = n[f(x, h(S)) - c] - \lambda nh(S) = 0 \tag{5}$$

$$\frac{\partial L}{\partial S} = n[\int_{o}^{x} \frac{\partial f}{\partial h} (z, h(S)) \, dz h'(S)] + r\lambda - nx\lambda h'(S) + g'(S) = 0 \tag{6}$$

Solving for λ gives

$$\lambda = nh'(S) \int_0^X \frac{\partial f}{\partial h} (z, h(S))dz/(r + nxh'(S) - g'(S)) \qquad (7)$$

λ represents the value of another fish in the water to the recreational sector. The numerator of λ is the annual value per representative angler of increasing the catch rate times the number of anglers (n) times the change in catch rate caused by a change in fish stock density $[h'(S)]$. The numerator is essentially the static part of the user cost. The denominator contains the dynamic element of the user cost: the discount rate (r) less the change in the growth function $(g'(S))$ plus the impact of changing stock on the anglers' catch: $nxh'(S)$. Thus the user cost is composed of a purely biological response $(g'(S))$, purely economic responses and the impact of stock density on the catch rate $(h'(S))$ which is a mixture. The term $h'(S)$, which shows how individual creels fill up as the stock density is higher, is the crucial element for management. Note that when stock density has no impact on the rate at which creels fill up $(h'(S) = 0)$, $\lambda = 0$ and, from the point of view of managing recreational fishing stock density does not matter.

Knowing λ at least implicitly is worthwhile for several reasons. First, λ is the marginal value of another fish in the water to sportfishermen. It is proportional to value of increasing fish stock density. For relatively small changes in the fish stock, the social value of the changes is given by $xnh'(S)\lambda\Delta S$. This is the additional social value induced by a change in the biomass density of magnitude S. The equation for λ can be manipulated to read

$$\lambda = \frac{n\int_0^X \frac{\partial f}{\partial h} (z, h)dz}{\frac{r - g'(S)}{h'(S)} + nx}$$

If $r \cong g'(S)$ or $h'(S)$ is very large, then $(r - g'(S))/h'(S)$ is close to zero, and

$$\lambda = \int_0^X \frac{\partial f}{\partial h} (z, h)dz/x$$

then λ is simply the incremental value of changing the catch rate per trip per angler. The relationship between h and S depends on the physical and environmental setting. If the physical distribution of fish is large, then $h'(S)$ will be small. It seems likely that $h(S)$ is a very small number, because h is the catch per trip of a representative angler, and S is the size of the total biomass of the species.

It is clear that λ is an ideal measure. To compute it, one must estimate a catch equation and stock size within reasonable error bounds. This is, at best, a difficult task. Estimating h(S), the relationship between stock density and the catch rate, is also difficult, and we have much less experience with this task. In one of the few empirical works, Stevens [1966] showed that the elasticity of catch with respect to stock of salmon, estimated from time-series data, was about one. Other than the work of Stevens, the h(S) function has not been estimated for marine sportfishing. Though the user cost of fish stock density may appear abstract, it is used, explicitly or implicitly, in policy decisions to change the level of the density.

This discussion has indicated that two crucial links in the connection between management of fish stocks and benefits to recreational anglers are (1) the relationship between fish stock density and fishing success by recreational anglers; (2) the relationship between fishing success by recreational anglers and the number of trips they devote to recreational fishing. Management of recreational fishing cannot proceed on any level other than the short run without better knowledge of these basic bioeconomic relationships.

SOME ECONOMIC ASPECTS OF SHORT-RUN PLANNING

It seems safe to say that fishery management plans and fishery managers do not solve dynamic programming problems. Instead they attempt to deal with a number of short-run problems in a rapidly changing world. The problems ·in this setting are still dynamic, in that fish stocks are growing and anglers may respond to changing fish stock densities. However, the lag between current actions which affect density and the realization of a change in the catch rate by anglers may be so long that h'(S), the change in catch rate with respect to a change in stock, can be assumed to be zero for the short run.

Because the initial focus of the FCMA was on rebuilding stocks, management plans have been concerned with the issue of how to reduce the current catch level. In particular, fishery management plans tend to deal with the total allowable catch and the restrictions invoked in achieving it. One of the roles of economics is to measure the foregone benefits from limiting the catch of the recreational sector. The total catch (C) in the recreational sector is

$$C = hxn \qquad (8)$$

There are three ways to reduce total catch: (1) restrict the catch per angler (h); (2) restrict the number of trips per angler (x); (3) restrict the total number of anglers (n).

The cost of a particular strategy is the impact on total benefits per year. Annual benefits are given by

$$B = n[\int_{0}^{x} f(z, h)dz - cx]$$ (9)

There are three different methods of reducing total catch. What is the difference in the change in B when the three methods cause the same change in catch?

Suppose the desired restriction in catch is ΔC. Then $nh\Delta x$ for regulating trips per angler; $\Delta C = xh\Delta n$ for regulating the number of anglers; and $n\Delta h[x + (\Delta x/\Delta h)]$ for regulating catch per trip. The following section attempts to show which of the three strategies will have the smallest reduction in total benefits.

Let ΔB_1, ΔB_2 and ΔB_3 refer respectively to the reduction in benefits from regulating trips per angler, the number of anglers, and the catch rate. Suppose first that trips per angler are regulated, and let x represent the equilibrium, or unregulated number of trips, and x_r for the regulated number of trips $(x > x_r)$. Then the loss in benefits from restricting trips to x_r is

$$\Delta B_1 = n[\int_{0}^{x_r} f(z, h)dz - x_r c] - n[\int_{0}^{x} f(z, h)dz - xc]$$ (10)

$$= n[-\int_{x_r}^{x} f(z, h)dz + c(x - x_r)]$$

The change in benefits per angler $(\Delta B_1/n)$ is shown in Figure 2 as the vertically striped area. Each angler can gain the vertical area by evading restrictions, so that the method of enforcement will become an important part of the considerations.

The reduction in benefits caused by restricting the number of anglers to $n_r(n > n_r)$ is given by

$$B_2 = (n_r - n)[\int_{0}^{x} f(z, h)dz - xc]$$ (11)

The loss in benefits from reducing trips per angler is less than the loss from reducing the number of anglers. This can be seen by noting that in each case the total reduction in trips is the same; the difference being that in the first case the number of anglers remains the same but the trips taken by each are reduced and in the second the trips per angler remain the same but the number

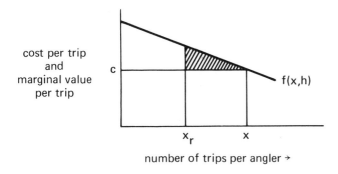

cost per trip
and
marginal value
per trip

Figure 2.   Effect of restricting trips.

of participants is reduced. However, in the case of reducing the number of anglers, the loss in benefits per trip is greater because higher valued trips as well as lower valued trips per angler are lost. That is, the marginal value per trip of an excluded angler exceeds the marginal value per trip of an angler who was not excluded. Hence, a management plan which proposes to achieve a given level of catch reduction by restricting trips can minimize the loss to the anglers themselves by restricting trips per angler rather than the number of anglers. Of course, management plans need to consider not only the loss to the anglers but the loss to taxpayers imposed by high costs of enforcing regulations, if they can indeed be enforced.

Now consider the loss that occurs from regulating h, the catch per angler. First, restricting h has two effects on total catch: (1) for a fixed number of trips a smaller h results in fewer fish caught; (2) a smaller h makes fishing less attractive and hence reduces the number of trips per angler, again reducing total catch. Let h be the unregulated catch rate, h_r be the regulated catch rate, and x_h the number of trips per angler that results when the catch rate is regulated. Mathematically the loss in benefits from restrictions on the catch rate is

$$B_3 = n[\int_o^{x_h} f(z, h)dz - cx_h] - n[\int_o^x f(z, h)dz - cx] \qquad (12)$$

$$= n[\int_o^{x_h} [f(z, h_r) - f(z, h)]dz - (\int_{x_h}^x f(z, h)dz - c(x - x_h))]$$

This change in benefits per angler $(\Delta B_3/n)$ is the horizontally striped area in Figure 3. By assumption the number of anglers is constant for changes in x

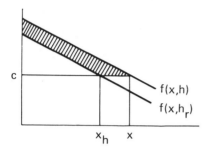

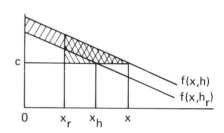

Figure 3. Effect of restricting catch rate.

Figure 4. Difference between trip restrictions and catch rate restrictions.

and changes in h, so that the less costly alternative reduces benefits per angler by the smaller amount. Figure 4 (which is essentially Figure 2 imposed on Figure 3) compares the costs of the two methods of regulation. In Figure 4, the loss from reducing the catch rate from h to h_r and hence indirectly reducing trips per angler from x to x_h, is the horizontally striped area. The vertically striped area is the loss from restricting the number of trips per angler from x to x_r such that the same reduction in total catch is achieved. The areas which are both horizontally and vertically striped cancel out. If the area which is only vertically striped exceeds the area only horizontally striped then trip restrictions are more costly than catch rate restrictions.

The better alternative depends on how the individual angler's trips respond to changes in the catch rate. At one extreme, if there is no responsiveness to changes in the catch rate, x_h will equal x, and there is no loss in benefits from constraining the catch rate. Hence catch rate restrictions are a better policy. At the other extreme, if trips per angler are highly responsive to changes in the catch rate, x_h will be very close to x_r, and the losses from catch rate restrictions will greatly exceed the losses from restrictions on trips.

Several conclusions emerge from this analysis of the choice of regulation approach to recreational fishing. First, in choosing whether to regulate trips per angler or the number of anglers, net losses to anglers are less when trips per angler are regulated. Second, the choice between restricting the catch rate (or bag or daily possession) and trips per angler depends on how responsive individual anglers are to expected catch. Only in the case where anglers do not respond to changes in expected catch will catch rate regulation have no impact on anglers' welfare. One facet of recreational fishing seems clear: anglers like to catch fish, and the more fish the better. Perhaps the most important conclusion from this section is that the behavioral relationship—how anglers respond to changes in fishing success—again appears as a crucial piece of information in determining appropriate strategies.

This analysis unfortunately ignores the methods of imposing regulations and their costs. For example, catch regulations are generally imposed on a maximum per day rather than a mean per year. This daily regulation will generally affect only a small number of anglers fishing on a particular mode. And the enforcement of regulations raises another issue which is primarily a political one. It seems difficult to make and enforce regulations without a simple system for licensing anglers. In addition, as noted, this analysis is short run and ignores the stock dynamics.

EXAMPLE

In this section, an example illustrates the conceptual issues addressed in the previous section using a substantial but imperfect data base. The example demonstrates the estimation of a demand curve and the use of the demand curve in making management plans.

The travel cost method, while the subject of considerable criticism, provides a well tested framework for estimating demand functions.[6] Because of the data shortcomings, the units of analysis are shifted from trips per angler to trips per capita, so that total trips equals population times trips per capita (rather than users times trips per user). The travel cost method essentially estimates a per capita demand function from observations on means of variables by geographical area or distance zone. In the example below, a travel cost demand curve is estimated using data from a survey on recreational fishing in Rhode Island. These data provide an example only, and should not be used by themselves for policy because they refer to fishing from shore during a two-month period (August-September 1978) only.[7]

The basic travel cost model is as follows: Let

trips_i = estimated total number of trips, region i to the shore

pop_i = population of region i

c_i = cost per trip, mean for region i

y_i = income per family in \$1,000's, mean for region i

u_i = disturbance term, $u_i \sim N(0, \sigma_i^2)$

x_i = $\text{trips}_i / \text{pop}_i$ = per capita trips, region i

The model estimated is

$$In \; x_i = a_0 + a_1 c_i + a_2 y_i + u_i \qquad (13)$$

The costs are measured as out of pocket expenses plus the travel cost of $0.15 per mile. The opportunity cost of time is implicitly set to zero. The data used here are preliminary, and do not permit the direct estimation of a catch rate coefficient. The estimated equation (see McConnell and Smith [1979]) is

$$In \; x_i = -1.92 \quad -0.102c_i \quad +0.038y_i \qquad (14)$$

$$(3.2) \qquad (3.6) \qquad (1.3)$$

$$R^2 = 0.32; \quad n = 37; \quad F(2,34) = 7.9$$

This is a per capita demand curve rather than a per user demand curve, and it is for a two-month period, not for the year. With these caveats in mind, we can analyze the foregone benefits of trip restrictions.

First, we can estimate total benefits for fishing during the period from the 37 regions in the study as

$$B = \sum_{i=1}^{37} pop_i \; [\text{benefits per capita, region i}] \qquad (15)$$

and

$$\text{benefits per capita} = \int_c^\infty \exp[a_0 + a_1 s + a_2 y] \, ds = -x/a_1 \qquad (16)$$

so that

$$B = \sum_{i=1}^{37} pop_i \; (-x_i/a_1) = \frac{-1}{a_1} \sum_{i=1}^{37} pop_i x_i = \frac{-1}{a_1} \; \text{total trips} \qquad (17)$$

(The peculiar result in Equation 17, that total benefits equals total trips times $(-1/a_1)$, is a consequence of the functional form of the demand function given in Equation 13.) The estimate of total benefits for the two-month period based on 135,000 trips is $1.3 million.

From the survey it is known that the total catch of all species from shore was 174,000 fish or 1.3 fish per trip. Suppose that we want to reduce the catch of all fish by 20% for the period, and suppose that the reduction is to be accomplished by cutting back on trips by 20%. (The question of how this restriction is to be achieved will go unanswered here, but it is a question which could be asked and answered of every regulation.) For simplicity, each region's total trips will be reduced by 20% also. The total loss in benefits is given by computing the loss per angler for each region, multiplying by population and summing over all regions

$$\Delta B = \sum_{i=1}^{37} pop_i [-\int_{x_i^r}^{x_i} f(z, y_i)\, dz - c_i(x_i^r - x_i)] \qquad (18)$$

This comes directly from Equation 10.

The resulting loss in benefits is $260,000. The distribution of the loss per region varies significantly by region, with the closer regions suffering more than the distant regions. By reducing benefits by $260,000, fishery managers could reduce total catch by 34,800 fish.

In this example, the effect of the catch rate on per capita trips has not been estimated. We can simulate this result by appending a catch rate coefficient to Equation 15. This will let us use a numerical example to show the impact of reducing the catch rate. Suppose the demand function were given by

$$ln\ x = a_0 + a_1 c + a_2 y + a_3 h \qquad (19)$$

and further, suppose that at the mean value of h, the elasticity of x with respect to h is 0.1:[8]

$$\partial ln\ x / \partial ln\ h = \%\Delta x / \%\Delta h = 0.1 \qquad (20)$$

From Equation 19 $\partial ln\ x / \partial ln\ h = ha_3$, evaluated at the mean of $h = 1.3$ gives

$$ha_3 = 1.3(a_3) = 0.1 \therefore a_3 = 0.1/1.3 = 0.077$$

so that the demand function which reflects this behavior at the mean is

$$ln\ x = -1.92 - 0.102c + 0.038y + 0.077h \qquad (21)$$

The constant term and the coefficients on c and y are as computed in Equation 14. Now it is possible to compute the reduction in the catch rate that it takes to achieve 20% reduction in total catch, when 20% of the catch is 34,800.

$$Total\ catch = \sum_{i=1}^{n} pop_i x_i h$$

$$\therefore 0.2\ (total\ catch) = 34{,}800 = \Delta h \Sigma pop_i x_i + h \Sigma pop_i\, (\partial x_i / \partial h)\Delta h$$

But Equations 19 and 20 imply that $\partial x / \partial h = x a_3$ so that

$$34,800 = \Delta h [\Sigma pop_i x_i (1 + a_3)] = \Delta h (1 + a_3) \Sigma pop_i x_i$$

Solving for Δh gives

$$\Delta h = 34,600/(1 + a_3) \, (\Sigma pop_i x_i) = 0.24$$

Thus reducing the catch rate on average from 1.3 to 1.06, a reduction of 18%, brings a 20% reduction in total catch. The loss in anglers' welfare brought about by this reduction in the catch rate can be calculated from Equations 18 and 19. The change in trips is about 2800, and the induced change in benefits is about \$25,000 or 2%. This number is much less than the change in benefits brought about by reducing trips by 20% because the elasticity of trips with respect to the catch rate is so low.

This example has shown two approaches to estimating the costs of restricting the total recreational catch. Each approach is feasible in that it can be carried out using survey data. In fact, with some supplementary information, the currently conducted National Marine Fisheries Service national survey of recreational fishing can be used to estimate travel cost demand curves of an imperfect but usable sort. The basic information needed is the number of trips from origin i, mean catch per trip from origin i, and estimate of the total number of trips, and mean measures of determinants such as income, or variables which are plausibly important determinants.

CONCLUSION

This chapter has dealt with some empirical approaches to obtaining the conceptual information needed for the management of recreational fishing. Given the current data base, it is not possible to engage in any "optimal" management of sportfisheries. In fact, it is questionable whether a benefit-cost analysis which included transactions and enforcement costs as well as gains to the anglers would ever show that management of sportfisheries is economically justifiable. Given the current methods of making management plans, the most productive role for economics seems likely to be in determining the management restrictions which attain the goals at minimum cost to society and to the anglers. Creel limits appear to be the least costly method although only a heuristic proof of this was offered herein.

Two basic relationships are needed to assess the impact of regulations on sportfisheries. The first, denoted h(S) in the text, is the relationship between fish stock density and the angler's catch of fish. Analogous relationships are equally valuable and similarly unavailable for commercial fishing. Because of the expense and uncertainty, it seems unlikely that we will ever have good estimates of h(S), though our understanding of the relationship between the distribution of ages, classes and the ability to catch fish will improve. The more important and more plausible relationship to know is between angler trips and expected catch. The magnitude of the response of trips to changes in expected catch is crucial in determining management strategy.

ACKNOWLEDGMENTS

We appreciate the comments of Richard Agnello and other conference participants, as well as the research help of Bruce Madariage. Agricultural Experiment Station Contribution Number 5959, Scientific Article Number A-2904.

NOTES

[1]The figures in this paragraph are taken from a forthcoming report on marine sports angling in Rhode Island by McConnell and Smith [1981].

[2]There are several important implicit and explicit assumptions in this paragraph. First is that the expected catch per trip is exogenous. It seems reasonable to suppose that individual anglers accumulate skills and are in part able to choose how many fish they catch. Second, the trade-off between catching fish and other types of quality variables, such as congestion and weather, may be endogenously determined. Both of these matters are within the purview of the household production function. For an analysis of the household production function within the context of recreational fishing, see Bockstael and McConnell [1980].

[3]This section is based on McConnell and Sutinen [1979].

[4]Clearly, h(S) and S(t) have to be in similar units or else another transformation is required.

[5]There is a growing literature in this area. See McConnell and Sutinen [1979], Bishop and Samples [1980] and Anderson [1980] for starters.

[6]The travel cost method has been used in Brown, Singh and Castle [1966] and discussed in Freeman [1979] and Dwyer et al. [1977]. There are many conceptual and practical issues which are not addressed in this simple example. The cost of time, the functional form, the certain pressure of heteroscedastic errors, and the bias from omitting the costs of substitutes are examples of but a few problems not considered here. The travel cost approach is taken here because of its relative simplicity. An alternative, some form of bidding game could prove useful, especially when results are needed quickly. The bidding game approach is basically an attempt to measure consumers' surplus direct from a respondent. For a review of such methods, see Currie and Kidd [1980].

[7]There are 37 regions, one for each town in Rhode Island. For details of the survey, see McConnell and Smith [1979].
[8]This is the lowest estimate given by Stevens [1966].

REFERENCES

1. Anderson, L. G. 1980. "An Economic Analysis of Joint Recreational and Commercial Fisheries," paper presented at International Symposium of Fishery Resources Allocation, Vichy, France, April 20-24.
2. Bishop, R. C., and K. Samples. 1980. "Sport and Commercial Fishing Conflicts: A Theoretical Analysis," *J. Environ. Econ. Management* 7:220-233.
3. Bockstael, N. E., and K. E. McConnell. 1980. "Estimating and Using the Household Production Function for Wildlife Recreation," unpublished.
4. Brown, W., A. Singh and E. Castle. 1965. "Net Economic Value of Oregon Salmon Steelhead Sport Fishery," *J. Wildlife Management* Vol. 29.
5. Burt, O. R., and R. Cummings. 1977. "Natural Resource Management, the Steady State and Approximately Optimal Decision Rules," *Land Econ.* 53(1):1-22.
6. Clark, C. W. 1977. "Control Theory in Fisheries Economics: Frill or Fundamental?" in *Economic Impacts of Extended Fisheries Jurisdiction,* L. G. Anderson, Ed. (Ann Arbor, MI: Ann Arbor Science Publishers, Inc.).
7. Currie, J. W., and J. Kidd. 1980. "Documentation of Bidding Games Used in Measuring Social Value," Battelle Pacific Northwest Laboratories, PNL-2798.
8. Dwyer, J. D., J. R. Kelly and M. D. Bowes. 1977. "Improved Procedures for Valuation of the Contribution of Recreation to National Economic Development," Research Report No. 128, University of Illinois, Urbana, IL.
9. Freeman, A. M., III. 1979. *The Benefits of Environmental Improvement* (Baltimore, MD: The Johns Hopkins University Press).
10. Krutilla, J. V., and A. C. Fisher. 1975. *The Economics of Natural Environments* (Baltimore, MD: The Johns Hopkins University Press).
11. McConnell, K. E., and T. P. Smith. 1979. "Marine Recreational Fishing in Rhode Island, August 1978 to January 1979," University of Rhode Island Marine Memorandum 62, University of Rhode Island Marine Advisory Service.
12. McConnell, K. E., and T. P. Smith. 1981. "Marine Recreational Fishing in Rhode Island—Report on a Survey," University of Rhode Island Sea Grant publication, Kingston.
13. McConnell, K. E., and J. G. Sutinen. 1979. "Bioeconomic Models of Marine Recreational Fishing," *J. Environ. Econ. Management* 6:127-139.
14. Stevens, J. B. 1966. "Angler Success as a Quality Determinant of Sport Fishery Recreational Values," *Trans. Am. Fish Soc.* Vol. 95.
15. U.S. Department of Commerce. 1973. "1970 Salt-Water Angling Survey," National Oceanic and Atmospheric Administration, Current Fisheries Statistics No. 6200.

COMMENT–CHAPTER 11

Richard J. Agnello
Department of Economics
University of Delaware

I enjoyed reading this chapter and found it to be clear and useful as far as it goes. My main criticism is that the paper might have gone somewhat further. At the outset, the paper provides a good background setting for recreational fishery analysis. For the future, it is argued that analysis of sports fishing may be very important due to an anticipated increased future demand for recreational fishing relative to commercial fishing. This is not a new argument and is based on the contention that prices of substitutes for commercial fishing (e.g., meat and poultry) are falling relative to prices of substitutes for recreational marine fishing (such as hunting and freshwater fishing). This is due to the intensive use of natural environments by marine fishing substitutes. Since the supply of natural environments is fixed, we expect the price of substitutes for marine fishing to increase relatively rapidly and thus the value of marine recreational fishing to increase relative to commercial fishing.

This is an interesting argument and may prove true. However, it seems to me that it is not obviously true for several reasons. One reason is simply that the issue is empirical in nature and what has been the experience in the past cannot simply be extrapolated into the future. In fact, since the agricultural sector is already quite efficient, future efficiency gains may be hard to come by.

Since all activities use the natural environment, supply constraints will impinge on everything, including agricultural substitutes for commercial fish. In addition, since leisure enjoyment is an important aspect of recreational fishing, substitutes which compete for an individual's limited leisure time become relevant. Technological change may have a large and unpredictable impact. What comes to mind is some sort of electronic sports fishing game.

The authors implictly are not optimistic about a grand future for sport fishing when in the paper's conclusion they mention that management of sports fisheries may never be justified by a comprehensive cost-benefit analysis.

The bulk of the chapter focuses on the basic economic relationships important for managing sport fisheries and the economic benefits of regulation. The chapter takes a narrow methodological approach. The emphasis is on fish stocks only and ignores the jointness between sports fishing and other recreational activities consumed along with sports fishing. The chapter is thus not a part of the current literature on hedonic pricing and recreation where the value of sports fishing is determined implicitly along with the values of other jointly consumed recreational activities. The authors argue that these other factors can be ignored if they are uncorrelated with (or I might alternatively add perfectly correlated with) catch information. Unfortunately the correlations are neither 0 or ±1, and the omitted factors would be relevant in a more general approach.

Let me discuss briefly the elements omitted from the paper before discussing the paper's findings.

1. No mention is made of the multispecies nature of recreational fish catch. Just as with commercial fishing, sportsfish catch is not homogeneous. Multiple species complicate demand and production function analysis for commercial fisheries and would presumably do the same for recreational fisheries.
2. Possible interactions between sports and commercial fisheries are omitted.
3. Most importantly, and I think the major criticism of this paper, is that the household production approach using the hedonic method for determining the value of nonmarket activities such as sports fishing is completely ignored. Since the authors have contributed to this literature, this is surprising.

The foundation of the hedonic approach is the derivation of prices for components of aggregate goods such as housing and vacations. House-hunters, given adequate time and a sufficiently rich assortment of houses to view, develop a good idea of what they can expect to pay for living close to work, having a nice yard, good schools, an extra room, a fireplace, etc. House-hunters gain this expertise by shopping and comparing the price of a house with a given set of characteristics with the price of a house with a slightly different bundle of characteristics. Attributing the difference in housing prices to the difference(s) in characteristic(s), the house-hunter has implicitly priced one or more characteristics for which there is no explicit market. This is the essence of the hedonic valuation procedure.

The hedonic valuation procedure is a two stage process. Expressed in the context of sportfishing, the first stage is to regress expenditures for a fishing trip or vacation activity on its characteristics such as quantity of each species caught, time spent fishing, length of the boat and any other characteristics of the trip. The derivative of the estimated expenditure function with respect to any given characteristic generates its implicit price (P_i) or marginal cost which the consumer faces in making his particular choices.

In the second stage, these implicit prices are combined with observations on the quantities of characteristics purchased and with other demand and supply determinants to estimate simultaneously a set of demand and supply equations for the separate sportsfishing characteristics such as fish caught.

Let me briefly review the main body of the paper. Although a very partial equilibrium approach is taken by the authors, the chapter is still quite useful to managers because what is done, although limited, is done well. Using some straightforward economic theory, the authors derive the marginal value of catch and eventually the net value of the right to access a recreational fishery.

They make explicit what variables fishery managers must change to influence this economic valuation and what controls are available to effect these changes.

They do this first for a static model and then expand it by including stock density of fish which is dynamic in nature although a steady-state equilibrium framework is assumed.

The end product of their modeling is to maximize the value of a recreational fishery and thus determine the marginal value of a unit of catch. Knowing this would allow managers to determine the optimal harvest of a fishery. The authors do a nice job of focusing on the elements of this calculation.

Unfortunately, many of these elements although clearly specified in theory are empirically elusive. The unknowns include (1) stock growth through time; (2) the effect of stock change on catch; and (3) the effect of catch rate on consumer willingness to pay. The paper makes a contribution in clearly pointing out the need to know these variables, and their theoretical linkages. It makes no contribution to their empirical measurement, however.

After abandoning the general management problem, the authors focus on the more limited and practical problem of regulating sensibly if you cannot regulate optimally. This is perhaps the paper's main contribution for management. The authors assume the goal of reducing catch as a very simple short-run management objective and analyze direct ways to achieve a catch reduction and the accompanying costs. They conclude, not surprisingly, that it is theoretically more efficient to either reduce the catch per angler or the trips per angler rather than the number of anglers. It is an empirical question as to whether reducing catch per angler is more or less efficient than reducing trips per angler.

This issue can be settled empirically and it does not seem too difficult to design experiments, whether it be surveys or field studies, to determine the willingness to pay of anglers for catch. Studies of this kind are surely needed if we are to make any headway in managing recreational fisheries. Unfortunately the Marine Angler's Survey conducted by NMFS does little to help us here. When its results finally become available, very good catch information but little economic information will be provided.

Another point that I would like to make is that the analysis by McConnell and Strand assumes the homogeneity of anglers. When this assumption is relaxed, the analysis becomes more complicated, and quantity restrictions might be shown to be generally less efficient than price controls since the former restrict the highest valued user the same as the lowest valued user.

The last part of the paper presents an example which, unfortunately, assumes away some of the modeling done in the paper. Although a demand curve is estimated empirically, this demand relation omits the rate of catch (i.e., catch per trip) from the demand function. Since the catch rate was one of the variables in the theoretical analysis (and I might say the most interesting variable), the empirical example only weakly correlates to the theoretical sections. Again the problem is surely lack of data, and I commiserate with the authors. Much more empirical work needs to be done in sports fishing analysis in order to better understand the motivations of the recreational fisherman. To do this, more data must be available than what currently exists. That state of managing recreational fisheries is certainly at its infancy.

CHAPTER 12

ECONOMICS OF DEVELOPMENT AND MANAGEMENT: THE ALASKAN GROUNDFISH CASE

Robert L. Stokes

Institute for Marine Studies
University of Washington

The purpose of this paper is to identify, from the experience of Alaska groundfish management, some of the contributions that economic analysis can make to the management of developing fisheries, those primarily exploited by foreign nations at present. To this end, three topics are explored: optimal yield adjustments, joint ventures and protection of incidental species. Each subject is considered (1) as it is treated in current practice, and (2) as it might be dealt with through a model of rational choice among competing social values commonly used in applied economic research.

ALASKA GROUNDFISH RESOURCES

Management of the groundfish resources of the Bering Sea and the Gulf of Alaska is one of the major tasks set by the Fisheries Conservation and Management Act (FCMA) of 1976. Although current U.S. groundfish harvest is small, the significance of the combined U.S. and foreign harvest (Table I) can be seen by comparison with more familiar magnitudes. In 1979 the foreign harvest of Alaska groundfish was 89% of the total U.S. allocation from all fisheries to foreign nations. The combined U.S. and foreign harvest equaled 54% of the U.S. harvest of all species. On a 30%-yield basis, the Alaska groundfish harvest equaled 115% of U.S. consumption of fresh and frozen

Table I.   1979 Output of Developing Alaska Fisheries (metric tons round weight)[a]

	Japan	Mexico	Poland	Republic of Korea	Canada	USSR	Taiwan	U.S. Joint Venture	U.S. Shore Based
Gulf of Alaska									
Atka Mackerel	544.5	36.3	0.4	74.6	–	10,262.0	–	–	–
Cod, Pacific	8,823.4	939.3	126.9	806.7	–	833.6	–	700	1,000
Flounders	12,331.7	113.1	18.6	597.2	–	366.5	–	100	400
Halibut	–	–	–	–	1,085.9	–	–	–	–
Ling Cod	–	–	–	–	–	–	–	–	–
Pacific Ocean Perch	7,334.0	457.0	5.3	821.7	–	1,066.2	–	–	300
Pollock, Alaska	32,114.2	8,676.9	19,551.2	25,549.2	–	17,176.7	–	600	2,100
Rockfish	1,068.5	6.6	18.7	183.5	–	121.7	–	–	–
Sablefish	5,866.0	54.7	–	758.4	–	150.4	–	–	3,300
Squid, Unclassified	260.6	12.6	9.1	143.2	–	1.2	–	–	–
Other Finfish	2,265.8	100.8	14.0	754.7	–	983.6	–	–	400
Total	71,608.7	10,397.3	19,744.5	29,689.2	1,085.9	30,916.9	–	1,400	7,500
Bering Sea									
Atka Mackerel	1,657.4	–	1.3	1,329.0	–	20,277.3	–	–	–
Cod, Pacific	35,480.3	–	16.5	3,232.8	–	2,615.7	39.4	–	600
Yellowfin Sole	53,482.9	–	–	1,348.7	–	41,258.7	3.0	–	–
Flounders	75,776.2	–	1.6	1,960.6	–	12,128.1	19.2	–	–
Halibut	–	–	–	–	–	–	–	–	b
Herring, Sea	1,707.8	–	–	107.6	–	5,529.5	–	–	–
Pacific Ocean Perch	6,875.1	–	1.9	281.2	–	21.6	2.6	–	–
Pollock, Alaska	779,003.6	–	18,229.9	83,787.7	–	58,715.5	1,928.6	–	–
Sablefish	1,691.0	–	1.8	425.3	–	49.2	6.3	–	–
Snails	537.2	–	–	–	–	–	–	–	–
Squid, Unclassified	5,739.2	–	24.5	1,232.7	–	6.4	14.2	–	–
Tanner Crab	14,953.5	–	–	–	–	–	–	–	b
Other finfish	52,672.7	–	5.8	3,962.2	–	8,054.4	–	–	600
Total	1,029,576.9	–	18,283.2	97,667.8	–	148,656.6	2,013.3	–	8,100
Grand Total	1,101,185.6	10,397.3	38,027.7	127,357.0	1,085.9	179,573.5	2,013.3	1,400	8,100

aSource: U.S. National Marine Fisheries Service (Annual a).
bU.S. fishermen took a total of 59,589 metric tons of tanner crab and 9,968 metric tons of halibut from the Bering Sea and Gulf of Alaska.

groundfish products. Globally, Alaska contributed about 9% to the world's groundfish supply. [United Nations Annual a,b; U.S. National Marine Fisheries Service Annual a,b].

Not surprisingly, these resources are seen as the single most important opportunity for further development of the U.S. fishing industry and of that part of Alaska's economy which relies on renewable resources. Alaska groundfish are also of vital importance to those fishing nations which currently depend on them for protein food supplies and for the employment of their distant-water fishing fleets. Alaska groundfish are also important to U.S. consumers, whether they consume groundfish produced by U.S. industry or imports from the world groundfish market which in turn depends on Alaska supplies. Finally, the management of Alaska groundfish discloses a number of issues equally applicable to other developing fisheries—elsewhere in the U.S. fisheries conservation zone (FCZ) or in the economic-resource zones of other coastal states, where it is often the United States that must adapt to the role of foreign fishing nation.

From an economic standpoint the distinguishing characteristics of Alaska groundfish management are the dominance of foreign fisheries and efforts by the U.S. government and fishing industry to establish a U.S. fishery. Each of the following policy issues is directly related to that effort. In the following sections each issue is discussed both as it would be viewed within a multiobjective model of policy choice, and as it has actually been treated so far by those responsible for management of Alaska groundfish. An appendix discusses some of the empirical economic tasks and problems that would have to be faced if the suggested multiobjective models are to be adopted as a guide to policy choice.

Multiobjective decision theory has a long history of application to the management of natural resources, particularly the evaluation of federally supported land and water resource projects. The general framework for multiobjective analysis is specified in the U.S. Water Resources Council [1973] principles and standards, as well as in a number of benefit cost analysis texts such as Howe [1971]. The essential logic is summarized below.

> In general, multiobjective theory provides the basis for moving from the objectives of society to system design in an iterative fashion. . . . Thus, the theory is concerned with the choice of objectives, and the final choice of a plan. . . . The choice of the objectives for planning is fundamental. The extent to which the objectives chosen are the right ones determines to a significant degree the success of a planning effort. Because for many planning operations . . . a very large range of objectives is relevant, even if only in small degree, and because planning resources are generally limited, some criterion is required for the selection of objectives to be studied. The criterion . . . is that those objectives should be included in analyses that are both important to society and are those on which the range of measures under consideration is likely to have some significant effect.

The application of this criterion requires judgment both on the part of the planner and on the part of the decision-maker. An iterative process should be at work. The initial set of objectives chosen for analysis on this criterion might not be the set of objectives that is really of importance. There should be checkpoints in the planning process to allow for expansion or contraction of the objective set as planning proceeds [Major and Lenton 1979].

A familiar textbook question in fisheries economics, whether to manage for physical or net economic yield, illustrates how multiobjective theory can be applied to fisheries management problems. The simple static model of an open access fishery with unit prices and unit costs, is displayed in panel A of Figure 1. Maximum economic yield (MEY) occurs at effort level E_1, where marginal revenue equals marginal cost. Effort levels below E_1 would be of no interest to a rational decision-maker, as they require sacrifices of both physical and economic yield. However, by increasing effort from E_1 to E_2 the decision-maker can sacrifice net economic value for increases in physical output. The nature of that tradeoff is indicated by the transformation function (F) in panel B. The curve denoted by F is the relationship between net profits and physical yield as is derived from what are assumed to be empirically estimable revenue (TR) and cost (TC) functions in panel A.

The indifference curves (W'), (W''), (W''') describe the preferences of a rational decision-maker who considers both net economic value and physical output to be relevant social objectives. Introduction of physical output as a social objective, independent of economic value, might reflect the commonly held view that contributions to food supply have a social signficance not entirely captured by their monetary value.

A decision-maker who adopts this view would presumably choose an effort level such as E_3, which maximizes neither net economic value nor physical output, but a social welfare function that recognizes the significance of both. In the terminology of FCMA, choice of E_3 might be regarded as a determination of optimum yield (OY).

In the following sections this multiobjective approach is applied to three issues in the management of Alaska groundfish. In each case an empirically estimable model is described which indicates both the economic research required and how that research could be used to derive one or more multiobjective transformation functions such as F.

The usefulness of such an approach depends entirely on the willingness of decision-makers to regard their task as rational choice among multiple social objectives. Hence, a discussion is also provided of how they might do so for each issue, and how each issue has been discussed so far. The reader who wishes to examine more carefully the implied standard of decision-maker rationally can turn to a variety of interesting works on the subject [Elmore 1978; Lindblom 1979; Wildavsky 1979].

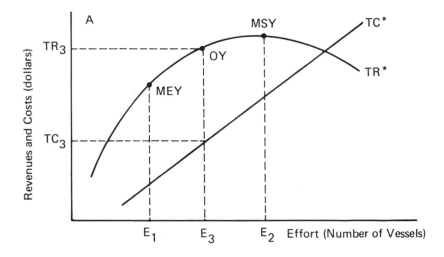

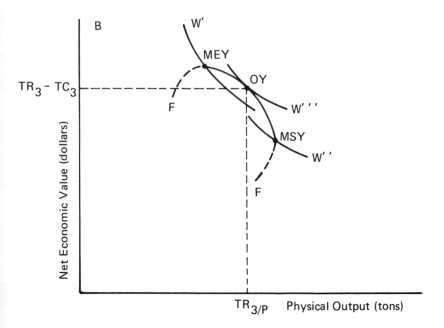

Figure 1.   Transformation function between net economic value and physical output.

OPTIMUM YIELD

In a developing fishery, the restriction of output to increase stock size presents economic trade offs different from the more familiar ones in a fishery fully utilized by the domestic industry. In the fully utilized fishery, it is the domestic industry which pays for the long-run benefit of a healthier stock in terms of short-run losses of output, profits and employment. In the developing fishery, FCMA imposes short-run cutbacks on the foreign components while conferring both short- and long-term benefits on the domestic industry. That is, output reductions alter not only the time distribution benefits but also their division between the foreign and the domestic fishery.

The population dynamics of a demersal fishery, and the preferential rights granted by FCMA to domestic fishermen, explain why the U.S. fishing industry always gains from output reduction. As long as the resource is at less than its virgin stock size, output reductions will incease the density of fish and their age distribution. The relationship between initial stock size and that which will support maximum sustained yield, of course, determines whether the effect on long-run total output will be positive or negative. However, where there is also a foreign component, FCMA imposes no quantity constraints on the U.S. fishery; hence the domestic industry will feel the economic effects only of the density and age distribution of the stock.

Long-run profitability will increase when unit (per ton) costs are reduced by spreading the essentially fixed daily fishing expenditures over the higher daily catch rates obtainable from a larger, denser stock. And, for some species such as Alaska pollock, revenue per ton may increase as well, since the value of pollock produced for sale in the U.S. market varies substantially according to size. At the low end, one third or more can be used only in the production of fish meal and oil, and under present economic conditions these fish are often discarded at sea. Of the larger fish suitable for human consumption, only a portion can be used to produce higher valued individual fillets. As the proportion of larger fish increases, some pollock should move from the fish-meal/discard category into human consumption and others from the fillet-block to the individual-fillet category, in each case increasing the economic value of the harvest.

However, some special characteristics of the pollock resources may offset these benefits. Parasitism, common in older and more densly concentrated fish, may reduce product quality and increase processing costs. Also, because pollock are cannibalistic, the greater proportion of older fish may eat so many of the young as to cause periodic shortages of recruitment. Finally, some of the older pollock may migrate into nonfishable areas off the continental shelf.

In the short run, reductions in output may improve prices and market opportunities for the domestic industry. There is widespread feeling in the industry that a reduction in the foreign allocation of any species will compel foreign nations to replace lost supplies with purchases from the U.S. industry. However, in cases where U.S. costs exceed prices, output reductions must increase prices by at least the amount of the deficit before the domestic industry will benefit. For some species such as tanner crab, where 90% of world supply comes from the U.S. FCZ, such a price relationship most likely exists. But, it remains to be seen whether this is also true for groundfish, where production from the U.S. FCZ accounts for only 9% of world supply.

Foreign fishermen will generally lose from production cutbacks which come entirely out of their allocations. If the long-run effect is to reduce output (initial stock size being equal to or greater than MSY stock size) there is little opportunity for eventual gain. And, even if output is increased in the long run, foreigners will benefit only if the U.S. industry proves economically unable to exercise its preferential rights.

Do any domestic U.S. values hinge on the level of foreign fishing? The common belief that foreign fishing is of no value to the United States, or is even a positive nuisance, cannot withstand careful examination. Even under present federal allocation policy the United States collects some (nominal) foreign fees and presumably also gains diplomatic leverage in the allocation process. The benefits to the domestic industry and to the public at large should increase if the present trend continues: namely, a policy of exchanging foreign allocation rights for efforts to develop specific fisheries and/or higher fees. If such benefits increase, the United States will, of course, also stand to lose more by any reduction or elimination of foreign fishing levels.

In the context of the multiobjective rational model, different levels of reduction of output can be seen as alternatives which vary in their contribution to the values of domestic and foreign fishing. The specific nature of the tradeoff depends on the combined influence of stock density, age distribution and price-elasticity effects, and on the initial economic position of the domestic industry.

The implied trade-offs are described in Figure 2 for three assumptions about the initial cost/revenue position of the U.S. industry. In the first case (C_1^0, R_1^0), the U.S. industry just breaks even at the stock size, CPUE, size distribution and world market price consistent with management for maximum sustained yield and the resulting level of foreign fishing (T_0). In this case, the cost and revenue effects of reduced foreign fishing (slopes of the functions C_1 and R_1) could be used to derive a transformation frontier (F_1) along which all reductions in foreign fishing imply some improvement in the prospects for U.S. fisheries development. Under the second set of initial cost conditions (C_2^0, R_2^0) the same cost/revenue effects would imply such a trade off only for those reductions which would bring foreign fishing below some critical level (T_1) sufficient to move U.S. industry at least to a breakeven point. Here a meaningful transformation function (F_2) exists only for levels of foreign fishing below (T_1). Finally, under the third and the least favorable set of initial conditions $(C_3^0,$

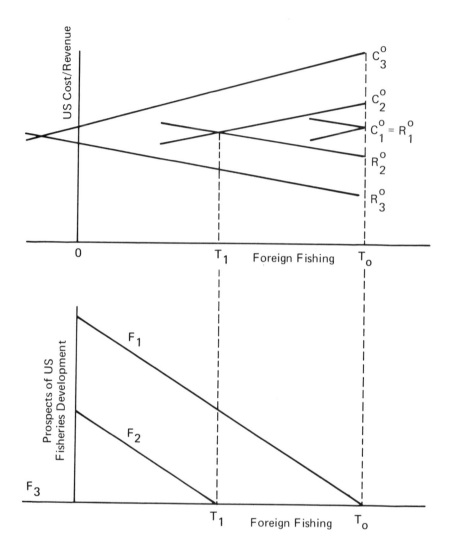

Figure 2.   Transformation function between U.S. and foreign fishing in a developing fishery.

R_3^0) that breakeven point cannot be attained even if foreign fishing is completely eliminated. Hence, as transformation function (F_3) indicates, the U.S. industry cannot benefit from any reduction in foreign fishing.

Suppose that decision-makers are considering reductions in foreign fishing to stimulate the domestic industry. Recognizing the relative importance of the contributions made by both foreign and domestic fishing, they seek empirical economic information on the current situation. In some cases, such research may indicate that the domestic industry is close enough to the break-even point so that either a large or a small reduction in foreign fishing will stimulate its development (F_1). One would expect the decision-makers then to respond by selecting that level of reduction which would express their view of the relative importance of domestic as opposed to foreign fishing. In cases where research indicated a substantial gap between prices and U.S. costs, which could be overcome only with large reductions in foreign fishing (F_2), the same preference function might lead either to adoption of such substantial reductions or to no reductions at all. Finally, if research indicated that elimination of foreign fishing would still leave U.S. industry below the breakeven point (F_3) one would expect decision makers to reject any output reductions, regardless of the relative values they place on foreign and domestic fishing.

The foregoing discussion has maintained a sharp distinction between the biological research which leads to an initial determination of maximum sustained yield and the subsequent consideration of social and economic factors (domestic industry development effects) which might justify a down-ward adjustment in optimum yield. Although this approach reflects the reasoning behind both elementary bioeconomic theory and FCMA, it is far from an accurate reflection of the real world.

Fisheries biologists widely recognize that maximum sustained yield is not a point estimate of the maximum quantity that can be harvested year after year from a particular stock. Rather, because abundance and harvestable surplus will vary with changing environmental conditions, any management policy seeking maximum physical output must rely on a continuous review of numerous indicators of stock abundance to determine annually varying quotas. MSY is simply the ex-post average of those periodic output decisions [Alverson 1975].

It is, however, these annual output decisions which determine both the harvest quotas and (after subtraction of expected domestic harvest) the level of foreign fishing. Because the biology which underpins these annual decisions does not yield point estimates or closely bounded ranges, what has emerged in the management of several developing fisheries—notably tanner crab, sable fish and Bering Sea herring—is an almost inseparable tangle of biology, economics, and politics. Typically, a plan-development team uses primary data provided by state or federal agencies to assess the status of stocks and to estimate maximum sustained yield. In doing so, both the agency and the team must necessarily make subjective decisions about how to gather, analyze and interpret the often sketchy information. If the resulting MSY estimate dictates a substantial reduction in foreign fishing, other biologists tend to question whether a desire for that outcome might have led the team and agency to make overly conservative subjective choices. The developers of the plan then respond, as one would expect, with a defense of their scientific objectivity.

Although the level of foreign fishing resulting from such a process may be identical to that produced by the more explicit trade off approach discussed earlier, the logic and informational content of the debate leaves a great deal to be desired. The credibility of fisheries biology declines to the extent that scientific choices are, or are suspected to be, influenced by the political purposes of those who make them. And economic information on the strength of trade offs between foreign and domestic fishing is seldom sought at all, in part because it is not supposed to be applicable to questions of "conservation" of the resource.

One possible solution would be a more explicit recognition, by council members and others, of the ambiguities in fisheries science which are now fully appreciated only by its practitioners. Councils might, for example, be asked to choose between the maximum, the minimum or the mean of a scientifically defensible range of MSY values. The social and economic basis for such a choice would presumably be the same as that described earlier. Choosing lower points in the range would, like setting OY less than MSY, reflect an increasing emphasis on domestic rather than foreign fishing.

JOINT VENTURES

The joint venture issue illustrates another common problem in the economic analysis of fisheries management questions: how to incorporate incomplete and sometimes contradictory legal and administrative policies into the structuring of economic research.

In each of the two joint ventures currently operative, American fishermen sell their catch to foreign processors: in 1979, these sales totaled 1400 metric tons of Alaska groundfish, or 15% of the U.S. harvest in the developing fisheries (Table I). American trawlers deliver their catch by tying off the filled cod ends of their nets to buoys in the vicinity of the foreign factory ship then immediately returning to work, leaving the fish for later pick up and processing aboard the factory ships.

The economic advantages of such at-sea delivery include an extension of fishing time and improved quality of the product. Furthermore, processing costs are substantially less on the foreign vessel than at U.S. shore plants because of lower wages and the lower economic opportunity cost of surplus factory ships.

Not surprisingly, U.S. processors feel that joint ventures impose unfair competition on U.S. processors who must pay American wages; bear the cost of American environmental, health, safety and other social legislation;

and, particularly, buy and finance new capital equipment. Seeking protection, initially from the regional councils but ultimately from Congress, the domestic processors obtained an amendment to FCMA (the Processor Preference Amendment) which permits joint ventures to process only that portion of the U.S. harvest which exceeds the capacity of U.S. processors. In defining that capacity, the Secretary of Commerce is instructed to consider such factors as the availability of equipment, proximity to fishing grounds, contracts with fishermen and so on; but completely unanswered is the prime question of what price a U.S. processor must be willing to pay. Nor is price mentioned in the committee report from which the legislative intent of the amendment might be inferred. Furthermore, the question of price has yet to be addressed by any other federal agency or regional council.

The first application of the amendment produced yet another dimension of ambiguity. A U.S. processor, Icicle Seafoods, argued that Marine Resources, the U.S./U.S.S.R. joint venture, should be banned from operating within 12 miles of Icicle's cod processing operation in the Aleutian Islands. The North Pacific Fisheries Management Council recommended that the Secretary of Commerce grant Icicle's request. However, the Secretary, in rejecting that recommendation, indicated that the Processor Preference Amendment could be applied only in cases where some issue of resource conservation was involved.

Such a position raises the question of whether the amendment can ever be applied as intended—to resolve conflict between join ventures and U.S. processors in favor of the latter. Presumably, conservation is affected by the volume and technical method of harvest, rather than by the national identity of those involved. Hence, in deciding between two processors to use a given quantity of fish, one must search among the technical differences to ferret out conservation issues that will permit application of the amendment. The North Pacific Council did this in the Icicle-Marine Resources case. They concluded that the joint-venture practice of storing cod ends at sea until pickup by the factory ship rather than immediately bringing them on board, would reduce the survival rate of halibut and other protected species which trawlers must return to sea. The council was not, however, able to obtain support for this position from its own scientific and statistical committee or groundfish plan development team. However, Icicle's 1980 operation ended before the issue could be resolved with the Secretary of Commerce.

Presumably these issues will arise again as joint ventures and U.S. processors are attracted to the same areas and stocks. The economists who will assuredly be involved in debate over future applications of the amendment will have to exercise considerable independent judgment in determining just what the legal and political objectives really are. Certainly the issue of equity between fishermen and processors was not so trivial to those who drafted the legislation that they just forgot about it! But what did they mean? Are fishermen to accept whatever U.S. processors offer? Are processors to fully match joint-venture prices, or is some intermediate position to be taken? Similarly, does the emphasis on conservation mean that those in the Department of Commerce who made that decision really consider that to be the point at issue? Or, instead, did they wish for some other reasons to restrict so sharply the potential application of the amendment?

A better guide to identifying values for inclusion in a multiple-objective model might be to look at the predictable effects of a decision to ban joint ventures from a particular area or species to protect U.S. processors. Equity must be addressed. Either the protected processors commit themselves to pay a price which in some way balances the interests of fishermen and of processors, or unconditional protection results in the most extreme position in favor of processors and against fishermen.

Application of the amendment will also affect the rate and direction of development of the U.S. fisheries. Joint ventures will necessarily be offshore operations, since their economic advantage lies in the use of existing factory ships and in operation at sea. U.S. processing may be either offshore or onshore, but only the latter allows use of existing plant capacity. Not surprisingly, the state of Alaska opposes joint ventures, which provide few benefits in the form of state tax revenue on shoreside employment.

Assessing the other effects of joint ventures on fisheries development is more difficult. Joint-venture advocates point out that lower processing costs and the operational advantages of at-sea delivery enable them to buy from U.S. fishermen in the near term, when U.S. processors evidently cannot because of higher costs. The result, they say, will be a trained and equipped domestic trawl fleet ready to supply U.S. processors whenever economic conditions permit them to enter the market. U.S. processors counter that their entry into the groundfish market is obstructed by the real or potential competition from lower cost joint ventures which prevents them from obtaining debt and equity financing.

Of all these issues the one most amenable to empirical economic analysis is probably the equity tradeoff between fishermen and processors. Figure 3 describes three empirically distinguishable multiple-objective transormation functions that might describe that tradeoff. Assuming that a U.S. processor meets the technical requirements for viability, availability of equipment, proximity to the resource, willingness to enter into contracts, etc., the principal remaining issue would be: How high a price must he offer U.S. fishermen to justify governmental intervention to make the resource unavailable to joint-venture competition? That is, how much must he pay American fishermen in return for protection? Let the horizontal distance to point A in Figure 3 refer to the economic profit U.S. fishermen can obtain by selling to

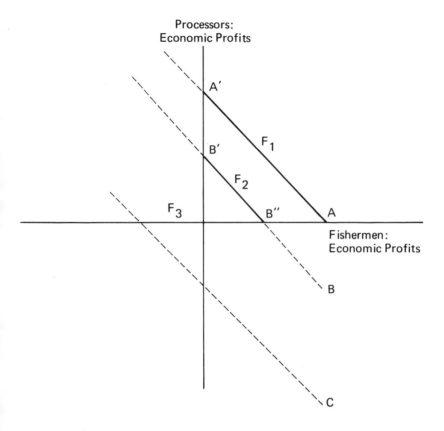

Figure 3.   Transformation function between processors' and fishermen's economic profit.

a joint venture: that is, the joint-venture price less opportunity costs of production (what fishermen and vessels could earn in the next best fisheries or non-fisheries employment alternatives). Let the vertical distance refer to a processor's economic profits (similarly defined) for varying prices paid to fishermen. Point A describes a situation where U.S. processors exactly break even by fully matching the joint venture price. Point A' describes the situation where, with the same processing cost structure, the processor earns a substantial economic profit but pays the fisherman only his nonjoint-venture opportunity cost. The slope of the transformation function F_1 between those two extremes would be -1. What any change in price gives to one, it takes from the other.

The alternative transformation function F_2 describes a situation where, because of higher processing costs, the U.S. processor loses money by fully matching the joint-venture price. That is, at point B fishermen are as well off as they would be with the joint venture but processors earn negative economic profits. Hence the relevant portion of F_2 begins at B″ where the processor is accorded protection in return for a price to fishermen which is somewhat less than that offered by the joint venture, but at which the processor breaks even. No decision-maker who places value on the profits both of fishermen and of processors would select B′, since at that point fishermen would lose and processors would gain only the economically valueless opportunity to engage in a breakeven operation. From B″ to B′, the slope of F_2 is also -1. But at any point along that segment, the total loss in profits by fishermen exceeds the total gains to processors. Finally there is the transformation function F_3 where U.S. processors cannot earn profits even if they pay fishermen only their nonjoint-venture opportunity costs. All choices along F_3, other than A, impose costs on fishermen with no corresponding gains to processors.

INCIDENTAL HARVEST

Incidental catch has long been a thorny issue for fisheries management. Moreover, of all the topics discussed here, it is the only one which promises to increase in urgency as the domestic trawl fleet displaces its foreign equivalent. Potentially, salmon, crab, herring and a variety of other species vital to most established Alaska fisheries could all be involved since, depending on the way it is used, trawl gear can take any of these stocks. However, it is the incidental halibut harvest which perhaps best illustrates the economic issues common to all the fisheries.

The long-line (hook and line) fishery for Pacific halibut has long been a mainstay of the Pacific coast fishing industry in both the United States and Canada. Also, the work of the International Pacific Halibut Commission provides one of the world's few biological success stories in the international management of fisheries for conservation purposes.

The principal elements of the commission's regime are (1) minimum size regulations, which ensure that only larger and higher valued mature halibut are taken, and (2) production quotas enforced by seasonal closures, which ensure that the total harvest by the long-line fishery is consistent with conservation of stocks. However, in calculating the total quota, halibut commission scientists must necessarily consider not only recruitment and natural mortality, but also the expected incidental harvest by the trawl fisheries which implies proportionately reduced quotas and shorter seasons for the long-line fishery.

The foundation for the halibut protection regime now established in the Bering Sea and Gulf of Alaska fisheries which includes a retention ban and time/

area closure for trawlers, was laid prior to extended jurisdiction, through negotiations between the U.S. and Canada and fishing nations of the eastern hemi-
sphere. However, those measures have been criticized both for their costs to the
trawl fishery and for their questionable effectiveness in protecting halibut.

The retention ban requires trawlers to discard all halibut, even though
most are dead or die soon after release. Thus, the share of the harvest taken
by trawlers must be wasted to achieve the intended goal of preventing trawlers
from deliberately targeting on the species.

The time/area closures are effective only if halibut concentrations in closed
areas exceed those found elsewhere. Such a clustering of halibut is more
pronounced in the Bering Sea than in the Gulf of Alaska where some scientists
think the closures merely shift trawl effort between areas of roughly equal
halibut concentrations. If they are correct, the results will be no significant
change in the overall halibut take but an adverse impact on the costs and
productivity of the trawl fishery.

The question of imposing the burden of time and area closures on the
domestic as well as the foreign trawl fleet was addressed in the initial development of management plans for the Gulf of Alaska and the Bering Sea fisheries.
In response to the council's selection of halibut as a top priority for protection,
the plan development team decided that time/area closures should, indeed, be
applicable to domestic trawlers after their annual output exceeded a minimum
level. However, when several new domestic groundfish trawling operations
entered the field by late 1979 and early 1980, it appeared that the harvest
would certainly exceed the allowable quota. The North Pacific Council was
then persuaded to delay imposition of the closures on domestic fishermen.
Current policy is to restrict the domestic trawl fleet only by the rentention
ban, pending review of the effect on the halibut stock.

The day of reckoning cannot be delayed forever, although the clouded
economic prospects for the U.S. groundfish trawl fishery may put it off for
some time. Eventually, increased domestic trawl effort will force the issue
back on the council's agenda. If nothing is learned in the interim, the issue
may remain that of imposing or not imposing time/area closures on the
domestic fleet. The question is: should the council, by imposing costs and reducing productivity, retard development in the one fishery FCMA specifically
identified as a development priority? Or should that fishery's unrestricted development be encouraged even at the cost of further decline in output and
economic distress in the halibut long-line fishery? Clearly, there should be a
high payoff to any activity that avoids a choice between these two alternatives.

Indications are that better alternatives can be developed through technological innovation and institutional change. To highlight the policy significance
of such potential innovations, we cast them in a model of multiple-objective

choice. Assume that the gross economic value of the combined groundfish and halibut harvest increases with every shift of halibut into the long-line fisheries. This will obviously be the case as long as trawlers are required to discard their halibut catch, and will most likely be true in any event, because only the long-line fishery is size selective. Therefore, if the shift of halibut into the long-line fishery involved no other costs, the net economic value of the total groundfish and halibut harvest (the vertical axis of Figure 4) would necessarily increase every time such a shift occurred. Also assume that the long-line harvest has a positive social value independent of its contribution of overall net economic value, a plausible assumption given the longstanding dependence of individuals and communities on that fishery. Three specific points along that second social objective (the horizontal axis of Figure 4) should be noted: the existing level of long-line harvest H_0, the level that would result from no incidental trawl harvest, H_{MAX} and the level that would occur if an unrestricted trawl fishery were allowed to develop, H_{MIN}.

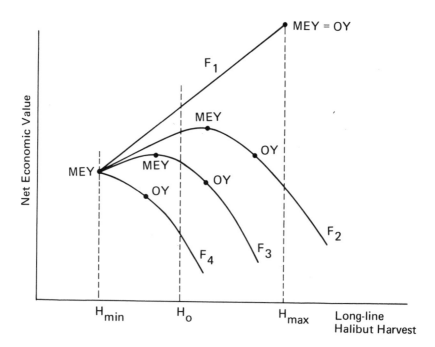

Figure 4.   Transformation function: control of incidental halibut harvest. Net economic value refers to the sum of groundfish and halibut exvessel revenues in both the trawl and longline fisheries, less the costs of fishing in both these fisheries.

If one accepts the unrealistic assumption underlying F_1 that control of incidental harvest is always free, then both the economic maximum (MEY) and the social optimum (OY) are obvious. No incidental trawl harvest should be permitted, and the entire allowable surplus of the halibut resource should be harvested by the long-line fishery. However, the control of incidental harvest by any means will not only be costly, but will most likely produce the economic phenomenon of diminishing returns, making transformation frontiers such as F_2, F_3 and F_4 more realistic. The economic maximum would occur where the marginal cost of incidental harvest control equals the increased harvest value resulting from shifting halibut to the long-line fishery. As F_2 has been drawn, the costs of controlling incidental halibut harvest are low enough to warrant an increased level of long-line halibut harvest to achieve the goal of maximum economic value. Furthermore, a social optimum, trading off some economic value for the social value of the long-line fishery, would result in an even greater long-line harvest. However, if the more restrictive technological alternatives described by F_3 prevail, the economic maximum would be more likely to dictate a reduction in long-line harvest. Finally, if technological alternatives were so limited that all reductions in incidental harvests would cost more than they could add to the value of catch, i.e., the F_4 curve, the economic maximum would indicate that the long-line harvest should be only the residual left by an unrestrained trawl fishery. Although the social optimum would call for a long-line harvest more generous than that indicated by maximum economic yield, even that would more likely represent a reduction from current levels.

American trawlermen have been quick to point out that the technological possibilities described by F_2 exist now, or could be readily developed. For example, many species of groundfish, including pollock, can be taken efficiently with midwater trawl gear which avoids most of the bottom-dwelling halibut. Even when trawling on the bottom, the vessel operator can often move away from halibut concentrations without substantially reducing his catch of the target species. Finally, even though halibut mortality will always be high, there is some room for improving the survival rate by careful onboard handling before return of the halibut to sea.

The institutional problem is that all these improvements are virtually unenforceable by the current procedures of aerial survey, boarding and the control of landings. It is hard to see how any changes in operating producedures could be effectively policed without onboard observers—as are presently required for a small portion of foreign fishing vessels. But, simply extending that requirement to domestic vessels will not completely solve the problem. Although foreign fishermen pay for their own observers, the money goes directly into the U.S. Treasury. The National Marine Fisheries Service then has to compete for funds for the overall observer program under the normal appropriation process.

Hence an increased number of observers assigned to protect the halibut stocks would most likely be taken away from other and perhaps most urgent tasks.

This requirement for funding would very probably preclude one of the most appealing possibilities for institutional change: an arrangement under which unobserved domestic trawlers could be made subject to time and area closures, while those willing to take on board and to pay for an observer would be unrestricted. That observer could monitor operating procedures to see whether, as they claim, U.S. trawlers will be able to take groundfish without an unacceptable high incidental harvest of halibut.

CONCLUSIONS

Two common points emerge from the issues just discussed. Many major questions in the management of developing fisheries are amenable, at least in part, to the kinds of empirical economic analysis that resource economists have done successfully to support the multiple-objective management of other natural resources. Particularly relevant are techniques for multiple-objective analysis of federal water resource projects. But it is equally true that the multiple-objective framework has not yet significantly affected the thinking of others, including many council members and management biologists who have the authroity to make real decisions.

APPENDIX: IMPLEMENTING MULTIOBJECTIVE MODELS FOR ALASKA GROUNDFISH MANAGEMENT ISSUES

Much of the information and analytical techniques required to estimate the multiobjective transformation functions described in Figures 2-4 can be obtained from existing or ongoing studies of Alaska fisheries. This appendix sketches an approach to estimating each, and provides a selected bibliography of sources the reader will find useful if he wishes to proceed further.

Optimum Yield (Figure 2)

The current financial feasibility of U.S. groundfish operations, $(R_0 - C_0)$ has been estimated for several species and production modes. Studies of groundfish biology (particularly for Alaska pollock) may eventually provide the biological basis for estimating two of the factors which go into determining the slopes of the cost and revenue functions (C, R) namely (1) attainable increases in CPUE, from which estimates of harvest cost reductions could be inferred;

and (2) estimates of attainable increases in size distribution, from which estimates of improved revenue per unit of harvest could be derived.

An additional slope component of the revenue function (R) could be estimated from the price effects of any reduction in optimum yield. Such estimates would be derived from the inverse of the demand curve for the stock or group of stocks being considered. The elasticity of such a demand curve would depend upon demand and supply elasticities in the product markets served by those stocks, as well as each stock's share of total supply. The initial, and easiest, task would be to define the relevant destination markets and shares of total supply. According to most credible assumptions about overall demand elasticity in destination markets, a resource that provides only a small share of total output will have a high elasticity of derived demand; hence, for these the price effects of optimum yield reductions would be negligible. In cases where the share was large, however, overall market elasticity of demand and supply would have to be examined. The following literature addresses each of these issues.

Financial Feasibility at Current Levels
of Foreign Fishing (C_O,R_O)

Published studies on this topic include Combs [1979], Jaeger [1977], Lamb [1980], Little [1978], Rogers [1979], Scott [1980] and Stokes and Offord [1980].

As far as ongoing work is concerned, private firms in Seattle, Washington, Alaska and elsewhere, maintain data files on the technical and economic feasibility of Alaska groundfish production. In some cases industry information is available to the public by special government industry arrangements: these include an industry-State of Alaska agreement with New England Fish Company (now bankrupt), a similar agreement with Icicle Seafoods; there is also an agreement between a West German firm, the 13th Regional Corporation, and the U.S. government.

Responsiveness of U.S. Costs and Revenues
to Reductions in Foreign Fishing

Increases in Catch per Unit Effort and Size Distribution Due to Optimum Yield Reduction. The only published study on this topic is Laevastu [1980].

Price Increases Due to Optimum Yield Reduction. The United Nations and most major fish-producing or consuming nations maintain statistics on production, by species, and trade, by major species/commodity groups. The following is a partial list of these documents.

Fisheries and Marine Service [Annual]
Ministry of Agriculture and Forestry [Annual a,b,]
Ministry of Food, Agriculture and Forestry [Annual]
Office of Fisheries [Annual]
United Nations [Annual a,b]
U.S. Department of Commerce [Annual a,b]

Price Elasticity in Destination Markets

Published studies in this area include Bell et al. [1970], Bockstael [1976], S. Crutchfield [1980] and Vidaeus [1977].

Joint Ventures (Figure 3)

Setting up transformation functions such as F_1, F_2 and F_3 for a particular fishery would be a relatively straightforward empirical task of the type already undertaken in several of the previously cited economic feasibility studies. Economic profits for both fishermen and processors would be estimated, except for exvessel prices, which, when varied in those profit functions, would permit calculation of net profits for both fishermen and processors.

Points A, B or C, maximum benefit to fishermen, would be calculated by inserting prices offered by the joint venture into both sets of profit functions. Fishermen's profits (horizontal distance) would reflect the value of the joint-venture market to fishermen over their best nonjoint-venture alternatives. The vertical distance would be the profits or losses of processors who had to fully compensate fishermen for the loss of joint-venture market opportunities.

Points A', B' or C', reflecting the opposite equity position, would be calculated by solving the profit functions for prices which yield zero economic profits for fishermen (returns equal to those attainable in the best nonjoint-venture alternative). These prices would then be substituted into the profit functions of processors to determine vertical distance of each point.

If processor profits are positive for both joint-venture and minimum (nonjoint-venture opportunity cost) prices to fishermen, transformation function F_1 pertains. Where processor profits are negative at both prices, F_3 is appropriate. Where they are negative at joint venture prices but positive at minimum prices, a third calculation must be made to determine point B'' on transformation function F_2. This would involve solving the processor profit function for an exvessel price that yielded zero profit, then substracting from the joint venture price to calculate the income loss such a price would impose on fishermen.

Much of the information required to develop processor and fisherman profit functions for analysis of the joint venture issue would be found in the bottom-fish feasibility studies cited above under financial feasibility at current levels of foreign fishing. Of those studies Jaeger [1977] focuses most directly on the joint venture issue.

Incidental Harvest (Figure 4)

*Tradeoff Using Existing Methods
Such as Time Area Closures (F$_2$)*

A paper by Low [1980] may be interesting in this regard.

Possible Tradeoffs Using Novel Methods (F$_3$-F$_4$)

Papers by Marasco and Terry [1980] and Westestad et al. [1980] could be useful here. The three papers cited above are being prepared as part of a broader effort by the North Pacific Council to address the incidental catch issue.

REFERENCES

1. Alverson, D. L. 1975. "Management of the Ocean's Living Resources: A Book Review and Perspective," U.S. National Marine Fisheries, Northwest and Alaska Fisheries Center, Seattle, WA.
2. Bell, F. W. et al. 1970. "The Future of the World's Fishery Resources: Forecasts of Demand, Supply and Prices to the Year 2000," U.S. Department of Commerce, National Marine Fisheries Service, Washington, DC.
3. Bockstael, N. E. 1976. "An Analysis of Investment Behavior and Price Determination: Analytical Input for the Formation of Policy in the Fisheries," Ph.D. Dissertation, University of Rhode Island.
4. Combs, Earl R., Inc. 1979. "Prospectus for Development of the United States Fisheries," U.S. Department of Commerce, Washington, DC.
5. Crutchfield, S. R. 1980. "Management of Foreign Fishing Rights: Theory and Policy," Ph.D. Dissertation, Yale University.
6. Elmore, R. F. 1978. "Organizational Models of Social Program Implementation," *Public Policy* (spring).
7. Fisheries and Marine Service. Annual. "Annual Statistical Report of Canadian Fisheries," Ottawa, Ontario.
8. Howe, C. W. 1971. "Benefit Cost Analysis for Water System Planning," American Geophysical Union, Washington, DC.
9. Jaeger, S. 1977. "Presentation to the North Pacific Fisheries Management Council on the Subject of Joint Ventures," North Pacific Vessel Owners Association, Seattle, WA.
10. Laevastu, T. 1980. "Holistic Simulation Models of Shelf-Seas Ecosystems," *J. Fish. Res. Board Can.*
11. Lamb, T. 1980. "Factory Trawlers for Alaska, Are They Economically Feasible?" *Nat. Fisherman* (November).
12. Lindblom, C. E. 1959. "The Science of Muddling Through," *Public Admin. Rev.* (spring).

13. Little, Arthur D., Inc. 1978. "Development of a Bottomfish Industry: Strategies for the State of Alaska," Alaska Governor's Bottomfish Coordinator, Juneau, AK.
14. Low, L.-L. 1980. "A Bering Sea Time-Area Closure Model," National Marine Fisheries Service, Northwest and Alaska Fisheries Center, Seattle, WA.
15. Major, D., and R. Lenton. 1979. *Applied Water Resource Systems Planning* (Englewood Cliffs, NJ: Prentice-Hall).
16. Marasco, R., and J. Terry. 1980. "A Rational Approach to the Incidental Catch of Prohibited Species," U.S. National Marine Fisheries Service, Northwest and Alaska Fisheries Center, Seattle, WA.
17. Ministry of Agriculture and Forestry. Annual a. "Statistical Reports of Fisheries and Cultured Fish," Japan.
18. Ministry of Agriculture and Forestry. Annual b. "Statistical Report of the Flow of Fishery Products," Japan.
19. Ministry of Food, Agriculture and Forestry. Annual. "Report on German Fisheries," Federal Republic of Germany.
20. Office of Fisheries. Annual. "Yearbook of Fisheries Statistics," Republic of Korea.
21. Rogers, G. W. 1979. "Critique of the Arthur D. Little, Inc. Analysis and Recommendations for State Policy and Directions for Developing a Bottomfish Industry for Alaska," Report to the Legislature, Juneau, AK.
22. Scott, M. 1980. "Prospects for a Bottomfish Industry in Alaska," *Alaska Rev. Sociol. Econ.* (April).
23. Stokes, R. L., and B. L. Offord. 1981. "Alaska Groundfish: A Financial Feasibility Analysis," *Ocean Devel. Int. Law* (in press).
24. United Nations. Annual a. "Yearbook of Fisheries Statistics: Catches and Landings," Rome, Italy.
25. United Nations. Annual b. "Yearbook of Fishery Statistics: Fishery Commodities," Rome, Italy.
26. U.S. Department of Commerce. Annual a. "Fisheries of the United States," National Marine Fisheries Service, National Oceanic and Atmospheric Administration.
27. U.S. Department of Commerce. Annual b. "Food Fish Market Review and Outlook," National Marine Fisheries Service, National Oceanic and Atmospheric Administration.
28. U.S. Water Resources Council. 1973. "Water and Related Land Resources: Establishment of Principles and Standards for Planning," *Federal Register* 38 (143), Part III).
29. Vidaeus, L. O. 1977. "Analysis of Foreign Demand for United States Fish Stocks under Extended Jurisdiction with an Application to the New England Herring Resources," Ph.D. Dissertation, University of Rhode Island.
30. Westestad, V., S. Hoage and R. Norita. 1980. "Methods of Reducing the Incidental Catch of Prohibited Species in the Bering Sea Groundfish Fishery through Gear Restrictions," U.S. National Marine Fisheries Service, Northwest and Alaska Fisheries Center, Seattle, WA.
31. Wildavsky, A. 1979. *The Politics of the Budgetary Process* (Boston, MA: Little, Brown & Co.).

CHAPTER 13

FISHERIES ECONOMICS AND FISHERIES MANAGEMENT

Robert L. Stokes

Institute for Marine Studies
University of Washington

To inject economic analysis effectively into fisheries management will not be simple. To be sure, many of the easier steps in that direction have been taken. Money has been appropriated for studies which involve academic and consulting economists. Other economists serve on plan development teams, scientific and statistical committees and other public advisory bodies. Economists also fill an increasing number of full-time staff positions in both the National Marine Fisheries Service and the regional councils. But what remains is the task of truly integrating their thinking with that of other participants in fisheries management, a group that includes at least fisheries biologists, oceanographers, anthropologists, sociologists, attorneys, elected and appointed officials and interest-group representatives.

This paper suggests that the task now at hand is to integrate the paradigms of two specialized fields—economics and fisheries management. Specific rules for accomplishing this task will not be found in either field, but more general factors will govern the success of any effort at paradigm integration. This chapter is a tentative exploration of those factors, and of their implications for the roles that individual economists can play in the management of fisheries under the Fisheries Conservation and Management Act (FCMA) of 1976.

The first two sections define the paradigms of fisheries economics and fisheries management, and provide historical examples of their successful integration. The next two sections examine how individual fisheries economists can advance such an integration in the future; what choices they can make and what institutional factors they should consider in making them.

WHAT IS A PARADIGM?

The Concept

This chapter is about paradigms; particularly about how they change and how that change can deliberately be influenced. The simplist and most universal elements of any paradigm are the specialized terms of any given field and their definitions, as well as some consensus on the subject of study. Additionally, but in a degree that varies between fields, the paradigm will also include accepted conceptual frameworks and laws which explain relationships between data. Finally, the paradigms of some fields include objectives which its practitioners feel a shared obligation to advance.

Any specialist studies the paradigm of his field, in the sense that he learns the terms, definitions, concepts, laws and values of his profession. But few seriously consider why those paradigm elements have become what they are. Such inquiry is limited to a relatively few scholars, some of whom identify with the field being studied and others with more general fields such as the philosophy and sociology of knowledge.

These scholars ask how the general intellectual questions of validity and significance are answered in particular fields, and how those answers change over time. What does, and does not, constitute an adequate argument in support of a conclusion? Why does one method of reasoning come to be regarded as superior to others? Why do the interesting and uninteresting questions change over time?

When examining such questions, scholars of knowledge consider a number of factors. First among them are the general principles of logical deduction and empirical inference commonly referred to as the scientific method. Other factors include the psychology of individual practitioners, the sociology of the practicing group and, perhaps most importantly, the political, social and economic circumstances of the broader society within which they practice their discipline.[1]

The Paradigm of Fisheries Economics

Ultimately, fisheries economics is just the accumulated thinking of fisheries economists or, more precisely, the common elements of that thinking which are attributable to their training and experience as economists. The following introspective opinion of what those common elements might be is offered in the hope that my training and experience are at least reasonably representative. The paradigm of the fisheries economist certainly includes positive microeconomics—a set of logically interrelated propositions which explain individual and firm behavior as the interaction of rational maximizing decision-makers within competitive or other market structures. It also includes welfare economics—the system of normative reasoning which evaluates society's collective decisions (public policy) against the revealed or inferred values of individuals.[2]

The failure of market institutions to utilize common property resources in a way which maximizes individual values has been the focus for most work by the fisheries economist. Historically, fisheries economists have concerned themselves with the efforts of states and international agencies to cope with such common-property problems. Now that the management of most U.S. fisheries has become the responsibility of a federal/regional council structure established by FCMA, many have turned their attention to how those new institutions might cope with the same problems.

The Fisheries Management Paradigm

When participating in FCMA fisheries management, economists encounter another group with a paradigm of its own. Given the shortness of my own involvement, the following outline of that paradigm must be considered as merely suggestive of what a more complete definition might contain. First, terms such as "optimum yield" and "total allowable level of foreign fishing" must be included. Next, specific facts are also important. What is the current level of U.S. and world fisheries output? What are the commercially and recreationally important species? What institutional relationships exist and, at a point in time, who are the personalities?

More complex concepts must also be included in the fisheries management paradigm. Everyone is supposed to understand the relationship between stock abundance, fishing effort and the sustainable yield of a resource. There are also shared values, among which conservation or sustained yield management is perhaps the most notable. Man has some right to harvest the sustained yield of a resource but not (apparently in deference to future generations or to the fish themselves) the right to pursue the stock to extinction.

The Essential Function of Paradigms

Paradigms serve an essentail function in facilitiating thought and communication. A specialized vocabulary, once learned, is a sort of shorthand which permits more precise and economical communication than does the general language. Relationships between phenomena, once derived, tested and accepted, can then be applied quickly and effectively in a wide range of related situations. Even the ranking of values serves an economizing purpose in that those who accept the primacy of a particular set of values can pass on to tasks of implementation while those who disagree can construct different and perhaps competing paradigms. By such a process of convergence and resolution, a discipline advances and grows rather than circling on the eternal "square one" of common knowledge and experience.

Many "interdisciplinary" efforts to study public policy have reacted to the frustrations of communicating across paradigms by attempting to eliminate the concept of paradigm altogether. Their central tenet is that no one should be excluded from the discussion of policy issues by the barrier of a specialized language or by requirements to accept the validity of particular logical and empirical relationships or of specified value positions. Insistence on a convergent paradigm, they argue, inhibits the introduction of that wide variety of ideas and values which provides the raw material for creative activity. Further, if taken to extremes, insistence on a common paradigm violates liberal principles, which support freedom of thought and expression.

To be sure, such tradeoffs exist, but they are mitigated to a considerable degree by the ever-present freedom of individuals to choose between differing and competing paradigms. Although the above qualifications are recognized, this article still assumes that the process of specialization and convergence of thought which has advanced the more traditional disciplines can be turned to the same good purpose in the management of fisheries.

EVOLUTION AND INTEGRATION OF PARADIGMS: SOME HISTORY

A distinguishing characteristic of well-developed disciplines is that they destroy their own history [Kuhn 1970]. That is, concepts which have evolved through decades of false starts, failures and conflict are normally presented to students as timeless and somewhat self-evident truths. However efficient this textbook view of a paradigm may be in training its practitioners, it is of little use to those who seek to understand and to influence the development of concepts. For information on the slow formulation of paradigms, one must look to their growth process and to how it was influenced by the outside world and by other disciplines.

Fisheries Biology

Recall that both of the conceptual elements mentioned as part of the paradigm of fisheries management have their origins in fisheries biology. Everyone (biologist or not) is supposed to understand the biologist's conceptual framework for relating stock abundance and fishing effort to sustained yield. And everyone is supposed to accept the value orientation implicit in the biologist's concept of sustained yield management. The success these concepts represents in integrating paradigms is indicated by the language of FCMA:

"The term optimum with respect to the yield from a fishery means the amount of fish which is prescribed as such on the basis of maximum sustained yield from such fishery, as modified by any relevant economic, social or ecological factor."

You start with the fishery biologist's calculations of what can be taken on a sustainable basis and then adjust for other factors. You do not start the other way around—for example, with the economist's notion of maximum economic yield or the fishing industry's notion of what they would like to have—and then consider the implications for long-term stock abundance and productivity. That no one seriously questions the implied primacy of conservation as a value illustrates how thoroughly this element of the fisheries biologist's paradigm has penetrated the broader fisheries-managment paradigm.

The same language reveals another dimension of success in the transfer of ideas. Maximum sustained yield is the starting point, not "relevant biological considerations." By making such a specific choice from among the technical terms and concepts of fisheries biology, the drafters of FCMA revealed their own general understanding of the field and required a similar understanding by others in the fisheries-management community. The admonition to consider "relevant economic, social, or ecological factors" neither reveals nor requires any such specific knowledge of the fields to which these terms refer.

The concepts and values of fisheries biology have not always held such a prominent position in fisheries management. In fact, their introduction into actual management practice, as opposed to mere profession as general objectives, is quite recent. The Pacific sardine fishery is but one of many that illustrates the lag between estimation of maximum sustained yield and its implementation in fisheries management. By 1929, fishery biologists with the California Department of Fish and Game had assembled sufficient information to recommend overall production quotas based on the sustained yield concept. However, for almost two more decades management was governed by quite different considerations. Seasons were set according to the industry's determination of when sardines were suitable for canning. The only quantitative restrictions were on the reduction fishery, and these were based on a general public aversion to producing meal and oil from fish suitable for human consumption. The result was what the biologists predicted but were unable to prevent—collapse of the sardine stocks after World War II and subsequent termination of the fishery [Ahlstrom 1970].

That this is neither an isolated nor a historically remote outcome is illustrated by one biologist's defense of fishery research, offered in 1968. His justification for spending public funds on fisheries research was not its current application but its future potential, when and if a variety of political, economic and social barriers could be overcome [McHugh 1968]. Perhaps that day has arrived with the codification of sustained yield management in FCMA. However, another biologist has voiced his reservations. He asks whether the requirement for a close correspondence between maximum sustained yield and actual catch quotas has caused decision-makers to bend their preferences to the concepts and calculations of biologists, or whether it has put increasing pressure on biologists to bend their results to decision-maker preferences [Alverson 1980].

Political recognition of sustained yield as a management objective has brought changes in the concepts of fisheries biology, but to some not all the changes have been for the better.

> The doctrine of MSY had effects on other doctrines, and the most notable was the impact on traditional limnology. For almost 100 years, working from a European base, limnologists had been developing holistic schemes of trophic status in which fish were part of a complex community for which the rate of harvest was best expressed in pounds per acre or kilos per hectare .... The believers in MSY had little patience for the systematics of zooplankton or the subtleties of lake classification. The fish, they argued, were the integrators of their environment and the object of our crass interest. "Study the fish" was the motto [Larkin 1977].

As one might expect, the response to political demands for conservation resulted in a shift in the focus of fisheries science toward development of techniques to estimate sustained yields for single, isolated species. Whether this objective has been worth its cost to fisheries science—reduced knowledge about multispecies and fisheries-environmental interactions—is moot. What should be kept in mind is that the things we know, and do not know, about the biology of marine fish have been determined in part by the demands of the political system. That observation has implications for fisheries economics as well.

Fisheries Economics

Fisheries economics has a shorter but similar history in which some, but by no means all, of the implications of positive and normative microeconomics have gained acceptance in the management community.

The literature on limited entry is for the most part an application of the general economic principle that external diseconomies may be corrected either by regulation or by taxation of activities which impose them. From a theoretical standpoint, both approaches have the same efficiency consequences but quite different effects on the distribution of income. Taxation confers the benefits of fleet reduction on the general (nonfishing) public, while regulatory approaches such as licensed limitation confer those benefits on the fishing industry. More specifically, license limitation, as presently implemented, confers benefits on the current generation of fishermen who are normally granted transferable licenses on the basis of historic participation.

Both taxation and license limitation raise problems of implementation. The setting and adjusting of tax rates requires extensive knowledge about the industry's continually changing costs, revenues and profits. Because license limitation usually allows the participating fishermen to expand the catching power of their vessels, however, the overall effect is often to increase the economic costs of taking a fixed total quota. To prevent this inefficient outcome, increasingly detailed regulation of vessel capacity would be requisite, based again on current awareness of changing costs, revenues and technical efficiency. Furthermore, where rules based on historic participation admit a large number of "part-time" fishermen, government must cope with the incentive this group has to respond to improving economic conditions by either becoming full-time fishermen or selling their transferable licenses to those who will.

There is little question that both fisheries economists and the fisheries-management community have chosen license limitation rather than taxation as the primary method of controlling fishing effort. Virtually all of the current effort-limitation programs are of this type, and much recent economic literature considers how to make this approach work. Few have chosen to study the alternative: how to implement a taxation program. Instead, taxation is usually dismissed out of hand as being unfeasible or inequitable. At best, taxes on fishermen are cited as an adjunct in implementing licensed limitation: for example, by providing a revenue source to finance the buy-back of vessels.[3]

A quite similar choice is now being made in what might be called the economics of "underutilized" species—those over which the United States acquired legal control under FCMA but which are allocated to foreign nations because the domestic fishing industry cannot profitably exploit them.

Two equally logical economic implications follow from the fact that foreigners can profitably harvest what the United States cannot. The first implication is that global economic efficiency calls for continued foreign fishing as long as U.S. costs exceed their foreign equivalents, regardless of the relationship between U.S. costs and product prices. That is, a policy of promoting U.S. fisheries development will detract from global economic efficiency whenever it substitutes higher-cost (U.S.) factors of production for lower-cost (foreign) equivalents. A similar conclusion about the net contribution of any given fishery to U.S. national income requires only that more foreign-earned economic rent be captured domestically in fees than a U.S. fishing industry could earn in net profits.

The second implication is that whenever U.S. costs exceed product prices, but foreign costs do not, some joint operation including American participants ought to be financially feasible. In other words, the seemingly impossible task of developing commercially viable U.S. fisheries for underutilized species at present prices becomes solvable. What must be determined is a mix of U.S. and foreign factors of production that will not only make money at present prices but will also involve U.S. citizens. A search for such solutions to the "fisheries development problem" is increasingly attracting the attention of fisheries economists, including among others, Munro [1981], Kaczynski [1979] and Stokes [1980 a,b].

The U.S.-foreign mix principle is also being applied. Several joint ventures are essentially combinations of U.S. factors of production (fishing effort) and foreign factors of production (processing capacity). The same economic principle is at the heart of the new "fish-and-chips diplomacy"—an approach to foreign fisheries allocation (recently codified in the American Fisheries Promotion Act) which gives preference in allocation to foreign nations who provide benefits to the U.S. fishing industry.

Yet no one, this author included, has explored the conditions under which U.S. fisheries development might, or might not, be economically efficient—that is, no one has challenged on economic grounds either the preference in allocation which FCMA gives to U.S. fishermen or the mandate to encourage domestic fisheries development. These questions, like the implications of controlling effort by taxation of fishermen, will remain poorly understood.

CHOICES

These examples illustrate something about the process of integrating paradigms that have significance well beyond the particular choices they represent. In each case the outcomes were the cumulative effect of many decisions by individual investigators. However, external factors had as dramatic an effect on those outcomes as might have occurred through the enactment of law or other explicitly stated institutional policies. Single-species production models developed, in large part, because they served the purposes of the conservation movement and of those in the fishing industry who feared collapse of the stocks upon which they depended. License limitation and fisheries development similarly flourish as branches of fisheries economics because they better serve the interests of the politically dominant fishing industry than do the alternatives. In a sense choice occurs by evolution. Beginning with a wide variety of poential ideas some develop more rapidly than others, as they and the investigators who advance them gain support from the outside community.

Not surprisingly, some branches of fisheries biology and economics have grown in response to external demands, while others, for lack of such demands, are overlooked. Philosophers of knowledge have explained the similar evolution of far more important disciplines. Much of the mathematics we use today developed, in part, because the ancient Egyptians needed to resurvey their fields after the Nile's periodic floods, and much of our present understanding of the solar system exists because navigators sought out celestial configurations to find their way about. Specialists in any field who respond to preexisting external needs are not only welcomed, but find their ideas more readily understood, accepted and supported than others who go about with "solutions looking for problems."

Still a balance must be struck, not only in the making of policy but also in development of the systems of knowledge (paradigms) used to understand its implications. A better balanced development of our understanding of entire marine communities, as well as of single-species production models, might have given us tools badly needed today to deal with multispecies fisheries management and with concerns about the relationship between environmental quality and fisheries productivity. In the case of fisheries economics the license limitation and fisheries development examples raise questions not only about who is, and is not, served by public policy but about whom the fisheries economist serves as well.

Informed rational choices will have to be made about the development of all the specialized subfields that support fisheries management, and the unambiguously correct answers provided by corner solutions will be no more obligingly at hand here than they are elsewhere. Acceptance, as well as balance, are goods. As with other constrained economic choices, the only clearly wrong answer to the question, "Which do you want?" will be "both."

Fortunately, the fisheries economist can do more than just choose from within his theory those concepts which are the most acceptable to a particular audience. He also has a considerable range of potential audiences to choose from. Several of these audiences are found within the plan development process itself. Members of plan development teams, scientific and statistical committees, industry advisory panels, council staff and council members themselves represent a wide variety of individual and organizational interests which will influence their receptivity to any particular form of economic analysis. The same holds true for those in the Department of Commerce review channel and, for the risk-prone, private groups, including foreigners, who may legally challenge fisheries management decisions. The diversity of professional backgrounds one finds among these groups and individuals— in particular the growing number of social scientists—must also be taken into account in considering audience acceptability.

Additional opportunities for choice are provided by the grant and contract research programs of agencies with an interest in or responsibility for supporting the management of fisheries under FCMA. These include the social and economic research programs of the National Marine Fisheries Service, regional councils, Sea Grant, state fisheries agencies and the newly formed fisheries development foundations. Offering more diversity of interest than the plan development process itself, these various bodies open up a greater range of opportunities for the development and acceptance of economic analysis.

If one considers the otherwise uninviting notion that research and professional contribution need not specifically be funded, then even more opportunities become available. These include contributions to scholarly publications in resource economics, resource management and marine policy; teaching; and participation in the increasing number of fisheries-oriented conferences and workshops. The now apparently well-established fisheries session incorporated in the annual meeting of the American Agricultural Economic Association is a notable example of the latter. Other meetings, while less formal, may be equally productive. Fisheries economists are routinely brought together to address specific, and typically short-term, policy questions. Although discussions often range some distance from the established agenda, one hopes that the organizers and funders of these meetings will recognize the contribution such "extraneous" discussion can make to peer group interaction and to the development of ideas.

But where does the individual economist go for information on the external factors which will influence the success or failure of the choices he makes among ideas and audiences? Some suggestions follow.

INSTITUTIONAL FACTORS

The Legal Rules

Legal factors governing the role of economics in the management of fisheries under FCMA are found in FCMA, the National Environmental Protection Act and Executive Order 12044. The common purpose of all these directives is aptly reflected in Siegal's [1980] summary of the purposes of Executive Order 12044. That order requires all federal regulations, including fisheries management plans, to:

> be designed to achieve legislative goals as efficiently as possible, minimize reporting burdens, and that a comparative analysis be performed on the benefits and costs of alternative regulatory schemes early in the decision-making process . . . . This analysis places increased emphasis on the benefits and costs of regulations and the need to examine a wide range of alternative means of achieving regulatory objectives.

These directives appear to establish a standard of informed rationality for fisheries management. All of the values at stake in a particular fishery (management objectives) deserve explicit analysis by staff, and serious consideration by council members. Equally explicit analysis and consideration is required of all the alternatives for achieving those management objectives. All alternatives presumably means all those discovered by a careful examination of the characteristics of the resource, the technology for its exploitation and available measures for the social control of market behavior. That, in any event, is this nonlawyer's interpretation of what the regulations require council members and their staffs to do; and of the standards the Department of Commerce is supposed to apply when it reviews the council's work for compliance with the national standards of FCMA and other applicable law.

However, the role of economics, even in this somewhat idealized decision process, is not well specified. When the Department of Commerce indicated specific social and economic factors that councils were supposed to consider, it identified a list of specific data items such as the following.

> Describe the value of the catch (ex-vessel) identify the method of value determination, especially when the value is estimated or based on non-market pricing. The description of the economic statistics of the commercial fleet should include: gross income, investment costs and revenues, measurement of effort, measurement of efficiency, and measurement of productivity. The description of recreational fishing should include: investment, revenues and tourism (50 CFR part 602).

What is missing, though, is any indication of how councils are supposed to consider such information, or how decisions would change if economic analysis were to arrive at one set of results rather than another.

How little the legal rules help in sorting out the significant from the trivial can best be seen by comparison with the role the same rules assign to fisheries biology. A lower calculation of MSY implies, within most management regimes, a reduced catch quota and shortened season. Hence, policy relevant biological research is that which improves the accuracy of MSY calculations, and required data is that needed to perform those calculations. By contrast what management measures change, and in which directions, if gross income increases, investment costs decline, tourism increases or any of the other economic descriptors changes one way or the other?

That economic analysis can be employed with greater precision is illustrated by federal procedures for evaluating water resource projects. The U.S. Water Resources Council [1973] Principles and Standards establish a test of economic efficiency, not "relevant economic considerations," as one standard for project evaluation. As a result, detailed national economic development accounting procedures, and an even more extensive benefit-cost literature, have been developed to implement that efficiency standard [Howe 1971].

By comparison with the sustained yield management standard of fisheries biology and the efficiency standard of water resource economics, the legal rules for fisheries management plan development and review provide little useful guidance. Informed rationality is required, economics must be considered and specific descriptive data must be gathered. Nothing is said, however, about what are, or are not relevant economic management objectives. Perhaps with time these will be defined in much the same way that maximum sustained yield is now specified as a relevant biological objective. When that happens the economist will, like the biologist, be able to infer from the legal rules the relevant research questions and the data required to anser them. Until then he must look to other sources such as the political process.

Political Factors

The political process also provides information on values and alternatives for their advancement. As far as political information is made public, it is presented at hearings, in plan development and review meetings, and during council debates. Some apparently regard the political claims presented in these settings as the universe of relevant social and economic considerations [North Pacific Fisheries Management Council 1978]. They are considerably less than that for reasons discussed below. However, to the economist who understands which values and alternatives they will identify and which they will ignore, political claims can provide useful guidance in the choice of research topics and audiences.

For many reasons some values will fail to be considered by the political process. The skills and resources required for political action are no more equally distributed than is money income. In fact, the very groups on whose behalf government intervenes in the market will often be the ones least able to advance their interests by making forceful "claims" on the political system.

Others, such as consumers and taxpayers, may have the ability to take political action but no rational reason for doing so. Although a given fisheries management decision may affect their aggregate interests, no single consumer or taxpayer will find it worth his effort to represent his interests directly, or even to support organizations to that end. As an example, when is the last time the shoe tariff changed? How much did it cost you? And what did you do about it?

The interests of those who, by choice or otherwise, remain unrepresented in the political process present a continuing challenge to the students of all forms of public policy. Although scholars have addressed the problem of unrepresented values with regard to representative government in general [Olson 1965] and for fisheries management under FCMA in particular [Pontecorvo 1977], they have discovered no particularly useful solution. But perhaps there is some benefit in knowing what we cannot cope with. An awareness of the nature and extent of unrepresented values may, for example, tell us how much faith to place in the common assertion that the political system "solves" the problem of trading off conflicting social values.

The political process identifies some, but again not all, of the management alternatives. Informed rationality would seem to require that attention be given to management approaches that require large changes in the distribution of benefits among user groups, or the employment of unfamiliar management measures, as well as those which continue or incrementally modify past practice. However, experience, as well as a considerable literature in political science, indicates that such "radical" approaches are seldom seriously considered. Instead council members, like most political decision-makers, start with past practice. Consideration of alternatives is usually limited to continuing past practice and to modification which only incrementally effect the distribution of benefits [Wildavsky 1979] or which employ management techniques that are already in place and quite familiar to the decision-makers [Allison 1969].

The social efficiency of such an incremental approach to decision-making has been debated extensively. In particular its supporters argue that incrementalizing a policy permits decision-makers to learn as they go about its consequences [Lindblom 1959], and that the use of established, familiar policy tools conserves on the time and talents of decision-makers [Wildavsky 1979].

One doubts, however, that even these supporters of incrementalism would suggest that we only need to know about alternatives which closely resemble past practice. Gaining knowledge about policy alternatives has considerably different costs and purposes than adoption of the policies themselves. "Radical" alternatives can be examined without the risks associated with their implementation. And the information obtained provides, at the minimum, an indication of the opportunity cost which society pays for the incrementalist approach.

But, if these qualifications are kept in mind, the political process still can provide useful information on alternatives as well as values. By observing the claims of interest groups and their interplay with effective decision-makers, one can learn what the politically represented values are. The next logical step of the course is to augment this knowledge with a serious study of how the policies being considered may effect those who, by choice or otherwise, do not represent their interests in the political process. The political process gives the same useful information on some of the alternatives, provided it is similarly augmented with a thoughtful analysis of the broader range of technologically, but perhaps not politically, relevant alternatives.

CONCLUSIONS

If the past is any guide to the future, fisheries economics will have a highly selective impact on the broader fisheries management community. Although individual economists have considerable discretion to choose questions and approaches to them, institutional factors will have a powerful influence over which approaches succeed and which fail. Except for requiring overall rationality and specifying a variety of data collection tasks, the legal rules for fisheries plan development provide little useful guidance in the choice of significant topics for economic research.

However, by carefully understanding what the political signals say, and particularly what they ignore, the economist may be able to identify some of the important values and relevant alternatives. And, of course, these political signals also tell him how the research he conducts will be received by any of the several audiences he can present it to. It is from this sort of information that one determines, at least in part, the interesting questions for applied research, and the data required to answer them.

In other words, fisheries economists, like it or not, are going to have to become politicians of a sort, not necessarily to influence policy choices through political activity of the usual type, but simply to practice applied fisheries economics. This requires both finding receptive audiences for particular ideas and developing interesting ideas for particular audiences. In short, we must learn as much about the interests and motives of those in the public sector, to whom we present our analysis, as we often claim to know about those in the private sector upon whom our analysis is centered.

NOTES

[1] For a sampling of readings in these fields and access to the broader literature, see Robinson [1962], Kuhn [1970] and Galbraith [1973].

[2] A layman's introduction to the paradigm of economics might include Samuelson [1976] for positive economics, Hyman [1973] for normative economics and Anderson [1977] for fisheries economics.

[3] A survey of the recent theory and experience with limited entry is found in Rettig [1981], "Symposium on Policies for Economic Rationalization of Commercial Fisheries [1979] and Stokes [1979].

REFERENCES

1. Ahlstrom, E. H., and J. Radovich. 1970. "Management of the Pacific Sardine," in *A Century of Fisheries in North America,* N. G. Benson, Ed. (Washington, DC: American Fisheries Society).
2. Allison, G. 1969. "Conceptual Models in the Cuban Missile Crisis," *Am. Polit. Sci. Rev.* (September).
3. Alverson, D. L. 1980. Paper presented at the Annual Meeting of the Pacific Fisheries Biologists Association.

4. Anderson, L. G. 1977. *The Economics of Fisheries Management* (Baltimore, MD: The Johns Hopkins University Press).
5. Galbraith, J. K. 1973. *Economics and the Public Purpose* (Boston, MA: Houghton Mifflin).
6. Howe, C. W. 1971. "Benefit Cost Analysis for Water System Planning," American Geophysical Union, Washington, DC.
7. Hyman, D. N. 1973. *The Economics of Governmental Activity* (New York: Holt, Rinehart and Winston).
8. Kaczynski, W. 1979. "Joint Ventures in Fisheries between Distant Water and Developed Coastal Nations: An Economic View," *Ocean Management* No. 5.
9. Kuhn, T. 1970. *The Structure of Scientific Revolutions* (Chicago, IL: University of Chicago Press).
10. Larkin, P. A. 1977. "An Epitaph for the Concept of Maximum Sustained Yield," *Trans. Am. Fish. Soc.* (January).
11. Lindblom, C. E. 1959. "The Science of Muddling Through," *Public Admin. Rev.* (Spring).
12. McHugh, J. L. 1968. "The Biologist's Place in the Fishing Industry," *BioScience* (October).
13. Munro, G. 1981. "Joint Ventures for the North Pacific Project," Institute for Marine Studies, University of Washington, Seattle, WA (in press).
14. North Pacific Fishery Management Council. 1978. "Procedures and Socioeconomic Data Needs for Determination of Optimum Yields in Fishery Management Plans," Scientific and Statistical Committee, Anchorage, AK.
15. Olson, M. 1965. *The Logic of Collective Action* (Cambidge, MA: Harvard University Press).
16. Pontecorvo, G. 1977. "Fishery Management and the General Welfare: Implications of the New Structure," *Washington Law Rev.* No. 641.
17. Rettig, B., Ed. 1981. "Workshop and Conference on Limited Entry," Institute for Marine Studies, University of Washington (in press).
18. Robinson, J. 1962. *Economic Philosophy* (Chicago, IL: Aldine).
19. Samuelson, P. A. 1976. *Economics* (New York: McGraw-Hill).
20. Siegel, R. A. 1981. "Federal Regulatory Policy for Marine Fisheries," Chapter 2, this volume.
21. Stokes, R. L. 1979. "Limitation of Fishing Effort: An Economic Analysis of Options," *Marine Policy* (October).
22. Stokes, R. L. 1980a. "Prospects for Foreign Fishing Vessels in U.S. Fisheries Development," *Marine Policy* (January).
23. Stokes, R.L. 1980b. "U.S.-Foreign Cooperation for Fisheries Development," *Marine Policy* (October).
24. "Symposium on Policies for Economic Rationalization of Commercial Fisheries." 1979. *J. Fish. Res. Board Can.* (July).
25. U.S. Water Resources Council. 1973. "Water and Related Land Resources: Establishment of Principles and Standards for Planning," *Federal Register* 38(174, Part III).
26. Wildavsky, A. 1979. *The Politics of the Budgetary Process* (Boston, MA: Little, Brown).

PARTICIPANTS
CONFERENCE ON ECONOMIC ANALYSES
FOR FISHERIES MANAGEMENT PLANS

Dr. Burton A. Abrams
University of Delaware
Department of Economics
Newark, DE 19711

Dr. Richard J. Agnello
University of Delaware
Department of Economics
Newark, DE 19711

Dr. Lee G. Anderson
University of Delaware
College of Marine Studies
Newark, DE 19711

Mr. William Bellows
Economic Analysis Staff (FX53)
Office of Policy and Planning
National Marine Fisheries Service
2001 Wisconsin Avenue, N.W.
Washington, DC 20235

Dr. Adi Ben-Israel
Department of Mathematical
   Sciences
University of Delaware
Newark, DE 19711

Dr. Richard Bishop
Department of Agricultural
   Economics
University of Wisconsin—Madison
1450 Linden Drive
Madison, WI 53706

Dr. Nancy Bockstael
Department of Agricultural
   Economics
University of Maryland
College Park, MD 20742

Dr. James Cato
Department of Food &
   Resource Economics
1170 McCarty Hall
University of Florida
Gainsville, FL 32611

Mr. Stephen Freese
Mid-Atlantic Fisheries
   Management Council
North and New Streets
Federal Building, Room 215
Dover, DE 19901

Mr. Art Gallagher
Pacific Marine Fisheries
   Commission
528 S.W. Mill Street
Portland, OR 97201

Mr. Louis Goodreau
New England Fishery
   Management Council
Suntaug Office Park
5 Broadway
Saugus, MA 01906

Dr. Wade Griffin
Department of Agricultural
  Economics
Texas A&M University
College Station, TX 77843

Mr. Richard Gutting
National Marine Fisheries Service
3300 Whitehaven Street, N.W.
Washington, DC 20235

Ms. Stacy Hall
Staff Economist
Pacific Fishery Management
  Council
526 S.W. Mill Street
Portland, OR 97201

Dr. Rǿgnvaldur Hannesson
Institute of Economics
University of Bergen
N5014 Bergen-U
Norway

Mr. Richard Hennemuth
Northeast Fisheries Center
National Marine Fisheries Service
Woods Hole, MA 02543

Mr. Mark Holliday
University of Delaware
College of Marine Studies
Newark, DE 19711

Dr. Suzanne Holt
272 Applied Sciences
University of California
Santa Cruz, CA 95064

Dr. Daniel D. Huppert
National Marine Fisheries Service
Southwest Fisheries Center
P.O. Box 271
La Jolla, CA 92037

Mr. David Keifer
Mid-Atlantic Fisheries
  Management Council
North and New Streets
Federal Building, Room 215
Dover, DE 19901

Mr. James Kirkley
Northeast Fisheries Center
National Marine Fisheries Service
Woods Hole, MA 02543

Ms. Pat Kurkul
National Oceanic & Atmospheric
  Administration
National Marine Fisheries Service
Northeast Fisheries Center
Gloucester, MA 01930

Ms. Pat Lavin
University of Delaware
College of Marine Studies
Newark, DE 19711

Mr. William Lovejoy
University of Delaware
College of Marine Studies
Newark, DE 19711

Mr. David Lund
Office of the Chief Economist
Department of Commerce
Washington, DC 20230

Mr. William MacKenzie
National Marine Fisheries Service
Office of Policy & Planning
Washington, DC 20235

Mr. Roger Mallett
Office of Regulatory Policy
Department of Commerce
Washington, DC 20230

Dr. Richard Marasco
Northwest & Alaska Fisheries
  Center
National Marine Fisheries Service
2725 Montlake Blvd. East
Seattle, WA 98112

Dr. K. E. McConnell
Department of Agricultural
  Economics
University of Maryland
College Park, MD 20742

Mr. Morton Miller
Economic Analysis Staff (FX53)
Office of Policy and Planning
National Marine Fisheries Service
2001 Wisconsin Avenue, N.W.
Washington, DC 20235

Dr. C. L. Mitchell
Acting Chief, Economic Research
Department of Fisheries & Oceans
Fisheries Service Directorate
235 Queens Street
Ottawa, Ontario
Canada K1A OE6

Mr. Ignacio Morales
Fishery Economist
Caribbean Fishery Management
Council
Suite 1108 Banco de Ponce
Building
Hato Rey, PR 00918

Mr. Joseph Mueller
National Oceanic & Atmospheric
Administration
National Marine Fisheries Service
Northeast Fisheries Center
Gloucester, MA 01930

Mr. Bruce Norman
National Marine Fisheries Service
Office of Policy & Planning
Washington, DC 20235

Dr. Virgil Norton
Department of Agricultural
Economics
University of Maryland
College Park, MD 20742

Dr. Fred Olson
International Fisheries Affairs
National Marine Fisheries Service
3300 Whitehaven Street, N.W.
Washington, DC 20235

Dr. John Poffenburger
Southeast Fisheries Center
75 Virginia Beach Drive
Miami, FL 33149

Dr. Giulio Pontecorvo
622 Uris Hall
Graduate School of Business
Columbia University
New York, NY 10027

Mr. Sam Pooley
Western Pacific Fishery
Management Council
1164 Bishop Street
Honolulu, HI 96813

Mr. Jeffrey Povolny
North Pacific Fishery
Management Council
P.O. Box 3136DT
Anchorage, AK 99510

Dr. R. Bruce Rettig
Department of Agricultural
Economics
219 Extension Hall
Oregon State University
Corvallis, OR 97331

Mr. James A. Richardson
North Pacific Fishery
Management Council
P.O. Box 3136DT
Anchorage, AK 99510

Dr. Kenneth J. Roberts
Marine Resource Economics
Knapp Hall, Room 259
Louisiana State University
Baton Rouge, LA 70803

Mr. David Rockland
University of Delaware
College of Marine Studies
Newark, DE 19711

Dr. Brian Rothschild
University of Maryland
Chesapeake Biological Laboratory
Box 38
Solomons, MD 20688

Dr. Francis M. Schuler
National Sea Grant College
    Program
NOAA
Rockville, MD 20852

Dr. Robert A. Siegel
National Marine Fisheries Service
Plan Review Division, F/CM6
Washington, DC 20235

Dr. Robert Stokes
Institute for Marine Studies
University of Washington
Seattle, WA 98195

Dr. John Stoll
Department of Agricultural
    Economics
Texas A&M University
College Station, TX 77843

Dr. Ivar E. Strand, Jr.
Department of Agricultural
    Economics
University of Maryland
College Park, MD 20742

Mr. Richard Surdi
Economic Analysis Staff (FX53)
Office of Policy and Planning
National Marine Fisheries Service
2001 Wisconsin Avenue, N.W.
Washington, DC 20235

Dr. Jon Sutinen
Department of Resource
    Economics
University of Rhode Island
Kingston, RI 02881

Dr. Stanley Wang
New England Fishery
    Management Council
Suntaug Office Park
5 Broadway (Rt. 1)
Saugus, MA 01906

Dr. James E. Wilen
Division of Environmental Studies
University of California, Davis
Davis, CA 95615

INDEX

309